THE CALIFORNIA GOLDEN SEALS

THE CALIFORNIA GOLDEN SEALS

A TALE OF WHITE SKATES, RED INK, AND ONE OF THE NHL'S MOST OUTLANDISH TEAMS

STEVE CURRIER

University of Nebraska Press | Lincoln

For Mom

CONTENTS

ILLUSTRATIONS

Following page 228

ACKNOWLEDGMENTS

To put together an accurate and amusing history of the Seals, it was necessary to find people who could help me fill in some blanks and provide stories few others had ever heard. My thanks go out first and foremost to the many people involved with the Seals who patiently sat through my awkward, bumbling interviews and answered question after question about their careers and their impressions of playing in the Bay Area. This is my first book, so rest assured, the conversations were bumpy and filled with rambling questions on my part, but everyone interviewed was incredibly patient, understanding, and, in many cases, helpful in contacting other great interviewees. I was fortunate to talk to two gentlemen who have been general managers in the NHL, a broadcaster who has called Super Bowls, a former 60-goal scorer, a Bill Masterton Trophy winner, and several All-Star Game participants. For that, I will be eternally grateful. Boundless thanks to John Bonasera, Bryan Campbell, Lyle Carter, Ted Hampson, Joey Johnston, Marshall Johnston, Wayne King, Ron Lalonde, Greg Lamont, Larry Leal, Jim Lingel, Larry Lund, Jack Lynch, Dennis Maruk, Howie Menard, Morris Mott, Dick and Sandi Pantages, Larry Patey, Scott Ruffell, Tim Ryan, Larry Schmidt, Frank Selke Jr., Leonard Shapiro, Gary Simmons, Joe Starkey, Tom Thurlby, and Cathy White for taking time out of their busy schedules to talk to me.

I would like to thank many of my fellow Society for International Hockey Research colleagues. Thanks to George Kloepping for answering my questions about the San Francisco Seals, to Todd Denault and Ken Reid for reading my manuscript and writing great blurbs for the back cover, to L. "Waxy" Gregoire for arranging an interview with Wayne King, and to Brad Kurtzberg for allowing me to quote several excerpts from his book *Shorthanded: The Untold Story of the Seals; Hockey's Most Colorful Team*. Thanks also to Rich Reilley of the Seals Booster Club for providing me with photos of his awesome collection of Seals memorabilia and for writing a great quote about Joe Serratore, to Dennis Turchek for providing me with some super photos of the Cleveland Barons, to Doug McLatchy of completehistoryofhockey.com for giving me a great deal on Seals photos, to the San Francisco Public Library, to the Manitoba Sports Hall of Fame, and to Mark Greczmiel and Elliot Lowe for allowing me to use several of their personal photos. I also wish to thank Pete Manzolillo for his stories about growing up as a Seals fan, Reggie Leach for reading an early draft of this book (and for having autographed it as well!), and my uncle Pete Tessier, who asked his friend Dan McCaig to reach out to Mr. Leach for me. More thanks go out to Marie-Claire Thauvette for asking her cousin, Bryan Campbell, to answer my questions about the 1967 expansion and his reasons for defecting to the WHA. Thanks to Adrien Robertson, for his invaluable feedback and advice during the early editing stages. Thanks also to Jane Curran for her help with the book's final edit, and the staff at the University of Nebraska Press, particularly Rob Taylor, Courtney Ochsner, and Elizabeth Zaleski, for taking a chance on a book about a little-known, unsuccessful, white-skated hockey team, and for answering all my questions about the publishing process. I would also like to thank my friends and family, my brother Chris, and my parents, Jim and Gisele Currier, for having always encouraged me to keep writing and for letting me fill their house with dozens of boxes of the *Hockey News* and other hockey memorabilia. Last but not least, I would like to thank my wife, Hope, for her love and support even when this project started to eat up way too much of our time, our son Emmett, also known around these parts as the world's cutest two-year-old, and our two kitties, Chilly and Blue, who could not help but walk in front of my computer screen or beg for treats every time I tried to get some work done.

Sections of this book had their origins in the following articles I first published with the Society for International Hockey Research: "When Garry Met Charlie: The 1971–72 California Golden Seals and How They Almost Got It Right" (*Hockey Research Journal* 15 [Fall 2011]: 91–96); "Turning Points: Ten Landmark Moments That Defined California's Seals" (*Hockey Research Journal* 17 [Fall 2013/14]: 50–56); and

"The Fickle Finger of Fate" (*SIHR blog*, March 8, 2015, http://sihr.ca/ _a/public/column.cfm?cid=3&aid=353). I wish to thank the Society for International Hockey Research for supporting and promoting my work and for providing me with the means to get my first articles in the hands of hockey fans and historians.

Some of the game statistics and statistical information used herein were obtained free of charge from and are copyrighted by The Hockey Summary Project. For more information about the Hockey Summary Project please visit: http://hsp.flyershistory.com or http://sports .groups.yahoo.com/group/hockey_summary_project/.

INTRODUCTION

Why the Seals? Why not write about the Montreal Canadiens or the Boston Bruins? For lack of a better word, the Seals were so *weird*, how could I *not* write about them? They weren't *Twin Peaks*–weird, but rather white-skates-on-white-ice-weird. Live-seals-as-mascots-weird. Since World War II, the Seals are the only NHL franchise to just vanish from existence, and this is because of a merger agreement hastily scribbled on a cocktail napkin in Czechoslovakia. And that was only after moving to an arena where sheep were known to roam nearby. Is that weird enough for you? Keep reading, it gets better . . .

When I was a kid, hardly a mention of this long-suffering franchise could be found. This being the pre-Internet era, I first learned of the existence of the Seals in my 1987 NHL sticker book. There were three players with a "CAL" abbreviation written into their career stats, Dennis Maruk, Gilles Meloche, and Charlie Simmer, and none of them had ever suited up for Calgary. I could see by their numbers that they had all been very good players, and I could have just left well enough alone, but my natural curiosity pushed me to find out what in the world had happened to "CAL"? I later found the answer (sort of) while perusing another sticker book, this time from the Esso gas station franchise. For a ten-year-old kid, this was heavy research. In this sticker book there was a brief piece about NHL expansion, but it didn't explain much. It went something like, "the old Seals just disappeared entirely." I couldn't accept this; nothing could just up and vanish into thin air, could it? I had to find out what had happened to this team, not to mention the Kansas City Scouts, Colorado Rockies, and Atlanta Flames. Then I plunged down the rabbit hole. I wrote to the NHL and asked them if they had any information on any of these teams. As fate would have it, someone at the league office photocopied the Seals' entire 1975-76 media guide and sent it to me. Who knows, if I had received an Atlanta Flames media guide, or even nothing at all, I might not have cared a lick about the Seals. To this day that media guide is the greatest piece of mail I've ever received. I studied that media guide from cover to cover. I brought it to school so I could read it when I finished my work. I knew I had to write a book about the Seals, so at the ripe old age of twelve, I got down to brass tacks and wrote the first version of this very book.

Hundreds, if not thousands, of books and articles have documented the best of hockey's expansion era, but little has been written about the very worst. That would be the California Golden Seals. The Seals (and their eventual successors, the Cleveland Barons) own one of the worst records in professional sports history: 229 wins, 488 losses, 141 ties, and a .349 winning percentage. In fact, of the fifty-one franchises to have played more than one season in the NHL or WHA, the Seals/Barons' winning percentage ranks fifty-first. By comparison, the Seals made the Charlestown Chiefs look like a well-oiled machine, yet the Seals are shrouded in mystery, except for the fact they briefly wore white skates and lost tons of games.

When I talked to the late Frank Selke Jr., former general manager, about my book, he asked me to send him an excerpt. I was delighted when he told me he liked what I had written and that my research and my conclusions were accurate. "It's got to be a labor of love, because I don't know why else you would do it," he said. That sentence sums the Seals up perfectly. Anyone who has ever been associated with the Seals will tell you it was a rollercoaster ride, and those who have survived to tell the tale are often baffled, bemused, and bewildered that anyone would want to dig up the Seals' grave.

How the franchise managed to hang on for eleven NHL seasons is an enigma that ranks up there with the meaning of life and the Kennedy assassination. The history of the Seals was indeed a challenge to write. As former Seals Booster Club member John Bonasera explained to me, "Everything that happened had a short shelf life. It was like trying to build homes in quicksand. . . . You're not looking at the New York Yankee dynasties of the '30s and the '50s. Anything that lasted more than two or three years is an anomaly when it comes to the Seals, and so it's got to be presented that way, so that whether it's a memory or a stat, it's all fleeting, because there's no backbone of history here."

The California Golden Seals remain the perfect example of how *not* to run a sports franchise: seven owners, four different nicknames, and five different color schemes in their history. The Seals' history is colorful in more ways than one. The retina-burning yellow-and-green uniforms just screamed out what the team was all about: horrifyingly brutal, at times even nauseating. The club's owners, coaches, and players have been the talk of many legendary stories. From its inception into the NHL in 1967 to its demise in 1978, the jinxed franchise was always the subject of some sort of nasty gossip. The Seals were always rumored to be moving somewhere, be it Vancouver, Buffalo, Long Island, Seattle, or Cleveland. The usual dedicated fan base of two to three thousand could be found at most games, but not many more paid to see the Seals play.

It wasn't the players' fault they had to wear white skates, it wasn't their fault ownership didn't give a damn about the product it was putting on the ice, and it certainly wasn't their fault the team was never located in the right place. They were just honest guys fighting for a small piece of the pie. They shouldn't be faulted for playing for the Seals; it was a job, and it *was* the NHL, as many players will tell you. Like professional wrestlers, playing for the Seals sometimes meant you had to put up with goofy gimmicks and horrible management practices, but the players persevered and got to fulfill their dream of playing in the pros. Some, like Charlie Simmer, Gilles Meloche, and Ivan Boldirev, were fortunate enough to put their Seals days behind them and become stars with other franchises. Others such as Reggie Leach, Craig Patrick, and Bill Torrey even won the Stanley Cup.

In 2017, the fiftieth anniversary of the Seals' first NHL game, there is something about this team that continues to fascinate people. There still exists a lot of love and passion for the team that never failed to fail, and that is what this story is all about. This is a love story about an endearing bunch of hockey players and their devoted followers.

Now let's see how this bizarre tale of hockey and heartbreak came to be.

1 SAN FRANCISCO TREAT, 1917–1967

The story of the California Golden Seals originates much further back in history than one would believe. While the National Hockey League granted San Francisco a franchise only in 1966, California and professional hockey had collided for the first time way back in World War I, months before the United States shipped its first troops off to Europe. Ushering in an exciting new era in hockey would be no less than the 1917 Stanley Cup Champion Seattle Metropolitans and the Montreal Canadiens. In the most technical sense, the storied Canadiens actually won their second world hockey championship in the City by the Bay. While no Stanley Cup banner hangs from the rafters of the Bell Centre to commemorate this victory, the Canadiens could have, at the time, proclaimed themselves the true hockey titans of the world. Before the Metropolitans and Canadiens could face off, however, they needed a suitable indoor rink to accommodate them.

On October 10, 1916, San Francisco's Winter Garden opened its doors to the public for the first time. It can be argued the California Golden Seals' origins lie with the construction of the Garden, which accommodated 1,800 people, housed a 210-by-90 foot sheet of ice—the largest of its kind on the Pacific coast—and contained approximately 55,000 feet of piping "necessary for the circulation of the cold brine which ma[de] the ice on the main floor."[1] The Garden gave many Californians not only the chance to experience for the first time the sheer joy of gliding nonchalantly down a smooth, pristine frozen surface, but also the opportunity to see the world's fastest athletes compete before their very eyes.

The *Oakland Tribune* did its best to encourage Bay Area residents to participate in activities that had already been a popular pastime in Canada and the northern United States for decades. "Ice skating, under agreeable and comfortable conditions, will be enjoyed by lovers of this healthy and exhilarating sport, when the immense new Winter Garden opens tomorrow evening," read the *Tribune*. The newspaper also lay to rest any fears warm weather lovers may have had about spending time in what many probably thought would be some sort of full-scale snow globe. "The Winter Garden, one of the largest and finest institutions of the kind in the world," the *Tribune* explained, "has a frontage on three streets—Sutter, Pierce and Post, and is afforded splendid lighting by day and a wonderful artificial illumination by night. It is steam-heated throughout, so that spectators and others will not suffer in any way from the cold."[2]

Dunbar Poole, the Garden's manager, and G. R. Percival made sure the Winter Garden's grand opening would be quite the social event even for those patrons who planned on staying off the ice. "A military band, under the direction of Charles Cassasa, leader of the park and exposition bands, will add to the enjoyment of skaters," read an article in the October 9, 1916, *Tribune*. "Norval Baptie and Gladys Lamb, exhibition skaters from 'Castles in the Air,' New York City, and their ballet of six girls, will be a feature for the opening days."[3] The October 1, 1916, *Tribune* explained, "For those who do not skate, however, things will be made very comfortable as hot air from the basement will be forced up under the seats allotted spectators. Another provision has been made for non-skaters, a ballroom being placed adjacent to the rink where dancing may be indulged in both afternoon and evening to the music of Cassasa's military band."[4]

While the Winter Garden was ideal for leisurely skating, there was an added incentive to building an arena in San Francisco: getting professional players to come over as a feature attraction. In late 1916 and early 1917 local amateur teams from Stanford University and the University of California were among the first to play organized hockey at the Garden, but it was not until March 31, 1917, that the first professional hockey game was played in California.

Five days earlier the Seattle Metropolitans of the Pacific Coast Hockey Association had defeated the Montreal Canadiens of the National Hockey Association to become the first American-based team to win the Stanley Cup. Unlike today's NHL, players and coaches of the championship team did not disburse after the season to enjoy the summer with friends and family; they often kept playing a little while longer. In fact, just two days after Seattle's triumphant victory the Metropolitans defeated the Canadiens again, this time in an exhibition contest, by a score of 9–7.

The game was a tune-up for an exhibition series that would be played at the Winter Garden from March 31 to April 4. At stake would be a $5,000 prize, with the winning team taking home 60 percent. The *Manitoba Free Press* reported that the two clubs "left Seattle at midnight for San Francisco," where they would play three exhibition games in a week. The *Free Press* continued: "They will introduce professional hockey in the Golden Gate city for the first time and according to advance accounts big crowds are expected to see the champs and runners-up perform."[5]

In ads leading up to the first game, the *Oakland Tribune* promoted the series like it was of monumental importance, boasting the Metropolitans and Canadiens would be playing "World's Championship Professional Hockey" and proclaiming, "this engagement has been made at an enormous expense and will be the *first Professional Hockey ever seen in California*."[6] Tickets were sold for between 50 cents and $1.50, which included skates, since ticket holders were also allowed to take to the ice themselves following the game!

The Canadiens won the first contest 5–4, in what the *Tribune* described as "a brilliant game."[7] Seattle stormed back to win game two on April 2 by a score of 5–2 thanks to a hat trick from Bernie Morris and 2 goals from Cully Wilson.[8] The third and final game was hyped up as though the Stanley Cup was actually on the line: "Hockey Title of World at Stake" read the headline of the small write-up tucked way down at the bottom of page 10 of the evening *Tribune*.[9] In retrospect, saying the world title was up for grabs was a slight exaggeration, but when Montreal won the final contest 6–2, there was more than a little boasting heard from the Canadiens' side. "We finished in a blaze of glory," said Canadiens' owner George Kennedy. "We have the better team—the finest aggregation playing hockey today."[10]

Interestingly, Kennedy believed California could sustain a four-team hockey league with teams primarily located in the Bay Area:

Do I think that the introduction of professional hockey in California would pay? Well, that's a pretty big question. There is no doubt that the people of San Francisco were highly enthusiastic over the games

3

there between the Canadiens and Seattle and I see no reason why other California towns shouldn't relish the fastest sport on Earth also. But—and here's where the rub comes—it would take an outlay of several hundred thousand dollars to build four rinks and get the game started. The question is—who is going to take the gamble? It might be a highly paying one at that.[11]

With the groundwork already laid thanks to these early professional teams, the California Hockey League began play in 1928 with four teams: the Oakland Sheiks, San Francisco Icelanders, Los Angeles Richfields, and Hollywood Millionaires. During the CHL's first season, the Sheiks emerged as the league's premier franchise, finishing atop the regular-season standings with 41 points in 36 games. The Sheiks continued to dominate the CHL as the Great Depression worsened, winning championships in 1930, 1931, and again in 1933 before the league was dissolved.

Four years after the demise of the CHL, Oakland had another club, the Clippers, that competed in the Pacific Coast Hockey League, but before the season ended the Clippers packed their sticks and shoulder pads and moved to Spokane. Bay Area hockey then went into a slumber for nearly ten years, supported only sporadically by college and amateur teams. It was not until 1945, with the creation of a new Pacific Coast Hockey League, that organized hockey returned to the Bay Area. The new PCHL became a senior amateur league, because the NHL had territorial rights to Seattle, Vancouver, and Portland, and the PCHL refused to pay a territory fee. Both the San Francisco Shamrocks and Oakland Oaks became mainstays in the new amateur league and enjoyed varying degrees of success.

In 1948 the PCHL once again became a professional circuit under the NHL's supervision. The Oaks moved to the top of the standings while the Shamrocks sank to the bottom. Despite the Oaks' strong season, the club suffered financially and disbanded just 29 games into the 1949–50 season. The Shamrocks, meanwhile, finished first in the Southern Division that same season with a 35-27-9 record. Attendance in the entire Southern Division, comprising the LA Monarchs, San Diego Sky Hawks, and Fresno Falcons, was pathetic, so all of the

California teams closed up shop, leaving the PCHL with only six teams for its 1950–51 season. In 1952 the PCHL merged with the Western Canada Senior Hockey League to create the Western Hockey League, but there would be no California-based franchises for a while.

While the California Seals' birth was still a few years away, the eventual franchise would greatly benefit from the Winnipeg Warriors, who were granted league membership in 1955. The Warriors experienced immediate success, winning the league championship their first season thanks to the likes of past and future NHL alumni Paul Masnick, Bill Mosienko, Eric Nesterenko, Mike Nykoluk, and Ed Chadwick. The Warriors mostly disappointed from that point on, finishing out of the playoffs three of the next five seasons.

After the 1955–56 season the Warriors reportedly made an $80,000 profit. After the 1960–61 season, however, the Warriors had lost an estimated $200,000 over their six seasons. Owner J. D. Perrin Jr. planned on moving the Warriors to San Francisco, but the league preferred setting up an expansion franchise there instead. The Warriors never moved to California, but they did take a leave of absence from the league, which eventually became a permanent withdrawal. Winnipeg's loss would greatly benefit the new Bay Area outfit.

In the meantime, Vancouver general manager Coleman "Coley" Hall, a hotel owner and cattle rancher, suddenly resigned from the Canucks and bid on an expansion franchise for San Francisco. On April 23, 1961, the Seals were born when Hall and the minority owner and San Francisco hotelier Melvin M. Swig won the rights to the franchise. The plan was for the San Francisco Seals to play their home games at the venerable Cow Palace in Daly City, contingent upon an ice surface being installed before the start of the regular season.[12]

The Cow Palace had character, to put it nicely, but not quite in the same way as, say, Maple Leaf Gardens or the Montreal Forum. Built in 1941, the 11,866-seat Cow Palace had not been designed to house a professional hockey team; thus it was inadequate in many ways. Jim Lingel, who would later become the Seals' vice-president for marketing, recalled that "between the goal lines there were only about 15 rows" of seats. "Most of the seats were in the corners for hockey," he continued. "It was like a big, square barn and it had terrible sight lines. The rink was also 15 feet short of the regulation 200 feet long. It was originally designed for rodeo." Future Seals head coach Fred Glover recalled, "The nets at each end were smaller at the bottom than at the top. They were bent in and couldn't fit on the pegs. The seats were up against the bench. There was just no room."[13]

The Seals, led by general manager Joseph J. Allen and coach Max McNab, were not a typical expansion team in that high-quality players were acquired from a few other minor-league teams rather than through a league-controlled expansion draft. Hall obtained many players from the Canucks, which, at the time, was the New York Rangers' farm club, and other players from friend Eddie Shore's Springfield Indians. Before the season started, the Seals also acquired several Winnipeg Warriors players, notably Nick Mickoski, Al Nicholson, Jean-Marc Picard, Tom Thurlby, and Carl Boone.

Even though the Cow Palace ice was not in place until mid-November, the season started without much of a hitch, except for the fact the Seals would be forced to start their history on a 14-game road trip! This little hiccup notwithstanding, high-level hockey was back in the Bay Area. Over nine thousand fans witnessed the Seals' home debut November 17, 1961, versus the Edmonton Flyers, and the fans were treated to a tremendous effort by their new heroes. Bob Solinger, who would lead the Seals in scoring that season with 85 points, gave the Seals a 1–0 lead just two minutes into the game, followed by a goal from Boone eight minutes later. The Flyers fought back the rest of the period, cutting the lead to one thanks to a goal by Forbes Kennedy. In the second period, the Seals refused to let the Northern Division leaders pull away from them; the period ended with the two teams deadlocked at 3 goals apiece. In the third period, Kennedy scored his third goal of the night on the power play and gave the Flyers the lead for good. Eddie Joyal scored an insurance goal at 18:29 to give the Flyers a 5–3 win.

Despite the loss, opening night was an overwhelming success. "From the roar of the crowd, there were more knowledgeable clients than mere night-outers," wrote the *San Francisco Chronicle*'s Art Rosenbaum. "The Seals were greeted with an outburst of applause when they took the lead, and as the game progressed the cheers

FIG. 1. The 1961–62 San Francisco Seals, prior to their home debut vs. Edmonton. Front row, left to right: Bev Bentley, Jim Hay, Tom Thurlby, Floyd Hillman, Gary Collins, Nick Mickoski, Harry Pidhirny, and Gord Redahl. Top row, left to right: trainer Bill Gray, Carl Boone, Al Nicholson, Jack Martin, Bob Solinger, Barney Krake, Jim Wilcox, Ray Cyr, Gary Edmundson, and coach Max McNab. Photo by Sid Tate, courtesy of San Francisco History Center, San Francisco Public Library.

increased for the home side and the boos grew for the currently detested and, as it turned out, victorious Flyers."[14]

Despite having just one goaltender in training camp and not enough players to make two full practice squads with substitutes, the Seals recovered from a shaky 4-10 start to finish third in the Southern Division with a respectable 29-39-2 record. In the playoffs the Seals were soundly defeated by Spokane in a best-of-three series by scores of 4–1 and 7–3, but fans remained enthused about the future. Fans came to the Cow Palace in droves: 194,530 to be exact, a figure that put them ahead of every other team in the league except Portland. The formation of the Seals Booster Club, a nonprofit organization, was announced on September 8, 1962. The club's first meeting, open to anyone interested in hockey, took place Tuesday, September 11, at

8 p.m. in the Round Up Room at the Cow Palace. The Booster Club would grow in stature over the next fifteen years, counting at one point, some have estimated, around a thousand members. In 2012, the club celebrated its fiftieth anniversary.

For the 1962–63 season Norman "Bud" Poile became the Seals' new coach and general manager. Offensively, the team was led by star forwards Nick Mickoski (95 points) and Orland Kurtenbach (87 points), and goaltender Jim McLeod won 43 games. The Seals became one of the more aggressive teams in the WHL, thanks to toughies like Kurtenbach, Larry McNabb, and Gary "Duke" Edmundson. "We had some pretty tough guys on our team," recalled defenseman Tom Thurlby, the WHL Seals' all-time leader in games played. "We didn't go looking for trouble, but it always seemed to find us, I guess, but we had some pretty good players on our team that could mix it up if the time came."

The Cow Palace became an extremely inhospitable rink for visitors. Over their five seasons in San Francisco, the Seals sported an impressive 113-59-4 home record. Thurlby remembers the Palace being an intimidating place to play "just because of the size of it compared to some of the other rinks, and it was a small ice surface there too . . . we had a lot of big guys on that team, and I think we just dominated at home. Teams coming in there were kind of shocked, I guess, at the amount of people that was there the first time they played there." He went on to add that the fan support the Seals received in San Francisco "was unreal, you wouldn't believe it, and we filled that old Cow Palace all the time . . . even though it didn't matter where we were in the standings." Over the Seals' six seasons in the Western League, the club's average attendance would vary between 2,700 and 5,600. Some teams, many in more traditional hockey markets, were only drawing a fraction of that.[15]

The 1962–63 season started much like the last one. The Seals opened the schedule splitting 2 games with Portland at the Cow Palace, before embarking on what would become a traditional, ridiculously long October road trip. This season it would be 12 games straight away from home. After 14 games the Seals' record was a disappointing 4-10-0, which included two 5-game losing streaks, but after a cushy

8

home stand in November and December, their record climbed to 18-14-0. The slow start cost the Seals a chance at the division title, but with a 44-25-1 record and a second-place finish, the team was a serious contender for the Lester Patrick Cup.

After disposing of Los Angeles 2–1 in a best-of-three first round, the Seals challenged the Portland Buckaroos, who had finished first overall during the regular season. The Seals had dropped 9 of 12 games against Portland during the regular season, and a disappointing outcome seemed likely early on when Portland won game one, 6–3. The Seals rebounded nicely in game two with a 5–2 victory and came away with a 6–3 win in game three, but they were then humiliated 5–1 in game four in front of 11,864 fans, to that point the largest crowd in San Francisco hockey history. Back to Portland the series went for game five, and the Buckaroos came out with a huge 2–1 overtime win, putting the Seals on the brink of elimination. This Seals team, however, played its best hockey when its back was against the wall.

The first period of game six concluded without a goal for either team. The scrappy Seals came out blazing in the second period as Moe Mantha slapped a 60-footer past Portland goaltender Don Head just 1:23 into the frame. Less than seven minutes later, Larry McNabb scored on a pass from Duke Edmundson. In the third period, captain Eddie "Can of Tobacco" Panagabko put the Seals up 3–0 with a goal at 13:39. Seals rookie Jim McLeod made 34 saves for the shutout.

The two teams would have to wait six days to play the seventh and deciding game of the series due to scheduling problems in Portland. The Seals had offered to play game seven at the Cow Palace, but the Bucks, having earned home-ice advantage, would have none of that. When the day of the big game arrived over ten thousand fans sat on the edge of their seats as the Seals and Buckaroos put on a great show. Orland Kurtenbach opened the scoring just 2:55 in, but Portland's Tommy McVie tied it up some six minutes later. The Seals pulled ahead in the second period when Danny Belisle took an innocent-looking shot from the blue line that found its way past a screened Head. The Bucks came out firing on all cylinders early in the third period, as the Seals' Len Haley sat in the penalty box for five minutes for having cut Portland's Jack Blonda with a high stick. McLeod was

FIG. 2. Nick Mickoski's San Francisco Seals jersey. Photo courtesy of Manitoba Sports Hall of Fame & Museum.

up to the challenge, stopping 41 shots. The score remained 2–1 San Francisco until Nick Mickoski scored with less than three minutes to play, giving the Seals a 3–1 win and a ticket to the Patrick Cup finals.

Jim McLeod had been the Seals' unquestioned MVP in games six and seven, but had it not been for the Seattle Totems, who had arranged for McLeod to play in San Francisco to gain some experience, the Seals might not have made the final at all. Ironically the Seattle Totems now had to get through the rookie netminder to get the Patrick Cup.

The championship series was unusual in that all games were played at the Cow Palace due to a scheduling conflict with the Ice Follies, who were performing in Seattle. As the series opened, the Seals looked like the better team by far, but it was the Totems who took a 1–0 lead on a goal by Don Chiupka late in the first. The Seals poured it on in the second period, but goaltender Al Millar performed miracles in the Totem net, including a breakaway save on Ed Panagabko. As Millar stood his ground, Bob Sabourin banged home a Bill MacFarland rebound to put Seattle up 2–0. Late in the period the Seals finally found a chink in Millar's armor as Mickoski scored with just 14 seconds left. The Seals then unleashed 17 shots on Millar in the third period, and with just 6:39 left to play, Haley scored on a pass from Ray Cyr to tie the game at 2–2.

After sixty minutes of exciting end-to-end hockey, the teams went to overtime. With just over two minutes to play in the period, the Seals made a poor line change, and Seattle's Jim Powers took advantage, breaking in alone on McLeod and beating him on the short side. "They're again one game down," said sportswriter Hugh McDonald in the following day's *San Mateo Times*, "finding themselves in that normal (for them), if unenviable position" of losing the opening game of a series for the third straight time. On paper the Seals had controlled the game's tempo from the opening faceoff, but they made many mistakes that came back to haunt them:

> What Millar and his forechecking teammates didn't do to the Seals they did to themselves. They showed about as much finish around the Seattle cage as a sculptor working with a wood chisel.
>
> Not that the Seals weren't trying. They overcame a two-goal deficit and had a crowd of 8936 in hysterics, but they missed more opportunities with wide shooting and poor positioning on rebounds than the bad guys miss in four full-length western movies.[16]

In game two the Seals jumped out to a 5–1 lead in the first period and should have walked away with an easy win, but the Totems clawed their way back. With just 15 seconds left in the period, Chiupka scored to make it 5–2. Then, just 3:02 into the second period, Chiupka scored again to make it 5–3. Seattle clearly had the momentum going into the final period, but when Powers and Sabourin scored within 1:33 of each other to make the score 5–5, the Seals were beside themselves. Fortunately for the Seals, just over five minutes into the extra frame, Kurtenbach gained control of the puck in the corner and sent a pass to Mickoski parked in front of the cage, who then hammered it home for a 6–5 win.

Even though the Seals had managed to steal game two and had home ice advantage the entire series, a certain uneasiness had seeped into their collective brains. In game three Seattle skated as though they had rockets strapped to their feet and destroyed the directionless Seals, 9–1. Poile was not at all impressed by his team's, and particularly his goaltender's, performance. "You can say that McLeod had an off night," he said after the game, "and I'm speaking conservatively." In the following day's *Pasadena Star-News*, it was said that McLeod was "spinning like a revolving door." He stopped only 16 of 25 shots, while Al Millar stopped 41.[17]

Game four, this time a 3–1 loss, was hardly better for the Seals. "About all that can be said for the San Francisco Seals," said *Oakland Tribune* sportswriter Merl Moore, "is that they looked better losing last night than they did in defeat the night before."[18] Millar was outstanding once again, making 39 saves for the win. The struggling McLeod had to deal with just 25 shots, but he still could not come through for his teammates.

Overall, game four was a chippy affair, with the Seals dishing out the majority of punches. San Francisco fans were ornery and angry, tossing paper cups, coins, hot dog wrappers, and beer cans onto the ice when the referee called the Seals for various fouls. The Seals may have lost the game, but something extraordinary happened as the minutes ticked away: they found their heart. In the third period the Seals got tough and changed the momentum of the series once again, and not a moment too soon. At one point Jean-Marc Picard nailed the Totems' Lou Kazowski with a solid left, Larry McNabb beat George

Konik in another fight, and Al Nicholson, according to Merl Moore, "pummelled and pounded upon Millar."[19]

Game five was all San Francisco. Moore said it best in the opening lines of his next-day summary of the game: "If the Cow Palace was a horse racing track, the San Francisco Seals would have had to take saliva tests after last night's bruising 8–0 slaughter of the Seattle Totems."[20] Haley led the Seals with three goals, all in the third period, while Mantha and McNabb each scored twice. Nicholson had four assists in the rout.

With the game firmly out of reach and just twenty-two seconds left, a fifteen-minute "battle royal" broke out, with players from both benches spilling out onto the ice. The melee started after Kurtenbach nailed the Totems' Bill MacFarland into the boards, and MacFarland fell to the ice in a heap. MacFarland recovered enough to yell some derogatory comments toward big Kurt, who had dropped the gloves with him earlier in the contest. Kurtenbach started wailing on MacFarland, who went down. "Bill MacFarland, he was a big guy, and never hurt a flea," remembers defenseman Tom Thurlby. "He was the captain of Seattle's team, and a real good hockey player. . . . I never saw how it started or anything, I just remember they were at center ice fighting, and it was quite a fight. Kurtenbach ended up knocking him down, as I recall, and that pretty well ended the fight. . . . They went toe-to-toe there for, I hate to say how long, but probably two or three minutes anyways."

The brawling did not stop there. Millar went after Mantha, and then both benches cleared. According to Merl Moore, "A blow-by-blow accounting would be as ridiculously inaccurate and inadequate as a shot-by-shot chronicling of World War II." In the end there were twenty-three penalties called in the game, including five-minute majors to Kurtenbach, Mantha, McNabb, MacFarland, Millar, and Konik.[21]

The two clubs were much more civil in game six, after league president Al Leader had warned both clubs that further brawling would result in fines. The 11,869 fans in attendance were treated to a classic contest, and they responded by hooting and hollering throughout. Konik opened the scoring at 14:07 of the first period, but Haley tied it up on a power play just 61 seconds later as he tipped in a shot by Kurtenbach. In the second period Mickoski stole the puck from Guyle Fielder and slapped a 20-footer past Millar to put the Seals up 2–1. Fielder redeemed himself at 8:13 of the third period as he feathered a pass over to Jim Powers, who then shot the puck through McLeod's legs. The scoreboard read 2–2 at the end of regulation time, meaning the series would be heading to overtime for the third time. Down three games to two, the Seals looked for a hero to push the series to a seventh game. The suspense of the extra frame would be short-lived as the Seals' Danny Belisle scored his second overtime goal at 2:02 to even the series 3–3. Seals fan Cathy White remembers Belisle fondly. "He was very much underrated," she believes. "He would set up the players. He had a lot of assists, not too many goals, but that's because he kept setting up the wingers." Everyone was thankful he elected to shoot more this series.

The climactic seventh contest, the Seals' seventeenth playoff game overall, worked the Bay Area into a frenzy. The gutsy, gritty, and deter-mined Seals had become a big deal in San Francisco. "Big, rough, tough and with heart to match their size," said the *San Mateo Times*'s Hugh McDonald, "the come-from-behind San Francisco Seals will meet the Seattle Totems at the Cow Palace tonight in the deciding game for the Western Hockey League championship."[22] The deciding match for the league championship was played before a record 12,404 screaming San Francisco fans. Overall, 59,260 fans had bought tickets for the entire series, which was an astonishing figure for California hockey. The Totems had hoped to play game seven in Seattle since evangelist Oral Roberts, who had originally booked the arena that night, agreed to let the teams play, but the league ruled against the last-minute change of venue. It would have been a shame for the fans of San Francisco to miss out on this game; like game six, game seven was a classic.

The Seals stormed out of the gate in the first period, outshooting the Totems 17–4, but the game remained scoreless. In the second period, Bob Sabourin's two goals in a span of a minute put the Totems up 2–0 before the halfway point, but Edmundson and Mantha erased that lead with goals before the buzzer sounded. Belisle scored his eighth of the playoffs 5:09 into the third period and put the Seals up 3–2, but Powers tied it up just a minute later. That's where the score stood as the buzzer signaled the end the third period.

"You won't need me to tell who wins it," pointed out play-by-play man Roy Storey.[23] The crowd was so agitated, either the roof would cave in from the excitement of a Seals win or all the air would be sucked out of the room in defeat. Throughout overtime, fans stomped their feet and pounded on anything they could find with their fists. Over the radio, fans at home could hear all sorts of horns and noise-makers go off in the background. Like the two previous overtime games in the series, it did not take long for someone to become a hero. "Danny Belisle shot the puck," recalled Orland Kurtenbach. "It hit [a] Seattle defenseman and bounced over to Larry McNabb. He shovelled it over to me. I shot from 10 feet out and it went in. I heard a 'pl-ing' as it bounced off the inside of the post."[24]

The crowd's reaction to Kurtenbach's goal was euphoric. Team-mates hugged and kissed Kurtenbach, and about a hundred fans poured onto the ice. Radio color man Bill King announced: "There's a lady out there—she can't be a day under 65 years of age—in high heels, and she came skidding and sliding on her posterior 20 feet." On the air the noise from the jubilant crowd was deafening. In the postgame celebration, two overjoyed Seals defensemen hoisted Bud Poile onto their shoulders. Captain Ed Panagabko proudly accepted the Patrick Cup and in his speech to the crowd, exclaimed, "Ladies and gentlemen, at the end of every hockey season, it's always hard for us players to say goodbye, even to one another . . . we don't want to say goodbye. We just want to say so long."[25]

The animosity that had developed between Kurtenbach and Mac-Farland was put aside as the two stars shook hands and hugged in a mutual display of respect. For Kurtenbach it was the perfect way to cap off a fantastic season. "I was wondering if I'd ever score another goal," Kurtenbach said after his big moment. "That was only the fourth in 17 playoff games."[26] When Kurtenbach and his 87 regular-season points left the Seals during the summer to join the NHL's Boston Bruins, it left the Seals with a huge void to fill. "Absolutely outstanding," is how

Seals fan Cathy White describes Kurtenbach. "I was so disappointed when they traded him, but he had a chance to go to the NHL. We were still Western Hockey League, but he was an outstanding center . . . He was big. He wasn't afraid to throw his weight around, but he wasn't dirty . . . Kurtenbach played with skill, but he wasn't dirty."

The city of San Francisco let the players know they were loved. Tom Thurlby recalls how well the players were treated by their fans and city officials. "Oh, it was fantastic," he said. "We drank champagne right on the steps of city hall with the mayor. We had a parade." Thurlby fondly remembers San Francisco, due in part to the many perks the players received there. "We were always invited to play golf on Monday afternoon at some really nice golf courses," he said. "We could hardly wait to get out of the rink after practice with the Western Hockey League team to see if we could get to the golf course first to tee off. And we never paid to play golf. . . . We just had to show up, and we were honorary members wherever we went."

When the 1963–64 season started, the Seals found themselves with a target on their back and struggled to regain the form that had made them so successful the previous year. "I kind of call it the championship hangover. That was part of it," said center Larry Lund. "Orland Kurtenbach was on that previous team, Danny Belisle, so there was a couple of players who were lost. . . . The other thing that happened is the other teams would get up a little more for the championship team."

The Seals stormed out to a 7-4-2 record, but things turned sour in a hurry. By Christmas the Seals' record had plummeted to 12-19-2, forcing the club to ponder the embarrassment of missing the playoffs just one year after winning the championship. The Seals turned things around in the New Year, climbing as high as one game over .500, but an 8-game losing streak starting at the end of January dragged the team's overall record down to a dismal 23-30-2. Bud Poile handed his coaching hat to thirty-seven-year-old Nick Mickoski, who also continued to play a regular shift. The Seals began to gel after the switch. "I think there was some leadership in the locker room," said Lund. "I guess it was probably at the point where guys started to take things a little more seriously, and when you have a winning team there's sort of a culture there that expects that, and I think it took a while for that to click in and probably towards the end of the year guys started to become the team that could do this. . . . And then, there was a coaching change too . . . A large percentage of the time, with a change, people take notice and step it up a few notches."

Even though the team qualified for the playoffs, there were many reasons for concern. The Seals sputtered to a 32-35-3 record, and their offense managed just 228 goals. The helmeted Charlie Burns had come over from the Boston Bruins before the season started and led the Seals in scoring (ninth in the league) with 69 points. "He was NHL caliber," said Cathy White, "but all of the teams were afraid, because he had [a] plate in his head, that he would become injured, so nobody signed him. Fortunately for us, he came to California and he was by far the best player. He had so much talent." Len Haley finished second with 68 points, but he and Burns were the Seals' only 30-goal men. In contrast, five players had scored 30 goals the year before. Mickoski, in particular, missed his line mate Kurtenbach and scored just 57 points. "The loss of the good center did hurt," Mickoski said. "That's part of it . . . there just weren't that many good ones left on the club to go around." In what might have been the understatement of the year, Mickoski admitted, "It was just a mixed up season."[27] It didn't help matters that the Seals also gave up a league-high 262 goals. New number one goalie Bob Perreault struggled throughout the season and finished with an inflated 3.65 goals-against average and no shutouts.

The WHL had been reduced to six teams for the 1963–64 season, so the road to the championship consisted of just two best-of-seven rounds. In round one the Seals brushed aside the second-place Portland Buckaroos in five games. As luck would have it, the first-place Denver Invaders, who finished 24 points ahead of San Francisco, fell to the mediocre Los Angeles Blades. In a stunning turn of events the WHL crown would go to one of two teams who had fought tooth and nail just to make the playoffs.

Mickoski felt optimistic about the Seals' chances, despite the fact LA had run roughshod over San Francisco, going 11-4-1 during the regular season. "Physically and mentally we are in good shape. Our spirits are up . . . we could win it all," said Mickoski. Even the local

17

newspapers were starting to believe. Spence Conley of the *Oakland Tribune* wrote, "It may be that a team of retreads and rookies, kids on their way up and veterans on their way down, *can* win it all. If they do it'll be one of the most uncanny sports comeback [*sic*] in Bay Area history."[28]

Early on it seemed as though the Seals were going to follow the same old script. The Blades scored a 3–1 win in game one, but Poile believed goaltender Jack Norris "was lucky against us tonight. Four of those shots hit the posts and they all went out."[29] Overall, Norris had to make just 22 saves, whereas Perreault made 35. Poile was right to feel confident; the Seals won game two, 5–4, and in game three the Seals scored two goals in the final minute to secure a 4–2 win. "It was grind, grind, grind, with everybody doing his job," said Mickoski about game three, but Panagabko and Mantha were the true standouts for San Francisco; each scored two goals.[30]

Over the last two playoff seasons the Seals had developed a reputation as clutch performers, earning the nickname "Adversity on Ice." No matter how dire the situation and no matter how close the Seals were to the edge of defeat, they always found a way to win. The Blades jumped out to a 2–0 lead just ten minutes into game four, but Thurlby, Haley, and then Thurlby again scored in the dying minutes to give the Seals a 3–2 lead. Thurlby played one of his best-ever games this night. "He had the best hip check of anybody I've ever seen," remembers Seals Booster Club member Cathy White. "Now, they've outlawed them since then. He had a way of taking out the wings or the center that took 'em out, but it didn't injure them. Nobody ever got hurt when Tom hit them. He was the most underrated player we had, I think."

Eddie Panagabko put the Seals up by 2 goals at 11:57 of the middle period, but the Blades fought back to tie the game at 4–4. In overtime Len Haley, playing with a broken rib and right hand, tipped an Al Nicholson pass for his second goal of the night and gave the Seals a huge win.

Up 3–1 in games and on the verge of back-to-back Patrick Cups, the Seals fell flat on their faces. The Seals fell behind 3–1 late in the second period of game five, but at the 5:09 mark of the final frame, disaster struck. Former Seal Camille Bedard scored to make it 4–1, followed by goals by Norm Johnson, two by Harold White, and another by Marc Dufour. Five goals in a span of 2:16 set a new league standard for quick offense, and the 8–2 win gave the Blades hope for game six.

Back at the Cow Palace 11,229 fans cheered on the Seals as they looked to bring home the championship for the second year in a row. The Seals jumped out to a 3–0 lead on goals by Ray Cyr and Gerry Brisson in the first period, and Al Nicholson at 12:48 of the second frame, but the Blades' Leo Labine cut the lead to 3–1 at 13:43. Willie O'Ree brought the Blades to within one at 4:51 of the third period, but Cyr returned the favor just four minutes later, making it 4–2, Seals. Not to be outdone, Labine scored his second at 11:53, but the Seals hung on to become WHL champions once again.

Despite the Seals' many regular-season problems, they became the first club in league history to win back-to-back Patrick Cups. Player-coach Nick Mickoski felt ecstatic, but drained: "I've never been so tired in all my life. Everybody seemed to knit. We grew together as a family. They wanted to get into the playoffs—they wanted to win. They had guts. It was a great inspiration to me . . . A fourth place club finishing first—this is the greatest thrill of my life."[31]

Popular team captain Eddie Panagabko was a huge part of the Seals organization in the 1960s. In his postgame speech at center ice he closed out the season with these memorable words: "Thanks for sticking with us through thick and thin. We are a team with a big heart, and we won this cup for a city with a big heart."[32] Panagabko finished his Seals career with 186 points in 207 games, but it was in the playoffs where he really shone, scoring 31 points in 28 games. "He just had those qualities," said Larry Lund. "He'd rally the team or if something needed to be said in the locker room between periods, he was the guy who would do it . . . he was the undisputed leader."

Despite the back-to-back championships the Seals knew they had been lucky. After all, they had qualified for the playoffs with a losing record and had taken advantage of the league's top club crumbling in the first round. Luck can only take you so far, so in an effort to defend their championship the Seals acquired an array of future NHL players such as Wayne Connelly, George Swarbrick, Gary Dornhoefer, Dallas

Smith, and Gerry Odrowski. Despite the influx of talent the Seals, once again coached by Bud Poile, started the season 5-14-0, and even though they went 26-23-2 the rest of the way, they missed the playoffs by two points and blew their chances at a three-peat.

To start the 1965–66 season 1960 U.S. Olympic hero Jack McCartan took over in goal, and solid forwards like Ron Schock and Wayne Maxner were added to the roster, but the Seals were listless early on. Charlie Burns suffered a ruptured disk during the season and was unlikely to return for the playoffs. When one visiting player was asked his opinion on what had befallen the once back-to-back champions, he said, "You can't make chicken salad out of chicken feathers." It was true; the Seals had become pushovers, and a trip to the Cow Palace had ceased to be an ordeal. Poile handed the coaching reins to Burns after just eleven games. In early March the Seals found themselves 13 points out of a playoff spot, but the team went on a 13-3-2 run to close out the season and finish one point up on Seattle for fourth place. Burns healed nicely from his surgery and returned to action while continuing to coach the team.

A late-season knee injury to McCartan could have spelled doom, but the Detroit Red Wings organization thankfully loaned the Seals Joe Daley. The young goaltender won six of his seven games, fashioned a 2.39 goals against average, recorded two shutouts, and helped launch the Seals into a playoff spot. Daley also earned a special award from the Booster Club for his inspirational play. Once again the inspired Seals looked like they were going to run roughshod on the rest of the league, but fate had other plans.

Daley's place in Seals' history might have been greater had it not been for the International League's Fort Wayne Komets. Once the Komets were eliminated from the playoffs, their goaltender, thirty-six-year-old Bob Gray, who was the Seals' property, became available, making Daley ineligible to play in the Seals' first-round series versus the Victoria Maple Leafs. The Seals pleaded with WHL president Al Leader to let the league's standby goalie, Los Angeles's thirty-nine-year-old Marcel Pelletier, play in the series. Even though Pelletier was at the arena for game one, Leader turned down the Seals' request. "All the other clubs are able to play pros," Poile raged, "I don't see why we should be forced to play an amateur."[33]

Fate certainly proved to have a twisted sense of humor. At the other end of the ice the Seals would be shooting at "Long" John Henderson, who had been sent to Victoria in January after having played ten so-so games for the Seals. "I know the Seals feel they know Henderson's moves," said Leafs general manager Buck Houle, "but John, on the other hand, feels he knows the Seals, too."[34] Seals sniper Wayne Connelly scored the series' first goal just 2:35 into game one, but Victoria returned the favor with four of their own before the teams retired to their dressing rooms. The clearly outmatched Seals lost 6–3, but that didn't stop Burns from taking a jab at Victoria's netminder. "Nobody, including me, played well," he admitted. "However, we all feel that with John Henderson in the net for them, we're in it all the way."[35]

Fortunately for the Seals, the league's three other playoff teams allowed the Seals to dress Pelletier, who would become the Seals' third goalie in three games. The Leafs didn't care who played goal for San Francisco as they deposited two pucks past Pelletier in the first seven minutes. Pelletier was outstanding blocking 43 shots, while his new teammates managed a paltry 21. The Seals' 3–1 loss meant they would be heading back to the Cow Palace down two games. Back in San Francisco, Victoria took a 2–1 lead in the first period, but the Seals responded with three straight goals to take game three, 4–2, and allowed just 28 shots.

With the Seals down 2–1 in the series, the teams were deadlocked at 2–2 in game four as the final buzzer sounded to signal the end of regulation time. Just 2:25 into overtime, Connelly passed the puck to Larry McNabb, who then shot it past Henderson to send the series back to Victoria tied up at two.

Momentum was in the Seals' favor when fate reared its ugly head once again. Goaltender Doug Favell, whose rights were owned by San Francisco, had just won the Central League title with Oklahoma City; therefore, the Seals told him to fly west immediately. Unfortunately, Favell's flight was delayed by bad weather, and the Seals had no idea if he would even make it on time, so Burns told a stunned Bob Gray just fifty minutes before face-off that he would be suiting up. Gray shook off the jitters from his game one debut and made 44 saves, while the well-protected Henderson only had to make 14. The score was tied 4–4, and the game seemed destined for overtime, but with just fifty-four seconds remaining, rookie Stan Gilbertson redirected Wayne Connelly's pass behind Henderson to give San Francisco the win. Gray was hailed as a hero, but he acknowledged the players protecting him. "The defense played fantastically and I'd have to say it's the best game I've ever won," he said.[36]

One would have thought the Seals would ride their hot goaltender until he collapsed, but Burns had other ideas. Fate may have been trying to tell Burns something by delaying Favell's earlier flight, but Burns had a hunch he needed to turn to Favell instead of the over-his-head Gray. Going back to the regular season, Favell became, incredibly, the *fifth* goaltender to don a Seals uniform in the last *thirteen* games! Victoria's Gordon Redahl rudely welcomed Favell to the series with a goal just 26 seconds into the game. Victoria controlled the game and increased their lead to 3–0 until Connelly scored at 13:24 to make it 3–1. The Seals' Ron Harris and Ron Schock stunned the Leafs with goals in the first two minutes of the final stanza to tie it up at 3–3. Victoria took the lead soon after, but defenseman Tom Thurlby scored with just 1:10 remaining to send the game to overtime. The Seals' recent play had harkened to the days of "Adversity on Ice," but in the extra period the Seals succumbed to the Leafs' challenge. Victoria's Bob Barlow deflected Bill Schvetz's shot past Favell at 12:37 to give Victoria a 5–4 win.

Favell had played out of his mind in game six, stopping 48 shots, so Burns again turned to him for the deciding seventh game. This time the Seals' hot hand flopped miserably. According to the *Hayward Daily Review*, Milan Marcetta "pushed a pass from the back and side of the net and goalie Doug Favell hooked it into his own goal" just forty-seven seconds into the game.[37] Favell faced 33 shots in the first two periods and allowed 5 goals, while the Seals were skating around looking for a road map to Henderson's net. Gray replaced Favell for the third period, but the Seals had run out of miracles, and Victoria took the series with a decisive 6–1 victory.

The 1965–66 season had indeed been a tumultuous one for the San Francisco Seals, but there were earthquakes far away that could be felt in the Bay Area. The WHL was seriously pondering the idea of turning professional, providing some competition for the NHL. Many Western League players had the chops to play in the NHL, but with just six major-league teams, only 120 full-time jobs were available. The Western League did have one advantage over the NHL: a monopoly over Western Canada and the Pacific coast. With major markets like San Francisco, Los Angeles, Seattle, and Vancouver in their grasp, and major-league–sized arenas in each of these cities, the WHL believed it could declare its independence from the NHL and, eventually, compete for the Stanley Cup. In August 1964 the Joint Affiliation Agreement with the NHL expired, and the WHL refused to sign a new one, meaning the senior league no longer had any control over the players skating in the WHL. Portland general manager Harry Glickman remembered how serious talks about joining the big time had become:

> In the winter of 1964, Leader called a secret meeting of representatives from Seattle, Portland, San Francisco, and Los Angeles at the Fairmont Hotel in San Francisco. . . . Leader carefully outlined the situation and told us we had two choices. One was to continue as a minor league and accept the dictation of the National Hockey League. The other was to stand on our own feet and either enforce the NHL to accept us as a division or to form an independent league of our own. Remember, the important consideration was that we had the buildings. We agreed that we should follow Leader's advice and present the NHL with an ultimatum to either accept us as a division or see us form a rival league. Leader further proposed that each club put $250,000 into a kitty to give the new league a total of one million with which to sign some of the NHL players if they refused to accept our division.[38]

Western League owners started talking tough. "I haven't met with any NHL people lately, but there are other ways of presenting our case forcefully," said James Piggott, owner of the Los Angeles franchise.

"And we do want in. And I can tell you it's not very far off, either."[39] Seals co-owner Coley Hall declared: "[The] time has come for the NHL to realize that Los Angeles and San Francisco can't wait; our hockey fans are just as major-league-conscious as fans of baseball and football and feel they should be up there. An angry feeling is developing."[40]

LA Times columnist Jim Murray believed California was ready for major-league hockey because other professional circuits such as major-league baseball had been experiencing success following expansion to the West Coast:

The National Hockey League makes a mockery of its title by restricting its franchises to six teams, waging a kind of private little tournament of 70 games just to eliminate two teams.

Other big money sports are expanding . . . but hockey likes it there in the back of the cave. Any businessman will tell you that in a dynamic economy you either grow or perish. Baseball had to be dragged kicking and screaming out of its rut. Football groped its way on the end of a short rope. Hockey just can't sit there in the dark forever, braiding buggy whips.[41]

Make no mistake, the WHL was a genuine threat to the NHL. After all, in the 1960s the American Football League emerged as a legitimate competitor to the established National Football League. To counter the AFL's ambitious plans, the NFL expanded, resulting in an increase in the league's popularity and eventually forcing a merger between the two leagues. The WHL felt it had the talent to compete with the NHL. "In the Western Hockey League," said Larry Lund, "there was a lot of older players, ex-NHL players, because at that time there was only six NHL teams, so if you looked down the rosters of Portland and Los Angeles, Vancouver Canucks . . . a lot of those guys were NHL quality but older."

On March 11, 1965, the NHL gave up its conservative demeanor and announced plans to accept applications for teams to comprise a new six-team division that would begin play in 1967–68. Los Angeles and San Francisco, the jewels of the Western League, intrigued the

NHL because of the size of their markets, but mostly because any U.S. television contract the NHL signed required the inclusion of both California cities.

Former Princeton goaltender Barend (Barry) Van Gerbig and five other investors (his brother Mickey, George Coleman, singer Bing Crosby, and senior partner Virgil Sherrill) applied for a team to represent the entire Bay Area. "As soon as we had the inside track on the team, our friends came out of the woodwork," Van Gerbig admitted. "Our friends all saw sellouts in the Original Six buildings and we had guys who really wanted to be part of it. The five of us owned over 50 percent of the team. I was the president, the figurehead, and I represented the team at NHL governors' meetings."[42] Eventually more than fifty people owned a piece of the franchise, including George C. Flaherty, president of the Shasta Corporation, which owned the Ice Follies, San Francisco 49ers quarterback John Brodie, Marco Hellman of Hellman's Mayonnaise, and publisher Nelson Doubleday, but the handsome twenty-eight-year-old Van Gerbig became the early face of the franchise.

Although the dapper Van Gerbig was filthy rich, he had absolutely no experience in the world of professional hockey; but his connections to California's rich and famous left an impression on NHL brass. The young man was also very well connected in the hockey world. "I had been very close to Bruce Norris of Detroit and Bill Jennings of the New York Rangers," he explained. "I also knew Charlie Adams in Boston and his lawyer, Charlie Mulcahy, was a friend of my father."[43]

Seals' principal owner Coley Hall had sold his interest in the club to a twenty-five-man group, led by Mel Swig, for a rumored $150,000 in the summer of 1964. Though Swig also applied for the new NHL franchise, the league turned him down, choosing Van Gerbig instead. Swig was a respected, elegant, well-connected San Francisco hotelier who would have made an ideal NHL owner, but the *Oakland Tribune*'s Spence Conley believes there may have been an ulterior motive in the league's decision to reject Swig's proposal: "Swig was truly a class act and was one of the nicest men in hockey. Swig also had the political

connections in San Francisco to make things happen; there were alle-
gations of anti-Semitism when he didn't get the Bay Area franchise."[44]

It was relatively easy for Van Gerbig to work himself into the NHL
expansion picture. "Charlie Mulcahy and I were both working on Wall
Street in 1965. One day, we were playing golf when Mulcahy mentioned that the Bruins organization owned an interest in the San Francisco Seals and that they were looking for a partner to take over their
interest when the NHL expands."[45] Van Gerbig became part owner
of the Seals. It was just a matter of dotting the *i*'s and crossing the *t*'s
before the Seals were part of the NHL. There was just one problem:
Swig was also part owner of the Seals, and the NHL wanted him out.
According to Van Gerbig:

> A bunch of good people led by Mel Swig owned a minority stake
> in the minor league franchise. Swig was a good man and well con-
> nected in San Francisco. The league said to us that Mel Swig and
> his group were "not acceptable partners." Mel Swig was a prince
> of a man. We should have kept him involved in the ownership of
> the team. There were apparently some [negative] feelings between
> the Bruins and the Swig group. I think, in hindsight, that was one of
> the things that prompted the Bruins to approach me about owning
> the team in the first place.[46]

Swig was pushed aside as the Seals marched into the NHL, but
before long, some of Van Gerbig's friends began feeling apprehensive and decided to bail. In April 1967 the Shasta Corporation asked
Van Gerbig if he would be interested in buying it out. Van Gerbig
and Shasta came to the conclusion that "the interest of the California
Seals would be best served by a realignment of ownership and a cen-
tralization of management." At his first press conference as majority
owner, Van Gerbig pledged to "saturate the area with sales promotion": "We are going to spend money, time and all our energies to
make our game a success." He said the team's primary goal was to
make a Seals ticket "the most valuable piece of property you can own."
Van Gerbig announced he had named Tim Ryan the Seals' vice president for public relations and Jim Lingel as vice president for sales.[47]

Most importantly, Van Gerbig announced Frank Selke Jr., son of the Montreal Canadiens' legendary general manager, would be the Seals' first president. At the time, Selke had been the vice president of the Canadien Arena Company, owner of the Montreal hockey club.

Selke was excited to be starting this new phase of his hockey life but fully realized the difficulty of starting up a new team in a nontraditional market. "My main problems are to fill the building . . . selling the game, which shouldn't be too hard because this is the greatest spectator game in the world." Van Gerbig was determined to make the Seals a financial success and promised, "Everyone is going to be sales oriented from now on. We're going to spend our money, time, and energies to saturate the area. . . . Our ultimate goal is to have every one of the 12,500 Arena [sic] seats held by a season ticket subscriber, and I think that's a fairly realistic goal in an area of three million people."[48]

One advantage the Seals would have over their expansion brethren was the fact they had already established a solid fan base. One month before the expansion draft even took place, the Seals had sold more than two thousand season tickets for the upcoming season. "And a lot of them are from San Francisco," said Van Gerbig, "proving again that there is no barrier between the two sides of the bay as some people claim."[49]

Besides the Seals, the Los Angeles Kings, Minnesota North Stars, Philadelphia Flyers, Pittsburgh Penguins, and St. Louis Blues all forked over the $2 million expansion fee to join the NHL. Baltimore, Buffalo, and Vancouver were also hoping to join the league, but all were rebuffed. The NHL's six expansion clubs were placed in the newly created West Division.

Although the NHL wanted San Francisco as part of the league, a problem soon arose since the city did not have a suitable arena that could house the Seals. The Cow Palace was rejected as the Seals' home rink because of the building's poor sight lines. The rink was dingy, cramped, and awkwardly shaped. The Cow Palace also smelled like, well . . . cows. There was no way the NHL was going to allow the Seals to play there. The club was shifted across the bay to Oakland, where a new arena would be built, but the decision would end up costing the Seals dearly.

Unlike San Francisco, Oakland was not perceived as a major-league city, so the name "Oakland Seals" was deemed unacceptable. There was one other major reason the team didn't want the "Oakland" label attached to it, and it had to do with the Seals' long-term future. "I got some assurances from some people who were well connected with the city government in San Francisco," said Van Gerbig, "that if we got a hockey team, we would have the impetus for a new arena in downtown San Francisco. I thought that we would be well placed. We would start the franchise in Oakland and then move to San Francisco when the new arena was built and we could maintain our fan base."[50]

Just before the 1966–67 season Van Gerbig and his group bought the Seals and moved them across the bay to Oakland, where they played their final WHL season as the California Seals. To get permission to move, the Seals were forced to pay the WHL, over the course of three years, $450,000 in indemnification. The other league owners had demanded $750,000, but the Seals threatened to suspend operations for a year if the price wasn't lowered.

After five seasons in the old, smelly Cow Palace, the Seals would play their home games at the state-of-the-art Oakland-Alameda County Coliseum Complex, also known as the "Jewel Box." The Coliseum featured a 50,000-seat stadium for baseball's Oakland Athletics and a 53,000-seat stadium for football's Raiders. The arena received universal acclaim. "It's big league from top to bottom," exclaimed then-coach and general manager Rudy Pilous. "In fact, it's so infectious that we're going first-class even in our dressing room by laying down a blue and green nylon carpet."[51] At the time only the Detroit Red Wings had a carpeted dressing room. "The players deserve the best," said Van Gerbig cheerfully. "These guys are our bread and butter. We can't do enough for them. A happy player is going to skate better."[52] Van Gerbig could not have been more delighted. "I've seen hockey in every major arena in the United States and Canada," he chirped, "and this has got them murdered."[53] George Flaherty, then-president of the Seals, waxed ecstatic on opening night. "This should warm the cockles of our Irish hearts," he gushed. "I'm busting with such fatherly pride, I feel I should be passing out cigars."[54]

The $30 million building gave the people of Oakland a reason to smile. Even though the Seals were still a minor-league team, they had a major-league rink that would make NHL teams jealous. "The building is beautiful," wrote the *Oakland Tribune*'s Spence Conley, "its high stretch of glass walls rising up from the green and blue padded seats to a ribbed concave ceiling of spectacular sweep."[55] The arena also had a state-of-the-art illuminated scoreboard.

"Seventy days early and 53 minutes late, the new window-walled Oakland-Alameda County Coliseum Arena opened with a movie script ending Wednesday night," read the November 10 *Oakland Tribune*.[56] The arena was not supposed to be available until much later in the season. With work moving ahead of schedule, opening night was moved up, but that didn't mean the Coliseum was ready. Seats were still being bolted down a few hours before the game's 8:00 start time. They had to be airlifted in, but about 150 didn't make it on time, so folding chairs were used instead. A truck transporting some aluminum extrusions got stuck in a snowbank on Donner Pass, creating another delay, but by game time most of them had been installed. In the hours leading up to the game, hot welding sparks fell onto the ice because workmen were still busy getting the arena ready. Workmen's footprints and even a few cigarette butts were still imbedded in the ice when the puck was dropped. Panes of glass were still being installed as the crowd of 9,413 made its way to its seats. Despite these small inconveniences, the game was an overwhelming success.

The Seals weren't at their sharpest, due in part to the fact they hadn't had a place to practice for a few days. The score was 5–5 at the end of regulation time, but Danny Belisle made sure fans went home happy by scoring the winning goal at 3:46 of overtime.

It was expected that with such a beautiful new arena and a more regional name like the California Seals that fans from both sides of the bay would come to the games, but that was not the case. Fans in San Francisco were upset the club was moving away from the city of its minor-league success, while fans in Oakland were miffed at the idea the NHL didn't think their city was good enough to carry the name of its team. Foolish problems such as this one were just the beginning of the headaches for the California Seals.

For one thing, there were cultural and economic divisions in the Bay Area, with sophisticated (some would say smug) San Francisco on the west side, and blue-collar Oakland on the east. Like the Capulets and the Montagues, neither city had much time for the other. According to Gary Simmons, who would tend goal for the franchise from 1974 to 1977, "All the hockey population was on the peninsula down in San Jose and in San Francisco, but they would not go across that bridge into Oakland. Oakland had a lot of crime, it didn't have a good name, and people just didn't go." Therein lay the problem: Oakland had the fancy new rink all ready to go, but San Francisco was where the money and fans lay, and the NHL desperately needed a franchise *anywhere* in the Bay Area to get their television contract.

For the 1966–67 season the Seals hired former Chicago Black Hawks bench boss Rudy Pilous to be both coach and general manager. Pilous had won a Stanley Cup with Chicago in 1961 and had compiled a 162-151-74 NHL career record, so he had excellent credentials, but expecting him to lead his team behind the bench did not make much sense considering he would be spending part of the season scouting NHL teams in preparation for the June 1967 expansion draft. Pilous stood behind the bench for the first 27 games, compiling a 10-11-6 mark, before Charlie Burns replaced him. The Seals took off under Burns, going 9-2-2, including 7 wins in a row, before Pilous returned. Under Pilous the Seals did a complete about-face and went 0-6-1, so he handed the coaching reins back to Burns, who righted the ship and led the Seals to a fourth-place finish. It had been a rather up-and-down season, and the playoffs were no better: the Seattle Totems bounced the Seals out in six games.

The most interesting thing to come out of the Seals' season was the tale of poor Tommy Green, who was called upon to play goal in the Seals' last regular-season game against the San Diego Gulls. According to the write-up in the April 3, 1967, *Oakland Tribune*, Green was a pari-mutuel clerk who filled in when the Seals decided to give Jack McCartan a rest. McCartan had played 30 games in a row and badly needed some time off before the playoffs. "There's absolutely no reason why we should have played McCartan," Burns said after the game. "We didn't want to take a chance of having Jack injured in a meaningless game." The previous night against Los Angeles, McCartan had been struck on the head and needed nine stitches to close the gash. Burns made it quite clear that they "weren't going to sacrifice him."[57] Rather, it was Green who became the sacrificial lamb.

Green had been used as a practice goalie by the Seals, so he had faced professional shooters before, but practice is not the same as an actual game before actual fans. In all fairness to Burns, his decision to rest McCartan made sense, considering the Gulls came into the contest with a pathetic 21-47-3 record, but the Gulls also finished the season winning five of their last six games. "That was a funny game," Tom Thurlby remembered, "because it was a nothing game for both teams . . . they had no way of making the playoffs, and we were already comfortably in the playoffs. [Green] hung around the team there, and he'd come out and practice with us the odd time, and they just put him in there just to say that he played a game in the Western Hockey League, I think." Asked if he remembered how Green felt after the game, Thurlby responded that he did not, but "I know he let in a lot of bad goals, I do recall that," and then he chuckled.

Before 13,363 San Diego fans, the Gulls took a 3-1 lead into the second period. Matters just got worse for Green when Len Ronson scored for San Diego at 9:03, making it 4-1, Gulls. Charlie Burns responded with a goal of his own just 43 seconds later, but the Seals were out of it from that point. Fred Hilts scored his second goal of the game at 12:28 and his hat trick goal less than a minute later. Light-scoring defenseman Gordie Sinclair scored at 19:20 to make it 7-2, San Diego.

After eight minutes of peace and quiet, the assault picked up again as former Seal Al Nicholson scored his 24th goal of the season. Thirty-one seconds later Jack Faulkner made it 9-2, and 1:11 after that, Jim Wilcox made it 10-2. Not done yet, Nicholson scored again at 14:40 to bring the final score to 11-2. Overall, the unfortunate pari-mutuel clerk faced 48 shots, while his counterpart Les Binkley faced but 29. Green even had to get stitches above his right eye. Surprisingly, despite the embarrassing score, the Seals acted very civilly; in fact, no penalties were called against either team. In the understatement of the year Burns said, "It was a very bad game from our standpoint, but after all, with absolutely nothing at stake it was hard to get up for the game."[58] Green must have felt relieved his hellish night was all for naught.

As the WHL became more and more of a distant memory, the California Seals prepared to embark upon their NHL journey. Though many former Seals from the Western League would pop in for an occasional visit to the Coliseum, it did not matter; the atmosphere at the Oakland arena was never the same as it had been at the Cow Palace. Tommy Green's night of horror turned out to be a chilling omen of things to come.

2

THE OAKLAND ERROR, 1967-1968

From 1942 to 1967 the National Hockey League consisted of six teams: the Montreal Canadiens, Toronto Maple Leafs, Boston Bruins, New York Rangers, Detroit Red Wings, and Chicago Black Hawks. Hundreds of talented young players who could not find a place in the NHL had to settle for a spot in the minor leagues. Someday, they hoped, they would get the call from the big team, asking them to sub for an injured Rocket Richard or Gordie Howe. NHL expansion meant 120 more full-time jobs. Players who had been buried deep in the minors were now expected to play major minutes and lead these new expansion clubs. Opportunity existed as never before, but playing for an expansion team would be a difficult adjustment for many.

After expansion the game would never be the same, for better and for worse. Gone were those simpler days when the league's uniform color palate consisted of red, white, blue, yellow, and black. With expansion came unconventional colors such as forest green, purple, gold, orange, and powder blue. While the NHL of yesteryear may have been a little conservative and drab, it oozed tradition; but if the league truly wanted to be *national*, it needed to open itself to experimentation.

Even before a game had been played, the California Seals' front office felt confident about the team's chances in the expansion division. In May 1967 Frank Selke predicted the Seals were "not going to be just contenders," they were "going to be better."[1] The Seals had every reason to feel confident; they had a huge advantage over all the other expansion clubs. "People in the sport tell me we will have more strength starting off than the other new clubs," said Rudy Pilous, "mainly because we're the only one already operating." He tried his best, however, to avoid promising Seals fans the world so early in the franchise's existence: "Sure we own 12 players outright, which is more than the other new teams have at the moment . . . But that doesn't mean that all these players are of National Hockey League calibre."[2]

Pilous gave the Seals instant credibility, even though the team had struggled with him behind the bench. Nevertheless, Pilous was gregarious and had a way with the media. "He was a really likeable guy. The media liked him. He was a fun guy to be around, he was friendly," said the Seals' then-broadcaster and public relations director Tim Ryan.

Unfortunately, as would often be the case with the California Seals, common sense took a backseat to folly. Barry Van Gerbig wanted to hire Vancouver Canucks coach and former NHL star Bert Olmstead to take over the Seals' bench because he felt Pilous was too laid back. "We felt we really needed a disciplinarian, and Bert Olmstead fit the mold. He had so much credibility as a player—he had an aura about him. We felt minor league players would respond to him as they wouldn't to Rudy."[3] Pilous agreed he was more suited as general manager and accepted Van Gerbig's decision to hire Olmstead as coach.

No one ever doubted Olmstead's heart and drive, but he could be oppressive and curt, often straining relationships with his players. "I remember one time," said Tom Thurlby, "he brought up about Charlie [Burns] coaching that last year in Oakland. Bert brought this up two or three times against Charlie, about what a poor coach he was … in front of all the players in the dressing room and stuff like that just to try to intimidate Charlie." Olmstead was just as blunt with members of the media. According to Tim Ryan, "Olmstead was a hero because of who he was in Canada, but by nature he was a shy, inward-looking guy who put a lot of pressure on himself to do well. Bert was always short-tempered with 'stupid' questions from the press."[4] There were reports his lack of communication skills cost him a coaching job with the New York Rangers. One anonymous player even said, "Olmstead has no use for minor league hockey players," which, if true, was a very bad sign for the California Seals, a team that would be loaded with minor leaguers.[5]

Olmstead had been a key component of five Stanley Cup winners in Montreal and Toronto. He had never been the most talented player in the league, but he had been an excellent playmaker who had played well alongside Bernard Geoffrion and Jean Beliveau in Montreal. He twice led the league in assists and scored 602 points in 848 career games. Geoffrion and Beliveau got to the Hall of Fame through superior skill and by capturing several individual honors along the way; Olmstead got in through guts and determination. When he became the Seals' coach, he expected his players, even those with minor-league credentials, to show the same tenacity and drive he had. "A minor league hockey player is a man that has to make a living like anyone else," he said. "But he has to have the ambition to try and better himself, to correct his bad habits that have kept him down, and be willing to work and keep himself in condition so he can be a winner and draw major league pay."[6]

Van Gerbig was hoping Olmstead's pedigree would rub off on the castoffs that were going to make up the opening night roster, but before Olmstead committed to anything, he insisted Rudy Pilous be fired. "I've forgotten the details," admitted Tim Ryan. "I just know that a lot of it had to do with the fact that once Bert was there it wasn't going to work. . . . Bert was making it clear he didn't want him to be the boss, and everything just got off on the wrong foot." Who would replace Pilous as general manager? Olmstead took that job too.

Pilous and Olmstead actually coexisted for a while, contrary to popular belief. For instance, in the book *Hockey! The Story of the World's Fastest Sport*, authors Dick Beddoes, Stan Fischler, and Ira Gitler claim, "When Bert Olmstead sat down at the Montreal draft meeting of June 1967, he had been general manager-coach of the Seals for a month." That was not true; Pilous was still general manager at the draft. "Without an astute general manager armed with informed scouting reports," the trio continued, "Olmstead was like a total paraplegic at a grab bag."[7] Hockey writer Gerald Eskenazi once claimed that "a month before the critical draft meeting was to be staged, van Gerbig fired Pilous. Olmstead suddenly was thrust into the role of general manager. He had to pick 20 players and was ill-prepared to make knowledgeable judgments, so he did not do well in the draft."[8] On the contrary, it was reported in the *Oakland Tribune* that Selke, Olmstead, Pilous, and chief scout Bob Wilson had "set up a huge blackboard in the club's executive office at the Edgewater Inn and ha[d] been exmaining [sic] draft potential of nearly 300 players." In the same article, Tim Ryan explained, "They've spent 10 to 12 hours a day, and will continue to do so until draft time, comparing age versus experience and youth versus inexperience."[9] Frank Selke explained in a May 2012 interview that Pilous, Olmstead, and Wilson worked together "quite diligently" to put together a detailed list of players they wanted.

Pilous was definitely the team's general manager at the expansion draft. In fact, in a June 6, 1967, article detailing the Seals' picks in the expansion draft, the *Oakland Tribune*'s Spence Conley clearly states, "With general manager Rudy Pilous naming the choices and coach Bert Olmstead at his right hand, the Seals continued by shifting to forward help in naming New York's Bill Hicke and Detroit's Billy Harris in third and fourth rounds." Furthermore, Pilous sounded pleasantly optimistic, which would be odd for a guy who had supposedly just been sacked. "Our draft is going much better than we had anticipated," he said. "Even though we drafted last for goalkeepers, I think we got two of the best."[10]

Pilous had signed a four-year contract with the Seals on May 18, 1966, but thirteen months later he found himself on the unemployment line. The contract called for Pilous to be paid $25,000 a year to coach the club, plus an additional $10,000 to be the general manager, and a $10,000 bonus if the club finished with a better record in the standings than three other clubs. Pilous took the Seals to court, suing pretty much everyone associated with the club: Barry Van Gerbig, the California Seals Inc., Shasta Telecasting Corp., San Francisco Hockey Co. Inc., San Francisco Seals, Ltd., Sports Investors, California Seals Hockey Club, and George C. Flaherty, to the tune of $105,000, including $15,000 for "lack of endorsements," which were not defined, and $5,000 for "damaged feelings."[11]

Even though the affable Van Gerbig was part owner of both Standard Oil and Union Carbide, his money and movie star good looks did little to convince hockey experts he was suited to be a NHL owner. Van Gerbig should have kept Pilous in the fold; he was a good hockey man who, because of his friendly relations with the media, would have been a great asset. Some believed Van Gerbig also had some commitment issues. According to Stewart Warner of the *Toronto Star Weekly*, Van Gerbig was "something of an absentee owner—he missed Oakland's 6–0 victory over Los Angeles [January 7, 1968], which snapped their

11-game winless streak, because he was helping organize the [Bing] Crosby golf tournament. But he kept sufficiently in touch with the team to decide he didn't like Pilous's style."[12]

Over the years Van Gerbig has gained the reputation as just another of the Seals' many absentee owners, but Tim Ryan insists Van Gerbig was a dedicated owner who has gotten a bad rap:

> He was terrific with the press, he was friendly, he was outgoing, he was willing to do whatever was required. Anything I asked him to do in terms of media, he did. He didn't hold back on the budget until we literally were running out of money. . . . The players liked him. He liked being around the players because he had been a player himself. He'd come to the locker room and the guys knew he was committed and I think in the second season, that a lot of them felt like, well, he's giving up, not on the players, but I mean, he was giving up on keeping the team there, and so I think that created a little more distance. I think, to a degree, that he was embarrassed that things weren't going better for the players, and I think he shied away a little more from being close to them because it was just harder for him to go into the locker room and tell the guys, "Don't worry, we're going to get through this" when he could see that we weren't going to get through it.

At the expansion draft the Seals stocked their roster with a few fading veterans and a slew of unproven youngsters waiting to get their feet wet. "I think the Original Six only gave up maybe six players or whatever," said Los Angeles King Bryan Campbell. "You could protect maybe, say, your twelve best players, and you lose one, and you fill one, you lose one, you fill one. . . . So they never really gave up that much. A lot of the expansion players came from the American Hockey League, the Central pro league, the Western pro league, so going into these cities, the Original Six, we were always considered underdogs."

The first two rounds of the draft involved only goaltenders, by far the most talented and recognizable names available, but the Seals had the last pick in each round. With their first pick, the Seals selected Charlie Hodge of the Montreal Canadiens, which turned out to be a smart move. Hodge had an excellent track record as a member of the Canadiens. He was named the league's best goaltender in 1964 and shared the Vezina Trophy with Lorne "Gump" Worsley two years later. In 1966–67, Hodge was runner-up for the award, proving he was still at the top of his game, but the Habs had no choice but to leave either him, Worsley, or Rogatien Vachon unprotected.

Hodge's back-up for the upcoming season, the twenty-three-year-old, 6'4" Gary Smith, was selected from the Toronto Maple Leafs, but he had only five games of NHL experience under his belt. Of those five games, one left a lasting impression. "My real ambition," Smith admitted a few years later, "is to be the first NHL goalie to score."[13] He never did score that goal, but he came close one time versus Montreal:

> The next time I had a shot I caught it and the wingers started peeling off and there wasn't anybody on our team near me. So I dropped the puck at my feet, put it on my stick and took off for the other end. I was gone . . .
>
> I reached the vicinity of the Montreal zone and J.C. Tremblay was standing there, just inside the blueline. J.C. Tremblay had never thrown a bodycheck in his life, but he stepped into me and decked me. I can remember I was spinning around off-balance and I happened to see Punch [Imlach], who was pulling his hat down over his eyes. The next thing I knew, Ralph Backstrom had the puck and he was heading the other way toward our end, and I was scrambling along behind trying to catch up. Backstrom took a shot and Marcel Pronovost, who was on our defence, had gone back into our goal crease and he made one of the greatest saves I've ever seen in my life. He still had the puck when I finally got back into the net.[14]

Smith's risky style of play often distressed his coaches, even though this kind of stunt usually brought the crowd to its feet. Unfortunately for hockey fans everywhere, no other goalie will ever take a rush toward his masked brethren. Rule 32, section i (aka "The Gary Smith Rule") of the NHL rulebook states: "If a goalkeeper participates in the play in any manner when he is beyond the center red line, a minor penalty shall be imposed upon him."[15] Smith's nickname was "Suitcase," not because of his tendency to wander all over the ice, but rather because he always seemed to be playing for a new team. By the time he retired in 1980, he had suited up for thirteen different professional teams.

As if Smith's on-ice antics were not enough, the flaky goalie often wore an obscene number of socks under his skates to protect his ankles and feet. In an October 2011 interview Ted Hampson recalled how Smith's superstitions could cause his teammates to panic:

> *There's* a guy that had superstitions. Before the games . . . he had about six suits of underwear he'd put on first. Or maybe not six, maybe three or four, and then he'd have, I think it got up to nine pairs of socks . . . and he'd be playing, and Charlie Hodge is sitting there looking at him and saying, "I hope this guy is gonna be ready to play, 'cause I'm not ready to play. I didn't even warm up to play. He's never gonna get dressed in time, so I'm gonna have to start." I think this was going through Charlie's mind, but it went through all our minds to a degree, but [Smith] always got ready.

Hampson need not worry about exaggerating the truth when describing Gary Smith. Talking one time about his sock superstition, the goalie once admitted, "My record is sixteen."[16]

Smith's antics didn't stop there. One time, in the middle of a game, while he was playing for Vancouver, his coach caught him eating a hot dog on the bench. Between periods, Smith had the strangest habit of stripping off all his equipment and taking a shower. He also had nasty diarrhea attacks before games, but anyone who has met a goaltender will tell you that diarrhea is not much worse than the vomiting that goalies such as Charlie Hodge would routinely do before facing a barrage of pucks. Despite his many eccentricities, Smith was fondly remembered. "Gary was a good goalie," said future teammate Howie Menard, "and was a happy-go-lucky guy. . . . 'Axe' was a lot of fun to play with, a good guy."

After the goaltenders had been selected, rounds three to twenty of the expansion draft were reserved for forwards and defensemen. Once again the Seals drew a short straw and picked fifth every round.

Pilous, Olmstead, and Wilson planned their selections around a defense-first strategy as there was no way they were going to get many goals out of the forwards available. Bobby Baun, the hero of the 1964 Stanley Cup finals, was chosen first. He had scored the game winner in game six of the final on an awkward blast from the blue line to even the series with Detroit en route to the Leafs' eleventh Stanley Cup. The fact he scored on what turned out to be a fractured ankle became part of hockey folklore. While Baun's offensive skills were limited, no one doubted his character, ruggedness, and defensive prowess. Baun was so keen on escaping Punch Imlach's doghouse that he took precautions in case plans fell through: "'Sit tight,' Bert said, 'you're going to be our number-one draft choice.' Well, I put down the phone and probably belted out a few bars of 'California, Here I Come.' My heart was set on rejoining Bert, and I even had my lawyer, Jim Blaney, draft a retirement announcement in case I was chosen by any other team."[17]

Seals president Frank Selke offered Baun a huge pay raise ($37,500 a year for three years), nearly one-third more than he was earning in Toronto. Baun's value to the Seals was evident even before he played a game. When Baun was voted interim president of the NHL Players Association, Olmstead sternly advised him to "duck that headache," as he would "have enough problems just concentrating on hockey" that winter.[18] Olmstead fined Baun $1,000 a day until he resigned from his position as head of the union. Disgusted, Baun considered leaving Oakland for good, but Olmstead convinced him to come back with the fine, now at $13,000, withdrawn. Baun stayed on as president for six months until Norm Ullman took over in March 1968.

Olmstead was nothing short of thrilled to have his former teammate patrolling the Seals' blue line. "I wish I had 16 like him," he gushed. "I don't know of a more honest hockey player. He has tremendous pride, the kind of guy you can build a team around. Any young kid coming into this league looks at the way Bobby comes off the ice with his sweater stuck to his skin with perspiration, and he soon realizes what you have to do to play in this league. We want Bobby to be our leader."[19] Everyone thought so highly of Baun that on opening night, he was handed the team captaincy.

As valuable as Baun was to the franchise, he could not do it all by himself. With their second pick the Seals selected 1963 NHL Rookie of the Year Kent Douglas from the Leafs, while the massive 220-pound Larry Cahan, a long-time New York Ranger, headed west with the fifth overall pick. So far, so good for the defense.

Offense, on the other hand, was a different kettle of fish. Based on career statistics at that time, the biggest offensive weapons chosen by the Seals were Bill Hicke (220 points in 455 career games) and Billy Harris (292 points in 634 career games). While no one was going to rejoice over those numbers, they were actually among the best of all the available players. Hicke had talent, but his frequent asthma attacks were distressing. He also had not played a complete NHL season since 1962–63. Hicke had such bad luck health-wise that he almost died *twice* during his big league career. While he was playing for the Rangers, Hicke had been playing golf with some of his team-mates when it started to rain. Before long, he was so sick that he fell into a coma for two weeks. Then, during his first season in Oakland, he almost died at practice. Olmstead was running the team ragged one day when Hicke's asthma started acting up. He skated over to the bench for a rest, but Olmstead sent him back out anyway. Hicke fell to the ice in a heap a few minutes later and was rushed to the hospital.

Despite the health issues, Hicke had talent in spades. In 1958–59 he won both the American Hockey League's Rookie of the Year award and the scoring title with 41 goals and 97 points before moving up to Montreal as a fill-in for the playoffs. In his first three full NHL seasons he scored 18, 20, and 17 goals and had a career-high 51 points in 1961–62. Afterward, injuries took their toll, reducing Hicke's effectiveness before he was finally dealt to the New York Rangers in December 1964. In the final year before expansion Hicke's production dropped to 7 points in 48 games, but the Seals gambled on him regaining his form.

The grey-haired, thirty-one-year old Billy Harris had also been a consistent 15–20 goal man at one time and had been one of the most popular Maple Leafs of the early 1960s. He was quick on his feet and was an excellent playmaker, but he never got along with Punch Imlach. Harris was traded to Detroit in 1965 after a couple of mediocre seasons in Toronto, but he played only 24 games with the Wings that season.

He spent most of the season and all of the next with the Pittsburgh Hornets of the American League winning the circuit's MVP award. For Harris, expansion was a chance to prove he still had what it took to play in the big leagues.

Pilous, Olmstead, and Wilson made some wise choices as most of the players drafted early on would play key roles in the coming season. Hodge, Baun, Douglas, Cahan, Hicke, and Harris all had excellent credentials and had enjoyed considerable success with their Original Six clubs. With the exception of Cahan, all had won the Stanley Cup. The Seals' problem was their inability to find gems in the career minor leaguers and youngsters available in the latter stages of the draft. Table 1 lists all of the players the Seals selected at the draft and their age at the time of the draft.

The California Seals were long on experience but short on skill, especially at forward. Some expansion teams, such as Pittsburgh and St. Louis, did the same thing as Oakland and relied on big name players to lead the way, while others such as Philadelphia and Los Angeles believed a roster chock full of youngsters was the way to go. Since there had never been an expansion draft before, no one knew which philosophy would lead to greater success.

The Seals hoped a few players with minor-league offensive credentials would provide some secondary scoring behind Hicke and Harris. Wally Boyer, for instance, had been a consistent scorer with the American Hockey League's Rochester Americans and Springfield Indians. In his five full seasons in the AHL, he had never scored fewer than 20 goals. Joe Szura also had similar credentials, scoring over 20 goals four times, including a career-high 46 goals with Cleveland in 1965–66. Not to be outdone, Alain "Boom-Boom" Caron had scored an AHL-leading 47 goals with Buffalo that same year. Ron Boehm was just coming off a season in which he had scored 18 goals and 24 assists and had won the WHL's Rookie of the Year award. While those gaudy statistics gave the impression the Seals were going to score a ton of goals, none of the above players, with the exception of Boyer, had ever scored one in the NHL.

Following the draft, many experts figured the Seals would win the expansion division. In fact, the October 14, 1967, issue of the *Hockey*

Table 1. Seals selections in 1967 expansion draft

GOALTENDERS

PLAYER	GP	W	L	T	GA	SO	GAA
Charlie Hodge (34) MTL	237	119	73	40	563	21	2.46
Gary Smith (23) TOR	5	0	4	0	14	0	3.62

FORWARDS AND DEFENSEMEN

PLAYER	GP	G	A	PTS	PIM
D Bobby Baun (30) TOR	602	25	110	135	925
D Kent Douglas (31) TOR	283	20	65	85	408
RW Bill Hicke (29) NY	455	87	133	220	228
D Billy Harris (31) DET	634	107	185	292	181
D Larry Cahan (33) NY	388	19	47	66	445
C Wally Boyer (29) CHI	88	9	23	32	36
D Joe Szura (28) MTL	0	0	0	0	0
D Bob Lemieux (22) MTL	0	0	0	0	0
LW Jean-Paul Parise (25) BOS	21	2	2	4	10
D Ron Harris (24) BOS	4	0	1	1	7
RW Terry Clancy (24) TOR	0	0	0	0	0
D Tracy Pratt (24) CHI	0	0	0	0	0
D Autry Erickson (29) TOR	160	3	13	16	134
LW Ron Boehm (23) NY	0	0	0	0	0
RW Alain Caron (29) CHI	0	0	0	0	0
C Mike Laughton (23) TOR	0	0	0	0	0
C Bryan Hextall (26) NY	21	0	2	2	8
D Gary Kilpatrick (24) CHI	0	0	0	0	0

News proudly boasted on its front cover: "Hockey News Poll Reveals Hawks, Seals Teams to Beat." Inside, the magazine elaborated on its prognostication: "In the West, hockey men figured the expansion division will be at least a three-way 'dogfight' for the top with California, Philly and Minnesota closely involved."[20]

Van Gerbig, for one, couldn't have been happier with the outcome of the draft. "Things just couldn't go any better for us," the twenty-eight-year-old owner chirped. "We've obtained just about everything we wanted so far. We're going to have the biggest, meanest and steadiest defense, possibly the best in the NHL. Nobody is going to shove us around."[21] Olmstead also felt confident, perhaps a little too confident, that the team he had helped draft would be successful. "We'll beat every team in the National Hockey League this season," he said. When asked if he meant the five other teams in the expansion division, Olmstead clarified his opinion. "No, I mean the old clubs."[22] The Seals were arguably the cockiest team in the NHL, and they had yet to play a single minute.

As the regular season loomed, the Seals tossed around different uniform designs. After toying with the idea of keeping the same uniforms as those from their WHL days, it was decided that a new big league team deserved a new uniform: forest green home uniforms with blue and white trim, while the away jerseys would be white with blue and green trim. A new logo, consisting of an abstract-looking seal holding a hockey stick and leaping out from a blue *C* was also designed. The Seals' stylish logo and uniform were winners and certainly ahead of their time. One press box observer described the Seals' attire as "flashy green and blue uniforms that looked like something from a psychedelic tailor."[23]

The California Seals' first-ever training camp opened on September 10, 1967, in Port Huron, Michigan. Nearly forty players were invited, including several from the WHL Seals and the twenty men selected in the expansion draft, but the players drafted in June were expected to make up the bulk of the roster. "They already had that team picked before training camp, as far as I could see," recalled Tom Thurlby. "Us minor leaguers were just there to get the NHL players in shape. . . . None of us, that I recall, ever played in an exhibition game. In fact, I remember, they went on the road there for, I think, a Saturday-Sunday game somewhere, I think it was Buffalo, and they just told the rest of us guys we could do whatever we want . . . there would be no ice for us to practice on."

44

At the conclusion of camp the final roster was pared down to nineteen players, including San Francisco player-coach Charlie Burns. Bringing Burns to the NHL was an easy decision for a team with few recognizable faces. "He was phenomenal," remembered Thurlby about Burns's play in the Seals' second championship run. "He just never quit. I bet he played 30, 35, 40 minutes a game; he just seemed to be on the ice all the time and he pretty well controlled the play anytime he was on the ice." Broadcaster Tim Ryan, who became close friends with Burns, said he was "a terrific guy. . . . He was kind of the heart and soul of the team, and a guy that was just really a minor leaguer, but played an NHL level when he got his chance." Expansion was an opportunity for Burns, who had played in the big leagues from 1958 to 1963, mostly as a penalty killer and power-play specialist, to prove he still had what it took to compete with the world's best players.

George Swarbrick, the 1964–65 WHL Rookie of the Year, and a 31-goal scorer in San Francisco, also eased into the Seals' roster as one of the club's top right wingers. "That guy could shoot with anybody in the NHL," said Ryan. "He wasn't too great at anything else, but he could shoot the puck. He was in like Bobby Hull's category of slap shots in those days." Other Western League Seals to play games for the NHL club that season included Tom Thurlby, Gerry Odrowski, and Ron Harris.

The team's first exhibition match on September 17, 1967, foreshadowed what was to come for the California Seals. J. P. Parise scored the NHL franchise's first-ever goal, but the Minnesota North Stars won the game 3–1. Olmstead was irate by his troop's supposed lack of motivation. "We have a few players who need their heads deflated and their bodies in shape. Today, we skate! We know what the problem is and we are going to solve it."[24] And skate they did, over and over and over.

Olmstead could not tolerate losing. Practice soon became draining to players, and after a while they stopped responding to Olmstead's drill sergeant tactics. "He was pretty good with a whip," recalled ticket sales manager Jim Lingel. "He made those guys bounce—and not in a good way—and they didn't want to play for him. . . . I don't know why he did it, but it just destroyed the team." Practices would sometimes last over two hours, exhausting the players, but Olmstead never needed to worry about getting winded himself. "As I recall," said Thurlby, "he'd sit in the stands, drink coffee, and smoke cigarettes, and blow the whistle. That's true! Over in that old rink over in Berkeley there. Very seldom we practiced in our home rink. . . . There wasn't such a thing as an easy practice, and if we lost the night before you know right well the next day it was going to be two hours of stops and starts."

Even a national holiday didn't stop Olmstead. He felt the team was lazy and unappreciative of their opportunity to play in the NHL. According to Charlie Hodge, Olmstead had told the players, "You guys are going to start acting like a regular working person; you would work the whole day." Olmstead called a practice, but after the players had showered he told them to come back to the rink. Hodge continued, "So we came back at 1 p.m. on Thanksgiving Day and he made us sit in the dressing room, doing nothing, until 4 p.m. We were waiting to go home for Thanksgiving dinner. We couldn't leave because Bert was in the next room."[25]

The Seals were off to a rough start, but there was a glimmer of hope. Around that time, legendary Montreal Canadiens goaltender Jacques Plante, then thirty-eight years old, pondered making a comeback. Plante already had a sales promotion job with a Quebec brewery, but when he went on vacation in September he turned up in Port Huron for the Seals' training camp. Plante had not played an NHL game since 1964–65, but he arrived at the same time Hodge was engaged in a contract dispute.

Several sportswriters claim Plante was originally brought in to be the Seals' goaltending coach, but in reality Plante came to play. In early 1967 Rudy Pilous had actually received permission from the New York Rangers to negotiate a contract with Plante, which would have seen him join the San Francisco Seals. The January 13, 1967, *Oakland Tribune* reported that Pilous said Plante wanted "to abandon his one-year retirement and get back into action." With the Seals then in the middle of a 7-game win streak and looking like a championship contender again, Pilous declared he was hoping to talk with Plante "to see what it would take to bring him out of retirement, possibly for the last half of [the] season." Pilous said, "He should be in good shape but we don't know just what to expect from him so we're going to have a long discussion."[26] In the end Plante never played a regular-season game for the Seals that season, but that didn't mean his comeback plans were scrapped.

Plante was signed to a try-out contract partly as insurance in case Hodge remained unsigned before the start of the season. According to Frank Selke, "Olmstead had a very good relationship with Emile Francis and Plante belonged to the Rangers. Somehow Bert made a deal with Emile to let Plante come to our training camp," which was good news for the Seals, who desperately needed some big names in their line-up not only to make them competitive but to draw fans as well.

Plante looked good enough in Port Huron to earn himself a shot versus Terry Sawchuk's Los Angeles Kings on September 21. Plante played the first thirty minutes and allowed two goals. "Plante directed his teammates [very] well," said Olmstead. "He handled the puck authoritatively and the fact he went 30 minutes his first time out is pleasing." Plante himself was more than satisfied with his performance. "I proved to myself that I could still play in the NHL. The two goals scored were well played by the other team. But I wasn't weak and I think to myself that if I had played those shots another way, I might have stopped them."[27] As is customary in preseason games, the back-up goalie, in this case Gary Smith, took over at the halfway mark. The Seals entered the third period trailing 3–1, but two power-play goals by Wally Boyer and Bill Hicke evened the score before the final buzzer.

Plante looked poised to take over the starting job from Hodge, but as would become the norm in Oakland, the club's best-laid plans were quickly dashed. The Seals could not work out a deal with the Rangers, so Plante was ordered to leave camp. Hodge came to terms on a new contract, and Plante never played another minute for the Seals. Plante had a different explanation for his sudden departure: "I want to play but I can't because of my family. The Seals wanted me to come here to help coach; that's why I came. There were others who didn't want me back as a player though."[28] According to Selke, however, Plante never planned on being the Seals' goaltending coach:

> He was looking for a job as a goaltender. He wasn't interested in being a coach. . . . Olmstead and Pilous, even before the draft, they had made arrangements to have the training camp in Port Huron, and I was in the process of moving family and all kinds of things so I didn't get to training camp in Port Huron until . . . probably the third or fourth day of camp. . . . He wasn't there very long for sure . . . He played enough to make the decision that this team wasn't good enough for him to play with, and frankly, knowing Jacques as well as I did . . . he would not have had a very happy time, for sure, so he made the right decision.

On September 30, 1967, Bill Hicke, Kent Douglas, and Billy Harris led California to a 3-1 victory over the Kings, the Seals' first win in seven preseason games. The Seals also won their next game 3-2 over Minnesota, but the good will the players had built up with Olmstead quickly disappeared in their final exhibition game, because the Seals actually *lost*, 4-3, to the American Hockey League's Buffalo Bisons.

Olmstead was furious. He felt his players showed little enthusiasm and that while the other expansion teams were "enthused with their opportunity," the Seals players weren't, and he was "going to find out why."[29] Pete Axthelm wrote in *Sports Illustrated* that Olmstead "felt players, especially rookies, were over-evaluating their services in some cases; a player who signed for a large increase might tend to become complacent, while one felt he was short-changed could turn resentful."[30] Coming from perennial Stanley Cup contenders in Montreal and Toronto, Olmstead expected the same type of winning attitude from his troops. But Bill Hicke was not Maurice Richard, and Kent Douglas was not Doug Harvey.

Tim Ryan believed Olmstead had tenacity and had always been a hard worker, but those qualities did not help him behind the bench. He could motivate himself, but he could not motivate others:

The biggest lack that Bert had was communication. He didn't know how to communicate the Bert Olmstead style of hockey to his players. And not only that, he expected, unrealistically, that they should all be like Bert, and they weren't going to be, and a lot of them didn't want to be. They didn't see the demeanor and the point of view toward the game that Bert had as being the way that they thought was to be successful, so our problems with the team were mainly the coaching situation, and I think really we kind of recognized it fairly early on, but, you know, here it is our first year, we don't want to be giving up on the coach, and it's his first year coaching.

Bobby Baun defended his coach's high expectations to *Sports Illustrated*'s Dick Beddoes. "He's right, like he always is about hockey," Baun said about Olmstead. "If you make fundamental mistakes you lose. If you don't make mistakes and you're anywhere even in talent, you win. Olmstead is the Lombardi of hockey. Under Olmstead, skating is the first commandment. Some days it is skating for two hours at a stretch without stopping."[31] Baun had no problem with tough practices; he was just glad to be away from the Leafs' Punch Imlach: "He makes Punch's practices look like nursery school. I feel like a young guy again. It's like starting over—with the advantage of experience. I'm even learning new things, and I've regained the enthusiasm that I lost in Toronto."[32]

Olmstead often butted heads with his players when he felt they weren't performing well. For instance, young J. P. Parise had a tremendous upside and good offensive skills, but once he had a verbal altercation with Olmstead, he was deemed expendable. After a preseason game in which Parise made a defensive gaffe and drew a subsequent penalty that led to a power play goal against the Seals, Olmstead allegedly made some derogatory remarks about French Canadians, which infuriated Parise, but Olmstead was judge, jury, and executioner in Oakland.[33] Parise was dealt to Toronto with Bryan Hextall for Gerry Ehman, a thirty-five-year-old right winger who had scored 59 points in 132 career NHL games. The Parise deal highlighted another problem that would plague the Seals throughout their history: impulsiveness. Instead of sending Parise to the minors and waiting for the right moment to trade him, Olmstead shipped him off as quickly as possible. While the Seals' penchant for trading promising young talent for immediate help benefited the team in the short term, in reality this practice proved harmful.

Gerry Ehman may have been short on NHL experience, but he was a proven veteran in other pro leagues across the continent. He had been the darling of the Toronto Maple Leafs in the 1959 playoffs, having scored 13 points in 12 games, but by 1961, his NHL career had all but evaporated. He had a brief stint in Toronto in 1964 but before long was shipped off to the sticks once again. In Oakland, however, Ehman went on to prove his weary legs still had much life. Captain Bobby Baun had many positive things to say about his new, yet familiar, teammate: "He was from Cudworth, Saskatchewan, and he looked like a square-jawed gunslinger, so we nicknamed him Tex. He had a knack for shooting the puck with a quick flick of his wrists. He wasn't the greatest skater, which is probably why he had been a career minor leaguer, but he had a great attitude and good hockey sense; you could always count on him to be on his wing."[34] Tom Thurlby remembers Gerry Ehman fondly. "That poor old guy, he worked his ass off every shift," he said.

Prior to the start of the regular season, the *Toronto Globe and Mail* suggested, "In expansion [Ehman] may score one goal for each year he has lived." The *Globe and Mail* article also warned: "[Unless] Olmstead can engineer other trades for scoring strength, he must expect to win a lot of 2–1 and 1–0 hockey games. Deals are remote because he does not have much to offer. The onus is on the defense and goaltending to make California competitive, so demanding a task that skepticism is the proper stance."[35] Thankfully for Olmstead, the other five expansion clubs also had rosters full of question marks.

On October 11, 1967, the Seals hosted the Philadelphia Flyers to open the first season of NHL expansion. Kent Douglas went down in history as the California Seals' first ever goal scorer at 3:23 of the first period, and the Flyers' Bill Sutherland scored the first goal against the Seals at 10:07 of the second. Overall, the Seals looked very good outshooting Philly 33–25, and Hicke, Douglas, and Ehman scored 3 points each in a 5–1 win. "I think it is unbelievable to have this kind of game played by a new team," Van Gerbig was quoted as saying. "It's the best coached team for this early in the season that I've ever seen." Indeed, it was a rather naive comment to make so early in the season, but it spoke volumes about the man at the top. "You just had to love Barry," explained Bobby Baun, "but he had no idea what he was taking on, other than he loved to be a jock. Bert and Frank had their hands full trying to give him a line to go on."[36]

Despite the rave early season reviews, building a fan base in Oakland would prove difficult; only 6,886 fans showed up for the season opener, but 9,000 had been expected. While San Francisco fans had been accustomed to having their own hockey team, Oakland had been without pro hockey for years. Even years later the fans hadn't quite learned the rules of the sport. In 1974 long-time New York Rangers fan Greg Lamont watched a game at the Coliseum with his wife, but they were left scratching their noggins. "When you grow up in New York, hockey was forever, going back to the twenties," he explained, "so everybody knew about offsides." Seals fans, however, were not quite so knowledgeable. "The announcer would go, 'That . . . was . . . a . . . two-line . . . pass' in a monotone voice, or he would say, 'That . . . is . . . an . . . offside' . . . but we're sitting there laughing like, 'You really got to tell the people that?'"

The Seals continued their winning ways in game number two by shutting out the Minnesota North Stars, 6–0. Hodge turned in the first shutout of the expansion era by blocking 20 drives. Harris scored twice for California while Ehman, Douglas, Cahan, and Szura picked up singles. The early season success had been predicted by hockey experts as far back as the expansion draft, but reality soon caught up to the California Seals. After the hard-earned victory over Minnesota, the Seals went 14 games without a win. By that time they were firmly entrenched in last place, and all the preseason fears that Olmstead had felt in his bones came true. To make matters worse, attendance was shrinking at an alarming rate. Game two had but 4,155 spectators, and game three had fewer than 3,500. "When I arrived there I didn't know all of the subtleties," admitted Tim Ryan. "I knew that only in a very general way that San Francisco people didn't go to Oakland for anything, and I met the reality of it, that was my job to somehow a) get those fans to come across the bridge and b) create new hockey fans, so it was twofold. . . . So, it was a bit of a task, to say the least, and I don't think that I succeeded, and I don't think that history shows that the following group under Charlie Finley succeeded either. I regret that fact; I wish we had had more time, but I'm not sure that even with more time, at that time in the late sixties, that we could have made it a successful NHL franchise producing enough ticket sales and television and radio rights and so on to make the thing pay off." Selling tickets in Oakland would be an ongoing problem throughout the team's history. Ryan believed that even "if P.T. Barnum had been the PR guy with the Seals, he wasn't going to fill a circus tent."

In early November Van Gerbig asked the NHL front office for permission to change the club's name, hoping it would entice local fans. "It was the desire of the league that we try to identify with San Francisco," Van Gerbig conceded. "This is a different situation from Minneapolis and St. Paul. The only way we could identify with both cities would be to play in the middle of the bridge. There should be no kidding ourselves. We're Oakland."[37] The club's name was officially changed to the Oakland Seals on December 8.

The Seals picked up a few wins here and there after the name change, including a surprising 2–1 victory over Montreal on November 18 during the Habs' first-ever West Coast trip, and a 4–1 win over Boston on December 15, to improve the Seals' record to 7-16-5. The Seals had gained a little momentum as 1967 drew to a close, but they then won just one of their next seventeen games.

On Christmas Day 1967 nothing went right for the Seals as they and the Bruins refused to promote any love and goodwill. Instead of exchanging presents, the two teams exchanged lots of fists in the Bruins' 6–3 win. Ken Hodge of Boston and Charlie Burns of Oakland started needling each other, and a fight broke out. Both benches cleared, and a total of five major penalties were handed out. During the brawl, a fan even threw a few punches at back-up goaltender Gary Smith, spurring Bert Olmstead to come to his aid. Never a shy player in his heyday, Olmstead rushed onto the ice with a hockey stick and hunted the fan around Boston Garden. "Hodge hitting Burns seemed a little uncalled for," Olmstead said later, "and the fan getting into it sort of went against my grain, too. I didn't think I could get him along the corridor so I went the other way—the wrong way. I realized afterward I should have gone the other way (down the aisle)."

"A fan has no business getting into that," the coach continued. "He doesn't pay to hit players, just to watch them. Oh, I wish I'd gone down the back way, I'd have gotten him."[38] The league fined Olmstead $450 ($200 for having chased the fan and $250 for having stepped onto the ice during the brawl) and fined each player who left the bench $50. As for the fan who attacked Smith, he was found by police and escorted out of the arena, but he was not charged.

Olmstead was quickly losing what little patience he had left, but no matter what he did, it never seemed to help the Seals win. "They're just not trying," he said. "I've tried everything to get them to snap out of it. I've insulted and I've threatened. But they've just quit." Later in the season, Olmstead once again blew up when the media confronted him about the club's poor play: "If I was a player, I don't even know whether I'd want to be associated with this bunch. I'd be tossing a few of them out of that dressing room on their cans. They have no pride. A lot of them are getting the chance of a lifetime, and they're reacting like playing in the NHL is a prison sentence." Olmstead was not a people person. Not only did the players have difficult relations with the cranky coach, but so did the media. He refused reporters access to the Seals' dressing room and refused to give out his home phone number. Eddie Dorohoy, a former WHL player, described Olmstead in an unflattering fashion: "If Olmstead did public relations for Santa Claus, there wouldn't be any Christmas."[39]

Olmstead may have bitten off more than he could chew by becoming coach and general manager of an expansion team. He often took out his frustrations on his poor players. "I'm not saying it was all on Bert," said Tim Ryan, "because I certainly believe that athletes getting paid should be giving their best all the time, but he didn't make that an admirable or an enviable task for our players to do. He'd lock 'em up and close the doors to the arena and make them skate laps when they lost or after a losing streak. Guys would be throwing up on the ice. . . . It just didn't work."

Tom Thurlby believed Olmstead was under tremendous pressure in Oakland, and that over time the pressure simply became unbearable. "The way I see it, Bert just hated so badly to lose," Thurlby said, "and he had such a good team there. Everybody said, 'Well, Oakland's gonna be number one,' and we ended being at the bottom, but I think it was just too much; he couldn't cope. And I was surprised he didn't end up in a mental hospital somewhere. He couldn't take it anymore, he just packed it in. He just got the hell away from it."

According to Ryan, when it came time to speak to the media before and after games, Olmstead would often delegate the task to someone else:

> It was very upsetting to Frank Selke and it was very hard for me to be trying to explain him to the media. He didn't want to talk to the media at all, and so all of those things made it harder for us to a) win, and b) create an atmosphere that would have helped to bring more people to the arena . . .
>
> He had hired an assistant coach, Gordon Fashoway who became his kind of drinking buddy more than anything else. . . . He understood that this whole world wasn't easy for Bert to be doing and he needed an apologist, so Gordon would kind of make up for him with the press and Bert would say, "Well, you go talk to the press, and if they want to know who's playing the lines tonight, you tell 'em. I don't want to talk to those guys."

After five consecutive December losses the Seals finally picked up a point against Pittsburgh. Oakland's Gary Smith and Pittsburgh's Les Binkley, both rookies, recorded shutouts as the game ended in a scoreless draw. Unfortunately this game started a string of four consecutive games in which the Seals were unable to score. The Penguins, Canadiens, Black Hawks, and Blues all took turns blanking the Seals.

On January 4 versus Detroit, following 276 minutes and 15 seconds of consecutive scoreless hockey, the Seals' Alain Caron mercifully put an end to the dubious streak with a 25-foot blast that eluded Wings' goaltender Roy Edwards. Wally Boyer and Kent Douglas also tallied for Oakland, but the happiness was short-lived as the Wings took the game, 9-3, dropping the Seals' record to 7-25-6.

With this latest winless streak now stretching to 11 games, Gerry Ehman took matters into his own hands on January 7 and registered the first hat trick in club history while Charlie Hodge, making his first start in 8 games, shut out the Los Angeles Kings, 6-0. The dependable Charlie Burns, playing on a line with Ehman and Boyer for just the second time, scored just his third goal of the season, giving the trio 7 goals since being placed together. Boyer picked up 3 assists while Larry Cahan and Ron Harris also picked up singles for Oakland.

Despite the occasional solid performance, it was painfully obvious that some changes were needed to pull the Seals out of the gutter. Kent Douglas became the fall guy for the team's lousy performances. On occasion, Douglas had been more trouble than he was worth. For example, he believed uniform numbers belonged in football, so early in the season he tore the numbers off his jersey. When Douglas scored 8 points in his first 5 games, Olmstead let that little offense slide, but when Douglas scored just 7 points in his next 35 games, his spunk became less appreciated. "Kent should be the best pointman on the power play and one of the best at getting the puck out of his zone in the league," Olmstead remarked.[40] Gordie Fashoway was even less kind in his assessment of Douglas: "If Kent doesn't pare a little suet off his hide, we'll take a slice out of his pocket. He's overweight, and it shows in his play."[41] Douglas did himself no favors by standing up to Olmstead, something few players ever had the nerve to do. "He was a hard-nosed defenceman who didn't take any shit from anybody," said Gerry Odrowski. "He'd talk back to Bert, but Bert knew better than to say anything to him. He had a heart of gold, but if he didn't like you—look out!"[42]

Olmstead traded the much-maligned defenseman to Detroit for forwards Ted Hampson and John Brenneman and defenseman Bert Marshall. The veteran Hampson was the key to the trade; he had been one of Detroit's better players that year scoring 27 points in 37 games. Brenneman did not have the greatest offensive skills, but he would score 10 goals in 31 games with Oakland. Marshall's forte was a steady, defensive game that included a knack for blocking shots. "We didn't give up on Bert," said Detroit general manager Sid Abel. "But we had to turn over something good to Oakland to get a defenceman of Kent Douglas' calibre."[43] Marshall would go on to patrol the Seals' blue line for the next six seasons.

Hampson was not at all thrilled about leaving Detroit: "My initial reaction was very negative. . . . I really enjoyed Detroit. I liked the team and the people on the team. I was devastated. Not surprised, but I was not happy." Detroit was in the midst of a terrible season, but Hampson believed the situation in Oakland "was more depressed because Bert Olmstead was the coach and he was a real taskmaster, and he was pretty hard on the players, so there was a lot of negative in that regard towards Olmstead."

The Seals and the Bay Area grew on Hampson before long, and a big reason for that was, ironically, Olmstead. "Bert Olmstead treated me really well. . . . I got to play more than I had ever played in pro hockey before," said Hampson. "More situations, more time; I'd come to the bench and get a short rest and then be back out again in some situations, so although he was tough on a lot of players he was the best thing to happen to me in that situation . . . the way Bert used me I just felt like a new player."

Most of the Seals' inaugural season was filled with misery and disappointment, but little did the Minnesota North Stars and Oakland Seals know that their matchup on January 13 would end in true sorrow. In what undoubtedly became the NHL's darkest moment, Minnesota center Bill Masterton lost his life due to injuries suffered during a game.

Masterton had been semi-retired for four years, and with a master's degree in finance from the University of Denver, he had several career options. But when expansion came calling he could not resist taking another kick at the can. "I had to give it a try," he said. "Once you're in hockey, you always wonder if you can play with the best."[44] In the years since his death, Masterton's name has become synonymous with determination and dedication. Players take great pride in winning the Bill Masterton Memorial Trophy because it is not about one's skill as a hockey player, but about one's love of the game.

Although the exact details of what happened to Masterton vary from one witness to another, according to the *Winnipeg Free Press*, during the first period Masterton "had led a rush into the Oakland zone when he was hit by one or two Seals defenders." Masterton fell to the ice, hitting his head hard against the frozen surface. "When I looked back at him he was falling," recalled North Stars public relations man Dick Dillman. "He fell as if he might have already been knocked out."[45]

Blood gushed from Masterton's head. He was subsequently lifted off the ice and placed on a stretcher. At Fairview-Southdale Hospital near Bloomington, Minnesota, a team of five doctors, including two neurosurgeons, could not save his life. Masterton died without regaining consciousness at 1:55 a.m., January 15, 1968, in the presence of his family. At the time of his death Masterton had recorded 4 goals and 8 assists playing on a line with Dave Balon and Wayne Connelly.

Ron Harris was one of the players who had hit Masterton. No one would have called it a dirty or malicious hit; it was a routine play. Even today Harris has difficulty talking about the incident, but in an interview with Seals historian Brad Kurtzberg, he opened up about that fateful night. "Masterton got squashed between a couple of players and fell," Harris recalled. "He hit his head on the ice. We realized right away it was bad."[46]

According to Billy Harris, who was also on the ice at the time of the incident, "It was a clean check; they didn't call a penalty. They say Bill Masterton dumped the puck in and put his head down." Wally Boyer was also there and recalled years later that "[Masterton] came across the blue line and I moved out of the way. Ronnie Harris hit him when his head was down and he fell backwards onto the ice. It was not a dirty check; it was just the way he fell that caused the injury. We didn't know at the time, we just sat around and looked. . . . It was sad; he was a nice guy."[47]

Fans had just taken it for granted that the large number of hockey head injuries had never resulted in a single fatality in NHL history. In a sport where its players have always prided themselves on being gritty, tough, and refusing to back down in the face of danger, player safety had never been a major concern. Wren Blair, the general manager and coach of the North Stars at the time of the Masterton tragedy, explained: "A player signs a professional contract and he plays without a helmet. The fans like to recognize the players and they can't when they wear helmets."[48] The one silver lining in the Masterton tragedy is that it forced players to reevaluate their views on wearing a helmet. Afterward, the helmet didn't seem so wimpy anymore; many of the sport's biggest stars began wearing them, and a new era in hockey began.

With the Seals in danger of falling out of the West Division playoff race, the second half of the season got off to a great start. On January 21, in the first game of a home-and-home series with Los Angeles, Charlie Hodge recorded a 3–0 shutout, and three nights later, the Kings were trounced 4–1 by the surging Seals. Then, just as the Seals seemed to be turning a corner, they lost 6 of their next 7 games, causing Olmstead to reconsider his career path. He wouldn't be the last member of the Seals' front office to do so.

According to ticket sales manager Jim Lingel, at the beginning of the season Olmstead "was very pleasant to me and everybody else around here," but later in the season the stress of coaching a last-place team got to him. Lingel said, "Nobody saw him, and that was his deal. . . . None of [the office staff] liked him . . . I wasn't going near him, I'll tell you that." Tim Ryan recalled one particular road trip when Olmstead opened up to him about how uncomfortable he felt coaching the Seals:

I can remember sitting at a bar somewhere, a hotel bar, after one of these painful losses, and several others, just with Gordon and Bert, and it was the first time that he kind of humanized himself in my presence. He said, "I can't take this anymore. When I get back, I'm going to resign." And I said, "Well, that doesn't sound like the Bert Olmstead I know. Maybe you never lost, whatever it was, ten games in a row or something when you were with the Canadiens, but personally, you were just never a quitter. I find that hard to believe that's what you're saying." And then he said, "Ah, you know," he's swearing and so on, "These guys don't want to play," he was just kind of dumping it on them and so I knew the handwriting was on the wall, and I called Frank and I told him what had ensued and I said, you know, "This doesn't look good. I think he's serious."

In the meantime, Billy Harris, who was mired in a season-long slump, was testing Olmstead's patience. "I've seen Billy Harris play better," said Olmstead, and thus he started using him sparingly.[49] In 41 games Harris had counted just 6 goals and 10 assists, a far cry from what was expected from him, but the bitterness between player and coach went much deeper than that. On January 20 during a game against the Rangers, Harris played the first period but found himself glued to the bench for most of the second. According to Gary Smith, during the intermission Olmstead told Harris, in front of the entire team, to take off his equipment because he believed he had shamed the team. Harris did just that, then put on his street clothes and walked out. Olmstead suspended Harris immediately.

Harris explained that the tension between him and Olmstead had reached a boiling point and that he (Harris) needed time "to think." "I asked Bert to play me or trade me," Harris said to a friend, who then repeated the story to the *Long Beach Press-Telegram*. Olmstead responded by giving Harris a third option. "I'm not going to do either one," said the coach, according to Harris's friend, "which leaves you one alternative—you can quit."[50]

It was a matter of time before the pot boiled over. "Bert Olmstead just rode him to death," remembers Tom Thurlby. "Poor Billy might as well have packed up and went home because he was so intimidated by Bert, it was unreal. Bert always picked on him too." When Thurlby was asked why Harris became a target for Olmstead's wrath, Thurlby said he hadn't a clue. "I think Bert expected more of him than what he was producing. That's the only thing I can think of, and Bert was like that; you had to produce or, boy, he'd just be on you all the time."

Olmstead's rocky relationship with Harris mirrored the situation just one year earlier when his Vancouver Canucks star Billy McNeill, a two-time league MVP, who could not stand playing for Olmstead, took off after just six games. While Harris lasted much longer than that, the situation and the result were practically the same. Both players were thirty-two years old, both played center, both had loads of NHL experience, and both did not respond well to the crack of a whip. Perhaps, as *Press-Telegram* sportswriter Rich Roberts mused, "Apparently, it's just that guys named Billy get Bert's goat."[51] There was talk that Harris's departure could trigger a player revolt, but this never materialized. Bobby Baun, who was a close friend of both Harris and Olmstead, felt uneasy about the bad blood between his long-time teammates: "As the season dragged on, it seemed Olmstead was always criticizing Harris, egged on by his assistant coach, Gord Fashoway. . . . The constant criticism strained, for a while, the very close friendship I'd enjoyed with Bert, although it has since been repaired."[52]

Olmstead decided the best way for him to evaluate his now last-place team was to watch it from the press box, so he handed Gordon Fashoway the coaching reins for a few games. At first the Seals looked their usual listless selves in an awful 5–2 loss to Minnesota, but the Seals soon woke from their slumber beating Toronto 4–3 on February 11, followed by victories over Philadelphia and Boston. The three consecutive wins set a club record, but more importantly, the Seals attracted 11,201 fans to the Coliseum for the Boston game.

A tie and a win versus Minnesota in the final week of February gave the team a total of 42 points in 61 games, but they were still dead last in the league. With Fashoway behind the bench, the team built a 5-game undefeated streak between February 24 and March 3 and lost only one of 9 games, dating back to February 11, but even that one loss was positive in a way.

A season-high 12,025 fans flocked to the Coliseum to watch the Seals battle the Chicago Black Hawks. Any time Bobby Hull made his way to town, fans would come out in droves. "I wish," said Selke, "that we had him all the time." The Seals were completely outgunned by the powerful Hawks, but the game remained scoreless with just three minutes to play. Then the "Golden Jet" took off. According to an article in the March 1968 edition of *Time*, "The scoreboard clock read only three minutes to play when Chicago's Bobby Hull swooped in from the left wing and scooped up the puck. Whoosh! he flashed across the Oakland blue line. Wham! he absorbed a brutal check from Seal Defender [*sic*] George Swarbrick that seemed to stagger him.

Hull's shoulders sagged, his curved stick came up, and for the briefest instant, Swarbrick relaxed. Whap! Hull's stick slashed downward; 25 ft. away, Goalie Hodge could not even begin to react as the rock-hard rubber disk, traveling at better than 100 m.p.h., whistled past his knee into the net."[53]

In early February, Olmstead passed the coaching reins to Fashoway permanently and delivered his most famous quote as a member of the Oakland Seals. "I was sick and tired of looking at them," he said, "and I'm sure they were sick and tired of looking at me. I had to get off the bench to keep my sanity."[54] While this may have been true, the fact he wanted to be by his mother's side while she lay dying back in Saskatchewan was another deciding factor. Olmstead's record was a sorry 10-32-11, but the Seals did not fare much better under Fashoway. After a quick 5-2-3 start to the Fashoway era, the Seals crawled to a 0-8-3 finish.

Tim Ryan believes that Bobby Baun, who was never one to complain about being overworked, took it very personally that Olmstead's time with the Seals came to such a sudden halt:

He was a fan of Bert's. He was the one guy who would go the distance and not complain and give everything. He was a leader on the ice, and he'd try to get the rest of the team to put into it what he did, but most of those guys, they couldn't wait to see Olmstead leave, and Baun kind of took it personally that he hadn't done enough to keep Bert's job, but that's just Bobby as a human being. That's how he would see things. He was a very special guy, and he certainly was as a player and a team leader, and he was the team leader by far.

One player who was certainly glad to see Olmstead gone was Billy Harris, who was welcomed back to the team and found his scoring touch, notching 13 points in 21 games. For the most part, however, Fashoway's promotion did little to fix the Seals. "In fact, I think it got worse," remembered Thurlby with a laugh. One time as the team was boarding the bus, Thurlby remembers Fashoway not taking too kindly to Gerry Odrowski's sense of humor:

I know it's funny, but it wasn't funny at the time. We were going to the airport, and the airport wasn't that far from the rink, really, but we had to take the bus. So anyways, Gerry was the last guy on the bus and he jumped in the bus and, I don't know, he cracked some kind of a joke and, of course, Fashoway was sitting right in the front seat, and he just jumped up, and he said, "Odrowski, get the hell out of here! This isn't a fun place to be!" I know Gerry was just shell-shocked and so was everybody else, so I don't think the morale picked up at all.

Odrowski remembered the incident well. "He responded by telling me that I was going to Vancouver and to pack my bags," he said. "That's what you call an asshole. We used to call him 'Liver Lips.'" Not wanting to make his coach look weak in front of his players, Olmstead grudgingly stood by the decision, but Odrowski eventually got even with Fashoway. "Years later, I was playing for the San Diego Gulls," he remembered, "and we were taking on Portland and he had his knuckles on the boards. I came by and rapped them with my stick and said, 'Take that you son of a bitch!'"[55]

Whether it was the grueling road trips or the endless losing streaks, something made Fashoway's character change. "I felt sorry for Gordon in Oakland, because he didn't represent himself as the person he was," said Thurlby. "I think the pressure he was under was unbelievable, and he turned out like Bert Olmstead; he took it out on the players, and he wasn't very nice compared to the way he was when I played with him in Portland."

With the Seals hopelessly out of the playoff picture and attendance figures sagging, rumors suggested the franchise was on the verge of moving. According to Tim Ryan, Van Gerbig was hoping the rumored sale would spur some interest in the Seals from the Bay Area sports fans:

I spoke to Barry Van Gerbig about it at the time, and he said, "You know, it's not going to happen, that we're going to move there, certainly not this year," but he said, "I have to consider it. The Vancouver people are serious, and maybe it will help us rather than hurt us." And I didn't necessarily agree with him, but I understood his thinking that the threat of moving might entice our local audience, "Oh, my God, we don't want to lose our hockey team, we just got 'em" kind of thing, and neither of those things happened.

Long before the first season ended, Van Gerbig realized that owning an NHL franchise in a nontraditional hockey market was an overwhelming challenge. It was difficult for his friends to see him struggle to keep his head above water. Selke had always enjoyed a warm relationship with the Seals' owner:

> Barry Van Gerbig treated me very well, and I think he got kind of caught up, the way a lot of us did in expansion, thinking that an NHL franchise was a license to print money. A lot of us made egregious mistakes. . . . I wish for his sake, and his brother, who was a decent guy, that things had worked out a little differently. I know they had a tough time for a few years, and it certainly wasn't fun for them . . . but we did the best we could do given the situation that we were faced with and thank goodness it's forty-five years ago.

Tim Ryan also got along well with Van Gerbig and does not blame him for the Seals' struggles. Ryan believes the minority investors bailed out on Van Gerbig when he needed them most:

> I didn't feel, ever, that the owners were saying "Oh, we can't afford that." That certainly didn't occur. . . . The financial problems happened in a more overall way in that when the first capital calls went out, the original ten-percenter type guys . . . didn't come up with the dough, and that put tremendous pressure on Barry and Mickey Van Gerbig. Some of these guys were friends of theirs, but they were dreamers. I guess they thought, "Oh, this will be fun, to say I'm a part owner of a National Hockey League team," and most of them hadn't had any connection with hockey at all . . . you had to be prepared for the fact that the principals may come back and ask for more . . . and when it did occur, these guys just said, "Oh, no way, that's not what I expected, and I'm not going to put up any

more money," so then the Van Gerbigs had to kick in more of their own and find some new partners and ultimately put the club up for sale in a very short period of time.

Despite the huge financial losses he had incurred thus far, Van Gerbig insisted the Seals would remain in the Bay Area: "We definitely will finish the season here and plan to stay many more years. . . . We aren't here for a trial—we are here to stay." Curiously, his denial and his commitment to the city came around the same time *Vancouver Sun* columnist Jim Kearney quoted Van Gerbig as saying, "For us to stay [in Oakland] we'd have to show a considerable increase in crowds after the football season ends. I can't see us doing that."[56] By March 1968 average attendance had risen slightly thanks to a string of large crowds (including one sellout), but the Seals were still a mess. The *Winnipeg Free Press* cleverly summed up the Seals' awkward situation: "For a team that can't win hockey games, can't draw fans, is reported in debt up to $700,000 and is being sued for $100,000, Oakland Seals are mighty popular."[57]

There were reportedly three groups interested in buying the Seals. First, there was Calgary millionaire Max Bell and Vancouver industrialist Frank McMahon. The two men were among a group of fourteen that owned the WHL's Vancouver Canucks, which had a brand-new fifteen-thousand-seat rink ready to accommodate an NHL team. Bell denied any interest in purchasing the Seals even though he was vacationing in California at the time and admitted Vancouver was ready for a big-league franchise.

A second group of potential buyers led by Oakland Athletics owner Charles O. Finley seemed much more promising to local fans since this group claimed to want to keep the team in the Bay Area. In the end Finley was unable to secure the franchise, but it was not the last anyone would hear of him.

Finally, there was the Labatt Breweries of Canada, the heavy favorites to land the ailing franchise. Frank Tatum, secretary and director of the Oakland Seals, claimed Labatt would pay off the Seals' debt to the NHL in exchange for control of the franchise. "Labatt's will provide us with funds to meet our commitment on the date it is due, May 15," said Tatum. "We owe the league several hundred thousand dollars, but not nearly as much as the published figure of $700,000." No money was going to change hands, however, if the Seals stayed in Oakland. "Labatt's have let us know in spades," explained Tatum, "that the brewery is in no way interested in operating a hockey club in northern California. They want control and operation to repose in Canada." And make no mistake, Van Gerbig, while rich, was desperate to unload his money pit. "If we don't pay the NHL by the termination date," admitted Tatum, "they can take back the franchise and we go down the tube. We've got a gun the size of a cannon pointed at our heads and the only way we can solve it is to come up with at least $2,000,000."[58]

Despite formal applications and desperate pleas from Labatt's, the league owners agreed the Seals should remain in Oakland. For one thing, the league's TV contract with CBS stipulated that a franchise be located in the Bay Area, then the fourth-largest market in the United States. Besides, according to Robert T. Nahas, president of Coliseum Corp. Inc., the Seals still had four years left on their five-year lease. Furthermore, the NHL's pride also kept the failing franchise from moving. In the months leading to the expansion draft, the league boasted about its ambitious plan to double in size. It would have been embarrassing for one of its new franchises to pack up and move after one season.

It also should not be forgotten that, at the time, the NHL was looking at Vancouver as a potential expansion site. The Canadian city had wanted to join the league in 1967 but was rebuffed, due in part to the fact they had too many investors, none of whom would have owned more than 10 percent of the team. However, with a potentially solid, more centralized ownership, Vancouver had suddenly become an interesting market, but in reality the league would never allow the Seals to move to British Columbia. After all, the NHL could charge the city of Vancouver a hefty $6 million fee in the next round of expansion. Moving the Seals would not bring the league a dime. In short, the Seals were going absolutely nowhere, at least for the time being. The NHL would be stuck with its problem child until one or the other could no longer breathe. Seals fans survived their team's first real scare, but their hearts would be severely tested over the next decade.

In the end a group emerged known as Puck Inc., consisting of Potter Palmer and a minor shareholder in his family's Palmer House Hotel, John O'Neil Jr., Palmer's brother-in-law and owner of several insurance and travel businesses, and George Gillett, president of the Harlem Globetrotters. The partners had invested some money in the Atlanta Braves baseball club and the Miami Dolphins football club, but they were not about to jump into the sticky ownership situation in Oakland with both feet. According to Gillett, "Barry van Gerbig still owned the team; we just had an option. We were not involved in the day-to-day running of the team; we were just involved in the marketing."[59] There was more to Puck Inc.'s option to buy the team. According to D'Arcy Jenish, author of *The NHL: 100 Years of On-Ice Action and Boardroom Battles*, "The Puck Inc. purchase was contingent upon a favourable tax ruling from the Internal Revenue Services."[60]

Despite Gillett's claims that Puck Inc. was not in control of the team, it was unclear who actually owned the Seals. "We started to attend league meetings," said Palmer, "but van Gerbig was also still attending them. I remember my lawyer attended these meetings and made a disclaimer speech before each meeting started stating that my being there didn't mean that I owned the team and what have you. I don't think I had a vote on league issues." Nevertheless, in the team's annual media guide, O'Neil was "chairman of the Oakland Seals Board of Directors," Gillett was "vice chairman," and Palmer was "president and member of the National Hockey League Board of Governors."[61]

Adding to the confusion was the fact Labatt lent the Seals $680,000 to pay off the NHL, even though the league had rejected Labatt's plans to move the club to Canada. In May 1968 Van Gerbig explained that the Seals agreed to call the relocation project off: "We're personally pleased with the way the LaBlatt [sic] people have treated us. LaBlatt [sic] has no financial interest in the Seals. They have loaned us the money we need and until it is repaid, we will be associates as well as friends. They will not have an equity."[62]

Despite what seemed an amicable agreement, Van Gerbig filed suit against the NHL, claiming that when the league refused to let the Seals move to Vancouver it had violated sections 1 and 2 of the Sherman Act. Van Gerbig believed the NHL was forbidden to prevent clubs from relocating. He also accused the league of refusing to let the Seals move because it wanted to keep the Bay Area market for itself to stop rival leagues from stepping in. This lawsuit would drag on until 1974, meaning the Seals would be prohibited from moving anywhere until then.

With the relocation rumors now firmly put to rest, and with Puck Inc. seemingly on the verge of making their ownership official, a few important changes were made to the front office. Team president Frank Selke was asked to handle the general manager duties, effectively ending the Olmstead era of Seals hockey. In September, William Torrey, formerly a scout with the Detroit Red Wings and once publicity director and business manager of the AHL's Pittsburgh Hornets, became the Seals' new executive vice-president.

At the end of the season a number of distressing facts stared team brass squarely in the eye: a last-place 15-42-17 record and an average attendance of only 4,960 per game. All the other expansion clubs, even those with lackluster attendance figures, had managed to contend for a playoff spot. The Seals, on the other hand, finished 22 points behind fourth-place Minnesota. To make matters worse, it was believed the club had lost $1.8 million over the course of the season.

Gerry Ehman led the club in scoring with a paltry 44 points, including 19 goals. Bill Hicke scored a satisfactory 21 goals to lead the team, but that made the rest of the team look bad, considering he managed that mark playing in only 52 games. Overall, the club potted just 153 goals, by far the worst total in the league, and was held to fewer than 20 shots on goal in 18 of 74 games. In November, while the Seals were in the midst of their first major slump, Olmstead commented, "I think if we ever got a two goal lead, Hodge wouldn't know what to do."[63] In October, many experts believed the Seals had drafted a winning roster, but it turned out to be just the opposite. "Of the 20 players each team drafted," Hicke said, "only six or seven are of NHL caliber."[64] That, however, did not explain the reason the five other expansion clubs, who drafted their team from the same talent pool, scored so many more goals.

The fact the Seals had drafted three defensemen with their first five picks was a likely factor in the team's impotence. Thankfully, the goaltenders also turned out to be solid draft choices. Hodge stood on his head most nights, finishing with an excellent 2.87 goals-against average and three shutouts. Smith was adequate as his backup, but he still had a tendency to let in soft goals. "Charlie was a veteran, and he gave you a solid performance every night," said Ted Hampson. "Gary could be spectacular, and he could be very erratic some nights too and was obviously a big kid, so a little more inconsistent."

In short, the Seals' inaugural season was a colossal disaster. In hindsight it is easy to see why the team could not set itself straight since costly mistakes and bad decisions had been made long before the first puck was dropped. Management hoped their San Francisco fans would make the trip to Oakland, but they rarely did. "We learned quickly that Oakland was just across the bay from San Francisco," said Van Gerbig, "but people from San Francisco don't cross the bay for anything. If Jesus Christ came on a donkey over there, they wouldn't come." Ticket manager Jim Lingel, like many other Bay Area citizens, felt there was a sort of psychological barrier between blue-collar Oakland and ritzy San Francisco. "Anything in Oakland was considered second- or third class," he explained. "The people in San Francisco were so smug and pseudo-sophisticated."[65] Renaming the club the *Oakland* Seals also did little to endear Van Gerbig and company to San Francisco hockey fans.

Even the storied Montreal Canadiens seemed to have something against Oakland. "The only team that stayed in San Francisco was Montreal," explained Seals Booster Club member Cathy White. "I guess, in their contract, they had something about having to stay in a four- or five star location, and our hotel just didn't measure up. [It] was very nice, and the fella that handled all our travel arrangements worked there, and we had all our trophies displayed in a case at this hotel."

Jim Lingel could see the writing on the wall and decided to leave the Seals at the end of the season. "The leader of buying tickets was not very good . . . that's me," he admitted. "I could see it coming." Lingel worked very hard to sell tickets in this nontraditional market, and to his dying day he believed his inability to sell enough tickets was his only failure in life. Lingel thought the Seals sold "about 1,000 season tickets and 1,000 to 1,500 per game in group sales," but the mistake was putting all of the team's eggs in one basket and not thinking about the casual fan. "After the season started, we didn't do much advertising for individual games," he said. "Our entire advertising was geared toward selling season tickets and groups."[66] When interviewed for this book, Lingel admitted he was "glad to get out" even though he enjoyed hockey.

Worst of all, it seemed as though no one had control of the team. There were too many investors at the start, and when they started to bail one by one, the man left standing, Barry Van Gerbig, was rarely around to set things straight. The fact that the sometimes-hated Olmstead was not only coach but also general manager only aggravated the control problem. All personnel decisions went through Olmstead, and players did not respond to his sour demeanor. In March, with the Seals out of the playoff picture, Olmstead put his house up for sale and expressed disgust in his team's performance, saying, "Finishing last . . . you get the first draft choice next year. Sometimes that doesn't matter much if you . . . need 18 draft choices in the first round to make a contender."[67]

Needless to say, the club was looking at a very bleak future. The team would have to start from scratch and eliminate people who were only making minimal contributions on and off the ice. Michael Watson of the *Hayward Daily Review* reported, "Only about seven members of this year's team figure to be around come October—Brenneman, Hampson, Baun, Burns, defenseman Larry Cahan, wing Bill Hicke and goalie Charley Hodge."[68] As it turned out, even those seven were not as essential to the team's future as believed.

3   THE THREE MUSKETEERS, 1968–1969

The Seals entered their second season on their knees begging their fans for forgiveness. Barry Van Gerbig, in particular, claimed he had learned the error of his ways:

> We were organized wrong. We didn't exhaust every effort to see that hockey in this area became something the people could be interested in.
>
> The fact remains we lost a lot of money last year. But we're willing to gamble this year. All we can do is hope that the community will realize what we have been through and will not make it any tougher on us.
>
> Hockey has been my life for the past five or six years. I will spend next winter and probably this summer here in trying to get everything back in shape. I will accept criticism for my absentee ownership in the past.[1]

Van Gerbig started making amends to the Bay Area fans by stabilizing the front office and handing the general manager duties to Frank Selke Jr. The latter was responsible for many of the Seals' key off-season acquisitions, and his leadership gave the Seals much-needed respectability. "Admittedly we made a lot of mistakes," said Van Gerbig. "We were amateurs in the business and now we are going to bring in the pros. We're not hurting in the hockey end, but we are hurting in the business end."[2]

Selke became the team's third general manager in a calendar year. Soon after accepting the position, he hired minor-league legend Fred Glover to coach the Seals. Like Olmstead, Glover preferred death over losing, but Glover came off more amiable than his predecessor. One *Oakland Tribune* scribe wrote, "Charitably said, [Glover] improved public relations 90 per cent BEFORE he smiled." "Whadaya know," said another reporter, "a nice guy."[3]

Glover knew his hockey too. In the AHL he had won two scoring championships and three MVP awards, and he had been named to seven All-Star Teams. By the time he retired from active duty, he had set AHL career records for goals (520), assists (831), points (1,351), and penalty minutes (2,402). Most of those totals had been accumulated with the Cleveland Barons, with whom he played from 1952 to 1968, but he had also played 92 games in the NHL, scoring 24 points. Glover had always been a winner; in 21 seasons he missed the playoffs only twice and won five Calder Cups.

Tim Ryan believed the players respected Glover. "They knew that he knew the game," said Ryan, "that he had been a hell of a player at his level, that he was a guy that played every minute of every shift, but he wasn't a tyrant like Bert was, and he didn't treat them badly. . . . It wasn't a country club, they still worked as hard, but they were more willing to work as hard, because he communicated with them."

Montreal Canadiens enforcer John Ferguson spoke glowingly of Glover. "He's the greatest competitor I've ever seen," he said. "I saw him get beaten in some fights and then go right back in and tangle with the same guy in the next game. I learned a lot from him. I'll always remember his advice 'never let anyone fight you off the puck.'"[4] Glover's no-nonsense attitude could be seen behind the bench and on road trips as well. While coaching Cleveland, Glover would fine his troops $100 if they were caught conversing with players from the opposing team.

One team Glover particularly despised was the Buffalo Bisons, in part because of a 1965 incident when Glover was fined for getting into a scrap with Buffalo general manager Fred Hunt and for failing to control his players from fighting with fans in the penalty box. The hatred was mutual, and Buffalo fans would let their feelings be known during a 1969 preseason game against the Seals. The Bisons were dominating the Seals that night, and when Glover argued a first-period call, the fans really let him have it. After the second period one fan followed Glover to the Seals' dressing room and made the mistake of poking him. Never one to let anyone, let alone a Buffalo fan, put his hands on him, Glover grabbed the fan and pinned him against a brick wall, triggering an all-out brawl involving a reported two hundred people. Glover's friend, Richard Carr, tried to help out but was sent to the hospital with a broken jaw. Selke received a cut to his hand in the melee while an unidentified Seals' reporter had his glasses busted. One fan even suffered a broken ankle.

Right away Glover made it clear the Seals would no longer be pushed around. "I like my teams to move the puck often and well, and to check the opposition in their own end," he said at his first Seals press conference. "Our team will try to control the puck and skate with it—that's the name of the game, and we've played it that way since my junior days in Galt."[5]

Glover was full of energy and drive, and this was apparent during practices. "Practices were usually very fundamental," remarked defenseman Marshall Johnston, who played for the Seals from 1971 to 1974. "At the start, you'd go through the skating routines . . . and then Fred would scrimmage with us. The joke was the team that Fred was on, you'd better let him win or else we'd be out there 'til three o'clock in the afternoon." Joey Johnston would play for Glover in the 1970s, and he recalled, "Let him score a goal, and that's the end of the practice. Twice around and in," he chuckled.

Ted Hampson, among others, recalled that not everyone on the Seals was on the same wavelength when it came to practices: "[Bryan] 'Bugsy' Watson said, 'You're not scoring any goals while I'm out there!' So we would say, 'Let him get *one*. We've been out here two hours.'" Howie Menard, who ended up with the Seals the following year, remembered that Glover "was quite a competitor when he played, and he always wanted to put the gear on, so the guys said, 'Christ, there's our chance to get him now.'" As most players of the era will admit, there was not much coaching strategy in those days; it was mostly about managing and motivating players. "The feeling was, with a lot of the coaches then," said Menard, "that you're good enough to be there, you should know what the hell to do. . . . Fred was a good guy and a good coach, but knowing how to handle a group of players, that was the main thing in those days." Glover's antics and lack of teaching skills aside, his practices worked wonders initially. Glover helped improve team morale, and he was able to get the maximum effort from his players.

With Bill Torrey now in place as the Seals' new executive vice president, the club entered a period of relative stability. Of course, in Oakland, as long as the team wasn't in immediate danger of folding, that meant stability. Ownership was still a bit of a mess, but Torrey, Selke, and Glover would be the most successful front-office triumvirate the Seals would ever employ. As Selke remarked, "We kind of considered ourselves the Three Musketeers, Glover and Bill, and myself, because, in effect, we had no ownership. We were *it*, and so we pretty much shouldered the responsibilities of running the operation, and we did it as the Three Amigos, and I have to say that I believe the relationship that the three of us had with each other was our salvation, really, and we got along very well." Selke and Torrey were particularly close during their time together in Oakland. "Bill Torrey and I, our families socialized," explained Selke, "and we probably kept each other sane, I think."

"We had a very, very good working and social, personal relationship," Selke continued. "To this day I consider Bill a good friend. I haven't talked to him for a little while, but we stayed in communication for years. He was my boss, in effect. He never treated me in that vein." Selke and Torrey had a relationship that went way back. "We lived near the [Montreal] Forum and many times Selke's Dad ran me out of the building," Torrey said about Frank Selke Sr., the Habs' legendary general manager.[6] It was rarely sunshine and lollipops working for the Seals, but since Torrey, Selke, and Glover got along well, they were able to put aside constant rumors of the franchise's impending doom and get down to the business of building a decent team.

Throughout the Seals' inaugural campaign it became obvious that Rudy Pilous, Bert Olmstead, and Bob Wilson had not made as many wise choices in the expansion draft as was initially believed. The players who had been expected to make the Seals competitive failed to generate much excitement on the ice. Bobby Baun, Larry Cahan, Charlie Hodge, and Bill Hicke met or exceeded expectations, but others such as Billy Harris and Kent Douglas were busts. Unlike the other expansion cities, few Seals came out of the woodwork to become stars. Gordon "Red" Berenson scored 51 points in 55 games for St. Louis and had a 6-goal game versus Philadelphia. In Minnesota, former San Francisco Seal Wayne Connelly scored a division-leading 35 goals. Pittsburgh's aging Andy Bathgate paced the entire West Division with 59 points. No one came close to those numbers in Oakland.

With Selke barely settled in his new position, he traded Wally Boyer (13 goals, 20 assists), Alain Caron (9 goals, 13 assists), prospect Lyle Bradley, and the Seals' first picks in the 1968 and 1970 amateur drafts to Montreal for forwards Norm Ferguson and Michel Jacques and defensemen Stan Fuller and François Lacombe. Ferguson, primarily known as a plugger who could score the odd goal, made the biggest impact on the Seals. The Sydney, Nova Scotia, native was just average with the Habs' farm team in Houston, but when Montreal loaned Ferguson to Cleveland in 1967, he scored 42 goals. Coming to Oakland gave Ferguson the chance to prove he could score like that at the big league level and play some major minutes, something that likely never would have happened in Montreal.

To help give the Seals' plodding defense some flair, Selke snatched Carol Vadnais from the Canadiens with the first overall selection in the intra-league draft. Vadnais was a promising offensive defenseman who had been the victim of the Habs' deep roster, playing behind such stalwarts as J. C. Tremblay, Serge Savard, and Jacques Laperriere. The Canadiens' wealth of talent turned out to be the Seals' fortune.

Carol Vadnais's rough edge earned him a lot of time in the penalty box, but he combined his aggressive nature with a deft scoring touch. Vadnais represented the spirit of the 1960s well. According to Spence Conley of the *Oakland Tribune*, the handsome, hip twenty-two-year-old was a "sartorial sensation when he arrived decked out in the latest fashions from Montreal, accentuated by long flowing hair."[7] Before long, Fred Glover ordered Vadnais to get his hair cut, but it didn't take away from the fact Vadnais was a true NHL star. "He's a mod guy," said Selke. "He has that special French-Canadian flair about him. They're a different breed of cat. A lot of guys in the league have the mod look, but not too many of them can carry it off as well as Vadnais." That didn't mean the rest of the team agreed. On the team's charter flight one time, Vadnais's teammates teased him about the cowboy boots and Continental-style slacks he wore. "I look," said Vadnais, "just like Jahn AUTREE, eh?" Vadnais spoke in a sort-of half-English, half-French hybrid, mainly because his English was not very good. "But he has improved a lot," said Glover. "I used to have trouble trying to figure him out. Now at least I can understand what he's saying."[8]

When the Habs' turn came up later in the draft, they selected Larry Cahan, the Seals' top scoring defenseman with 24 points. Pittsburgh selected Charlie Burns, who had led the Seals with 26 assists.

While smaller pieces of the puzzle were acquired throughout the off-season, a major trade involving All-Star Bobby Baun occurred at the end of May. Baun had requested a trade at the end of the season, because "the disorganization and lack of hockey interest got to [him]," but Selke hated seeing the rugged defenseman go. "If we'd had eighteen Bobby Bauns, we'd have no problems," he said.[9]

Baun and fellow defenseman Ron Harris were sent to Detroit in exchange for Gary Jarrett, a twenty-five-year-old left winger, Doug Roberts and Howie Young, both defensemen, and Chris Worthy, a twenty-year-old goaltending prospect. Jarrett, the key acquisition in the trade, brought some blazing speed and scoring punch to the Seals' weak left-wing position. Jarrett had picked up 18 goals in Detroit, which was more than all but two Seals had mustered. Teamed with Bill Hicke and new team captain Ted Hampson, Jarrett became part of the Seals' most consistent scoring threat, the Assembly Line.

In season one, no line combinations had stood out, and there hadn't been any real team identity, so Van Gerbig invited seventeen members of the team to Montreal, where the NHL draft meetings took place, so they could mingle with one another and get to know Glover and Selke. "We want our players to know each other and have confidence in both coaching and management," Van Gerbig said. "We don't want them to be strangers when they come to training camp in September," said Selke. "We want them to know each other as teammates, and to know the coach." Perhaps the most important goal of the two-day event was, as Selke put it, "to build some pride." The players needed to be reassured things would be different at the top of the Seals' hierarchy. Only by changing the atmosphere in the dressing room could the team hope to succeed. "If we can bring them together in a common spirit of building for success, then we have taken a giant step toward success next fall," said Van Gerbig.[10]

The team building that had been so emphasized in the off-season paid off in spades. Players were so motivated they steamrolled their way through the exhibition schedule and finished with a league-best 6-0-2 mark. "Our primary objective was to do everything possible to build a totally new feeling, a new spirit among our players," explained Selke. "With Glover and the type of young, enthusiastic players we have, it was a surprisingly simple job." Selke was happy to see that after such a positive training camp, the team was returning to Oakland with players who felt "a great sense of pride in both themselves and the organization."[11]

The Seals opened the regular season in Oakland on October 11 with a disappointing 5–1 loss to Minnesota. Two nights later, the Seals tied Los Angeles 4–4, and three nights after that the Seals fell to Boston 2–1. Oakland's first win of the season did not come until they hit the road. After another loss against St. Louis on October 19, the club rebounded to beat Chicago the following night and Minnesota a few nights later.

After nine games the Oakland Seals had shown little, if any, improvement on their inaugural campaign, yet they were tied for first place in the West with an underwhelming 2-5-2 record and still no wins at home. The team had also scored just 19 goals at that point, so Glover placed defenseman Carol Vadnais on the left wing on November 1 against Chicago. The move made Glover look like a genius. "I knew Carol could play wing," Glover beamed after the contest. "He came up in that position at Montreal, but had some trouble so was shifted to defense." The coach was still stunned his little experiment produced immediate dividends. "I didn't think he'd get off this fast in his first real test out there," said Glover.[12]

Early in the first period, Vadnais skated into the Hawks' territory with Ted Hampson trailing behind. As Vadnais turned Pat Stapleton inside out, Hampson made a bee line for the net, providing the screen. With Hampson firmly in Denis Dejordy's face, Vadnais unleashed a 15-footer that bulged the twine 5:16 into the game. Eight minutes later, Norm Ferguson scored his second of the season to put the Seals up by 2. Vadnais scored again to put the Seals up by 3 before Bobby Hull broke through the Seals' defense and scored. Bill Hicke scored at 12:20 of the final frame to restore the Seals' 3-goal lead, but Ken Wharram made it 4–2 just four minutes later. The Seals, however, refused to cave under the pressure. With just 46 seconds left, Gary Jarrett scored to give the Seals an impressive 5–2 win, their first at home.

Two days later the Seals fell 3–1 to the Pittsburgh Penguins before 2,166 Oakland fans. Lou Angotti, Gene Ubriaco, and Val Fonteyne all scored during for Pittsburgh during a four-minute span in the second period. The defeat pushed the Seals back into a second-place tie with Philadelphia, one point behind division-leading St. Louis.

The losses kept coming after the meltdown against Pittsburgh. By the time the Kings hosted the Seals on November 12, the Seals had lost three in a row. Hoping for a better result, Glover inserted rookie Chris Worthy into the net for his first career NHL start. Thus far Hodge and Smith had split the goaltending chores almost equally, but overall both had turned in uneven performances.

Despite Worthy's 30 saves, Los Angeles still managed a 3–1 win. Bill Flett scored twice for the victors in the second period. Ehman replied for the listless Seals with his fourth goal of the season midway through the third period, but Jim Peters restored LA's 2-goal lead with under three minutes to go to put the Seals on ice. The loss dropped the Seals to 3-9-2, and Selke was particularly critical of his club: "I guess some of our guys just don't want to win bad enough," he said, although he believed Worthy and the scrappy Hampson had played well.[13]

Despite the loss, Glover stuck with Worthy the following night versus Detroit. Gary Jarrett continued his fine early season play, scoring the game winner, his seventh goal of the season, on a pass from Ferguson with only forty-eight seconds to play. Jarrett's 25-foot blast gave Oakland a 2–1 win. Worthy was sharp in goal once again, stopping all but one of Detroit's 25 shots. "There was a lot more chatter in the dressing room before the game," said Worthy. "The guys knew they'd all have to pull together to win and we needed a win to prove to our fans that we are a better hockey team than we've been showing."[14]

As had been the norm since the franchise was born, the Seals could not build on the momentum of their goaltender's solid performance. That isn't to say everyone on the team was performing poorly. Hampson, Hicke, and Jarrett were all on pace to set career highs in almost every offensive category, and youngsters like Vadnais, Ferguson, and Worthy proved they belonged in the NHL. The problem was that whenever the goaltender had a great game, the big guns went silent. Whenever the Assembly Line lit it up, the goalies would let in floaters from the blue line.

With the Seals going nowhere fast, management traded Billy Harris, who had managed just 4 assists in 19 games, to Pittsburgh for Bob Dillabough. Although Dillabough became a useful player later in the season, the turning point for the Seals came when the club called up center Mike Laughton from the Cleveland Barons.

The night Harris packed his bags, the Seals hosted Montreal before 8,105 fans, the largest crowd of the season. Laughton, playing in Hampson's spot on the top line, scored his first goal of the season at 16:08 of the first period to give the Seals a 1–0 lead. In the second period Jean Beliveau tied it up with a goal fifty-two seconds in, but Hampson put Oakland up 2–1 with his eighth some five minutes later. Jacques Lemaire responded at 11:43 with his tenth, but Hampson scored another to put the Seals up 3–2, and Hicke scored his fifth on an assist from Jarrett to make it 4–2.

Hicke gave the Seals a three-goal lead at 2:29 of the third period, but the defending Stanley Cup champs refused to let the Seals have their way. Beliveau scored on the power play at 14:33, and Gilles Tremblay made it 5–4 with just 1:37 left, but the Seals kept the puck in the Habs' zone the rest of the way, preserving the victory.

For the first time in franchise history the Seals would actually play consistent hockey for more than just a few games and would mount a serious charge at the playoffs. A big reason for the turnaround was the Seals' outstanding performances at home. While the Seals had begun the season with a 1-6-2 record at home, they went 16-8-5 the rest of the way. The Oakland Coliseum had finally become an unfriendly place to play.

Although the Seals' offense was running smoothly behind the Assembly Line of Hampson, Hicke, and Jarrett as well as youngsters Norm Ferguson and Carol Vadnais, it took nearly two months for the goaltenders to play up to par. Smith had a 5-4-2 record with no shutouts while Hodge was winless in seven starts and had lost his roster spot to Chris Worthy. Taking Glover and Selke's criticism to heart, Smith came through for his teammates on December 6 versus Philadelphia, blocking 24 shots en route to a 4-0 shutout. "Smitty didn't get any criticism he didn't deserve," commented Glover. "I hope he stays mad tomorrow too. If getting him mad is the way to make him play better, then that's the way it'll be. It's nice to see an angry hockey player once in a while."[15]

Six nights later Smith collected his second shutout as the Seals humiliated Detroit, 6-0. Ferguson scored another 2 goals, while Hampson scored a goal and 3 assists. Many fans around the league were now beginning to believe in miracles, and considering the mess the Seals had been in just a few months earlier, it was truly miraculous they were gunning for first place in the West.

In late December the Seals ran into an old friend tending goal for St. Louis. The un-retired Jacques Plante showed off his best stuff in the Blues' net. The lethargic Blues managed only 14 shots on Gary Smith, but the one that actually rippled the back of the net turned out to be costly. Tim Ecclestone's goal at 17:43 of the first period was controversial as Bert Marshall had been in the sin bin for what Glover believed was an unwarranted holding penalty. "We played a very good game," he said. "It should have been a 0-0 tie. There never should have been a penalty on Marshall."[16] Undeterred, the Seals dominated the rest of the way. As time was running out, the Seals pressured Plante relentlessly until referee Bob Sloan called Gary Jarrett for boarding. That was the end of the Seals' momentum, and Plante picked up the 1-0 shutout. In 13 all-time games versus St. Louis, the Seals had yet to win a single one.

Despite the Seals' recent solid play, attendance officially bottomed out as only 1,829 people showed up at the Cow Palace on December 22 for a rare game in San Francisco versus Philadelphia. Even though the Seals were in a tight playoff race, they couldn't pay enough people to fill the rink every night. Low attendance meant little money in the coffers, which in turn spelled disaster for the Seals' new owners. Van Gerbig recalled, "[Puck Inc.] thought they would use the Globetrotters to fund the losses until they got it going. We [Van Gerbig and his partners] kept the franchise as collateral and we ended up having to take it back."[17] Making matters difficult was the fact the Seals' convoluted ownership situation left almost everyone scratching their head. Puck Inc. had had an *option* to purchase the Seals from Van Gerbig and his fifty-plus partners (San Francisco Seals, Inc.), but Van Gerbig and company actually owned the players as well as the lease at the Coliseum Arena. Since Puck Inc. did not have the necessary capital to keep the franchise afloat, Van Gerbig had to take it back. Who actually owned the Seals was anybody's guess. On January 21, when the league governors got together to discuss the different options in dealing with the Seals' future, Van Gerbig brushed off the meeting to play in the Bing Crosby Golf Tournament.

Rumors began to circulate that the drowning Seals were being pursued by a group led by Seymour Knox III, a millionaire banker representing Niagara Frontier Hockey Inc., and his brother Northrup. Bill Torrey was shocked to hear the news since no one in the organization had even heard of such plans. "I can say point blank that not a single thing has been done, either at a league or club level, to transfer the franchise to Buffalo," he said. League president Clarence Campbell was also shocked by the news the Seals were moving east. "There is no official foundation for this premise as far as the league is concerned," said Campbell. "I have no knowledge along these lines and there is nothing current in league circles. Of course there has been speculation, but that is all."[18]

It was believed Niagara Frontier Hockey Inc. had purchased the Seals for more than $2 million, but to move the franchise to Buffalo the Knoxes needed the support of at least nine of the twelve NHL clubs, which Labatt had failed to get. That didn't stop some newspapers, like the *Winnipeg Free Press*, from jumping to conclusions, stating matter-of-factly that "the Seals become the first NHL expansion team to move of the six that were created in 1965 [*sic*]." To be fair, Seymour Knox also gave people the impression the sale was a done deal: "There are hundreds and thousands of fans on the Niagara Frontier who at the present time cannot see major league hockey action and I'm sure that this development will be great news to them," he stated.[19] Buffalo seemed to be an ideal location for a NHL franchise. The AHL's Bisons were drawing crowds twice as large as the Seals. Representatives from Buffalo had also applied for an expansion franchise two years earlier but were rebuffed by the NHL. Now the city of Buffalo was planning to increase the Memorial Auditorium's seating capacity from 9,800 to 16,000.

Unfortunately for Buffalo hockey fans, not everybody in the NHL was thrilled about the Knoxes' ambitious plans. "In the end," recalled Selke, "the league refused to let them move the team. The NHL wanted to preserve the Buffalo territory so it could sell another [expansion] franchise along with Vancouver."[20] Thanks to the NHL's new $6 million price tag per expansion franchise, league owners looked forward to a nice little windfall in the near future. The league would have gained nothing had the Seals moved to Buffalo. The good news for Van Gerbig was that despite the league's refusal to move the team to Buffalo, the Knoxes remained as minority owners and brought in some much needed capital.

To recap, Van Gerbig had tried to sell the Seals *three* times over the course of a calendar year, and one by one each potential buyer, whether it was Labatt Breweries, Puck Inc., or the Knox brothers, ran into some sort of road block to keep the sale from going through. Van Gerbig must have lied in bed awake at night wondering what he had to do to unload his albatross of a hockey team. Enter ownership contender number *four*, Trans-National Communications (TNC), led by chairman and former radio announcer Ellis "Woody" Erdman, TV producer Bill Creasy, former New York Yankees star Whitey Ford, and ex–New York Giants Pat Summerall and Dick Lynch. For $4.5 million, TNC bought 80 percent of the club while the Knox brothers would own the remaining 20 percent. In the event the Knox brothers acquired their desired Buffalo franchise, it was presumed TNC would take over their share of the Seals. Creasy, TNC's thirty-nine-year-old president, became the Seals' new president.

The league certainly seemed impressed by TNC's enthusiasm and commitment. "They went after this franchise with hammer and tong," said NHL vice president for public relations Don Ruck. "They were willing to take it over under the terms set down by the NHL—that the club stay in Oakland and under no circumstances be allowed to move."[21]

Not only was TNC listed on the stock exchange, but it was a conglomerate claiming assets of $10 million plus another $1 million in the bank. According to Seals historian Brad Kurtzberg, TNC claimed to own "everything from farms to film companies." Selke recalled that TNC "owned the Bank of Philadelphia—in a tiny upstate village, Philadelphia, New York (population: 870). It also owned a vegetable farm in Florida. It claimed in its prospectus that 'if all the radishes they grew were placed end to end, they'd reach from Florida to New York!'"[22]

The Seals were just one of the many businesses under the TNC umbrella. Creasy recalled that in the beginning, "It was me, Pat Summerall, Woody Erdman, Dick Lynch and a bunch of lawyers and accountants. My job was to get new properties. Somehow, the subject of the Seals came up and I said to Woody, 'What would you think of owning a hockey team?' I had known Clarence Campbell, Stafford Smythe, Bruce Norris and John Ziegler through my work on NHL TV broadcasts. We paid Barry van Gerbig approximately 80 percent of what he paid for the team. Perhaps it was $1.6 million, plus we assumed a lot of debt—approximately $3 million."[23] Broken down, the debt included $1.9 million in losses accumulated since the first puck drop, as well as the remainder of the $2 million expansion fee still owed to the league, an undisclosed sum Van Gerbig owed to Shasta Corp., the $680,000 loan to Labatt Breweries, an undisclosed sum to Hockey Investors Inc., and settlements to the contracts of Rudy Pilous, Bert Olmstead, and Gordon Fashoway.[24]

Bill Torrey could not have been happier about the change of ownership: "We feel our family is now complete from top to bottom. We've had the bottom—Selke, Glover, the players—since the start of the season. This gives us the top."[25] When the technicalities of the deal were worked out and the deal finalized, Bill Torrey and Fred Glover were immediately signed to new three-year contracts. Frank Selke still had two years remaining on his four-year deal, which seemed to indicate the Seals' front office would be stable for a long time. In reality, this seemingly shrewd decision to sign the Seals' Three Musketeers for the long term would be a major factor in the team's eventual dismantling.

The confident TNC, meanwhile, was warm to the idea of staying in Oakland. "We have no plans for moving the club, because we have entertained no thoughts of attendance failing in Oakland," said Erdman, who became the Seals' chairman of the board.[26] "We've done our homework," Erdman added. "We've got market studies and with the combination of both the consumer's spendable income and the average family income, and the added asset of an improved exciting team, we think it will go."[27]

The Seals' new owners wanted to improve attendance and increase the club's visibility in the Bay Area. "I wanted a whole new marketing plan," said Creasy, the Seals' new representative on the league's board of governors. "I hired an ad agency and we placed newspaper ads, started a radio advertising campaign and got the team on the local ABC radio affiliate. We put bumper stickers on cars and send [*sic*] out mailers. We tripled our season ticket sales. Unfortunately, there were only 300 or so season-ticket holders when TNC took over the club."[28]

TNC's ultimate goal was to move the Seals back to the Cow Palace and get San Francisco's rich business community interested in hockey again. Mel Swig and Creasy became close around this time and even talked about building a new arena, but the NHL entertained no thoughts of moving the team back across the bay. The Seals would have to suffer in Oakland a few more years.

Despite the turbulence at the top of the Seals' pyramid, the players continued to play inspired hockey. On Christmas Day the Seals defeated the heavily favored Bruins 3–1 in Beantown. Bill Hicke enjoyed a 3-point performance and increased his season totals to 12 goals and 22 assists, good for thirteenth in league scoring. Gary Smith stymied the mighty Bruins with 36 saves and improved his record to 10-9-2. On the final day of 1968 the Seals owned second place with a record of 13-19-5, eight points behind St. Louis.

In the meantime the NHL Writers Association gave many Seals some recognition in the All-Star Game voting. This season the West Division All-Stars would face the East Division All-Stars in a game with much pride on the line. Hampson, Jarrett, and Hicke were all voted to play in the game, although Jarrett was forced to sit out because he had been injured in practice. The practice rink in Berkeley was not very well lit, and at one point a Mike Laughton shot deflected off Doug Roberts's stick and hit Jarrett in the eye. West All-Stars coach Scotty Bowman selected Carol Vadnais to replace Jarrett. The West had obviously matured now that its member clubs had one year under their belts; the surprising expansionists fought the established East Division to a 3–3 draw, but all three Seals were held off the scoresheet.

The Seals played inconsistently after the All-Star break. They were able to gain points against the East's best clubs—Boston, Montreal, and Toronto—but could not defeat weaker teams such as Detroit and Los Angeles. As impressive as the Seals' season had been, the team was still prone to the occasional meltdown. The Los Angeles game on February 1 proved to be a difficult one to digest. How bad was the game? According to *Oakland Tribune* reporter Spence Conley, "Fred Glover could have stacked Gary Smith and Charlie Hodge on top of each other in the goal mouth and got a better game than they delivered in the 8–5 pasting the Oakland Seals took last night. . . . The two Seal goalkeepers, missing shots with flawless precision, each yielded four goals but at the same time got very little help from an inept defense. So you might say it was a total team effort."[29]

The Seals could take solace knowing that at the other end of the rink the Kings' Gerry Desjardins had not been much better than his counterparts. The Kings took a 2–0 lead in the first period on goals by Howie Hughes and Gord Labossiere, both of which were shrouded in controversy. On Hughes's goal, ex-Seal Larry Cahan took a shot from the point that then rang off the post. The puck slid under Smith and back into the goal crease. Everyone stood around looking clueless until Hughes spotted the loose puck and shoveled it home. Labossiere's goal was equally frustrating for the Seals. Lowell MacDonald made a centering pass that was kneed by Labossiere over Smith's shoulders and into the net. The Seals protested, but referee Bill Friday let the goal stand.

The Seals took out their frustrations on Desjardins, scoring 3 goals on 3 shots in three minutes. Oakland narrowed the gap to 2–1 at the

11:34 mark, and then the floodgates gave way. Mike Laughton sprung into action, scoring twice in less than a minute to give the Seals a 3–2 lead. But that was as close as the Seals would come to a "W." The Kings scored three in a row to take a 5–3 lead and never looked back.

With the Seals down 8–4, Bill Hicke scored his nineteenth goal to whittle the gap to three. As the puck crossed the goal line, Brian Perry drove Larry Cahan into the boards and broke his nose, leading to further tension. Less than a minute later Hicke and the Kings' Dale Rolfe got into a scrap. According to Hicke, "I tried to check him and was down on the ice when he gave me a two-hander across the back." Rolfe disagreed with Hicke's version of the story. "He rammed me into the boards and hit me here with his stick," he said, pointing to an ugly abrasion on his chin. Rolfe was not entirely without fault, however; Hicke was left with a huge welt on his back.[30]

Glover was extremely upset over the unnecessary act of violence: "Rolfe didn't just try to injure Hicke," he exclaimed. "He darn well injured him!" Indeed, the Seals' star right-winger was forced to miss the next few weeks of play. Nevertheless, LA coach Leonard "Red" Kelly was quick to defend Rolfe's actions: "When you're attacked, you fight back," he answered after the game.[31] Whether Rolfe acted in self-defense was not the issue to Seals fans. The fact of the matter was that the Assembly Line, still without Gary Jarrett, would be short another man.

Although it would never rival the animosity that developed between the Canadiens and Leafs, a genuine hatred had started to fester between the Seals and Kings. The Seals and Flyers would have some nasty games a few years down the road, but almost everyone interviewed for this book agreed that it was Los Angeles who was the Seals' biggest rival. Los Angeles and the San Francisco–Oakland area have never gotten along well, so when Kings fans started showing up at the Coliseum wearing regal purple and gold, Seals fans took exception, calling their rivals the LA Queens or Jesters.

At the time of his injury Hicke was tied with Hampson for the club's scoring lead with 49 points, and both were among the league's top twenty scorers. Jarrett had 19 goals and 14 assists. Ehman had been solid as well, scoring 14 goals and 18 assists, while Vadnais led all

Oakland defensemen with 13 goals and 27 points, both already club records for that position.

Rookie scorers were also taking the spotlight in Oakland. At the top of the list was Norm Ferguson with 35 points. His 21 goals were the most on the club and tied Minnesota's Danny Grant for the league lead among rookies. Mike Laughton also emerged from out of nowhere to score 31 points in 36 games. He had played 35 games for the Seals the year before and scored but 2 goals and 6 assists, mostly because his skating needed work. When he was called up to the big club in November, his skating had clearly improved. "Mike worked hard all summer and has matured as an athlete," said Selke to Fran Tuckwiler of the *San Jose Mercury News*. "He works hard all the time now. He isn't fancy and he has to work to force the play. When he does, he is very effective."[32]

Searching for the final piece that would put his club over the top, Selke sent George Swarbrick, who had gone from 13 goals in 49 games the previous year to just 3 goals in 50 games this season, Tracy Pratt, and Bryan Watson to Pittsburgh for Earl Ingarfield, Gene Ubriaco, Dick Mattiussi, and cash. Ingarfield, the key player in the deal, was a wily center with a nose for the net. However, his career highs of 26 goals and 31 assists came with the New York Rangers back in 1961–62, and his last 20-goal season had come in 1965–66. Thus far his 1968–69 contribution had been limited to just 8 goals and 15 assists in 40 games. Once he arrived in Oakland, however, he looked reenergized.

The greatest beneficiaries of the Ingarfield trade were Ted Hampson and Gerry Ehman. Hampson, for one, greatly appreciated being put on the same line as Ingarfield:

I enjoyed very much playing with Gary Jarrett and Bill Hicke, but my real pleasure was when they made the trade for Earl Ingarfield. . . . [We] had instant chemistry. Earl hadn't played the wing—he was a centerman too—but he was, I think, quite happy to play there because things went so well for all three of us. . . . Earl was a very smart player, and a good playmaker, and a good shooter, and a pretty gritty guy. Gerry was one of the best checkers in the NHL over a long period of time, but he was also a sniper; he could really shoot the puck. And I think I gave the line some energy and tried to get the puck to those guys. . . . So we had that chemistry and it was a real pleasure.

As the season progressed, the Seals made it clear their surprising run was no fluke. They plowed through the stronger Original Six clubs like a hurricane on a straw hut. Oakland's outstanding run included a 5–1 home ice victory over Montreal on February 5 in which both Mike Laughton and Brian Perry recorded a club-record 4 points. Then, on February 8, the Seals embarrassed the Leafs, 4–1. The next night they tied the Boston Bruins 3–3, and on February 12 they beat the Rangers, 3–2. A 5–2 victory over Chicago on February 19 before over ten thousand home fans was the Seals' thirteenth against the East that season, compared to just four wins the previous year.

During the Seals' hot streak they even managed to beat the St. Louis Blues. In fifteen previous contests with St. Louis the Seals' record had been 0-12-3. They finally got the elusive win, but it did not come easily. After Laughton's 2 goals and Hampson's single marker in the first two periods, the Blues stormed back with two of their own in the third. In the dying seconds of the game, with their net empty, the Blues tried to gain the tie but were unable to find the back of the Seals' net. The game ended 3–2 for Oakland, a great moral victory, but the Seals were still miles behind the first-place Blues.

While in the midst of their streak, the Seals met the Minnesota North Stars on February 26, this time at the Cow Palace, and played one of their most spirited games ever. With the Seals down 3–0 at the end of the first period, Glover rallied his troops by delivering a great pep talk. "We've been down three goals to these guys before, and we pulled one out," Glover said to his players, referring to a 3–3 tie against Minnesota on November 27. "But we aren't working the way we are capable. We've got 40 minutes left and if we get going maybe we can come back. Let's try."[33]

The pep talk worked wonders. Chris Worthy came on in relief of Gary Smith and was outstanding for two periods. "Chris gave our guys a big lift. His attitude alone was enough," Glover beamed. "He had some problems in the third period, but he played well right from the time he took over."[34] Hampson led the Seals' attack with two goals. First, at 1:46 of the second period, he scored on a nifty backhand shot 18 feet from the net. Just under ten minutes later the captain scored his 23rd goal of the season. Hicke and Jarrett, both fully healed from their injuries, picked up assists on both markers. In the third period, when Jarrett scored his 20th goal to give the Seals a 4–3 lead, Hampson picked up an assist, giving the reassembled Assembly Line 8 points on the night. In the final period the Seals opened up a huge 6–3 lead. Minnesota tried a similar comeback on late goals by Danny O'Shea and Bill Orban, but fell one short of accomplishing the feat. Final score: Seals 6, North Stars 5.

The Seals were flying so high the local press was even talking championship! The *Oakland Tribune*'s Ed Levitt, in his daily column, said:

These guys are so fired up they just may win the Stanley Cup Play-offs in April.

Little ol' Oakland, leading the National Hockey League in empty seats, a franchise with 53 owners pulling 53 different ways, a club that was rumored to be moving just about every day in the week, now being talked about to take hockey's greatest prize?

That's right, baby.[35]

While the Seals had improved by leaps and bounds, it was a tad presumptuous to be handing them Lord Stanley's mug. For instance, on February 27, versus the Boston Bruins, Worthy got the nod in goal once again, but before long he was probably hoping Smith would take his place between the pipes. The Bruins scored early and often, starting at 2:25 from the opening face-off when Ed Westfall's 25-foot shot went through Dick Mattiussi's legs to find its way through Worthy's pads. Then the normally slow-footed Phil Esposito managed not one, but two breakaways on the Seals' rookie goaltender. The hockey gods took pity on Worthy as Esposito rang the first shot off the right goal post and then the second shot off the left post as the buzzer sounded.

Worthy's luck ran out in the second as the Bruins ripped four shots past him on 13 shots and then another 4 goals on 11 shots in the third,

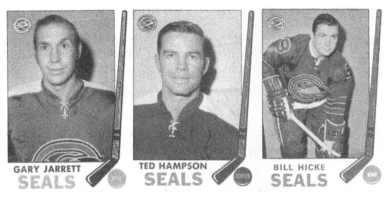

FIG. 3. For half the 1968-69 season, the Assembly Line of Gary Jarrett, Ted Hampson, and Bill Hicke was the West Division's most potent unit. Topps O-Pee-Chee trading cards used courtesy of The Topps Company, Inc.

making it 9-0, Boston. Esposito scored 3 points, including his league-leading 97th to tie the NHL record for points in one season, previously set by Bobby Hull and Stan Mikita. "If you're looking for a bright spot, that last one was it," said Glover after the massacre. "We sure didn't have any."[36]

It took the Seals a while to recover from the embarrassing defeat; three more losses and a tie followed. In one of those games, on March 8, the St. Louis Blues wrapped up the West Division title with a 5-2 win. In the meantime Oakland led Los Angeles in points, 58-51, in the race for second place.

Although the Seals had not been able to overtake the Blues in the West standings, there were other important matters to be settled. For one, Norm Ferguson was closing in on Nels Stewart's all-time single-season rookie goal record of 34, set in 1925-26. Ferguson was closely pursued by Danny Grant, but Ferguson downplayed what was seen as a rivalry between the two young stars. "I really don't feel there is a duel between Danny and myself," Ferguson said. "You try to not think about what you read and yet it's there subconsciously. And it hurts your game on the ice."[37] On March 16, in a 7-2 thrashing of the Pittsburgh Penguins, Ferguson added his 29th and 30th goals, putting him just one behind Grant.

On March 23 Ferguson scored in the Seals' 4–0 shutout over Los Angeles to bring his total to 31. He scored two more in a 5–4 win over LA the following night to help the Seals clinch second place in the West. The goals allowed Ferguson to temporarily surpass Grant, who had but 32, but the Stars' freshman caught up before long. By the end of the regular season the two rookies equaled Stewart's 34 goals, and there was no doubt they would be the top two contenders for the Calder Memorial Trophy, given to the NHL's Rookie of the Year.

The Seals finished the season 29-36-11, a 22-point improvement over their first season. The Seals' first-round opponents would be their state rivals, the Los Angeles Kings, who finished fourth. On paper, the Kings seemed less talented than the Seals, but the boys from Hollywood were a tight and pugnacious bunch led by coach Red Kelly.

In game one of the best-of-seven series the Coliseum's 5,449 guests were treated to an outstanding, suspenseful contest. Ingarfield drew first blood for the Seals with a shorthanded goal at 11:59 of the first period while Dick Mattiussi was in the sin bin. Gary Croteau replied for the Kings about five minutes later, but Joe Szura regained the Seals' one-goal lead at 16:21. Kings goaltender Gerry Desjardins was replaced by Wayne Rutledge after the second goal because of a lower-body injury.

In the second period the teams continued their tug-of-war. The Kings tied the score with a goal by Croteau at 3:07, but the Seals' François Lacombe regained the Seals' lead with just 19 seconds left in the frame.

For the third time in the game the Kings tied the score, this time on a goal by Eddie Joyal, but unlike the previous two times the Kings then took the lead on another goal by Joyal. The home team was down 4–3 with less than three minutes left in regulation time when Gene Ubriaco tied the score, setting the stage for overtime. The favored Seals had the opportunity to win the all-important first game of the series, but after just nineteen seconds of extra time, Ted Irvine knocked in a rebound past Gary Smith to give the Kings game one. At the time it was the fastest overtime goal ever scored. "I saw the puck lying there and took a forehand swipe at it," Irvine said after the game. "I didn't see it go in, but I saw it in the net."[38]

Fred Glover was fuming, to say the least, at the conclusion of the game. "We'd better come back," said the coach, resisting the temptation to bite some reporter's head off. "We went flatter than a pancake out there and just gave away a precious item—home ice advantage, if there is such a thing."

"Not everybody was doing their job," he continued. "They had their minds on something else. And the biggest problem was in our own end—just plain give away. I think there was one stretch there where at least 10 passes wound up on King sticks."[39]

In game two the Seals took the lead a little over a minute in on a goal by Hampson. The Seals stayed in the lead until the Kings struck early in the second period on a goal by Ted Irvine. The Kings took a 2–1 lead when Howie Menard deflected a Gary Croteau shot off his skate and into the net. Gary Smith and the rest of the Seals protested that Menard had kicked the puck in, but the goal stood. Referee Art Skov was none too impressed by the Seals' protest, even giving defenseman Doug Roberts a ten-minute misconduct and a game misconduct for flapping his gums a little too much.

Both clubs were in a pretty bad mood after the Kings took the lead. Bill Hicke checked Rutledge behind the net, which set off a series of scrums. The Kings' Brent Hughes went after Hicke, hitting him from behind and knocking him to the ice. Other players joined the fray behind the LA net, while the Seals' resident pugilist, Carol Vadnais, took on Bob Wall just a few feet away, but neither received fighting majors. Hicke and Rutledge picked up minors for roughing while Hughes picked up two minutes for charging.

Once Hicke got out of the box, he and Hampson went to work. With less than two minutes remaining in the second period, Hicke skated on the left side and rang a 20-foot shot off Rutledge's right post, but Hampson tapped in the rebound to make it 2–2. Jarrett then made it 3–2 just 2:54 into the final frame on a nice pass from Laughton that went through the LA goal crease. Bob Dillabough sealed the deal with an empty-net goal, giving the Seals a 4–2 win and evening the series at one game each.

The Seals were back in the series, but the boys in green and blue were feeling battered and bruised. "If this (checking) keeps up, I may not be alive at the end," said Hampson, the Seals' little sparkplug who, once again, had played his heart out. "LA means business and they're playing their best. We just happened to be a bit better out there." Vadnais said he was "almost too tired to take my uniform off." Norm Ferguson was in worse shape, however. "I just couldn't sleep last night," he said, revealing he had spent four hours in the dentist's chair getting an abscessed tooth removed. "And now he says I've got another."[40] Glover realized his troops were hurting and cancelled the noon practice that was scheduled for the following day.

Over nine thousand fans greeted the Seals and Kings for game three at the Great Western Forum, but most of them would leave the rink disappointed. The Kings drew first blood at 10:21 of the second period on a goal by Real Lemieux, but Gary Smith held down the fort afterward, making several big saves. Joe Szura responded for Oakland just one minute after Lemieux's goal, and the Seals never looked back. Jarrett made it 2–1 three minutes later, while Ingarfield lit the lamp just 13 seconds into the final period. By the time the dust had settled, the Seals had taken a 2–1 series lead with an impressive 5–2 win. Nevertheless, like the Seals had done in game two, the Kings rebounded from a tough loss to tie the series with a 4–2 win in game four. "We let them off the hook after getting a quick goal on them," said Glover after the game. "Instead of taking the game to them, we sat back and waited for them to come to us."[41]

Glover was very disappointed with his club's effort during the first four games of the series, declaring that his Seals had been giving a "spasmodic effort."[42] Back in Oakland for game five, Laughton gave the Seals a 1–0 lead just sixty-six seconds into the game on a pass from Hicke. Croteau tied the game with four minutes remaining in the first period, squeezing a puck through Smith's pads, but the young netminder was not fazed. "Earlier in the season that goal that went between Smitty's legs would have upset him," said Glover, "but he's come a long way since then and has learned to cope with things like that." Speaking about the one goal he let in, Smith admitted, "I hit it in myself. Croteau shot it from the side and I poked at it to clear it to one of our guys. It hit the heel of my stick and I pulled it between my legs."[43]

In the second period, Bob Dillabough scored his second of the game to put the Seals up 3–1. It was a sweet night for Dillabough, who had been left for dead by the Pittsburgh Penguins earlier in the season. "I didn't get off the bench for 22 games and I never felt so low. I felt I was a nothing. When I arrived in Oakland, the man (Glover) told me he brought me here to play. I got my confidence back."[44]

Glover's Seals thrashed the Kings 4–1 to take a 3–2 lead in the series. "I think they decided they are a better club than they have shown before in this series," said Glover. "If they play like they did tonight, they could wrap it up tomorrow."[45]

In game six, with their season on the line, the Kings gelled together before 7,846 home fans and played one of their best games of the series. LA built a commanding 3–1 lead in the first period, but the Seals tied it up on goals by Brian Perry and Gene Ubriaco. The Kings came on strong in the second period, outshooting the Seals 12–7 and winning the battles along the boards. Mike Laughton went down with a groin injury in the second period. With about five minutes left in the second period, the inevitable happened; the Kings took a 4–3 lead on a goal by Bill Flett. The Kings pushed hard to increase their lead in the final period, outshooting the Seals 12–2 and flexing their muscle as well. Bob Dillabough, already nursing a torn shoulder muscle, was checked hard into the boards in his only shift of the third period. Gary Smith shut the door, but the Seals could not take advantage of their goaltender's heroics, and the Kings skated to a 4–3 victory.

An enthusiastic crowd of 9,348, the largest of the series, greeted the Seals and Kings for the climactic seventh game at the Coliseum. Just 0:46 into the game, defenseman Bert Marshall was tagged for elbowing, and with the Kings on the power play, Ted Irvine put LA up by a goal. Less than two minutes later, as the teams played four-on-four, Vadnais unleashed a good shot from 35 feet out and, with Hampson screening Gerry Desjardins, sent the puck into the net. At the 12:14 mark, Billy Inglis took a 20-foot shot that Smith blocked, but with no Oakland defenders near him, Irvine scored his second goal of the game on the rebound, putting the Kings up 2–1.

With about two minutes to play in the first period, Perry dug out a loose puck that Desjardins had been sitting on and scored, but the goal was called back because referee Art Skov had already blown the whistle. Shortly afterward Perry had another great scoring chance but missed an open net. The teams went to the dressing room with the score still 2–1, Los Angeles.

Earl Ingarfield, who led the Seals in playoff scoring, tied the game on a 25-foot hummer that flew past Desjardins at 9:51 of the second frame, but Bill Flett returned the favor some five minutes later to put the Kings up 3–2. "I remember passing the puck to [Flett]," recalled the Kings' Howie Menard. "I kept it in at the blue line, and I remember Bill was cutting in on the right hand side and I just rifled it towards the net and he managed to tip it in. That broke their backs right there." The score remained the same until 7:53 of the third period, when Lowell MacDonald scored on a breakaway to make it 4–2, LA. Undaunted, Gerry Ehman scored his second goal of the playoffs to reduce the Kings' lead to one.

The Seals continued to push, but Desjardins was up to the task. The drama finally ended at 18:26 when Menard scored on his own rebound to give Los Angeles a 5–3 lead. This time, the Seals were not going to mount a comeback. "They wanted it more than we did and they played their game," Hampson said after the game. "We made too many mistakes, then had to play catch-up from a goal behind all the way. You can't play catch-up all the time and also expect to take away their game. They checked, checked, checked."[46]

Vadnais, one of the Seals' most persistent and pugnacious customers, agreed with the captain. "That's all they did and it worked. Every time we'd get something started they'd check us right off the puck."[47]

Despite the disappointing end to the season, Hampson felt optimistic about the Seals' future. "There is no reason we shouldn't be even better next year," he said. "We didn't do it right out there tonight but there's always next time."[48] This was clearly a different team than the one that had limped to the finish line a year earlier. When Hampson said the Seals "didn't do it right," you could see he and his teammates *expected* to win; they had been the clear favorites.

Long after the Stanley Cup had been won by the Montreal Canadiens in a four-game sweep of the St. Louis Blues, the NHL handed out its annual player awards. Norm Ferguson scored a rookie record 34 goals but narrowly lost the Calder Trophy to Danny Grant by a vote of 119–112, due in part because Ferguson had only 54 points while Grant had 65. Bill Torrey was dumbfounded: "Fergie's 34 goals helped us finish second and what did Grant's 34 do for Minnesota, a last-place club? Fergie played on a third line that totalled 50 goals. Look at the linemates Grant had—Larose and O'Shea."[49] The *Sporting News*, however, agreed with Torrey and awarded Ferguson its Rookie of the Year honor.

Ted Hampson capped off a fantastic season by winning the Bill Masterton Memorial Trophy, given to the most perseverant and dedicated player. Hampson is the only Seal to ever have his name engraved on a major NHL award. He also finished second to Detroit's Alex Delvecchio for the Lady Byng Memorial Trophy, given to the player who best combines gentlemanly play, sportsmanship, and skill. Back in Oakland, Hampson was named the winner of the Larriburu Brothers Trophy given to the Seals' Most Valuable Player. The Seals' Charlie Hustle led the team in assists (49), points (75), and power play goals (9), and finished second in goals (26).

Several other Seals enjoyed career seasons, including Bill Hicke (25 goals, 61 points), Gerry Ehman (21 goals, 45 points), Gary Jarrett (22 goals, 45 points), and Mike Laughton (43 points in 53 games and winner of the Seals' Most Improved Player award). Gary Smith took a huge step forward in his development, recording a 2.96 goals-against average, 4 shutouts, and a 22-21-7 record, the first and only time a Seals' goaltender would finish with a winning record. On a side note, the NHL had always claimed Smith compiled a 21-24-7 record in 54 games, but according to Seals' game summaries Smith actually compiled a far better record. Charlie Hodge's record was actually 3-8-2 in 14 games, not 4-6-1 as the league claimed; Chris Worthy went 4-7-2 in 14 games, while the league claimed he went 4-6-3.

While most of the Seals' top players set personal bests, the player who stood out the most was Carol Vadnais. "I got him to use his shot differently," Fred Glover said. "Instead of putting it up at the crossbar, he's shooting it down low where it belongs. There, the goalie can't see it if he's screened and can't glove it. And one of our guys can do something with it—deflect it, maybe—with his stick on the ice." Vadnais scored 15 goals and 42 points, the top marks among West Division defensemen. Vadnais greatly appreciated the opportunity he received by playing in California. "I became a regular right away and an important player," he admitted. "I got a chance I might have waited years for in Montreal."[50]

Fred Glover was rewarded for his club's surprising turnaround season. The Jack Adams Award, given to the NHL's top coach, was only introduced in 1974, but the *Hockey News* handed Glover its annual Coach of the Year award, which was no surprise. The *Oakland Tribune*'s Ed Levitt believed "Glover inherited the toughest job in hockey. The Seals had every problem imaginable and the way [Olmstead] handled the boys, you wondered if the players didn't belong in some cell rather than on some ice."[51] Thanks to Glover, and some smart managerial moves, the Seals became one of the best offensive clubs in the West. "My biggest problem," said Glover, "was to convince these guys that they had the talent to win. We also made trades to get people who not only were gifted, but who had played on winning teams and had a winning attitude.

"We ended up with players who could get along and not cause trouble. We wanted to get one happy and talented family and not just 18 individuals each going his own way," something Olmstead had never been able to accomplish.[52] Hampson still does not know why the Seals had been so much better in 1968–69, but he believes part of their success was due to the acquisitions Selke had made before and during the season. "In year two, I think it was just a new lease on life," Hampson recalled. "We really got along well as a group. That was probably very important. . . . It wasn't any one player. Everything kind of fit together in year two. I think we had a lot to prove."

The 1968–69 Seals definitely had Selke's fingerprints all over them. At the end of season one the Seals had been as big a mess as could be imagined: bad morale, no confidence, ready to pack up and go. One year later the team seemed poised to challenge for first place in the division. Bill Torrey credited his friend Selke for the Seals' amazing turnaround: "He has spent more time and energy in this one area than anywhere else. He has established a good rapport, understanding and total respect between the players and the front office. . . . There is no limit to what he'll do. He is willing to take that extra step to assist the players in whatever area they need help. . . . He knows them not as just hired hands, but as individuals. He cares who they are, not what they are."[53]

It seemed like a lifetime had passed since Bert Olmstead was running the Seals ragged. A certain warmth had developed in the team over the course of a calendar year. The Oakland Seals had ceased to be a collection of individuals and had become a family. They had accomplished one important goal: they had gained league-wide respect.

4

Shortly after being acquired at the 1968 intra-league draft, Carol Vadnais became the new face of the Oakland Seals. He was everything the Seals had hoped he would be: flashy, tough, hip, handsome. As the Seals geared up for the 1969–70 season opener, the *Oakland Tribune* published a series of articles hyping the team's best players. Sports editor George Ross compared Vadnais to Joe Namath and O. J. Simpson, blue-chippers who immediately excelled at the professional level, but Ross believed Vadnais was "that, plus." Ross explained, "The plus is image, presence, the mod young guy's instinctive ability to groove. They said of the collegiate Joe Namath that he tilted the field at Alabama. Vadnais tilted the ice in Montreal at 18."[1]

Vadnais's future was brighter than anyone else's on the Oakland roster. During the Seals' training camp in Oshawa, Ontario, a local sportswriter said, "The last instant superstar to come into hockey was Bobby Orr, from right here with the Oshawa Generals. . . . Carol Vadnais will be at least as big a name with Oakland." The same sportswriter also highlighted the fact Vadnais had scored an impressive 15 goals and 42 points, marks that eclipsed the 13 goals and 41 points Orr scored as a rookie three years earlier. "I think you'll see Vadnais become a much better player, a crowd pleaser," said Fred Glover. "He's the electrifying type of athlete."[2]

Word around the league was you didn't mess with the 6'2", 200-pound Vadnais. Ed Levitt of the *Oakland Tribune* declared Vadnais had "split open more eyelids, bloodied more noses, loosened more teeth, knocked down more NHL players and drawn more penalties fighting than any other guy on ice." Levitt also believed Vadnais was the only player in the league who had "never lost a beef."[3]

Levitt recalled one particular incident where Vadnais demonstrated his policeman role on the Seals:

Here last Friday night, Pittsburgh's Tracy Pratt, a 6-2, 195-pound ruffian, picked on the Seals' Ted Hampson, who is 5-8, 160.

Twice Vadnais rushed over to warn Pratt to keep his hands off Hampson.

Pratt didn't heed the advice. He went on to slug Hampson against the boards after the period had already ended.

At the time Vadnais was on the other side of the rink. But seeing his teammate in distress, he came flying across the ice, leaped over three players and threw a haymaker at Pratt.

And down on his prat went Tracy Pratt.[4]

Another youngster who had made a major impact was Norm Ferguson. While he may not have won the Calder Trophy, "Ferguson was an unknown quantity in the league," said Glover. "One of the younger guys groping their way. Now, with the benefit of a year's experience, we're hoping his progress continues. He and Vadnais are quality players."[5] Mike Laughton, the Seals' less-heralded rookie, had also surprised with 20 goals and 43 points in just 53 games. At the amateur draft the Seals selected a promising young forward named Tony Featherstone with their first pick, seventh overall. With the eighteenth overall pick the Seals chose Ron Stackhouse, an offensive-minded defenseman.

With a committed new owner, a young, talented roster, and a clear agenda, the future seemed limitless in Oakland. Not only were the Seals expected to make the playoffs, but they expected to represent the West Division in the Stanley Cup Final. Furthermore, Trans-National Communications (TNC) had made it clear the Seals were definitely staying in the Bay Area. Since the team had exceeded all on-ice expectations in its second season, the new priority was to increase attendance to make sure they did not have another midseason ownership crisis. The Seals had improved on the ice, but attendance had bottomed out at 4,584 fans per game. By September 1969, the team had sold only 1,100 season tickets, which was an improvement, but not nearly enough to make the club solvent.

TNC concentrated on group sales, at first exclusively in the Bay Area and then throughout Northern California, peddling tickets to a clientele ranging from high school students to factory workers. Two additional sales people were added to the organization, and Dick Lynch, TNC's vice president of sales, worked full-time in the Bay Area to help sell season tickets. Team president Bill Creasy could also breathe easily knowing the NHL had eliminated all Seals' Sunday night home games, meaning the club would no longer have to compete with the NFL's Oakland Raiders for local fans. TNC also increased the Seals' presence on Bay Area radio, signing an agreement with station WKGO to broadcast thirty games during the 1969–70 season.

Persistence paid off. In February 1970 Creasy chirped to the media: "After 27 home games we're already 42,712 admissions and $160,493 in cold cash above what we took in at a similar time last year." He elaborated that "average paid attendance is now 6,000. Last year at this time it was 4,300. . . . If we can keep going this way maybe by next year we can get up around 9,000 or 10,000 a game, and then we will have turned the corner."[6] Not long before, it seemed like just a matter of time before the moving vans would be backing up to the Coliseum doors.

The Seals entered the 1969–70 season bursting with optimism. With the exception of the St. Louis Blues, the Seals had arguably the best all-around team in the West. Oakland's goal-scoring threats were spread evenly across three solid lines. First there was the Assembly Line of Bill Hicke, Ted Hampson, and Gary Jarrett, which, according to the Seals media guide, had collected 181 points in 1968–69, although they did not actually play the whole season together. Norm Ferguson's shocking 34 tallies led all Oakland scorers. Earl Ingarfield looked rejuvenated upon arriving in Oakland, scoring 23 points in 26 games, mostly on a line with Hampson and Ehman.

If there was one area the Seals needed to upgrade, it was on the back end; the Seals' goals against total had risen from 219 to 251. The Seals took advantage of the fact the New York Rangers wanted to discard the 1966–67 Norris Trophy recipient, Harry Howell. The thirty-six-year-old had undergone a spinal fusion to correct his ailing back, but the Seals looked past his health and saw his experience as a huge asset, so they bought his contract. Howell had always been a strong defensive player, and even though he would not be ready until December, he planned to make an impact with his new team. "I think they see me as I see myself, as a steadying veteran of a young club," he said. "That was my role with the Rangers."[7] With 1,160 games under his belt, Howell became the Seals' most experienced player.

The Seals were expected to finish in the top half of the West Division once again, but something felt off from the very beginning. Complacency and a lack of consistency permeated the Seals' dressing room, and no one could quite explain how it got there. There were signs in training camp that this was not going to be a banner year. In late September the Seals lost 3–2 to their Providence farm club, and Glover was none too pleased. "It's the kids who are doing the fighting—nobody else," he said. "The others are afraid to get their face cut or suffer a fat lip because they're afraid it would make their wife or girl friend unhappy. Well I've got 400 stitches in my face and it doesn't look so bad."[8]

Glover did not mince words when it came to Gary Smith's early-season performances either. "Smitty is lost in the woods somewhere," Glover said. "We thought progress had been made with him last season, but it all went down the drain." Smith rarely reacted well to his coach's motivational tactics. "They think every time they light a fire under me I'll play better. All Glover does is bum-rap me. I'd rather he let me alone. I'd just as soon let one of the other guys play so I wouldn't have to take the aggravation. I'm not that crazy about the game. If there was something else I could do, I'd rather do it."[9] As goalie on one of the league's expansion teams, Smith was under a lot of pressure to succeed. Fans could be especially cruel to a goalie on a team that lost more than it won. "The fans in our section, and we sat in the end zone," remembered Seals fan Cathy White, "used to get [Smith] . . . and I got so tired of them giving him a bad time, that I stood up and I said, 'This is his mother!'" She then pointed to her friend Vivian Bolton, obviously not the goalie's mother, sitting right next to her. "Silence," she continued. "Nothing was said from that point on, but if I hadn't done that, they would have been on Gary forever."

Norm Ferguson also had a difficult preseason. "I lost 10 pounds in training camp and didn't feel good," he said. "I didn't have any stamina. Plus, I was having trouble with both touch and timing. But

I'm getting over the humps one by one and I'll be OK from now on."[10] Ferguson started the season well, scoring 3 goals and an assist in his first 6 games, but then he hit the skids. If he had been the only player to see his points decline, the Seals would have been okay. The previous year, injuries had been few and far between, and most players hit career highs in goals and points. This time around, the infirmary filled up fast.

One of the biggest secondhand victims of the injury bug was captain Ted Hampson. He scored 7 points in 9 preseason games, but he struggled once the season started. Earl Ingarfield missed the early part of the season with a wrist injury, which meant Hampson had to take on extra shifts on the penalty kill and power play. In the meantime, Ingarfield was replaced by rookie Don O'Donoghue, and Hampson took it upon himself to look after the youngster. "When we put O'Donoghue with Ted at the start of the season, for some reason Hampson felt he had to do Don's job as well as his own," said Frank Selke. "He got a little confused trying to do both jobs at once. Then when we switched Jarrett in for O'Donoghue, the problem carried over. I think that if Teddy had let O'Donoghue play his own game and not worried so much about him, he wouldn't have gotten himself into this mixup." Glover also refused to blame Hampson for his slow start. "He's trying to do too much," Glover said. "He feels a great responsibility to this team, and when things are going bad he tries that much harder."[11]

Hampson refused to blame anyone for his poor production. "Of course I'm not too pleased with the way things are going," he admitted. "It seems as though I can't get that little extra jump. But I'm feeling better and I'm encouraged by the way things have been going, especially in the last few games. The problems have certainly not been caused by my linemates. Once I get started, I'll be all right."[12]

Even though Hampson, Ehman, and Ingarfield played terrific hockey together in the second half of the previous season, Glover split them up. "It was a disappointment for us, it was a disappointment for management, coaching," Hampson said about the playoff series loss to Los Angeles, "so at some point they decided during the off-season to put Earl back at center, and the three of us that had so much success, we never played another shift together."

The Seals desperately wanted to prove their second-place finish hadn't been a fluke, and after eight games they did just that, compiling a solid 4-3-1 record, but reality soon set in. On November 7 the Seals took a big-league beating at the hands of the New York Rangers. Juha Widing opened the score at 2:32, and the Rangers did not stop there. In fact, by the time the first period had ended, Arnie Brown, Bill Fairbairn, Rod Gilbert, Dave Balon, and Jean Ratelle had all scored to make it 6-1. Gary Smith could not even take solace in the fact his team, as a whole, was badly outplayed in that first period. "He really put us in a hole," said Selke, placing the blame for the first four Ranger goals squarely on the goaltender's shoulders. "All four of those goals were bad."[13] Glover removed Smith after his twenty disastrous minutes, but just two minutes into the second, Walt Tkachuk greeted Charlie Hodge with the Rangers' seventh goal. Arnie Brown added an eighth in the third period to make the final score Rangers 8, Seals 1. The Oakland–New York contest was a complete and total embarrassment; the Rangers outshot the Seals 45-19. Vadnais and Balon received five-minute fighting majors as well as misconduct penalties for their part in a round of fisticuffs, but this was not an unusual occurrence for Vadnais, as he had set a league record with twelve fighting majors the year before, an unusual amount for a player of his talent.

As bad as the Seals' earlier 8-1 loss to the Rangers had been, things did not get much better a few nights later when the boys in green and blue visited Boston. The Seals stormed out of the gate, thanks to Mike Laughton's fifth goal of the season 2:33 into the contest, but the Bruins then reeled off 4 goals to take a commanding 4-1 lead through two periods.

The questionable performance of referee Ron Wicks, who blew several penalty calls, tried the patience of both benches. After Dallas Smith scored Boston's fifth goal just eighteen seconds into the third period, Gary Smith's frustrations boiled over as he argued Jim Harrison had invaded his goal crease. "Harrison was holding me," argued the Seals' netminder. "He had me hooked with his stick and I couldn't move. I tried to tell Wicks, but he told me to go back into the net. When I turned around, I stumbled over Dick Mattiussi's foot [bumping into Wicks in the process]. It was an accident."[14] Honest mistake or not, Smith was immediately ejected from the game after having faced a whopping 47 shots.

Hodge took over in goal, but his luck was no better. Ehman replied for Oakland at the 8:11 mark of the third, cutting Boston's lead to 3 goals, but Johnny McKenzie scored three minutes later to make it 6–2, Bruins. Overall the Bruins fired 64 shots at the Seals' beleaguered goaltenders. Final score: Bruins 8, Seals 3.

It did not take long for the Seals to nosedive into the nether reaches of the West Division. Before long, the LA Kings were the only club with a worse record than Oakland. Following a 4–2 victory over Minnesota on November 19, the Seals lost four in a row, then after a 1–0 win over Detroit on November 30, the Seals went on a five-game winless streak, bringing their record to 6-16-4. About the only thing going for the Seals was the fact that the final playoff spot was still just 2 points away because most other West Division teams were also struggling early in the season.

The Seals got back into the win column on December 12 when the Penguins paid a visit to Oakland. Vadnais, who was playing his second game of the season at left wing, scored his sixth and seventh goals and picked up an assist on a Bill Hicke marker to lead the Seals to a 4–1 win. Ingarfield picked up 3 assists for the second consecutive game. In the Oakland net Smith made 32 saves while Pittsburgh's Les Binkley stopped 22 shots.

The Seals were hoping for a similar result when they played Chicago a week later. The first period was scoreless, but when Bobby Hull gave Chicago a 1–0 lead in the second it turned out to be all the offense goalie Tony Esposito would need. Cliff Koroll, Jim Pappin, and Gene Ubriaco—formerly of the Seals—also added insurance goals, and Esposito easily turned aside the Seals' 23 shots. The 4–0 win was Esposito's fifth shutout of the campaign. The Seals could take solace in the fact over nine thousand people showed up at the Coliseum.

During this same game Vadnais and Chicago's Keith Magnuson engaged in a long, violent game of cat and mouse. The unending needling and chirping surprised few; both men were among the league leaders in penalty minutes and rarely backed down from a fight. The two players' constant bickering eventually led to three separate altercations. In the end, Magnuson needed six stitches to close a gash on his lip while Vadnais suffered a broken nose. Vadnais was given three minor penalties, two majors, and a misconduct, while Magnuson received two minors, two majors, and a misconduct.

Vadnais's ornery behavior was perhaps a result of the Seals' eighteen-day road trip covering both the Christmas and New Year's holidays. Earl Ingarfield summed it up best for his teammates: "It's a heck of a note. I sent my wife and kids home to Lethbridge for Christmas and said I'd see them when we got back. It's grim. And if you happen to be in a slump, a trip like this is even worse."[15] This certainly did not help team morale. Partly as a result of the lengthy road trip, the Seals found themselves a hair out of the West Division basement, barely ahead of Los Angeles, but surprisingly within reach of a playoff spot.

Despite the outstanding campaigns being put together by players like Vadnais and Ingarfield, more often than not the Seals were outclassed. On January 7 the Boston Bruins humiliated the Seals, 6–1, and as had become the norm that season, Gary Smith was left to his own devices. He often came up big, one time making a beautiful glove save on a Wayne Carleton blast from the top of the face-off circle. Unfortunately for Smith, Johnny Bucyk had the Seals' number on this night. In front of some seven thousand Oakland fans, Bucyk scored twice, the 299th and 300th goals of his career, providing the only real excitement of the game.

Four days later the Bruins embarrassed the Seals again. Under intense fire Smith allowed six more goals this time around, including a hat trick by Phil Esposito. Dick Mattiussi, Earl Ingarfield, and Norm Ferguson responded for Oakland, but it was not nearly enough as the Bruins went on to win 6–3. Smith was bombed with 42 shots while his counterpart Ed Johnston faced just 29. Smith was quickly becoming the league's favorite target. Not only did he start the majority of Seals games, but in most of them he could not afford to blink an eye for fear he might miss one of the 40 or 50 shots coming his way. Smith could have become a test dummy for bullet-proof vests and not even flinched.

Glover was so irate following the game he refused to tell his players when the next morning's practice would take place. "I won't tell them," he said. "If by this time they don't know when they practice, they never will. That's their trouble. They don't think."[16]

Glover did not even care if his players found out in the morning paper that he had insulted them, claiming "they'd probably complain to their shop steward or the players' association." One player surprisingly in Glover's good graces was Gary Smith. Glover believed Smith should have sued for lack of support. The coach was also impressed with defenseman Harry Howell, saying he played "steady" and "kn[ew] what he [was] doing," while of workhorse Ingarfield, Glover said, "[He's] playing better on one leg than most of them are on two." Carol Vadnais was "working and playing good hockey," and Ted Hampson was "working hard as usual." On the other hand, Glover had some harsh words for Mike Laughton and Gary Jarrett. The coach believed that if Laughton didn't "use his muscle," he was in trouble. As for Jarrett, a simple two-word comment summarized Glover's feelings: "No comment." Overall, the coach believed his team needed to "see a psychiatrist."[17]

Winning regularly, particularly on the road, had become a major issue for the Seals. Gary Smith had a good explanation for the Seals' horrible season. "We're having our troubles," he admitted. "But some of the reason is the schedule we've been following. It could best be termed ridiculous. We had a 17-day road trip and a 19-day road trip. With the three-hour time difference and the competition it's really been ridiculous."[18]

The Seals hit the turning point of their season just before the All-Star break. Coming into the Montreal Forum with a disappointing 9-25-7 record, the Seals shocked the Habs with a 3-0 victory, only their fifth in twenty-five games away from Oakland. The shutout broke Montreal's five-game unbeaten streak and helped propel the Seals in the right direction.

The Seals soon got the ball rolling and closed to within one point of fourth-place Pittsburgh with a convincing 6-3 win over Toronto on January 23. Earl Ingarfield and Doug Roberts scored in the first period while the Leafs had two men in the penalty box. The Leafs closed the gap to 4-2 in the middle period, but it was not enough to shut down Ingarfield, who was firing on all cylinders. The veteran center scored twice more in the game to give his team a 6-2 lead, earning himself his second hat trick of the season. Two nights later Mike Laughton rose to the occasion and scored another hat trick to lead the Seals to a 4-1 win over Minnesota. Gary Smith was sensational once again, stopping 43 shots.

The Seals lost three straight between January 28 and February 1, but they soon got back to their winning ways. On February 4 before a Coliseum crowd of 5,920, the Montreal Canadiens fell 5-2 with two goals coming from Vadnais and singles from Hampson, Ferguson, and Ehman. Two nights later in a 2-1 win over St. Louis, Ferguson appeared to have broken out of his season-long scoring drought by netting two more goals, only his 10th and 11th of the season. They turned out to be the last ones he would score that season.

The Seals needed just a win in their next game against Toronto to climb into third place, but the motivated Leafs were fighting just to stay alive in the East Division playoff race. Smith faced another ridiculous barrage, 54 shots in all. In the early going Smith was flopping and diving everywhere, even breaking a suspender strap trying to keep Norm Ullman from scoring. The Leafs outshot the Seals 21-10 in the opening frame and even recorded another 20 shots in the third period in a 5-1 win.

During the game Smith turned back the clock a few years to his days with the Leafs. That night the *Hockey Night in Canada* commentators noted that of all the goaltenders in the league, Smith and the Rangers' Ed Giacomin would be the most likely candidates to score a goal. Perhaps Smith overheard them way down in his crease, because with about thirteen minutes to play Suitcase stickhandled past the blue line in an effort to clear it out of the Seals' zone as the crowd roared its approval, but he dumped the puck out instead of attempting a shot on goal.

On February 13 over eight thousand fans greeted the Seals at the Coliseum, where they prepared to meet the league's first-place team, the New York Rangers. The game remained scoreless until the second period. Dave Balon gave the Rangers a 1-0 lead, but Mattiussi tied it up for Oakland early in the third period. The Rangers did not give up easily; former Seal Orland Kurtenbach scored a minute after the Seals had made it 1-1. From that point on, however, it was all Oakland.

Howell, Laughton, and Ingarfield each scored a goal to give the Seals a 4–2 win. As always, Smith was outstanding, stopping 33 shots; the Seals managed only 18 as the worrisome trend persisted.

Howell was in a particularly jaunty mood following the win. "It felt really good to get one against my old team. After all, we needed the win more than they did." The suddenly cocky Howell even went so far as to say he "wouldn't mind if [the Seals] played New York in the finals." When he was asked if he actually believed the Seals were good enough to make it all the way through to the finals, he replied, "stranger things have happened."[19]

Although the Seals had languished near the West basement most of the season, in early February the club was in position to challenge for third place thanks to a stretch of 4 wins in 5 games, but the Seals suffered a severe blow in a February 20 loss to St. Louis. Earl Ingarfield, the team's hottest scorer, broke his thumb and, after a brief layoff, was forced to play the rest of the season with his injury.

Even though the team had pulled itself out of the gutter and had propelled itself back into the playoff race, it was painfully obvious the Seals were not displaying the same intensity that had shot them into second place the previous season. Norm Ferguson admitted years later that he and his teammates were "a little complacent," although he didn't know why. "We expected bigger and better things," he said, "but they didn't happen. Maybe it's because we stood pat and didn't make enough changes."[20] Hampson, Vadnais, and Ingarfield were contributing regularly, but the team lacked enthusiasm, and Glover was frustrated. He believed the players thought they were better than they really were. "Even when they've been beaten 6–1," he said, "some of them will go out of this dressing room telling themselves they've played a good game. . . . Oh sure, there are a half dozen who are putting out and getting nothing in return. But the others think they got as high as they did last year on finesse, instead of hustle and muscle, and they're content to play finesse now and it's not working."[21]

Almost everyone was scoring less than they had the previous season. Entering March, Hampson led the club with just 38 points. Hicke had got off to a great start for the third consecutive year, but he ran into his usual injury problems and had counted just 32 points.

Jarrett struggled with consistency all season long and sat well behind the leaders with just 24 points. After returning from his eye injury the previous season, Jarrett was accused of being apprehensive, even soft, and as a result heated words were exchanged with both Glover and Selke.

Norm Ferguson, in particular, had slid far down the depth chart due to his season-long slump. He had worked on his skating and his shooting during the off-season, but his lack of pure goal-scoring talent had become evident, and he had been stuck at 11 goals since February 6. He had always been a plugger and a checker, and now he was playing like one again. "The only problem with Norm," Glover said years later, "was that he went the same way all the time. He'd deke inside and go outside at the blue line. The opposition caught on and his numbers were never the same."[22]

Late February and early March were difficult times for the Seals, but after six straight losses, the Seals lost only 3 of their next 13 games. The hot streak could not have come at a better time: the Minnesota North Stars were fighting neck and neck with the Seals for fourth place.

One of the Seals' most crucial games of the season came on March 24 in Minnesota. The Stars opened the scoring in the first period on a goal by Tommy Williams, but the Seals' Wayne Muloin scored a power-play goal to tie things up later in the frame. Minnesota regained the lead in the middle frame when sniper Bill Goldsworthy scored. The score remained 2–1 until the 11:12 mark of the third period when Laughton scored for Oakland. Had Laughton not scored, the Stars would have gained two more points in the standings, but with the 2–2 tie, the Stars remained only one point ahead of the now fifth-place Seals.

The Seals won two important games in a row to distance themselves from Minnesota. First, Ingarfield scored in a 3–2 triumph over Philadelphia on March 22; then the Seals defeated St. Louis by the same score, bringing Oakland's overall record to 21-38-13. The West standings were so close in the final few weeks of the season that any of the clubs seeded second to fifth had a chance of either making the playoffs or falling completely out of the running. St. Louis led the division with 80 points, followed by Pittsburgh (59), Philadelphia (58), Oakland (55), and Minnesota (52). Philadelphia and Oakland had but four games remaining while Pittsburgh and Minnesota had one game in hand each.

The Stars were not about to let the Seals take the last playoff spot from them. Like a flash of lightning, the Stars won two in a row—including an 8-3 bombing of the Seals in Oakland—and the Seals were back in fifth place. But by April 1 the Seals had a game in hand on the Stars.

In the meantime the Flyers were collapsing in spectacular fashion, adding another interesting element to the playoff equation. Just a month earlier the Flyers seemed destined to finish in the top four, but a 5-18-8 stretch spelled doom. On the last day of the regular season the Seals and Flyers were tied for the final playoff spot with 58 points apiece, while the Stars were fifth with 56. The Seals lost their final regular season game to Los Angeles, 4-1, meaning Philadelphia needed only one point in their final game, against Minnesota, to qualify for the playoffs. In the event of a fourth-place tie at the end of the regular season, the Seals would qualify as a result of more wins.

More than fourteen thousand fans packed the Philadelphia Spectrum for the tense showdown. The Stars and Flyers refused to let their guard down and give up the first goal. It was not until the final period that the Stars' Barry Gibbs finally managed to slip one past Bernie Parent. Lorne "Gump" Worsley, on the other hand, blocked everything that came his way. The 1-0 loss kept Philadelphia out of the postseason for the first time in their three-year history while the Seals graduated to the playoffs once again, but just barely. Interestingly, the Seals qualified for the postseason with only 58 points while the East's fifth-place club, the Montreal Canadiens, failed despite an excellent 92-point season.

Even though the Seals were advancing to the final eight for the second year in a row, it was no secret that this year's club had underachieved and had benefited from playing in the weaker West. Although the club got off to a strong start for the first time in its history, it played inconsistently right up until the last few weeks of the season. Between October 31 and February 1, the Seals went 8-26-7; in the other 35 games, the club went 14-14-7. The question now was which Seals would show up to face the Pittsburgh Penguins in round one of the playoffs.

Goaltenders Les Binkley and Gary Smith were at their best for game one in Pittsburgh. Pittsburgh outshot Oakland 35–29 before 8,051 fans, but few pucks found the back of the net. Not surprisingly, the game winner was an ugly one, as it often happens when two hot goalies face each other. In the third period, with bodies sprawled all over Smith's goal crease, Pittsburgh's Nick Harbaruk managed to squeeze one past the goal line for a 2–1 lead. Smith argued the Pens' Glen Sather had interfered with him while Harbaruk scored. To the hot-headed Smith's chagrin, referee Bruce Hood let the goal stand.

After the goal Carol Vadnais got into a shoving match with rookie Michel Briere, but Vadnais was then blindsided by former Seal Bryan Watson, who connected a few punches. The always-willing Vadnais left Watson with a right eye resembling a golf ball thanks to a single punch that landed just before the officials jumped in.

In his summary of game one the *Oakland Tribune*'s Spence Conley described how the Seals felt about the disputed goal:

> You could have cut the air of bitterness, disgust and pure anger in the Oakland dressing room after it was over.
>
> There was plenty of cursing and slamming down of equipment and Coach Fred Glover was seething: "That was an illegal goal," fumed Glover. "That man (Sather) had all the time in the world to get out.
>
> "Nobody was holding him. He must have had at least five seconds anyway. It was an illegal goal and he (Hood) blew it. And he knows he blew it.
>
> ". . . We could have won it. The guys played great, all of them. This is a tough way to lose a hockey game. Damn tough," Glover said.[23]

Smith was in an equally sour mood after the game. "[Harbaruk] came in, knocked me over and just held on," said the goaltender. "I didn't even see the winning shot. How could I? The man was on top of me."[24] Smith called the controversial goal "disgusting," adding that not only was Harbaruk in his goal crease but that he had been "in the *back* of the net."[25]

It was all downhill from there for the Seals. The result of game two pretty much matched that of game one: another loss and more controversy surrounding Smith. This time Gary Jarrett opened the scoring, but Harbaruk scored his second of the playoffs to tie the game 1–1, and before long the Penguins put away two more goals to take game two, 3–1.

"After we went ahead with those two goals within 34 seconds of the second period," said Pittsburgh coach Red Kelly, "the Seals were through for the night. They just caved in . . . our two quick goals took all the fight out of the Seals."[26]

Poor Suitcase had received little defensive support throughout the game, but that was pretty much how the entire season had gone for the Seals' netminder. Making matters worse, Pittsburgh fans chanted "Kill Smith" at the exasperated goalie. Frustrated, Smith tripped a number of Penguins roaming his crease, but his actions were futile; he was assessed two minor penalties. "When a goalie gets frustrated," explained Glover, "he's got to do something about it. Gary's a big man. You can't tie him to the net . . . you can't blame Smitty for our loss."[27]

Despite being down 2–0 in games, the Seals felt confident. "We'll come back, I guarantee," said Vadnais. "Three years ago," said Harry Howell, "Montreal lost the first two playoff games—then won four straight to win the Stanley Cup. We could do it the same way."[28]

Nearly nine thousand fans attended game three at the Coliseum, and the Seals got off to a good start once again. Ingarfield gave his team a 1–0 lead in the first period, but the floodgates soon opened and drowned the Seals. Harbaruk, Ken Schinkel, and Jean Pronovost reeled off three consecutive goals in the second period to put the Seals in a 3–1 hole. Schinkel made sure there would be no Seals comeback by scoring twice more in the final frame. Final score: Penguins 5, Seals 2.

With the Seals down 3–0 in games, Carol Vadnais sparked the team early in game four by scoring on a power play just 2:34 in, but just like in games two and three, the Penguins tied it up soon after. Vadnais scored another power play goal early in the second period to put Oakland up 2–1, but Bob Woytowich scored just two minutes later. With the score tied 2–2 at the final buzzer, the Pens and Seals went to overtime.

The last time the Seals had played in overtime—game one, versus Los Angeles the previous year—they were beaten just 19 seconds in. This time, Smith and Binkley absorbed puck after puck for the first 8:28 when the inevitable happened. "I went to clear the puck," said defenseman Bert Marshall, "and hoped to get our player away on a breakaway. My feet slipped out from under me. The puck went free and there wasn't a damn thing I could do about it."[29] The loose puck skidded toward the Pens' Jean Pronovost, who passed it over to Val Fonteyne, who then took a shot on Smith. The Seals' goalie made the save, but the rebound went over to Michel Briere, and he buried the biscuit to give Pittsburgh a hard-fought 3–2 win and the series sweep.

People associated with the Seals still talk about how great a series Briere had played. "They used to give us fits," remembers fan Larry Schmidt about the Penguins. "They had a guy on that team . . . and God rest his soul, this guy, this kid, could have been one of the greatest of all time . . . This kid was twenty years old and he played against the Seals in the playoffs, and he killed us." Sadly, Briere's series-winning goal turned out to be his last. Briere was badly injured in a car accident over the summer and spent the next eleven months in a coma before passing away in April 1971.

Although the Seals qualified for the playoffs, the team's lack of drive and determination left a bitter taste in everyone's mouth. "They had a taste going from last place to second and thought things would happen for them that didn't," said Glover. "They thought their skills alone could get them there."[30] Executive vice-president Bill Torrey promised the players would be "dancing to different music" come the 1970–71 season opener.[31]

Selke made several scathing comments to the media in the days following game four. "Our hockey team showed it didn't have any pride," he said. "You don't win anything, from ping pong or tiddly-winks, if you don't have pride in yourself and the team. It was a case of stubbornness on the part of our players to accept the fact that we aren't going to overpower anybody physically. The only way we can play is to go all out all the time." Selke did, however, give praise to a few players who had elevated their game over the course of the season. "Without [Smith] we wouldn't have even come close to the playoffs," he said.[32] Smith played brilliantly on most nights, but more often than not he was hung out to dry by his teammates. His 19-34-12 record and 3.12 goals-against-average simply did not do him justice; he faced 40 or more shots on 18 different occasions!

As for Earl Ingarfield, Selke believed the veteran player "contributed lots more than we had a right to expect considering his injuries."[33] The veteran center was an offensive leader throughout most of his injury-plagued season. He missed six weeks after severing tendons in his wrist at training camp, then injured his eye in January, and broke a thumb in March; yet he finished second in goals (21) and points (45) and scored two hat tricks in just 54 games. "We were lucky to get a player of his calibre," Glover remarked before the season. "He's always been one of the better centres in hockey."[34]

On Vadnais, Selke admitted, "To be moved around like he was to plug holes here and there, and still to produce the way he did, he has to get a lot of credit. If we had a dozen guys with his spirit we'd still be playing now."[35] To the Seals' delight, Vadnais had become a legitimate star in the expansion division. He scored 24 goals and 44 points to place second (with Toronto's Jim McKenny) among NHL defensemen, behind only Bobby Orr. Unlike McKenny and Orr, Vadnais played most of the season at left wing with center Ingarfield, so technically, he had not really played much defense that season, but his performance was impressive nonetheless.

In the span of a calendar year the Seals had become a listless, lifeless team, and they had been thoroughly embarrassed by a team that was no better than they were. During the regular season the Seals had showed little spunk, with the exception of the tenacious and determined Vadnais, whose 212 penalty minutes represented a quarter of the team's total time in the box, and defensemen Doug Roberts and Bert Marshall, who each picked up another 100. The *San Mateo Times*'s Hugh McDonald summed up the season best when he said, "In truth, the Seals were a fairly tame lot of pussycats in the NHL jungle. . . . While possibly Glover's own tenacious personality dragged the Seals into the playoffs, he at the same time should be held responsible for failing to teach them any team play worth mentioning."[36]

A year earlier the Seals seemed poised for greatness, mixing high-scoring veterans, solid defense, and talented rookies. By April 1970, the Seals' future looked bleak. Father Time had held off on the Seals for the 1968–69 season, but now he was staring many players squarely in the face. Hicke was thirty-two years old, Hampson was going on thirty-four, Ingarfield was almost thirty-six, while Ehman and the grey-haired Howell were pushing thirty-eight. Hampson led the club once again in assists (35) and points (52), and he was named the team's MVP, but he had not been as effective as he had been the two previous seasons. In the playoffs Hampson scored only 2 points in 4 games. His former linemate Hicke dropped from 61 points to just 44.

Many of the younger players who were expected to complement the veterans had experienced major scoring droughts. Jarrett dropped from 45 points to 31, and Laughton's point total declined from 43 to 35, even though he played 23 more games. Ferguson's shocking decrease from 54 points to 20 was even more distressing. "Our goal-scoring production from players who were paid very well for doing that, was disappointing. Sure it's possible for a 10 or even 20 per cent falloff," explained Selke. "But in some cases it was 50 per cent. We had a right to expect more. It may be understandable in the case of Norm Ferguson . . . because he certainly isn't the first rookie, nor the last, I'm sure, who had a bad second year. But you don't expect that from players with five or even 10 years of NHL experience."[37]

The club's rebuilding process would be accelerated in the off-season by the addition of two new NHL teams, the Buffalo Sabres and the Vancouver Canucks. Each established club could protect only so many players in the upcoming expansion draft. New faces would have to be found to replace the draftees, whether team management liked it or not. A few key figures would be moving on to greener pastures for the 1970–71 season.

5

FOOLS' GOLD, 1970–1971

In the summer of 1970 the Oakland Seals underwent another change in ownership, keeping the annual team tradition alive. The Knox brothers were awarded the Buffalo Sabres expansion franchise in 1970 and were therefore forced to give up their stake in the Seals. Furthermore, TNC could no longer stand the heavy financial burden of owning the Seals. Even though attendance had improved to over 6,000 fans per game, the Seals still lost money despite TNC's earlier claims that it would need to sell that many tickets to break even. Ironically, playing two playoff games at the Coliseum actually *exacerbated* the problem. Before game three of the Pittsburgh series, Bill Torrey explained, "We must draw 20,000 customers for our weekend games or we'll lose money being in the playoffs." They drew only 14,000. With the Seals already well in the red, they still had to send the league a percentage of the Coliseum gate receipts as part of the $575,000 playoff pool. "It's easy, of course for a club such as the Chicago Black Hawks to make a big profit from the playoffs," Torrey said. "Besides drawing bigger crowds, they charge higher prices. They're getting $10 and $12 for a playoff ticket—which is almost double what we're asking. But we're building. These established clubs have been in business for 30 years. We've been operating only three."[1]

According to Frank Selke, attendance was not the only reason for the club's financial problems that year:

> In reality, [TNC] had little or no money. Dick Lynch figured he could teach us how to market the team and was none too diplomatic in the process. Bill Creasy was a television producer who was a front man with nothing to back it up, and the others made one visit to announce their ownership and then disappeared. Under TNC, we had less operating cash than ever. They had radishes maybe, but cold cash, nope. . . . TNC was a cruel hoax, further proof that the NHL would try anything to keep up appearances without any con-

sideration for the fans, the players, their families and the organization. The less said about TNC, the better.[2]

According to a report in the April 13, 1970, *San Mateo Times*, league president Clarence Campbell "wasn't overly impressed with the performance of Trans National Communications, Inc." While talking to a fan during game two of the Oakland-Pittsburgh series, "he intimated that he couldn't see why with sound financing and businesslike operation the club couldn't become a solid attraction in the Bay Area. He pointed out that Pittsburgh, like Oakland, had problems at the gate, but in Pittsburgh there weren't the recurrent rumors of moving the franchise."[3]

Woody Erdman, TNC's founder, was believed to be a swindler and a sweet-talker who cut deals with unsuspecting rubes even though he had little capital to back him up. The court indicated he "was the subject of numerous legal proceedings both state and federal" and had "multiple judgments totaling several million dollars and federal tax liens of over $1 million."[4]

According to the *Toronto Star*'s Jim Proudfoot, the Seals "had to turn down deals just because they couldn't afford them. Many times, in fact, the players themselves were worried by rumors that their pay cheques would bounce. And there wasn't even enough money for a proper scouting program."[5] Bill Creasy said TNC was "so deep in debt that we bought the Boston Celtics just to get their assets on our books. I remember part of the deal was that Ballentine Beer could use Pat Summerall in their advertising."[6]

Erdman had big plans for his two sports franchises. Rumors had it that TNC was entertaining the thought of moving both the Seals and the Celtics to Long Island, to the dismay of the New York Rangers, who claimed such a move would infringe on their territorial exclusivity. The Rangers also alleged the Seals still owed them $15,000 from the purchase of defenseman Harry Howell. Erdman threatened to sue the NHL and force a move anyway if he was denied his right to relocate the Seals.

Erdman's threat was nothing more than hot air since TNC was in absolute chaos. The bigger issue was the accusation TNC had defaulted on four loan payments, totaling $1.6 million, including $991,000 to Wells Fargo Bank, $450,000 to Barry Van Gerbig's Seals Ltd., $83,000 to Mel Swig, and $89,000 to Van Gerbig's hockey investors. Erdman denied any default existed, but Van Gerbig disagreed. The May 24, 1970, edition of the *Oakland Tribune* explained that the money owed to the Wells Fargo Bank of San Francisco was in fact paid, and that "the debt responsibility was TNC's, but TNC officials said last month it would not be paid, so the bank called the note on its guarantors, Van Gerbig and 30 others. They paid."[7] Van Gerbig was accused of making the payment to solidify his case, but he denied it: "We were obligated to pay. It's as simple as that. Wells Fargo has been unbelievably cooperative. Perhaps they even should have called the loan sooner. When the loan was called, we had to come up. We didn't do it to solidify our default claim."[8]

TNC's holdings and investments turned out to be nothing more than smoke and mirrors, but that didn't stop Van Gerbig from drawing blood from the proverbial stone. TNC may have been flat broke, but they did have one interesting asset left: the Oakland Seals. Van Gerbig took TNC to court hoping he could regain control of the club and sell it to Charles O. Finley, the Chicago insurance tycoon and eccentric owner of baseball's Oakland Athletics. According to the June 1, 1970 *Oakland Tribune*, "Finley and the Van Gerbig interests have negotiated a purchase agreement in which the baseball owner would put up $3.4 million, waive a $700,000 future expansion windfall, and assume specified current liabilities."[9] The agreement would expire on June 30, meaning everyone involved was in a rush to close the deal.

Judge Robert Schnacke was assigned to the case. He declared that Van Gerbig would in fact regain control of the Seals and could sell them to whomever he wanted, but Schnacke never gave Van Gerbig control for operational purposes. Van Gerbig disagreed with the decision since he hoped Bill Torrey, and not Bill Creasy, would represent him at the league's June meetings, but Creasy was in fact the Seals' president and an NHL governor. Van Gerbig's hands were tied. Nevertheless, Van Gerbig was free to sell his club to Finley, providing NHL governors approved, which would be no easy feat.

Finley was a strange one indeed. It was easy to see why he alienated so many people. "He was a lot of talk, like a used car salesman," recalled Ted Hampson. "He was full of ballyhoo, whatever you call it. And we felt like the used cars." According to former ticket sales manager Jim Lingel, Finley's bluster got in his employees' way and made working for him difficult. "Frank [Selke] wanted to run it like a hockey team and this guy didn't want to," Lingel said. "[Finley] wanted to be a hot-shot."

During Finley's time as owner of the Oakland Athletics, most Major League Baseball owners perceived him as a boorish Rodney Dangerfield–type invading their respectable, buttoned-down country club. The establishment hated him because he believed in carnival tactics to promote his teams. For example, when Finley grew dissatisfied with the Athletics' venerable elephant mascot, he replaced it with a live mule and named it after himself, since Finley could never let an opportunity for self-promotion go by. If ever there was an animal that best exemplified Charlie Finley's character, it was the stubborn mule, and he absolutely loved this one. Finley wanted to bring "Charlie O." to Comiskey Park for a game against Chicago, but White Sox owner Arthur Allyn would have none of it, declaring, "If I let Finley ride that mule around the park, I won't be able to tell which one is the jackass."[10]

Despite his often crass demeanor, Finley knew his baseball, so he was respected in that regard. Bay Area broadcaster Joe Starkey, who got his professional start with the Seals, believes "it was extraordinary what [Finley] achieved with the Oakland A's. He put in new rules. He had a lot to do with the designated hitter. He put players in colorful uniforms. Nobody wore anything but white and grey, home and road, before he got involved. He knew his players. He was his own scouting staff. He was the owner, but he was the guy who found Reg Jackson and Sal Bando and a whole bunch of other stars of those '70s teams. So he knew the game, but he was also an incredibly difficult person."

For better or worse, one man was responsible for introducing Finley to the NHL board of governors: Munson Campbell. He had been involved in hockey for many years, having been raised by the Norris family, which owned the Detroit Red Wings, and he was friends with the Wirtz family, which owned the Chicago Black Hawks. He attended Yale University with Bruce Norris in the 1940s. As a result of his close ties with two of hockey's most famous families, Campbell had many acquaintances on the board of governors, making it easy for him to gain their support when he introduced them to Charlie Finley.

Campbell met Finley in 1968 while promoting his company's white baseball shoes to the Oakland A's. When the Seals came on the market in 1970, Campbell suggested Finley buy the franchise. Thanks to Campbell's influence, league governors voted 12–2 in favor of selling the franchise to Finley for $4.1 million. Van Gerbig was thrilled to finally unload his albatross, and Finley thanked Campbell for his help by naming him the Seals' new vice president.

Judge Schnacke was one hour away from handing Finley the keys to the car when U.S. District Judge Gerald S. Levin accepted a petition that gave TNC more time to pay off its debts before the Seals could be sold to anyone else. TNC used this time to initiate bankruptcy pro-ceedings, blocking Finley from purchasing the club. In the meantime St. Louis Blues' owner Sid Salomon III was looking for a way to keep Finley out of the NHL. Salomon was friends with Missouri senator W. Stuart Symington, who despised Finley in part due to the fact Finley had been troublesome when he had owned the Kansas City A's, which he later moved to Oakland. Salomon convinced a group led by Oakland Roller Derby owner Jerry Seltzer to purchase the Seals for $400,000 more than Finley had offered. Seltzer also submitted a detailed 120-page application, and he was well liked in the Bay Area. He had also convinced owners of four American Football League teams to join him. Finley, on the other hand, was loathed by the Bay Area media and fans. His application was as amateurish as it got: one page. Seltzer left quite the impression on Judge Schnacke, who recommended the Seals be sold to the Roller Derby king. "It seemed like the odds were 100 per cent in Finley's favor," Seltzer said. "Now it looks like I'll go before the NHL governors as the court-approved bidder, and I'll have the highest bid."[11]

Seltzer's deal was simply too good to be true for the financially troubled TNC, but the court still ruled that the NHL should decide whether Finley or Seltzer had the strongest claim to the Oakland

Seals. "I'd be shocked if they didn't [give the franchise to the Seltzer group]," said Erdman. "They're offering more money and some of the league traditionalists won't want to see the franchise go to a man like Finley. . . . Hockey doesn't need fireworks and live seals—the sport itself is electrifying enough."[12] As for Van Gerbig, he just wanted his money, and whether it came from Seltzer's pocket or Finley's was irrelevant.

After having met with both candidates, the NHL governors shook hands with the Devil, awarding the franchise to Finley. In the end, Finley equaled Seltzer's $4.5 million offer and gained full control of the troubled Seals, which he claimed could be turned into a successful operation. NHL governors "apparently preferred the fact that Finley was a sole proprietor and they shied away from any association with Roller Derby," which had a rather low-brow reputation.[13] The league's history with the Seals' disorganized ownership groups may have convinced the governors that Finley was the right man to run the Oakland Seals. Besides, as Bill Torrey put it, "It seemed ludicrous to the Board of Governors that Trans National Communications was trying to promote a successor [Seltzer] after not being able to run their own shop." Looking back, Seltzer believes he had no chance of obtaining the franchise no matter how professional his pitch might have been. "I think the vote was rigged," said Seltzer. "The chairman said one group had bid more money but that Mr. Finley had come up with the difference so we could judge the two groups equally." Of course, there were also the usual backroom dealings that the NHL of the early expansion era has become famous for. Seltzer admitted, "The Rangers representatives told us they would vote for us if we let them have Carol Vadnais. . . . I sort of danced around that."[14] The NHL played dirty, and in the end the league got what it deserved; it could have gotten rid of a huge problem, that being the Seals' convoluted ownership situation, but instead they cordially invited a much larger problem to sit at the dinner table.

Charles Oscar Finley was born February 22, 1918, in Ensley, Alabama, but grew up in Gary, Indiana. Even at a very young age, Finley was a hard-working, sweet-talking, crafty salesman. He would also stretch the truth, even outright lie, if it meant more money in his pocket. Ted Hampson was not exaggerating when he compared Finley to a used car salesman; he was, in fact, quite the wheeler and dealer, but Finley's early adult life was spent peddling insurance, not Buicks. According to G. Michael Green and Roger D. Launius, in their book *Charlie Finley: The Outrageous Story of Baseball's Super Showman*, during World War II "he would work at the ordnance plant, and nights he would make appointments and talk to families about ensuring their future livelihood should the principle breadwinner die or become incapacitated. His father-in-law, who sold insurance, encouraged him to enter this profession."[15]

In 1946, while in the hospital recovering from a bout of tuberculosis, Finley realized that most of the doctors who were treating him did not have disability insurance. Finley smelled a potential gold mine. He studied insurance statistics, found out how much doctors earned, what their expenses were, and put his plan to work. Initially, Provident Life and Accident Insurance refused to underwrite Finley's program, but the young man persisted. He went back to see them after having been turned down by almost every other company, but this time they thought Finley was onto something, so they gave him a shot. Before long, he had formed Charles O. Finley and Company and went on to sell insurance to 92 percent of the doctors in the Chicago area. Within two years of founding his company, Finley was a millionaire. According to Green and Launius, "the Finley empire would soon cover more than 50 medical associations, with memberships of more than 70,000 doctors, and generate $20 million worth of business annually."[16]

With his financial future now secure, Finley decided to dabble in one of his oldest interests: baseball. Finley became majority owner of the Kansas City Athletics in 1960. Life would never be the same for the poor baseball fans of the Midwest. The bombastic Finley expected everyone associated with the Athletics, whether they were managers, players, reporters, or city officials, to bow to his every demand. Finley loved getting involved in the day-to-day operation of his teams. He gave new meaning to the word *micromanager*. In a 2011 interview Joe Starkey explained just how demanding Finley could be: "Without having a lot of knowledge, both with his baseball team and with the

Seals, [Finley] would call managers, general managers, staff people at any time of the day or night, whenever it suited his whim to do so, and didn't worry about their personal lives or anything else. He just didn't care . . . he'd chew you out for anything of significance at all or insignificance, and that's just the way he ran things. He was a bottom-line guy."

Ernie Mehl, a Kansas City sportswriter, wrote many unflattering stories about Finley. In one article Mehl wrote about Finley's poor treatment of manager Hank Bauer: "[Bauer's] decisions on the field have been criticized . . . second guessed by the very men who should have been sympathetic with him. He has had to alter his pitching rotation to satisfy the whim of the owner, make line-up changes against his better judgment." Mehl later went on to say, "There never has been a baseball operation such as this, nothing so bizarre, so impossibly incongruous."[17] In retaliation Finley held an "Ernie Mehl Appreciation Day" on August 20, 1961, and had ordered billboards that read "ERNIE MEHL APPRECIATION DAY—POISON PEN AWARD FOR 1961." The billboards were then attached to both sides of a flatbed truck while the organist played "Who's Afraid of the Big Bad Wolf?" Finley staged a distasteful "Poison Pen Award" ceremony, but Mehl had no time for such silliness and declined his invitation. Athletics broadcasters Bill Grigsby and Merle Harmon, neither of whom worked for Finley, refused to promote such a ridiculous stunt on air, and when Finley confronted them about this, he threatened to fire them, something he had no authority to do at all.[18]

In Finley's mind he was *always* the victim. Someone was always trying to take advantage of his generous nature. By 1968 Finley felt victimized enough, so he packed up his Athletics and settled in Oakland. Senator Symington responded to the news by stating, "The loss [of the A's] is more than recompensed for by the pleasure resulting from our getting rid of Mr. Finley. . . . Oakland is the luckiest city since Hiroshima."[19]

Besides his erratic behavior and volatile personality, the other huge knock on Finley was his legendary stinginess, the effects of which Joe Starkey clearly remembers:

The entire front office, at one point, of the Oakland A's baseball team was like nine people. I mean, that's everybody! I'm talking scouts, ticket sales, you name it. . . . He didn't spend a penny he didn't have to. He didn't do any kind of marketing. A statistic that would blow you away, when you look at things today: the biggest attendance he had in three straight world championship teams which had what, four Hall-of-famers, the biggest attendance he ever had was 1,100,000 for any of those three teams in Oakland, because he didn't get involved in that part of the business, and he should have.

Finley always felt he could improve whatever sport he was involved in, to the dismay of his employees. In baseball, for example, he unsuccessfully tried to sell the idea of walking batters with just three balls instead of four. The A's were also the only club in baseball history to have a player listed as a "designated runner" in their annual media guide. In 1963 Finley broke with baseball tradition and dressed his team in his favorite colors: kelly green, gold, and white. Even the players' shoes were white! Yankee legend Mickey Mantle once quipped, "They should have come out of the dugout on tippy-toes, holding hands and singing."[20] In Kansas City Finley hoped to increase attendance by sponsoring cow-milking contests and greased-pig chases. There were also occasional discounts given to bald men, and another contest where helium-filled balloons containing game tickets were released into the sky. He built a miniature zoo, including six capuchin monkeys, six German shorthaired rabbits, two peafowl, and a German shorthaired pointer behind the bleachers in left field and even had sheep grazing nearby.

The strangest of all Finley innovations may have been Harvey, which Rex Lardner of *Sports Illustrated* described as "a rabbit with blinking eyes, wearing an A's uniform, that r[ose] from an invisible spot in the grass to the right of the plate umpire." Between Harvey's ears was a cage of baseballs that would open so the umpire could help himself. As the rabbit ascended from his spot in the grass, a whistle with a rising pitch sounded. Of course, the scene would have been incomplete without a descending whistle as he disappeared. All the while, the organist would play "Here Comes Peter Cottontail."[21]

Finley actually believed these kinds of cornball stunts were going to lead to success. To make the Seals' home opener a truly magical night, Finley had all sorts of shenanigans planned. "The first game he ever owned the Seals in Oakland," recalled Seals fan Larry Schmidt, "he put a fake guy out on the ice dressed up like a jackass, like Charlie O., the mule." When the poor saps stuffed in the donkey suit skated onto the ice, the fans started to boo. There were also two swing bands and eight dancing girls, but the crowd didn't care. "The next day in the papers, the press described it as 'Finley's Follies Hit the Ice,'" remembered director of group sales Frank Sanchez. Finley also planned on bringing in two white seals as mascots and calling them Stella and Seymour, because it apparently just made that much more sense to have both a male *and* a female seal. Even Finley eventually relented on that idea, but just a tad. "Finley insisted that we get a live seal as a mascot and introduce him to the crowd opening night, which we did," remembered Bill Torrey. "The only problem was that this trained seal preferred the cold ice and all he did in front of the crowd was lie down and sleep on the ice. End of mascot!"[22]

Finley had an affinity for animals, especially those that could be used to entertain crowds. The man must have owned stock in a petting zoo or animal sanctuary, because it seemed as though he couldn't go more than a day or two without using a creature for some sort of publicity stunt. One night Finley had the idea of inviting a bunch of chimpanzees to participate in a penalty shot competition, but the results were predictably disastrous. "I knew it was going to be a rough year when one of the chimps scored on Gary Smith," recalled Wayne Muloin to the *Hockey News* many years later.[23]

With the arrival of Finley, the circus had truly come to town, but wait, it gets better. "The A's had white cleats made from kangaroo leather," explained the Seals' Gary Croteau. "Mr. Finley wanted us to have skates made of kangaroo leather but fortunately somebody explained to him that we needed something stronger on skates."[24] Ah yes, old Charlie was planning a glorious future for his new club, conjuring up ideas that would have made Andy Warhol shudder. "At the moment I have no plans to replace the ice with pistachio sherbet, but what's wrong with colored ice?" Finley mused.[25] Luckily for everyone, Finley never followed through on that plan.

The Finley era of Seals hockey did not start off promisingly. "I know absolutely nothing about hockey," he announced at his first press conference as owner.[26] One can only wonder whether those in attendance felt an unsettling shiver at the moment of Finley's statement, but this quote proved to be a chilling omen of what was about to be unleashed upon the NHL. In front of the Bay Area media Finley held up a cartoon picture of a hockey player with his own face, balding head and all, superimposed on the body. On the front of the uniform was a giant *O* and the cartoon Finley wore cute little white skates. It likely dawned on a few people that even though *O* was the first letter in *Oakland*, it was also old Charlie's middle initial. Above all else Finley craved being the center of attention. If he were still alive today, he would love this modern age of blogs, reality television, and Twitter, so he could be in the spotlight 24/7 and keep everyone on planet Earth abreast of each and every one of his musings.

Finley's fake publicity photo was odd, but it was just the beginning of the insanity that would envelop the franchise. At a "welcome back" dinner organized for the team, Finley announced he was changing the franchise's name. "I know I may get cut up to pieces for this, but I've given it serious, considerable thought," he said. "I decided officially and this has nothing at all against Oakland that we want the team to be known as the Bay Area's hockey team. As of tonight and in the future, the new name is the California Golden Seals."[27] Officially the franchise changed names on October 14, 1970 . . . after *two* games had already been played.

One could tell the local media had already put up with plenty of Finley's shenanigans in the short time the A's had been in Oakland. For example, the *Fremont Argus*'s Steve Tadevich, in his report of Finley's big announcement, wrote, "Perhaps the best idea came from an Oakland evening newspaper that just referred to them as the Oakland Seals and let Finley call them anything he likes."[28] The media's indifference toward Finley's changes continued for years afterward.

FIG. 4. A likeness of Carol Vadnais was featured on many Seals items during the Finley era, such as this sticker and wall pennant. Author's collection.

In January 1973, two-and-a-half years after Finley had announced the name switch, the *Oakland Tribune*'s John Porter *still* referred to the team as *Oakland* Seals and rarely, if ever, used the team's true name in his articles. By the 1973–74 season, when few people actually remembered the team's old name, Porter simply referred to them as "the Seals."

What did Finley plan on doing to the uniforms, you ask? "Fort Knox gold and Kelly green are the only two colors in the country," chirped the excited Finley. The eccentric multimillionaire changed the team's home jerseys from the standard white base to bright yellow with kelly green pants, and retinas across the Bay Area would burn for years to come. The road uniforms were easier on the eyes, but just barely: a kelly green base with white and yellow trim. Furthermore, the stylish leaping seal logo was removed from the uniforms to be replaced with the word "Seals" stitched in strange italicized lettering. Finley also insisted his club's jerseys be the first in the NHL to include the players' names. One anonymous Seal was quoted as saying, "With the names on the uniforms, it might help the newspapers get the names right."[29]

Finley also gave his hockey club green and gold skates, which was only marginally less nonsensical than the white skates he had originally wanted his players to wear. When Bill Torrey heard about Finley's plan, he tried to reason with him. "I told him, 'Charlie, this isn't the Ice Capades. On white ice they're going to look like crap," Torrey said, but Finley was unconvinced. When training camp opened, the white skates were nowhere to be found. "We trained in Oshawa, Ontario," Torrey remembered, "and played exhibition games in Oshawa, Hamilton and Sudbury. Before one game I'm handed a note that says: 'Bill, where are my white skates? I'm downstairs. Charlie."[30]

Torrey entered the Seals' dressing room and made history by becoming the first man in the NHL to utter the following words: "Here is a pair of white skates. [Finley] wants to see what they look like on a player in a game. Anybody want to volunteer?"[31] Willie O'Ree may have been the first player to break the NHL's *racial* color barrier back in 1958, but some twelve years later Gary Jarrett broke a color barrier of his own by becoming the first player to wear anything but black skates.

Amazingly, old Charlie listened to reason! Sort of. He said to Torrey, "Bill, you're right. They look like crap. But I'm going to get some green skates with gold toes," and that's what the Seals went with for the 1970–71 season.[32] Surprisingly, this bizarre idea proved to be more popular; a few other teams, notably the St. Louis Blues and Pittsburgh Penguins, also used colored skates for a while.

Old Charlie had such an obsession with green and gold one would have thought he had been a leprechaun in a previous life. Morris Mott, who played in Oakland from 1972 to 1975, remembers what it was like traveling on the road with the now-legendary, Finley-conceived, California Golden Seals luggage: "They gave us these great big suitcases, they're green and yellow, and I would never go take luggage in that thing. . . . But when you put the whole team together . . . it didn't look that bad . . . but I never used that suitcase except when I was traveling with the Seals. I still got it as a souvenir in the basement of my house, but I would never travel with it."

Another classic Finley promotion was Barber Night on October 12, 1970. It was a $15,000 promotion that included a dinner at Goodman's on Jack London Square and free hockey sticks and pucks for all barbers who attended. Finley, in his infinite wisdom, believed that since barbers talked to their customers while cutting their hair, barbers could be used as a promotional tool: "We realize barbers represent an important link with countless sports fans and potential Seals fans," Finley claimed. The media was less enthused about Finley's latest promotional effort. "So far," said *Oakland Tribune* sports writer John Porter, "Finley hasn't announced a bartender's night, another spot where fans congregate, or a mailman's night, although he has the

FIG. 5. Fred Glover refused to travel with Finley's tacky green and gold suit-case. This still–mint condition Skyway Luggage Travel case stayed in Glover's closet until his death and then was given to equipment repairman and close friend Joe Serratore. Photo courtesy of Rich Reilley.

postal department busy," referring to the half million brochures Finley sent out to entice the locals to buy tickets.[33]

Jarrett remembered how happy Finley was that night: "Young man! I'm proud of you!" Finley said to him, "and [he] praised my play to whoever was there. The next night he had a reception for barbers. If they came, they got two free tickets to the game of their choice. The players were invited so we could mingle with them. When I got there, Charlie asked me where my barber shop was located!"[34] At the banquet three beautiful blondes sang while officials of the barbers union gave the Seals their full support. The barbers were impressed with the Seals' new owner, and while Barber Night had no lasting effect on the Seals' attendance, opening night was a rare sellout.

Though oddball promotions often made the Seals and their owner look like a joke, there were perks that came with working for Finley. When he was in a good mood, Charlie loved spreading the wealth. After the Seals beat Boston 2–1 on November 15, Finley was so delighted he bought each player a $25 steak dinner and a $200 suit. Marshall Johnston, who played for the Seals from 1971 to 1974 and coached the team afterward, remembered Finley fondly. One time in New York, Johnson recalls, "[Finley] took us all down and bought us all Gucci [alligator] shoes, and he bought us all bright green jackets one year, and we all had nice luggage . . . we were the only team that flew first class, and that was something innovative that was a long time before charters came in and things like that. You know, on a six-hour flight from San Francisco to New York, it was kind of nice."

The problem with Finley was that he believed players would respond positively to green luggage and matching suits, but in reality all the players wanted was for money to be spent on improving the team. Johnston remembered how Finley could be incredibly generous with his players while still being stingy where it mattered most:

> I was a player rep at the time, and we didn't have some of the new amenities that were coming in, like video, for example, off-ice training equipment. I don't remember the exact dollar amount, what it was costing him to fly us first class, but I went to see him, and I said . . . everybody looks at you like you're a big sugar daddy . . . for the money that it would cost to get video and some off-ice training equipment, things like that, I said, would be less than what you're paying us to fly first class. "Ah well, you know," and he'd kind of laugh, but that was him.

Adding to the complexity of Finley's character were his erratic mood swings and unpredictable changes of heart. Mike Laughton remembered how Finley nixed a little tradition he started at the Coliseum because it became too expensive for the owner's taste:

> After our home games, win or lose, I'd go out on the ice with a bucket of 20 or 30 pucks and flip 'em up into the stands. The fans

loved it! Kids would yell and scream . . . there'd be five hundred or so people at one end of the rink waiting for me to flick them the pucks. Freddy Glover came up to me one night and told me to cut it out or he'd deduct the price of the pucks from my paycheque! That was Finley's way: worry about the cost of pucks but treat the players like crap.[35]

Finley was the very definition of an enigma. One minute he could be mean, cheap, and boorish, yet he could be warm, generous, and fatherly the next. "You could call him Charlie," remembered Johnston. "Nothing 'Mister,' he was Charlie."

As the season opener approached, Finley stated he was dissatisfied with his club's poor performance the year before. He believed many of his players hadn't pulled their own weight, and the team had underachieved, even though he hadn't even been associated with the Seals at the time and was in no position to criticize. Naturally, Finley *raised* ticket prices! Another of Finley's solutions was to rudely dictate what salary his players were going to earn for the upcoming season. If they didn't accept, Finley was prepared to stock his club with rookies and minor leaguers. When Finley took over the club, many players were excited since he had deep pockets and a large media presence, two luxuries the Seals had never enjoyed. Before long, the uniform changes, the take-it-or-leave-it contracts, and the talk about live seal mascots made many players change their opinions of Finley.

In the meantime, Frank Selke had several roster issues to deal with. The biggest was the June expansion draft, where the Vancouver Canucks and Buffalo Sabres would officially join the NHL. Charlie Hodge and Bob Dillabough headed up the coast to Canada, while Buffalo selected Brian Perry and Howie Menard.

Expansion once again opened doors to players with little or no NHL experience. On May 22 the Montreal Canadiens sold twenty-seven-year-old Dennis Hextall to the Seals in what seemed like a low-key transaction. Although Hextall was not very big (about 5'11" and 175 pounds) he became one of the league's fiercest competitors. His father, Bryan, had starred for the New York Rangers in the 1930s and 1940s and had won the Stanley Cup with the Blueshirts in 1940. Dennis's brother Bryan Jr. was originally drafted by California in 1967 but never suited up for the Seals. Bryan's son, Ron, later became an All-Star goaltender for the Philadelphia Flyers in the 1980s and 1990s.

After the playoffs, Glover had announced the Seals badly needed "four big so and so's up front who aren't afraid of anybody."[36] With Dennis Hextall, Glover got one of the most vicious, temperamental players in the NHL. More often than not, when there was a tussle somewhere on the ice, wolverine-like Hextall was either the cause of the disagreement or one of its main contributors. "I probably lost any chance for [the Lady Byng trophy] on my first shift in the first game of the season," Hextall quipped.[37] Hampson described Hextall's style of play as "ultracompetitive," in part because he "was looking to establish himself as an NHL player. . . . He would battle anyone in the corners or drop the gloves with anybody bigger or smaller than himself. He would also use his stick."[38] He was just as aggressive at practice, often upsetting his teammates. Despite his willingness to fight, Hextall didn't see himself in that role: "I was never a fighter," he believed. "For me, physical play had much more to do with survival out on the ice."[39] From the press box and on television it probably didn't always look that way. In 1970–71 Hextall smashed Carol Vadnais's league record 12 fighting majors by squaring off 21 times! The fiery redhead impressed Glover immensely in training camp. "He's far and away the most impressive hockey player in camp," he said. "He never stops. No matter who his wingers are, his line produces."[40] He would play most of the season with Gary Croteau and either Norm Ferguson or Tony Featherstone. Their competitive nature got them dubbed the "Battle Line," which became the Seals' most productive combination.

Gary Croteau was selected from the roster of the Detroit Red Wings at the intra-league draft. He had earned himself a reputation with Seals fans in the 1969 playoffs when, as a member of the LA Kings, he scored 3 goals in the 7-game series. The twenty-four-year-old Croteau was a big, rugged, 200-pound mucker who was difficult to dislodge from the corners. "Gary Croteau was a workhorse," remembers Seals fan Larry Leal. "His nickname was 'The Bull,' and he had a look in his face. . . . I called it the 'Croteau Stare,' and you could always tell when he was mad or upset about something, and he was gonna take it all under his own hand." The biggest asset he brought to the lineup, however, was his strong defensive game thanks to his powerful skating style. The Seals, aside from Vadnais and Hextall, were not a particularly aggressive bunch, so they needed Croteau's skills badly.

The Seals also traded defenseman François Lacombe and their first round selection in the 1971 amateur draft to Montreal for forward Ernie Hicke (Bill's brother) and the Canadiens' first round selection in the 1970 draft. At first glance the trade seemed rather innocuous; if anything, the Seals picked up another Canadiens' castoff who could jump into the lineup right away, but Montreal general manager Sam Pollock had a sinister motive in initiating the innocent-looking deal. He knew the Habs would need the first overall draft pick to get coveted Quebec Remparts superstar Guy Lafleur. At the time, in order to get the number one overall selection, a team had to finish last in the regular-season standings. Pollock believed there was a chance the Seals could finish last, so he convinced Selke to make the move by telling him he wanted to help out the poor Seals and throw a few prospects their way. Pollock had little to lose and everything to gain. Even if the Seals did not finish last and Lafleur went somewhere else, Pollock could still turn the Seals' pick into a winner. That draft would also include future stars Larry Robinson, Marcel Dionne, Terry O'Reilly, Richard Martin, and Rick Kehoe. Just to be safe, Pollock also negotiated similar trades with Minnesota, Los Angeles, and St. Louis, giving the Habs a whopping six picks in the first two rounds of the 1971 draft.

The Seals' season started badly with a 5–3 loss to the Red Wings in Detroit. With newcomers Croteau and Hextall in the lineup, the Seals had more muscle up front, but the team was still pushed around and taunted, and not just by the Wings. Detroit fans were not particularly kind to their guests from Oakland: "Their gaudy green and gold uniforms earned Finley's skaters the treatment from a hockey-wise Detroit crowd of 14,039. . . . The partisan fans let loose with giggles, wolf whistles, ripples of snickers and even some applause as the 1970 Oakland club skated onto the ice for a pre-game warmup."[41] The following night in Chicago, Finley's boys were trounced, 5–1.

The Seals returned to the Coliseum for their home opener and their first official game as the California Golden Seals in front of a sellout crowd of 12,089. Unfortunately, the defending Stanley Cup champs from Boston couldn't have cared less. Bobby Orr scored his first 2 goals of the season, and Phil Esposito added 4 points en route to a lopsided 5–1 win.

Even the expansion Vancouver Canucks kept the Seals out of the win column. In the teams' first-ever meeting on October 20 Wayne Maki scored 24 seconds into the second period to put Vancouver up 1–0. Andre Boudrias then scored 1:33 later. Charlie Hodge kept his former teammates off the scoreboard until Dick Mattiussi scored with less than two minutes to go. In all, Hodge stopped 34 shots in the Canucks' 2–1 win.

After nine games, the Seals' record was a dismal 0-7-2, and they had been outscored 33–14. Everything finally changed for the better on October 30 against the Sabres. The Seals' offense came to life, pelting Buffalo's goalie tandem of Joe Daley and Roger Crozier with 48 shots. Bill Hicke scored 2 goals while Carol Vadnais also added a pair. Daley, the maskless ex-Seal, started the game for Buffalo, but he was injured in the middle period when a shot deflected off Earl Ingarfield's stick and hit him in the face. The puck opened a twelve-stitch gash on his temple, forcing him out of the game, but Crozier could do no better as the Seals went on to win 6–1.

The taste of victory became contagious in the Seals' dressing room. Soon after, California defeated the Rangers, 3–1, and then overwhelmed the Maple Leafs 8–4 a few days later. In the latter game, Toronto got off to a quick start, taking a 1–0 lead less than two minutes into the contest, but as the *Oakland Tribune*'s John Porter put it, "it turned out the Leafs were just blowing in the wind."[42] The game stayed close in the first period; the Leafs and Seals scored 2 goals apiece. In the second period, the Seals pulled ahead 5–2 on goals by Jarrett, Featherstone, and Mattiussi. Featherstone scored again early in the third period to open up a 4-goal California lead. Toronto rallied on goals by Guy Trottier and Ron Ellis to close the gap to 6–4, but Ehman and Croteau answered with goals in the last three minutes to put the game away.

When the Montreal Canadiens visited Oakland, the Seals were gunning for a fourth straight win. In the opening period the Seals set the pace outshooting the Habs 16–5 and scoring the only goal of the period, a Gary Jarrett rebound that eluded goalie Phil Myre. Later in the period the Canadiens' Serge Savard made the mistake of getting in Dennis Hextall's face and was handed a complimentary beating for his offense. Hextall pulled Savard's sweater over his head and scored a decisive victory. "I got in four or five good hits and he didn't hit me," Hextall said after the game.[43] No one on the Canadiens even jumped in to save Savard from the wolverine.

Ernie Hicke scored his first NHL goal at the 17:39 mark of the first period to put California up 2–0. "I just hope the next one doesn't take as long as that one," the younger Hicke said.[44] During the final few minutes of the contest, the Montreal offense kicked into high gear, pressuring Smith to crack under the barrage of shots, but he held his ground and preserved the 2–0 shutout to up the Seals' record to 4-7-2.

While the Seals were basking in the joy of their latest victory, Finley started meddling in his employees' affairs. Finley had asked Selke, Torrey, and Glover to sign new contracts at greatly reduced salaries, but Selke refused since he still had a year remaining on his contract. "It was a joke, to do what [Finley was] trying to do," explained Selke's close friend, Jim Lingel. "Frank didn't like it. He didn't want to work with him." According to Selke, "Finley insisted the courts awarded him the franchise and the player contracts only—not management and coaching. So, Finley was under no legal obligation to us in his mind. The NHL provided no support or information. We had to accept Finley's word, like it or not."[45]

Charlie Finley was never one to let his employees dictate what was and wasn't fair, and he started breathing down Selke's neck. After the team had returned from training camp, Finley asked Selke if he was going to accept his contract offer. "In a very fatherly gesture," Selke recalled, "he put his arm around my shoulder and said—as best as I can recall—'Son, you are a nice young man. I've met your wife and kiddies and you have a nice family. If you are thinking of legal action, let me tell you if you are going to get into a pissing contest with a skunk, I'm the biggest pisser in the U.S.A."[46] Selke stood firm.

In November, the tension between Finley and Selke escalated. One night around supper time Finley phoned Selke and asked if he was going to sign the contract. "I asked him, in response, if he was going to honor my contract. He said no, I said no and then he said, 'Get your ass out of my office by tomorrow. You're through.' He hung up and I finished my dinner."[47]

In the November 13 *Oakland Tribune* Selke explained: "I neither resigned nor quit, but I am simply refusing to accept less than that to which I am entitled." Selke stood his ground despite Finley's persistence. "Mr. Finley does not recognize his liability under the four-year contract I signed when I first joined the Seals' organization in 1967," Selke explained. "Through my attorney," Selke continued, "and in personal conversation with Mr. Finley I have advised him that I expect my existing contract to be honored and that the document which he has tendered to me is not acceptable."[48]

Of course, Finley had a very different version of the story, one that contained much more fiction than fact. Finley not only claimed he was not responsible for the contracts Selke, Torrey, and Glover had signed with previous owners, but he also made it seem as though he genuinely did not understand the situation in which he found himself:

Selke has done a fine job, and I hate to see him go, but I did not inherit the contracts of these three gentlemen. I told all of them when I bought the club that I would like them to stay and they all indicated they would.

I bought the club July 10 and continued to pay them all their salaries.

It seems the Seals, Inc. (first owners of the club) owe Selke a substantial amount of money, and before he could sign with me, he had to see where he stood.

Glover's and Torrey's contracts were with Niagara, and I understand they had similar problems.[49]

Selke's one regret in life was not taking his father's advice and turning down the Seals' general manager position.[50] When Selke was interviewed for this book in April 2012, he shied away from giving many details about his unpleasant time in Oakland. "Personally and professionally, this was not a happy chapter in my life," he admitted. "It's forty-five years ago, and I've done my best to forget some of the awful things that we had to go through there. Obviously, there was some good times, there were some great fellows that I worked with, and some of the players were quality people that I had, and still have, a great amount of respect for. . . . I worked for five different ownership groups in three years. It was an unbelievable trial, and there are certain aspects of it that I'd just as soon forget happened." He did, however, want to make it clear that there were many people in the organization he remembered fondly. "I've done the best I can to forget the issues that were really not very pleasant," he said, "and I've done the best I can to remember the good things, the Bill Torreys, the Teddy Hampsons, and the Carol Vadnais, and Bert Marshall, and the fellows that gave us something to be proud of while we were there."

Selke leaving the organization was a huge blow. He had managed to make the Seals look respectable after their disastrous first season, even though they were always out of money and rumored to be on the move. He would become vice president of *Hockey Night in Canada* the following year and remained there for twenty years. More importantly for Selke, he was an ambassador and fund-raiser for the Special Olympics, a cause that remained dear to him until he passed away March 18, 2013.

While the NHL Seals' ownership had been a mess from day one, the front office had always been stocked with knowledgeable hockey men. Bill Torrey, for example, when given the chance to do his job without interference, proved to be an incredibly astute, forward thinker. When the New York Islanders joined the NHL in 1972, Torrey handled the selection of players at the expansion draft. Resisting the urge to trade away draft picks for a quick fix, Torrey turned the Islanders into a Stanley Cup winner in just eight years.

The Selke-Torrey team should have thrived for many more years, but in a few short months Finley single-handedly tore down the franchise. When Selke was dismissed, Torrey was offered the general manager's post, which was a wise decision by Finley; but like Selke,

Torrey was not about to sign a new contract for less money, and on November 25, during the second intermission of the Seals' 3–1 loss to Los Angeles, he resigned.

Finley was completely clueless when it came to hockey matters, but that didn't stop him from micromanaging the Seals. "[Finley] violated the non-interference clause in my contract so often," Torrey said, "that it got to the point where I had my lawyer talking to his lawyer." Torrey thought that by putting together a contract that would have ensured Finley stay far from the general manager's chair, he would be in good shape. Finley refused to sign. According to Torrey, Finley said, "'Do you have your lawyer on a monthly retainer? Jesus, they're expensive.' He was, in a sense, trying to tell me that I couldn't afford to take him to court. He told me once that he'd never been sued by an employee and lost. He did in this case."[51] With Selke and Torrey out, that left Fred Glover as the only person already on staff qualified enough to assume the general manager's job. He signed a new two-year contract with the club, interestingly enough, on the same terms he had agreed to with TNC, and shouldered the coach and general manager responsibilities.

The day after Torrey's resignation, newspapers were filled with his carefully worded statements concerning the entire unpleasant situation:

> Mr. Charles O. Finley, present owner of the Seals, has tendered a new contract to me asking that I remain as both vice president and general manager. While I am flattered by the offer, it does not meet the terms or conditions of my present contract, which remains in full force, and I am naturally unwilling to accept anything less than that which was agreed to when I first joined the Seals. . . .
>
> It is with a regret deeper than mere words can express that I announce my immediate departure from the Seals' Hockey Club. Circumstances not of my doing nor liking force me to make this decision.
>
> A dispute over contractual [*sic*] obligations is the basis for this decision. Three years ago when I joined the team I did so with a clear understanding as to my duties, responsibilities and obliga-

tions. Likewise, the terms under which I would be compensated were not in doubt.[52]

Finley, of course, believed he was being more than fair, and as always, he got up on his soapbox and preached to the masses: "Mr. Torrey was tendered a contract which provided him with the same annual salary he had been receiving from the previous owner, Trans National. According to information furnished us by Mr. Woody Erdman, president of Trans National, neither Selke nor Torrey ever had a contract with his company." That last bit was a new twist, and one that was completely unfounded. "Both Torrey and Selke have requested additional benefits which were not provided them by TNC. The Finley Co. has not and will not agree to these demands," the owner concluded.[53]

A few months earlier, after Finley had bought the Seals, Torrey had been ecstatic, believing Finley would give him every opportunity to make the Seals a better club. "At first I got along really well with [Finley]," Torrey said. "People told him I knew what I was doing and he should listen to me. He didn't listen to anybody, and he didn't know a left wing from a right wing."[54] On October 16, Steve Tadevich of the *Fremont Argus* wrote: "We wonder what Torre [*sic*] will think in six months when Finley decides his team didn't finish high enough and starts fireing [*sic*] everyone in sight, and even some not in sight."[55] In fact, it took all of six *weeks* for the Seals to lose both their executive vice president and general manager.

The players had also had enough of Finley, as Ted Hampson recalled in 2011:

We were pretty enthused at the start of the year because of Finley . . . but as we got into the season we found things much different than we expected from that end. You can't blame the ownership for play on the ice, but you know, the painting of the skates. . . . Skates were getting heavier by the week. . . . Everything was kind of negative. . . .

I think our first victory against an Original Six team was in Boston, and we were pretty pumped up about that. This was fairly early. We had a good relationship with Mr. Finley at that time . . .

and to commemorate that win we ordered a plaque or a plate or a trophy or something that we were presenting to Mr. Finley for the first victory.

Well, [the gift] was quite a long time in coming. . . . It was like about a month later by the time it came, and by this time we were so disillusioned with Mr. Finley that I said to our guys, "What should we do with this trophy, this plaque?" And to a man, everybody said, "Just scrap it!" So we never presented it to him. Barry Keast, I think, was our trainer, and I said, "Barry, put this somewhere. Maybe we'll use it sometime in the future." And it went in the closet, and I never knew what happened to it.

Back on the ice, the Seals looked to extend their winning streak to five games. Their opponents, the expansion Buffalo Sabres, looked like easy prey, but on this November night rookie sensation Gilbert Perreault, celebrating his twentieth birthday, scored in the opening period to give Buffalo a 1–0 lead. The Seals overcame the deficit with 2 goals in the second period from Croteau and Jarrett, but Skip Krake knotted the game at 2–2 later in the frame. Paul Andrea, a former Seal who had been sold to Buffalo for $30,000 the previous week, scored the game-winning goal in the third period. To assure the Sabres' victory, Larry Keenan scored on a rebound later in the game to make the final score Sabres 4, Seals 2.

After the Seals' team-record four-game win streak ended, they won just three of their next fourteen games and dropped to last place in the West with a 7-19-2 record. Hoping for a reversal of fortune, the club played host to the Detroit Red Wings on December 16. California led the game 2–0 after twenty minutes but could have led by several more goals. "We really bombarded in the first period and still it's 2–0," said Ehman. "We could have been leading 5–2 in the third period, but we're fighting to stay in front by a goal."[56] Vadnais scored his seventh of the season early in the final period to give the Seals a 3–1 lead, but Tom Webster cut the lead to one with about four minutes to go. Doug Roberts scored an empty-netter with just thirteen seconds left to lift the Seals to a 4–2 win. Overall it was a solid effort by the green and gold: an 18–5 edge in shots in the final period, a 31–20 edge overall, and 3 assists from Ernie Hicke.

A few nights later the Seals pulled even with sixth-place Los Angeles with a 1–0 shutout over Philadelphia. Norm Ferguson, having recently returned from a shoulder injury that had cost him twenty-one games, scored the only goal, at 5:49 of the third period.

The good news did not stop at Ferguson's successful return. On December 20, California thrashed the Red Wings, 7–3. The Hicke brothers were particularly deadly as they each scored twice. In the Seals' next game versus Chicago, the brothers held the spotlight once again. Before a hometown crowd of over eight thousand, Ernie scored 2 more goals; Bill had a goal and an assist in the Seals' 5–2 victory.

Once again the Seals had won four in a row, bringing their overall record to 11-19-2. The Seals had finally escaped last place and had closed to within 5 points of fourth place, held jointly by Minnesota and Philadelphia. Despite the Seals' recent surge, they had become very difficult to read: the players looked aggressive and determined for stretches, but passive and lifeless on others. When the Seals embarked on a five-game road trip following the Christmas break, all games ended in defeat, including a 9–3 loss to LA on December 26. The Seals were relegated to the basement once again.

In the meantime, Carol Vadnais was honored with a third con-secutive trip to the All-Star Game, but he was unable to participate due to a fractured thumb. Doug Roberts was selected to replace him in the game, but Vadnais could not be replaced in the Seals' lineup. In Vadnais's first three seasons in Oakland he had become the face of the franchise. Without Vadnais anchoring the blue line, the Seals were not the same team. Vadnais would miss eighteen games as a result of his injury. When he came back on February 24 against Mon-treal, Vadnais tore ligaments in his knee and was forced to miss the remainder of the season.

A few days prior to the All-Star Game, Gary Smith and Toron-to's Jacques Plante engaged in an amazing goaltending duel. In the opening period Smith was outstanding as he faced 19 Leaf shots, but the Seals opened the scoring on a goal by Gerry Ehman. Paul Henderson beat Smith nine minutes later on a heavy shot that caught the top shelf to tie the game, 1–1. The overworked Smith managed to stop everything else directed at him that night. The Seals' burly netminder was brilliant, stopping 50 of 51 shots. Plante was also sharp in the 1–1 draw, stopping 35 California shots.

After the All-Star Game the Seals continued to keep pace with the rest of the division, but just barely. Dennis Hextall got his turn to shine a few nights later when the Rangers came to Oakland. He scored the game winner, his 14th goal of the season, in the Seals' 3–1 victory. Smith was sensational once again and blocked 38 shots. It had almost become a nightly ritual to see Smith perform his magic; since the start of the season, his backup Bob Sneddon had played just 224 minutes. Nevertheless, Fred Glover must have wondered once in a while if it was worth Smith's sanity to keep playing him as much as he did. Smitty might have been losing his marbles from being overused. During the Seals-Rangers game Smith came closer than ever to scoring that elusive goal. In the dying seconds of the game, with the score 3–1, California, the Rangers pulled goaltender Ed Giacomin in favor of an extra attacker, and according to the *San Mateo Times*'s Hugh McDonald, Smith "brought the house to its feet as he stickhandled up to the red line and essayed a missing shot on the Ranger goal." Glover couldn't help but shake his head after the game and said, "I think it's the ambition of his life to score a goal."[57]

The Seals got one step closer to a playoff spot with a 6–2 thrashing over Minnesota on January 27. Gary Croteau continued his fine rookie season by scoring his first career hat trick, and earning a $300 bonus from Finley. "The funniest part of this whole thing," said Croteau, "is that as a kid I used to go watch [Minnesota goaltender Cesare] Maniago when he was playing for the Sudbury Wolves in the Eastern Pro League. Now I have my biggest night against him."[58]

Unfortunately for the Seals, at the moment when they needed to transform into the hostile Mr. Hyde, it was passive Dr. Jekyll who showed up. A 2-17-2 rollercoaster ride stretching from late January to mid-March officially buried the Seals in last place. During that stretch the Seals allowed 5 or more goals twelve times. While the Seals' playoff chances were reduced to nil, the North Stars continued to battle for a playoff spot in the tense West Division. The Stars realized they needed to add some strength up the middle to bolster their anemic offense, and they were eyeing Ted Hampson. In late February, the Seals dealt Hampson and Wayne Muloin to Minnesota for center Tommy Williams and defenseman Dick Redmond.

After three years in the Bay Area, Hampson and his family were disappointed to be leaving Oakland. He has a theory on why he was traded. The Seals were in Chicago on the way to Minnesota when Hampson was paged at the airport. Some players told him Finley was on the line, but Hampson thought "the guys were pulling [his] leg." Ultimately, Hampson decided against answering the phone. "I said, if it *is* Charlie Finley, I know what he's going to be talking about," Hampson said. "He's going to want me to cut up the coach because . . . there was a lot of talk about Freddie losing his job, and I said, if that was Finley, 'I'm not talking to him, because I'm not going to answer questions about the coach.'"

Once Hampson was traded to Minnesota, he began to think about the missed phone call: "That's when I said, 'It probably was Mr. Finley on the phone.' I was traded about a week later and I never did talk to him," Hampson said, laughing, still wondering if he had caused his own trade.

Although Williams was younger than Hampson, the Seals were trading away their heart and soul. In 246 games with Oakland, the Seals' captain had scored 61 goals and 123 assists for a franchise record 184 points. He enjoyed his finest season in 1968–69 when he scored 75 points, took home the Bill Masterton Memorial Trophy, and participated in the All-Star Game, but now at the age of thirty-four, the classy Hampson had shown signs of slowing down and had scored just 10 goals and 20 assists in 60 games. In his last 24 games he had scored only twice. "It's been a frustrating season here for everybody," he admitted. "The whole team wanted to win and was trying but couldn't get rolling." He also bore no grudge against the man who traded him. "I have no bitterness whatsoever. Coach Glover treated me fine. I'm just sorry to leave so many friends."[59]

The thirty-year-old Williams had very good offensive instincts, but he was also struggling following the sudden death of his wife.

The Stars dropped him from their roster because he could not get along with management and coach Jackie Gordon, but the Seals took a gamble on him. Williams had accumulated a Stars team record 52 assists the previous year, but in his 41 games with Minnesota this season Williams had scored just 10 goals and 13 assists.

Williams played extremely well for the Seals down the stretch, scoring 17 points in 18 games, but the Seals went winless in 9 games between February 24 and March 14 and made it look as though they resented anyone taking last place from them. During that stretch the Seals allowed 7 or more goals five times.

The Seals could have occupied the entire floor of a hospital, so numerous were their health problems in the second half of the season. "We've had so many injuries," said poor Fred Glover, "you'd think our guys were run down by a truck. Hell, Norm Ferguson had a shoulder separation; Bert Marshall a broken wrist; Tony Featherstone a concussion; Mike Laughton a damaged knee; Gary Croteau a sprained shoulder; Harry Howell a back injury; and Gary Jarrett got his forehead busted open by a flying stick. He's carrying a scar that looks like a zipper."[60] Glover didn't even mention Vadnais's broken thumb, Joe Hardy's broken wrist, and Ingarfield's broken kneecap. "We've got so many guys hurt," said Glover, "that we have no flexibility."[61]

When the Seals were healthy, they had skated to a 11-19-2 record and were just a few points out of the playoffs. The players seemed to have put their lackluster 1969–70 season behind them with inspired efforts against some of the better clubs in the league. After the injury bug hit and the playoffs became unattainable, everyone began to play for themselves. At least, that is what Glover believed. "Some of them just think of 'I and me' instead of 'we and us,'" he said. "Certain players used [injuries] as an excuse for our misfortunes. They themselves didn't play well and used an injury to someone else as a cop-out."[62] Not long after, Glover reiterated that his team was not playing with enough drive and heart: "Also, we've lacked a team leader, a take-charge guy, a fiery fighter who will show the others how to go all-out to win. Some of the players are not putting out. I've warned them that if they can't straighten themselves out during our remaining seven home games, they won't be around next season."[63]

The Seals had to call up a collection of rookies and minor leaguers to ice a full team. On March 10, twenty-one-year-old Dick Redmond was brought up to round out the terribly depleted defense, and he got to experience firsthand how difficult a season it had been in Oakland. That night, the Bruins visited the Coliseum. Boston had steamrolled its way to first place overall with no fewer than four players among the league's top five scorers.

From the moment Bobby Orr opened the scoring in the first period with his first of two goals, the Seals were out of the contest. Orr's goal was something else too. Johnny McKenzie skated along the boards to the left of Gary Smith and sent a pass into the slot, toward which Orr was moving. Orr shuffled a weak backhand toward Smith, who made a nice save, but in doing so deflected the puck into the air. Undaunted, the Bruins legend then tipped the airborne puck past Smith while actually skating *behind* the net!

Later in the game, Phil Esposito tied a league record with his 58th goal while Johnny Bucyk scored his 45th. Overall, the high-powered Bruins launched 40 shots at the helpless Seals duo of Gary Smith and Chris Worthy. Mike Walton, Wayne Carleton, Don Awrey, and John McKenzie also scored for the Bruins in an 8–1 rout.

Debacles such as this were hardly uncommon for Smith, not that he should have been blamed. At the end of the season, the man sounded burned out. "I don't know where you draw the line," he said, having played in 71 of his team's 78 games. "[A] goalie needs a lot of action to stay hot. But he'll get stale if he's used too much."[64]

Finally, on March 17 versus Pittsburgh, the Seals broke what had become a 9-game winless streak. The Pens opened the scoring early in the first period, but the Seals took a 2–1 lead in the second period on goals by Featherstone and Croteau just fifteen seconds apart. Ehman scored his first of the night just sixteen seconds into the frame, while Jarrett and Ehman put the game away later in the period to win the game 5–2.

Once in a while the Seals showed a glimmer of hope, whether it was a hat trick or a big performance from Smith, but for the most part they were awful. Publicly, Glover put on a brave face as his team crawled to the finish line. "We may be out of the race," he said, "but I hope and trust we'll be battling everybody just like we were going for the championship."[65] It must not have been easy for him to say that. In reality, the players had developed a poor attitude. "We had a few guys who didn't care," remembered Dennis Hextall. "Harry Howell, for example, really wanted to win. Some other guys didn't have that attitude."[66] In the Seals' final eight games they allowed a whopping 46 goals. On March 28 the expansion Canucks clubbed the Seals, 11–5, for the Golden Ones' 51st loss of the season.

In the second-last game of the season, also against Vancouver, the Seals lost their 52nd game, 7–2, to tie the 1969–70 LA Kings for the all-time record. Leave it to those same Kings to hand the Seals a 6–4 loss on the final day of the schedule to rid themselves of the dubious record. In a span of three short months, the Seals had gone from a few points out of a playoff spot to the laughing stock of the NHL. Even though Finley's Follies were closing out one of the most disastrous campaigns in NHL history, Glover was not all that worried about getting fired by the unpredictable owner. "He's a very patient man," Glover calmly stated. "Under the circumstances, it could be worse."[67]

To say the 1970–71 Seals had problems is an understatement. For one thing, there were only 208,953 paid admissions to the Coliseum compared to 236,555 the previous season. By comparison, the NHL attendance leaders, the St. Louis Blues, had sold over 700,000 tickets. Finley admitted to losing approximately $700,000 over the course of the season. A league worst 20-53-5 record buried the Seals deep in the West cellar, 10 points behind the East doormats, the Detroit Red Wings, and only the Minnesota North Stars' 191 goals were fewer than the Seals' 199. The players performed badly for long stretches, despite the fact they set, and later tied, a club record for consecutive wins (4). It seemed as though the Seals only showed up for half their games, going a decent 17-21-1 at the Coliseum, but just 3-32-4 on the road.

It is difficult for a team to play consistently when its players simply aren't good enough, but Glover still felt the Seals should have been a playoff contender. "When we started the season, our roster was a good one," he said. "It was capable of doing the job and making the playoffs."[68] Injuries played a key role in the Seals' collapse, but Father Time certainly had something to say about it too. The Seals had hinted at a decline in fortune the previous year when they barely qualified for the playoffs, and while players like Croteau, Hextall, Featherstone, and Stackhouse were brought in to make the roster younger, the greybeards were all retained. History would not repeat itself. Harry Howell had turned thirty-eight and was traded to Los Angeles for cash in February. Gerry Ehman scored 18 goals, but now thirty-eight years old, he called it a career. Earl Ingarfield was riddled with aches and pains and scored just 13 points in 49 games, so he also retired. That left thirty-three-year-old Bill Hicke as the team's elder statesman, but his days in Oakland were numbered.

Nevertheless, the Seals' many rookies gave the team a flicker of hope for the future. Ernie Hicke led the team with 22 goals, and his 47 points were second to Dennis Hextall's 52. Gary Croteau had got off to a great start but tailed off as the season unfolded, and he finished with 43 points. Another rookie standout, defenseman Ron Stackhouse, finished with 8 goals and 24 assists, helping fill the void left behind when Carol Vadnais went down. Despite the young talent in the organization, the Seals were not going to contend for the Stanley Cup any time soon. With the retirement and discarding of the Seals' expansion era stars, it would be time to rebuild and look toward the future.

6

YOUNG BLOOD, 1971-1972

The 1971–72 season was a pivotal period for professional hockey and the California Golden Seals. Little did most people imagine that less than a year later the World Hockey Association would not only challenge the NHL for hockey supremacy, but would forever change the way the venerable league did business. In October 1971, however, the WHA was nothing more than a few businessmen with little hockey knowledge looking to gain a foothold in the lucrative world of professional sports. Few people took the WHA seriously at the time, but before long they would.

As the Seals prepared for the new season, Charlie Finley named thirty-five-year-old Garry Young the team's new general manager, discharging Fred Glover of one of his duties. Young was relatively unknown at the time, but he had gained valuable experience as a scout for the Boston Bruins. As a seventeen-year-old, Young had been a promising Toronto Maple Leafs prospect, but a severe back injury put an end to his playing career.

Young wasted little time determining the club's needs: youth, depth, and a backup goaltender to take some pressure off Gary Smith. In the first of many shocking moves Young dealt leading scorer Dennis Hextall to Minnesota for prospects Joey Johnston and Walt McKechnie. The trade was a huge risk, but Johnston and McKechnie quickly became mainstays in Oakland.

The twenty-two-year-old Johnston was originally the New York Rangers' eighth overall selection in the 1966 amateur draft. From 1969 to 1971 he produced three straight 20-goal seasons in the CHL and AHL. In 1970–71, while playing for the Cleveland Barons, he was named to the AHL's first All-Star Team. He played briefly for the Minnesota North Stars in 1968–69 but did not stick with the big club.

California was ready to give Johnston a shot at the NHL once again. He soon became one of the most popular players to ever put on a Seals jersey. Johnston played a rough game and could skate well. "Jet" became his nickname as his career gained momentum. He also had a unique physical trait that served him well on occasion. "He had kind of a lazy eye," remembers former Seals stick boy Scott Ruffell, "so he looked like he was going to shoot it in the corner, and a couple times he scored a goal because the goalie was looking at the wrong eye. The other guy thought he was gonna make a pass and he'd take a shot right on net and, boom, surprised the goalie a couple times."

Walt McKechnie was no less skilled at scoring goals. The promising young center won the WHL's Rookie of the Year Award in 1967-68 while playing for Phoenix and was then drafted by the Stars. Blessed with a lanky 6'2" frame, the twenty-four-year old McKechnie also displayed an aggressive edge when the opposition got rough.

Like Johnston, McKechnie became one of the cornerstones of the Seals franchise, but whatever noise McKechnie was able to stir up on the ice paled in comparison to the clamor that supposedly arose one night from his hotel room. During his first season in Oakland he roomed with the eccentric Bobby Sheehan, a newcomer who, on one road trip, allegedly brought nothing more than a bottle of hooch and a toothbrush. McKechnie despised Sheehan's slovenly behavior, and legend has it "McKetch" hung Sheehan by his ankles from a hotel window until he agreed to pick up after himself. Lyle Carter, who started the season as one of the Seals' two goaltenders, had played with Sheehan for two years in the Montreal organization. He knew Sheehan well, but he was skeptical when he heard the story. "It seems a little far-fetched to me," he said. "It's comical though; it made me laugh." No one else interviewed for this book was able to confirm the story, either.

"Bobby was full of life," said Carter. "He was popular with his teammates. He was a really likeable guy. He had all kinds of talent. He had talent to burn. He could just fly in those skates." Eventual Seals coach Vic Stasiuk remembered one game when the Seals were down 5-1, and Sheehan "broke in at the end of the game and boomed one straight at the goalie and didn't score. Well, he was going so fast he didn't make the turn. He just jumped on the glass and almost climbed over. Scared [the] hell out of the people in that section."[1] Sheehan certainly brought a lot of flair to the Seals. Oscar-winning actor Tom

Hanks grew up in the Bay Area and followed the Seals closely. Bobby Sheehan was his favorite player. "He sent me a letter and I sent him a signed picture, which he put up on his wall," Sheehan remembered. "That was great, hearing from him like that."[2]

Sheehan proved to be a bit of a discipline problem wherever he went, but few people doubted his talent. "Bobby Sheehan was an exciting forward," Carter remembered. "He didn't have the big game every game, but at times he did.... I'm not knocking him when I say this, [but] if Bobby Sheehan could have been more consistent every game, he could have put together some real big NHL seasons. It's too bad, because he had a lot of talent." Sheehan had a good sense of humor, but he also a bad habit of partying to all hours of the night, and he often broke curfew. According to McKechnie, when Sheehan went to the bar, which was often, he "would be dancing on top of the bar, doing splits. He could dance as good as anybody."[3] He was also kicked off the U.S. National Team for having stayed out too late one night. He was naturally inclined to break the rules. As a youngster Sheehan played in New Hampshire under the pseudonym Bob Terry because his school in his hometown of Weymouth, Massachusetts, did not permit its students to play for outside teams.

The crafty 5'7", 155-pound Sheehan had been in the Montreal Canadiens organization since the 1969–70 season and had scored 8 goals in 45 career games. However, the Habs, who already had centers Peter Mahovlich, Jacques Lemaire, and Henri Richard, had little use for Sheehan. They sold him to California for $25,000 in May 1971.

Sheehan's presence would help the Seals, but there were still many question marks at center entering the 1971–72 season. Tommy Williams was a shoo-in to fill the top spot, and Sheehan and McKechnie had the inside tracks on two more, but neither had proven they could score consistently. At the intra-league draft Young acquired Bruins' center Wayne "Swoop" Carleton, a swift-skating 22-goal scorer who had never had the opportunity to show what he could do. In one stint with Toronto he had not got along well with coach Punch Imlach, so he received little ice time, and since Boston had an embarrassment of talent at forward, Carleton craved the opportunity to shine. Still, 22 goals were not bad, either. Young could not have been happier to acquire the strapping lad, claiming, "In this division, with the ice time we'll give him, Carleton could be an all-star."[4]

Carleton, however, was not happy about going to Oakland. He had been part of the 1970–71 Bruins team that had scored a league record 399 goals. The Seals had scored half that. Defenseman Paul Shmyr, who was later acquired in a deal with Chicago, said Carleton "was a legend in his own mind. He was a good guy, but he came here with an attitude that he was Wayne Carleton and we had to look up to him. That wasn't going to work with our guys. It took awhile to get used to him but it turned out he was a good guy."[5] There were other reasons for Carleton's unhappiness. "What really ticked me off was that after I'd won a Stanley Cup in Boston and gone to Oakland as the first overall pick in the [intra-league] draft, I still had to go to salary arbitration, which I lost. . . . Basically I was so disenchanted with the Seals after the arbitration hearing that I was anxious to get out."[6] Carleton came to camp ten pounds overweight, which upset Glover. "You would have thought my stomach was hanging over my belt or something," said Carleton many years later.[7] Glover told Carleton to go to the Coliseum's football stadium and run laps wearing a rubber suit.

Older players and broken bodies were shipped out to make way for the Seals' new talent. In September, Young sold Bill Hicke to Pittsburgh, ending his tenure in California with 180 points in 262 games. Mike Laughton, the last original Seal, had suffered a serious knee injury during the 1970–71 campaign, and scored just 1 point in 25 games, so he was sold to Montreal in October. Also on the outs was Tony Featherstone, who had failed to realize his potential in Oakland. He was dealt to Montreal for goaltending prospect Ray Martyniuk, another first-round bust.

The biggest move of the summer saw workhorse Gary Smith dealt to Chicago for fellow netminder Gerry Desjardins, forward Gerry Pinder, and minor leaguer Kerry Bond. Smith could not have been more relieved to be leaving the shooting gallery. He had just suffered through two of the most trying seasons a goaltender had ever experienced: 136 games, 82 losses, and incredibly, 4,456 shots against. Smith asked to be traded, if anything, to save his sanity. "It was simply too many games to play," he admitted. "I had a nervous breakdown after the season. I felt bad when we lost. I was facing 50 to 60 shots per game, we were never winning and there was nobody in the stands. . . . I was literally in the hospital and I thought I was going to die."[8]

For the Seals, the key to the deal was Desjardins, a talented, young goaltender who had appeared in twenty-two games with the Black Hawks the year before and had recorded an excellent 2.42 goals-against average. The plan was for him to tend the Seals' net for years to come. Pinder had just come off a 13-goal campaign, but he had the potential for much more. "I think Gerry gave us a lift," remembered Lyle Carter. "He came from Chicago, a team that was up higher than we were, and I think he brought pretty good experience, and he was a pretty good two-way hockey player."

Young spent the rest of the summer stockpiling talent and replenishing the Seals' bare cupboards. He acquired former San Francisco Seal Stan Gilbertson, a Boston Bruins prospect and 31-goal scorer with the AHL's Hershey Bears. Young then picked up defenseman Marshall Johnston, goaltenders Gary Kurt and Lyle Carter, and forwards Craig Patrick and John French, all of whom had recently played in the Canadiens organization. If the Seals had been able to take advantage of the amateur draft to build their team, it would not have been necessary to scrounge the scrap heap for cheap talent. Desperate for help, Young took on all the misfits, castoffs, and prospects the big boys had no use for.

Unfortunately, the Seals' habit of trading away first-round picks came back to haunt the club in the summer of 1971. Montreal general manager Sam Pollock proved to the sporting world that he was indeed the Einstein of hockey. At the end of the 1969–70 season, he had traded the Canadiens' first-round pick in 1970 for the Seals' first-round pick in 1971. In order to ensure the Seals would finish dead last in 1970–71, and to have the rights to the first overall pick, Pollock traded three players, including the slumping Ralph Backstrom, to Los Angeles to help the Kings finish ahead of California. The rejuvenated Backstrom scored 27 points in 33 games, and without him the Canadiens won the Stanley Cup anyway.

Montreal selected Hall-of-Famer Guy Lafleur with the Seals' pick. The Seals desperately needed a star of Lafleur's magnitude, but they could have made the pain of losing him somewhat tolerable had they taken Larry Robinson, Craig Ramsay, or Rick Kehoe, who were all available when it was the Seals' turn in round two. Instead, California selected defenseman Ken Baird, who would go on to play just ten career NHL games. The deal that ultimately sent Lafleur to Montreal was rated in the *Hockey News*'s April 3, 1998, issue as the most bone-headed trade in NHL history, but the scouts should bear at least part of the blame in making the deal look so bad.

Finley openly complained about the previous administration's decision to trade draft picks for veterans. Before Finley arrived the Seals had traded away their first-round picks in the 1971, 1972, and 1973 drafts. They had also traded the number five pick in the 1970 draft but later acquired the number ten pick (Chris Oddleifson) from Montreal. "I cannot simply pay out big bonuses to land the best young talent as I did in baseball," Finley lamented. "I am limited to the amateur draft and we, like many other expansion teams, had, before I came in, traded away years of No. 1 picks for old players, which was simply stupid."[9] For once, the used car salesman was making sense; it *was* stupid, and he was *not* responsible for the mistake. While Finley is often blamed for pulling the trigger on the deal that cost the Seals Guy Lafleur, it was actually Frank Selke who held the smoking gun. The trade was registered with the league on May 22, 1970; Finley did not become owner until a month later.

The club was banking its entire future on minor-league prospects and young NHL rejects, a plan that, while often a winning long-term strategy, in the short term almost always guarantees a few years at the bottom of the standings. Glover was not overly concerned about coaching a potential train wreck: "There's no question about it," he said, "we had serious shortcomings and it would be a mistake to let our various problems conceal that fact. We've got to rebuild and I think we made a good start last season with some of the youngsters we worked into the line-up. Now, with all those young legs, we'll be able to put together the kind of skating, hustling club I prefer. I think we'll be heard from."¹⁰ Confident words, considering Glover was not exactly at the helm of the Boston Bruins or Montreal Canadiens.

Fortunately, the Seals sold programs at the Coliseum, because even the most dedicated fan would have had trouble identifying half the players on the opening night roster. One vet Garry Young had no interest in moving was Carol Vadnais. The defenseman's string of injuries the previous season had been a major reason for the Seals' second-half debacle. Young was confident his offensive leader would be back and better than ever: "Carol Vadnais is the guts of our hockey club. If we trade him, it won't be my doing." Finley did not hesitate to declare his feelings about his star player either: "As much as anything else, we need gate attractions. Vadnais not only is our best player, but our best draw. We're hanging on to him."¹¹ Vadnais was so valuable to the Seals he was elected the new team captain, and he became, literally, the poster boy of the franchise. His likeness was printed on team pennants, programs, and media guides, even years later when he was playing for *other* NHL teams.

In the preseason the club won just a single game and, for the most part, looked disorganized. The goaltending situation would have rattled even the calmest veteran coach. Gerry Desjardins had been expected to pick up where the brilliant Gary Smith had left off, but Desjardins was in no condition to play come training camp. He had broken his left arm in two different places during a game the previous season, but the Black Hawks' doctors had assured the Seals Desjardins was fully healed. When the goaltender arrived in Oshawa, Ontario, for the start of training camp, however, he failed his physical. Finley sent Desjardins to the Mayo Clinic, but the goalie was told his arm would have to be refractured and have a plate inserted.

Interestingly, in July Desjardins had claimed he had only regained 10 percent use in his injured arm. He spent five days in rehab in a Chicago hospital, improving his mobility to 70 percent. During the summer he even rode horses and taught at a hockey school. According to Finley, the Hawks "assured [him] Desjardins was 100 per cent recovered" when the deal was finalized on September 9, but Finley did not lay any blame on the Hawks for what could have been perceived as a scheme to unload an injured player. "In no way are we saying they slipped me a mickey," he said. "No accusations of fraud or anything like that. I think the Black Hawks made the deal in good faith."[12]

The blustery Finley hemmed and hawed and even threatened to withhold his team from playing. "I did not get a sound hockey player," he complained, "and will not stand for the deal as is. I talked with [NHL president] Clarence Campbell every day last week and he knows I won't put a team on the ice without a goalie with NHL experience." Then, in a truly Finleyesque vote of confidence to his players, he declared, "the team is bad enough as it is." Of course, Finley being Finley, he recognized the people who were lining his pockets with oh so much green: "Now we don't have an NHL goalie. We won't gyp the fans."[13]

Until the case was settled, Campbell decided that none of the players involved in the trade were allowed to play. For the Seals, Campbell's decision was difficult to accept since their roster was already razor thin. Making matters worse was the fact they could not even demand the Hawks send Smith back since Suitcase had broken his finger in practice and would be out for three weeks.

Looking for a veteran presence in goal, the Seals offered the Montreal Canadiens $150,000 for Phil Myre, but Sam Pollock turned the Seals down. The Seals then borrowed Marv Edwards from the Maple Leafs, and he recorded the Seals' lone preseason win, but the two teams could not work out a deal, supposedly because Finley had upset certain members of the Leafs' front office. Edwards went back to Toronto, leaving the Seals with nothing but rookie goalies. The Seals started the season in the unenviable position of having Gary Kurt as their number one goalie and the equally green Lyle Carter as his backup. Total NHL games played by the Seals' goaltending duo: zero.

In the opening contest of the 1971–72 season against Los Angeles, Kurt made his debut but had to settle for a 4–4 draw. California had a 4–2 lead in the third period and seemed in control of the contest. Carol Vadnais, Bert Marshall, and Marshall Johnston were laying out Kings left and right, but with three minutes to go Al McDonough drew the Kings to within a goal. With just fifty-five seconds left to play, Mike Byers scored the game-tying goal, sending the sparse Oakland crowd of 5,594 home disappointed.

Two nights later the Seals and Maple Leafs tied 3–3. If there was a silver lining to the game, it was that the Seals came back from a 2-goal deficit in the third period. Carleton scored 2 power-play goals, while Sheehan picked up assists on each tally. These Seals may not have been pretty, but they were feisty and could score. "I think you've just seen what kind of team we have," Carleton said. "We didn't quit. We may be young and we may make mistakes but I think you won't see a repetition of last year."[14]

Two ties were a nice start, so when the Seals took to the ice on October 13 to face Philadelphia, no one knew that a huge shake-up was coming. The Seals displayed that same persistence that Carleton had alluded to, coming back from 3–1 and 4–3 deficits to tie the Flyers. Norm Ferguson had an excellent outing, scoring three times, and the Seals seemed poised to finish with yet another draw, but Gary Dornhoefer scored for Philly with just fifty-one seconds left to win it 5–4. Gary Kurt had an awful outing, at one point letting a sharp-angled shot deflect off his goal stick and into the net. Twenty-four seconds into the second period Kurt did not cover one of his corners properly, and Bobby Clarke shoved the loose puck past the goal line for another weak goal.

Young did not like the way the season was starting and suggested to Finley that the Seals needed a change of leadership behind the bench. Fred Glover was fired and replaced by Vic Stasiuk, who signed a one-year deal with the club, intending to negotiate a new contract at season's end. The forty-two-year-old Stasiuk had once played on the famous Uke Line in Boston with John Bucyk and Bronco Horvath. He had gained experience as a coach guiding the Flyers from 1969 to 1971, amassing a 45-68-41 regular season record.

Stasiuk was introduced as the new coach at 3:30 on the afternoon of the Seals' next game, to the surprise of many, including Fred Glover's wife. "This has never happened to us before," she said. "If there was a real good reason, I'd understand. Fred told me he could have understood it at the end of last season. But he and Mr. Finley have got along very well. Fred felt he had a good team this year and if we had Desjardins in goal the team could go a long way. It seems so strange to happen this way, without the team even knowing about it. I don't understand it." The coaching change was a surprise. There had only been three games played, and the Seals had picked up points in two of them. "It's all a mystery to me," Fred Glover said. "I have some things to do and I'll stay around and finish them up. Otherwise, I have no comment."[15]

Hugh McDonald of the *San Mateo Times*, a staunch supporter of Glover, had many kind words to say about the departing coach: "[Nobody] was more dedicated to hockey than Glover, no one gave straighter answers to questions and he was a real man on and off the ice. This isn't an obituary, because it's a pretty safe prediction to make that Glover will be back in hockey before too long." McDonald smelled something fishy in the Seals' camp. Young had never been a big fan of Fred Glover, and there were rumors Young had planned on firing Glover during training camp. Young denied everything and claimed the coaching change was not made in haste. "Well," McDonald responded, "training camp was two weeks ago and the coach is fired after the third game of the season, and if that isn't sudden there's a helluva credibility gap somewhere, Mr. Young."[16]

Although Young was ultimately responsible for the decision to fire Glover, there were clues that pointed to Finley looking to make a change behind the bench. Before the 1971–72 season Finley had a verbal agreement with NHL great Bernard "Boom Boom" Geoffrion to let him coach the Seals. Geoffrion resigned from the New York Rangers thinking he had another job waiting for him on the West Coast, but Finley decided not to hire him after all, which irked several people around the league. The affable Geoffrion was left unemployed until Rangers general manager Emile Francis rehired him. The Rangers had also agreed to lend right wing Mike Murphy to the Seals but called off that deal when Finley left Geoffrion out in the cold.

Stasiuk was behind the bench when his new club took on the Vancouver Canucks, and before the end of the game he surely understood the problems Glover had had to deal with. Despite Sheehan's hat trick and a commanding 5–1 California lead, the Canucks' rebounded to win 9–6. "Six goals," the defense-preaching Stasiuk commented after the game. "I don't think I've ever seen my team with that many goals." He then added wryly, "It isn't funny."[17]

Not everyone had a positive spin on the Stasiuk era. "They got rid of Freddy Glover and brought in Vic Stasiuk who didn't like anybody who wasn't big and stupid like him," recalled rookie left winger Frank Hughes. "Stasiuk was a real dinosaur, one of those guys who thought you couldn't possibly be a hockey player unless you were built like a brick outhouse. I could see the writing on the wall [standing just 5'10", 180 pounds], so I ended up asking to be sent back down to Phoenix just to get some ice time."[18] Stasiuk was never afraid to show his emotions, which could be difficult to take. "When we were good, he was jovial, but when we were bad, he was not too pleasant to be around," recalled Bert Marshall. "He was old school."[19]

Overall, however, Vic Stasiuk's influence on the Seals' young players was positive. Gary Jarrett, for instance, enjoyed playing for his new coach. "Vic was a totally different type of guy," he said. "He was fun-loving. He had an NHL career and was more easygoing, more humorous. He got to know you more as a person and not just as a player."[20] Gilles Meloche also remembered Stasiuk fondly. "Whenever we played Toronto or Montreal [Stasiuk] would give us a pep talk about how the game was being seen coast to coast on *Hockey Night in Canada*," he said. "That meant friends and relatives of the players would all be watching so it was a chance for the guys to show off for them. We found out later that sometimes the games would be seen only in Toronto or Montreal, and sometimes they wouldn't be on TV at all. He knew that but he always gave us the same pep talk anyway."[21]

The Seals' needed a coach who stressed *X*'s and *O*'s more than his own personal need to prove he still had what it took to play in the NHL. Vancouver scout Phil Maloney, who was not at all impressed by the Seals' latest performance, commented, "Vic will teach the Seals fundamentals. This is a stick. This is a puck."[22] While this seemed like a derogatory comment, there was a certain amount of truth in it; the Seals *did* lack fundamentals. They could skate, they could hit, they could score, but they were also always digging the puck out of their own net. With 25 goals allowed in 5 games, the club's gaudy 5.00 goals against average was the highest in the league.

After seeing that Gerry Desjardins' broken arm still had not healed properly, the NHL voided the deal in which he was involved, forcing the Black Hawks to take him back. In exchange, Chicago sent the Seals defenseman Paul Shmyr and another goalie, rookie Gilles Meloche, who was taken aback by the trade. "I couldn't believe it," he said. "In the paper they say they want a goalie with experience."[23] Within weeks, the trade would make Young look like a genius. Meloche had all the skills to be a solid number one NHL goaltender.

At that point Meloche had done little to prove he could withstand the pressures of playing in the NHL. With the Verdun Maple Leafs of the Quebec Major Junior Hockey League, Meloche could do no better than a 16-26-1 record and a goals against average of 5.00. In 1970–71, with the Flint Generals of the IHL, Meloche's numbers were still unimpressive: a 12-13-4 record and 3.34 goals against average.

Meloche had made his NHL debut with the Black Hawks on March 16, 1971, defeating the Vancouver Canucks, 7-4. What the final score did not reveal, however, was that Meloche made an impressive 42 saves for the win. Three nights later the Hawks marched into Oakland to face the Seals, who at that point were buried in last place. Meloche had it much easier this time around, facing just 26 shots, while the Hawks had peppered Gary Smith with 48 in the 5-2 win.

Fred Glover was less than impressed with the kid who would eventually stand in the Seals' net. "The guy who had the most work played better by a long shot," he said afterward. "If the other guy would have had that much work, he would have folded." It was true the Hawks, with a stacked roster, played exceptionally well in front of their rookie goalie. According to newspaper reports, Meloche "was shaky on a few long shots Oakland mustered up and it was a race to see whether Chicago could build up a sizeable lead before the Seals could get going."[24] Nevertheless, it was obvious Meloche had potential, but he was not going to supplant Tony Esposito anytime soon.

Paul Shmyr had much more big-league experience and was expected to shore up the Seals' rickety defense, but he provided a lot more than that. "Paul hated to lose," remembered Gary Croteau. "He was not the biggest guy, but he'd battle game in and game out. In the dressing room, he'd let you know if you were letting the team down." Shmyr was also tough as nails. "He was a tough S.O.B.," remembered Walt McKechnie. "In Philadelphia, he had two fights in one game with a cast on his hand."[25] Lyle Carter remembered Shmyr as a player "who certainly stood up for the team physically and could really throw the knuckles. . . . I remember him as a steady defenseman, small defenseman, of course, but very capable and very respected around the league for being able to handle himself." The Seals had been bullied long enough; Shmyr would make sure that never happened again.

The other player involved in the original trade, Gerry Pinder, was frustrated by league president Clarence Campbell's decision to keep all of the parties in question on the sidelines. "This Pinder comes to play," said Young. "How do you think I felt when I told him about the freeze? He was our top scorer in training camp. He made the power play go." Pinder was ecstatic about being in Oakland. "Oakland is great. I just want to play," he said. Not surprisingly, Pinder was welcomed back with open arms when he made his debut against Pittsburgh on October 17. "I told Gerry 10 minutes before the game that he could play in the game. Everything was settled," said Young. "You should have seen his face light up."[26]

Despite the additions of Meloche, Pinder, and Shmyr, the Seals were still winless after six games, so Young traded defenseman Ron Stackhouse to Detroit for forward Tom Webster. It was seen as a good deal for both teams. Webster had led the Wings in scoring a year prior, with 30 goals and 67 points, while Stackhouse was emerging as an excellent offensive player. In the end, the trade was a bust for California. Webster picked up a goal and an assist against Pittsburgh on October 27, but "as I was settling in," Webster recalled, "I had my first experience with a bad back and I was out for the rest of the season."[27] In all, Webster played only seven games with California.

Fortunately, the young Seals began to gel as a team once they hit the road. Thanks to a Pinder hat trick, the Seals trounced Detroit 6–3 in the Motor City on October 24, their first win in eight games. Pinder also picked up 2 assists for a club record of 5 points in one game. For his efforts, Finley rewarded Pinder with a $300 bonus. "That Pinder," exclaimed coach Stasiuk, "has great moves for a little guy. He knows what to do with the puck."²⁸ The Seals followed up that game with a 6–4 victory over Pittsburgh three days later.

The Seals' surprising offense had the hockey world rubbing its eyes in disbelief, but there would be more shocked faces when the red goal light finally stopped giving California netminders sunburns. Gary Kurt had struggled badly as the Seals' number one goalie, giving up 20 goals in 4 games, so Lyle Carter took over and picked up the team's first two wins of the season. Carter was given the night off October 28 against Boston, so Meloche made his Seals debut.

Meloche's debut could have happened sooner had it not been for a fateful decision to drive to Oakland after his trade from Chicago. Paul Shmyr had wanted to drive his car to Oakland and asked Meloche to come along for the ride. "Shmyr told me the Seals would want us on a plane immediately," Meloche recalled. "He said, 'Check out of your hotel room right now and come to my house. We're driving to California.'"²⁹ Meloche and his wife Nicole tagged along with Shmyr, his wife, and their two kids for a three-day trek across the country. The Seals had no idea where their new players were, and had search parties and the highway patrol out looking for them. The Seals could not wait forever though, and they flew into Detroit for a game against the Red Wings.

To say Meloche's debut was astounding is an understatement. Eleven seconds into the game, Meloche handled an easy Wayne Cashman shot, which was very important for the young rookie. "I start getting mentally ready for a game as soon as I wake that morning," he said. "I like to get to the rink several hours before game time. By the time I'm ready to go on the ice I'm covered with sweat but I relax during the pre-game warmup and after I stop the first shot I'm really ready for whatever comes."³⁰

At the end of the first period the Bruins had outshot the Seals 15–5, but Norm Ferguson had put the Seals up 1–0. The Bruins continued to pour it on in front of the Boston crowd, but Meloche resisted. Dick Redmond scored at the 6:26 mark of the third period to give the Seals a 2–0 lead, and Meloche made 34 saves for his first career shutout. Stasiuk could not have been happier, and he gave the young netminder a big, wet kiss after the game. "He was great, he was fantastic, he acted like he'd been in the league 10 years," Stasiuk beamed.[31] No one had shut out the mighty Bruins in nearly a year. "That was the first time I actually cried at a hockey game," Stasiuk remembered. "I have only cried a few times in my adult life. After the game, I went into our dressing room to congratulate the players. I couldn't stand it. I had to go out in the alley where no one could see me and I cried like a baby. I don't know if I was crying because I was so happy for our young goaltender or selfishly for myself. I guess it was for everyone on the team."[32]

Today, Joey Johnston believes Meloche's debut was the most memorable game he played in as a member of the Seals. When asked to describe the game, Johnston did so in four words, "Two nothing. *We won*," he said emphatically and then chuckled, seemingly still amazed the Seals actually beat the Big Bad Bruins.

With a 3-1-1 record in his first five games, Meloche earned the number one goalie job, and Lyle Carter would be forced to ride the pine for the time being. After tying Buffalo in Oakland on Halloween night, the Seals defeated the Pittsburgh Penguins 5–3 three days later. This fifth straight game without a loss tied another club record for the Californians and pushed them into a playoff position. All the while, the goals kept on coming for the Seals. After fourteen games only the New York Rangers and the Montreal Canadiens had scored more.

Against Toronto on November 7 the Seals turned in their most decisive victory of the season. "There were more missed passes, poor defensive plays and bad goaltending efforts than you could shake a hockey stick at," said the *Hayward Daily Review*'s John Hickey. "There was only one difference. The team making all the mistakes was not wearing the Seals' green and gold, but the blue and white of the Maple Leafs." The Seals were merciless, outshooting the Leafs 40–15. With the Seals already up 5–0 in the third period, Vadnais, Patrick, and Pinder all scored in the span of 2:08 to put the Seals up 8–0. Meloche would have earned himself a shutout if not for Dave Keon's goal with just 3:31 left in the game. "I should have never had that one go through me," Meloche admitted afterward. "But I'm glad that the goal didn't cost us."[33]

FIG. 6. Gilles Meloche won 270 games over an 18-year NHL career. Topps O-Pee-Chee trading cards used courtesy of The Topps Company, Inc.

Many young Seals were cruising along beautifully. Teamed with left wing Ernie Hicke, newcomers Sheehan and Pinder quickly rose up the scoring ladder. Sheehan was tied for seventh in the league with 16 points, including 10 goals, while Pinder had 14 points in 10 games. Dick Redmond led all Seals defensemen with 11 assists and 13 points.

Redmond had flourished as the main man on California's blue line after Carol Vadnais was sidelined with an ankle injury in the second game of the season. "Bird Dog" provided the Seals with all-star performances and became the power play leader in Vadnais's absence. The handsome, casually dressed twenty-two-year-old with shoulder length blond hair was the typical early 1970s athlete full of flair. From the blue line Redmond could unleash a booming slap shot rivaled by few others in the league. As youngsters, he and his older brother, Red Wings star Mickey Redmond, had practiced shooting in the family basement. Before his first game after an early-season injury, Redmond would not let the team trainers tape up his injured shoulder because according to him, it affected his shot.[34]

The Seals were really rolling in mid-November when Garry Young traded prospects Chris Oddleifson and Rich Leduc to Boston for twenty-two-year old center Ivan "Ike" Boldirev, who would score 15 points in his first 18 games with the Seals. Stasiuk had nothing but praise for his young centerman. "If I were still playing," he said, "I'd be dying to get on Boldirev's line. He's so smooth. Any winger would look good with him."[35]

Boldirev has the distinction of being the first-ever Yugoslavian-born player in NHL history. He moved to Canada when he was two. Not speaking much English as a child, he became rather shy and introverted, but he was appreciated by his teammates. After being taken eleventh overall by Boston in the 1969 amateur draft, Ike put together seasons of 67 and 71 points with the Oklahoma City Blazers, but the Bruins already had Phil Esposito, Fred Stanfield, and Derek Sanderson at center. Boldirev was limited to just thirteen games over two seasons with Boston, but playing time would not be a problem in Oakland. In fact, he scored a goal in his first game with the Seals, a 7–5 win over Buffalo on November 18. Long-time Seals fan John Bonasera believed Boldirev was the team's most underrated player: "He obviously had talent and skill and was one of the top players when he was with the Seals. Again, not a flashy guy, not somebody that immediately drew your attention, but somebody that was obviously a skilled, top-notch player. I thought he was overshadowed by a few of the bigger name players while he was on the Seals. Interestingly enough, when he moved on and he went to the other teams, he was very, very successful everywhere he went."

While Boldirev was getting settled in Oakland, rumors were spreading that captain Vadnais was heading to Boston for popular but inconsistent Derek Sanderson. California fans had been using Vadnais as a target at which to vent their frustrations. After recovering from his early season injury, the captain was a few pounds overweight, and as a result, he was not playing as well as everyone had hoped. A chorus of boos and hisses often accompanied one of his shifts at the Coliseum.

By January Vadnais's popularity had sunk to even lower depths. Management and journalists criticized Vadnais's defensive play, which they claimed he sacrificed in order to put up big offensive numbers. During the All-Star break he demanded a trade. "What am I supposed to do?" Vadnais asked. "They want me to score goals all the time like Bobby Orr, but there's only one Bobby Orr."[36] The deal for Sanderson never materialized, but it was clear Vadnais's days in Oakland were numbered.

Despite California's vast improvement over the first quarter of the season, there were awful outings here and there. Sunday, November 21, saw the Seals play arguably the worst game in franchise history. On the heels of a 5–1 loss to Toronto on the weekend, the Seals skated into Madison Square Garden looking for a better result. The Rangers had already beaten the Seals 8–1 earlier in the season, and the G-A-G (Goal-a-Game) Line of Rod Gilbert, Jean Ratelle, and Vic Hadfield had been on fire all season.

In the years since, the game has been recalled several different ways, sometimes containing more fiction than fact. Many people believe the Seals scored the first goal in the opening minute of the game before the Rangers got mad and massacred the youngsters from Oakland. At the end of the game Joey Johnston supposedly asked his teammates, "Who's the ass hole who scored and pissed them off?"[37] While many players have confirmed Johnston's words, it was, in fact, the Rangers who scored the first *four* goals of the game. They were well on their way to an easy win when Ferguson potted one with 2:07 left in the second period. The red light never went on, but referee Art Skov ruled it a goal. A television replay showed the puck had in fact crossed the line, but the Rangers, without the benefit of instant replay, believed they had been robbed.

Ferguson's controversial goal may have been the catalyst to one of the worst twenty-minute ass-kickings in the history of professional hockey. In the third period, the Rangers smoked the Seals for 8 goals, tying the single-period NHL record. When Meloche was pulled midway through the third, he left the ice shedding tears. Eight seconds later the Rangers' Pierre Jarry greeted Lyle Carter with his second goal of the game. The G-A-G Line scored five times in the 12-1 rout. "We had guys who didn't want to go on the ice or wouldn't go on," recalled Joey Johnston. "So I went on. I think I was a minus eight that game, but I didn't care about my plus minus. If somebody wanted to come off, I went on."[38]

Even forty years later, Carter recalls the game like it was yesterday:

I remember the game well. Meloche came to the bench and wanted out with the score 9-1. I gave up 3 goals of the 12, I believe. . . . I was never a quitter, and nobody could say I was, and I went in there and tried to play. My two legs were practically asleep, being a tall guy and on the bench and cramped up, and all of a sudden, anybody who knows anything about hockey knows that you throw a [player] who has been sitting for [51] minutes of a game . . . it's tough enough for them. You throw a goaltender out there, and they're throwing pucks at you 80, 90 miles an hour, and your reflexes are just not there. I'm lucky I didn't get killed . . . it certainly didn't do a heck of a lot for my NHL goals against average. . . . It was a tough situation.

A crushing 12-1 defeat could have destroyed the confidence of this team full of impressionable rookies, but the Seals regrouped and embarked upon a five-game unbeaten streak in early December. They surged into third-place with 10-16-5 record. The last game of that stretch was a hard-fought 3-3 tie with Montreal on December 19. After spotting the Canadiens the first 2 goals, Redmond took matters into his own hands. The Seals' defenseman slammed into the Habs' Dale Hoganson behind the Montreal net, and as a result, a small scuffle ensued. Montreal's Frank Mahovlich came to his teammate's aid and was sent to the penalty box with Redmond.

During the first intermission, with the score still 2-0, Stasiuk remained calm as he walked around the quiet dressing room and rallied his troops. In a video highlighting the game, available on *YouTube*, one can hear Stasiuk telling his players in a rather soothing voice that they were "not scared enough," that they were "behind the eight ball," and that they could come back if they "learned from their mistakes." Thirty-two seconds into the second period Walt McKechnie scored on a rebound after Ken Dryden had made a nice stick save on Stan Gilbertson. About twelve minutes later Gilbertson tipped a Paul Shmyr point shot to tie the game 2–2. Claude Larose helped Montreal regain its lead with 2:22 left in the period, but the Seals did not give up.

In the second intermission Stasiuk encouraged his players one by one to step it up. As in the second period the Seals struck early. At 1:26 of the third period Wayne Carleton drilled a 45-foot slap shot past Dryden to make it 3–3. Meloche and Dryden played brilliantly the rest of the way, preserving the tie for their respective teams.

As 1971 came and went, the California Golden Seals had gone from doormats to rising stars. Charlie Finley had always believed that "S plus S equals S. This means sweat and sacrifice bring success. It is that simple."[39] He was right. The abundance of exciting players gracing the Coliseum ice was often credited to Garry Young, and deservedly so. He was one of the most popular figures in the Seals organization and became a compassionate father figure to many of the young men finding themselves in the big city for the first time. He gave the players a reason to play as a cohesive unit. "Garry had done a lot for us and we feel bad if we let him down in a game," one anonymous player was quoted as saying. "As long as he's with the team, I want to stay right here, but if he ever goes, you better believe that I'll be interested in what the World Hockey Association has to offer."[40]

The player's quote certainly said something about his dedication to Young but also hinted at problems plaguing the Seals. One of the Seals' biggest problems was Charlie Finley, who just could not leave well enough alone. In January 1972 Finley took his sartorial dreams to the next level. A year prior he had toyed with the idea of giving his players white skates, but when he saw what they looked like, he switched to green and gold. Others around the NHL were not too keen on white skates either. Finley admitted, "one governor told me they'd be fine but the fans in his building would wave hankies and blow kisses at the players."[41]

Gerry Pinder remembers the moment he first laid eyes on the most notorious piece of equipment in NHL history: "we were in the Hilton Hotel in Detroit or Minnesota. Mr. Finley was there and the skates were delivered to the lobby . . . Finley said we had to wear those skates *tonight*. We said 'No way,' and [Vadnais] had to explain to Mr. Finley that new skates need to be broken in before we could wear them for a game. It takes at least a week. They were stiff and not sharpened—heck, they were still in the box."[42]

Regardless, Finley was determined to get those white skates into the NHL, so the Seals started using them during home-ice practices in December 1971 to break them in. On January 14, 1972, against Vancouver, the fancy footwear was unleashed upon the world. Lost in the hype was the fact the Seals' 5–3 win was the one hundredth in franchise history.

Scribes were ready with their best jokes even before the white skates made their debut. "Always a bridesmaid, never a bride has been the lament of the Oakland Seals and the rest of the expansion clubs in the National Hockey League," wrote the *Oakland Tribune*'s John Porter just hours before the game. "Tonight the Seals will don their wedding-gown white skates for their first game use with an 8 o'clock faceoff against the Vancouver Canucks at the Arena."[43]

It did not take long for the white skates to irritate the players. "We took plenty of kidding out of them," remembered Marshall Johnston. "I remember in Boston one night, some guy hollered out of the old Garden there, 'Hey Johnston, where's your purse?'" Johnston then started to laugh at the thought. "But that was part of it. The worst of it was for the trainers 'cause they had to keep . . . putting the white polish and the green paint on all the time." Meloche admitted many years later that "they looked kind of silly. We heard comments everywhere we went. They [opposing players] said we looked like sissies or figure skaters."[44] Ironically, when Stasiuk was hired as coach, he said he believed in brisk, tough practices full of sprints, scrimmages, and drills, "not figure skating."[45]

Former stick boy Scott Ruffell revealed the many problems associated with suiting up players in white skates. Trainer Jimmy Pickard told Ruffell, "We're not supposed to have any black marks on these skates; [Finley] wants them all white," but the problem was finding an appropriate substance to cover the skates. At first they tried some sort of shoe whitener, but that didn't work. "We started painting them

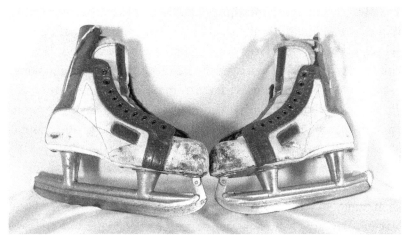

FIG. 7. A white and green variation of the Seals' infamous skates, circa 1972–73. Photo courtesy of Rich Reilley.

with . . . latex house paint," Ruffell admitted, "and I can remember a couple players going . . . 'These skates fuckin' weigh like fifty pounds a pair!' They didn't like that very much. That didn't help their play either, I don't think." One of the biggest Seals jokes that still resonates with players today is the weight of the infamous skates. "I thought they were alright," remembered Wayne King, who played in the Seals organization from 1971 to 1977, "but it was a pain for the trainers, 'cause every game they had to paint them, 'cause they'd get the black tape marks and puck marks, and they had to be looking good on the ice. Actually, they got heavy 'cause they got layers of paint on them. Keep putting a coat of paint on everything, it's going to get heavy." Before long, Finley added a bit of green to the white skates, but they still looked terrible. "Those white and green boots . . . made them look as if they were cut off at the ankles," said Munson Campbell a few years later. "In Canada, only girls—and Lord knows I have nothing against girls—wear white skate boots. This has to give hockey players an inferiority complex."[46]

Fans also thought the white skates were a goofy idea. "I thought it was a joke," said Booster Club member Larry Schmidt. "I think they should have just had black skates. I heard the players hated them. . . .

They would fall apart and things like that." Fellow Booster Cathy White agreed that the white skates were not appropriate attire for a hockey player. "When I was growing up," she remembered, "I had a girlfriend whose father managed the ice rink . . . and we used to skate. I always wore white skates, so it didn't make any difference to me. I didn't see any difference in it, but the players certainly did. They were embarrassed by the white skates . . . and it had a very detrimental picture for them."

Morris Mott, who would join the Seals the following season, didn't have a problem with the skates per se, but even he would not have been caught dead wearing them during a pickup game. "When I was playing," he said, "you took your skates with you in the summer and maybe a pair of gloves if you were lucky, and if you were by yourself or with a bunch of other guys on the ice they just made you look like an idiot. But in the context of the whole team they didn't look that bad. . . . So that didn't bother me that much 'cause most of the time when you had them on there were nineteen other guys, so it all kind of blended in."

In the end Finley's white skates got him the attention he craved. "The Seals' white skates and uniforms are what everybody remembers," said Bert Marshall. "Nobody remembers the players. They remember the uniforms. Charlie would be happy about that."[47]

Before the white skates got heavy and cumbersome, the Seals held down a playoff spot into January 1972. On the 28th Meloche recorded his third shutout of the campaign, stopping 30 Toronto Maple Leaf shots. Boldirev, Sheehan, and Carleton all scored in what turned into a solid 3–0 Seals victory. Two nights later Meloche repeated the feat, blanking the Canucks 2–0 in Vancouver. This time he turned away 29 shots, including 16 in the third period to preserve the all-important victory. Meloche became the first Seals goaltender to record back-to-back shutouts, and this, his fourth, tied Gary Smith's club record. Finley awarded Meloche a $300 bonus for every shutout.

There had been a lot of buzz surrounding the kids from Oakland, and the Seals seemed energized for the first time since 1969. The *Oakland Tribune*'s John Porter explained how much the team's attitude had changed over the course of a year:

Three-hundred and sixty-five days ago the Oakland Seals lost their love for hockey.

There aren't many of those players left on the club now, but Norm Ferguson remembers what it was like and so does Ernie Hicke.

"No one even wanted to go to practice," recalled Fergie.

"Hockey was a job. We had nothing to accomplish. Ernie and Hex (Dennis Hextall) had good years, but the team was down in the basement."[48]

In the same article Hicke admitted, "We didn't feel like doing anything. Everybody was working for himself." Ferguson described the 1971–72 season as "a new life. It's great, just great."[49] Young expressed similar sentiments. "You should see the enthusiasm on this club," he exclaimed. "I talked to Tommy Webster and he said we'll be as good as anyone in a couple of years."[50]

The Seals were still holding onto third place in the West, but their position was tenuous due to a disastrous 1-7-6 record between February 2 and March 3. Hoping to rouse the Seals out of their slump, Young pulled off his biggest blockbuster deal. In late February Young traded Carol Vadnais and Don O'Donoghue to Boston for Reggie Leach, Rick Smith, and Bob Stewart. Having worked in the Bruins organization for years, Young knew exactly what he was getting in exchange for Vadnais. Leach was a natural goal scorer blessed with incredible speed. Seals Booster Club member Sandi Pantages believes that some of the young prospects in the organization "with better coaching . . . might have been more promising, and I think Reggie Leach might have been in that category. I think he had promise to be a very good player." Her husband Dick chimed in that Leach "turned out to be a very good player later, after he was gone. He was very young when he was with us." Smith had decent offensive skills, but he was brought in for his defensive attributes. "Rick Smith was a hard-nosed defenseman and was a pretty rough-and-tumble defense guy," remembers Dick Pantages. Bobby Stewart would eventually become the Seals' captain and all-time leader in games played (414) and penalty minutes (691). "Bobby was a good defenseman, tough, he didn't put up with nothing," said future teammate Wayne King. "He was a good checker and . . . a good leader too." Joe Starkey believes that while he was broadcasting Seals games, Stewart was the toughest player on the team: "Good solid guy, good person," he says, "but on the ice, don't mess with him. He was a tough player, played it straight up, didn't look for fights but could definitely handle himself." Young felt very proud of his newest acquisitions. "This trade will put us in the playoffs," he happily exclaimed after the deal was made. "Reggie and these players are the future of this club."[51]

Even though Vadnais had become a bona fide NHL star in Oakland, he welcomed the chance to play elsewhere. In his final game with the Seals, a 4–4 tie against St. Louis, Vadnais scored his first career hat trick, but he did not even come out to salute the fans after being named the game's first star. Did he believe the fans had taken his talents for granted? Once in Boston, the disgruntled ex-Seal was quoted as saying: "I didn't mind Oakland, although . . . I was tired of losing. I was tired of being blamed for losing. I was sick and tired of being chewed up by everybody. Maybe they expected too much from me. I don't know what they expected. But management was giving me more aggravation than I cared for."[52]

Seals Booster Club member Larry Schmidt remembers the tremendous pressure Vadnais was under in Oakland. "He was one of the first guys, when they didn't have enough scoring," he said, "they pulled him up to wing, and he scored a lot of goals, because he was such a great skater, but he just got tired of playing here because he had to do everything. He was unhappy." After Vadnais's departure, Bert Marshall, one of the few veteran players left on the roster, was named the new team captain.

The night of the trade Leach, Stewart, and Smith were in the lineup to face their old Boston teammates before 10,492 California fans. In the opening minutes of the contest it seemed as though everyone would walk out of the building smiling. The Seals scored early and often, humiliating the Bruins at every turn. The Seals looked like they were finally going to teach the Bruins a real lesson after having endured so many previous beatings.

Dick Redmond opened the scoring just 2:51 into the game and added a second just over ten minutes later. Boston's Fred Stanfield cut the lead to 1 with a goal at 17:37, but Gary Croteau restored the Seals' 2-goal lead at 19:52. Carleton, Croteau, and Patrick added goals before the game was half over, putting the Seals up 6–1. The Bruins were reeling and looked nothing like the team that had outscored the Seals 33–8 in six games the year before. Nothing went right for Boston until Mike Walton stole the puck from three Seals who were fiddling with the disk in front of Gilles Meloche, and the Bruin got a good shot away, but the rookie goalie made a great save with his left pad. Walton then grabbed the puck again, this time dishing it off to Orr, but he too was stopped by Meloche. Wayne Cashman then skated into the Seals' crease and batted the rebound over Meloche's shoulder at 14:36 to make it 6–2, California.

Just over two minutes later, Bert Marshall tripped up Stanfield, and the Bruins were awarded a penalty shot. Stanfield skated in on Meloche and directed a high, hard wrist shot to the top left corner of the net, but the Seals' young netminder stood tall like he had all season, making a brilliant glove save to preserve the 4-goal lead. The enthusiastic Oakland crowd roared its approval as the Seals' bench flooded the ice to congratulate their unquestioned MVP.

When play resumed, Bobby Orr feathered a beautiful pass to Stanfield at the Seals' blue line, and it was off to the races. Rick Smith tried in vain to stop Stanfield with a series of hooks, but the Bruin still managed to put the puck past a surprised Meloche, who weakly kicked out his left leg while still standing on his right. It didn't really matter much since the Seals still led 6–3 going into the final period. There was no way the Bruins were going to score three more times in the third. Besides, the Seals had already beaten the Bruins twice that season. There was no reason to believe they couldn't go for the trifecta.

Less than three minutes into the final frame, Orr blasted a shot from inside the blue line that beat a screened Meloche, making the score 6–4, but surely the Seals were good enough this season to hang on to a 2-goal lead for another seventeen minutes.

At the 5:59 mark, the seemingly possessed Fred Stanfield completed his hat trick after receiving yet another tape-to-tape, blue line–to–blue line pass courtesy of Orr. Stanfield took the puck into Seals territory all alone and deked out a helpless Meloche to his left, making the score 6–5, California. *Now* the score mattered.

The Seals hung on as best they could for almost nine more minutes when disaster struck in the name of Phil Esposito. Ed Westfall skated in along the boards to Meloche's left, and directed a perfect flip pass to Esposito, who was coming in on Meloche's right. Before the puck even settled onto the ice, Esposito picked it out of the air and sent it past the helpless goaltender to even the score, 6–6.

Less than three minutes later Esposito tipped in a weak shot from Wayne Cashman, who was standing on the lip of the face-off circle near the boards to the right of Meloche. Incredibly it was now 7–6, Bruins.

In the dying seconds of the game Vic Stasiuk pulled Meloche in favor of a sixth skater. Boston's Derek Sanderson broke in on the Seals' vacant net despite Reggie Leach's persistent hooking and took a clear shot at the cage. Redmond valiantly stood in the way of the shot, making perhaps the best save of the night, but Sanderson picked up the rebound and scored. Redmond viciously slashed his stick against the post, angry that the Seals had blown what should have been an insurmountable 5-goal lead to the eventual Stanley Cup Champs. Final score: Boston 8, Seals 6.

When it came time for Stasiuk to face the media, the Seals' bench boss said all the right things and calmly explained what he thought were the reasons for his young team's collapse. "You really can't blame our defense though," he said. "They played their guts out. Our forwards just quit checking them in their zone, and Boston just came charging back. Nobody wanted to make the sacrifice of checking for us and they kept coming back like a tidal wave."[53]

Redmond was far less diplomatic in his choice of words. His disgust was evident on the ice, and after the game he was still seething. In a profanity-laced tirade, cleaned up for the newspapers, Redmond stated rather matter-of-factly: "Boston is good. . . . But to blow a five-goal lead?"[54]

It was a critical loss and undoubtedly a traumatic experience for the young Seals. The club had been slumping badly the entire month of February, and Stasiuk knew very well that the way his players reacted to the disappointment would determine their fate. "It's all up to the players," he explained. "They either come back or they keep right on skidding, right out of the playoffs."[55]

As the Seals imploded on the ice, the front office collapsed as well. Shortly after the Vadnais trade, team vice president Munson Campbell, who had not been on speaking terms with Finley for over a month, mailed in his resignation to the Seals' owner. According to the *Oakland Tribune*'s John Porter, Finley's radical ways conflicted with many of Campbell's friends around the league. Despite the problems he had had with Finley, Campbell was able to look back with pride at his two years with the Seals. "Two years ago Finley and I pooled our talents to obtain, reorganize and rebuild the Bay Area's hockey franchise," he said. "As long as I could continue to make a contribution it was fine. I think we are years ahead of a reasonable pace. Not many people knew what horrible shape the franchise was in.... There was no farm system, just a couple of stray scouts.... We had had no No. 1 draft choices for three years ... Now, we have something better than half the clubs in the NHL."[56]

While cracks started to appear down the stretch in the Seals' front office, the West playoff race tightened. Chicago and Minnesota had all but clinched the first two positions, but California, St. Louis, Philadelphia, and Pittsburgh were vying for the coveted third and fourth spots. On March 17, at home before 12,089 fans, the Seals and Blues tied 2–2, but no one was happy in the California dressing room. The Seals led the game 2–1 late in the third period when they broke into the Blues' zone. The puck hit Paul Shmyr's skate only to be grabbed by Frank St. Marseille, who then sailed toward the Seals' goal. Redmond dove out trying to steal the puck from St. Marseille but failed. St. Marseille got a good shot away from twenty feet out and beat Meloche. "I guess my dive took Meloche's eye off the puck momentarily and it went by him," Redmond said after the game. In the final minute Stan Gilbertson's shot deflected off goalie Jacques Caron's pads and ended up on Joey Johnston's stick, but the Jet couldn't slam the puck into the vacant cage. "It was too close to my feet and I couldn't get the puck up. It went into his pads," Johnston said.[57]

After the heartbreaking draw with St. Louis, Redmond said, "The boys will regain their stride and go get Pittsburgh tomorrow."[58] Near the end of the game and with Gary Kurt pulled in favor of a sixth attacker, Gerry Pinder scored his team-leading 23rd goal with just nine seconds left to give the Seals a 3–3 tie. It wasn't a win, but the Seals' play in the clutch was encouraging and moved the team to just a point behind St. Louis for third place.

Knowing every remaining game was a must-win situation, the Seals traveled to the Twin Cities to face the North Stars. A win would vault the Seals into third place, but a loss would put them perilously close to losing their grip on a playoff spot. No one would have been surprised had the North Stars just phoned it in that night; they had no reason to exert themselves at this point. It was the Seals, surprisingly enough, who laid a giant egg. The Stars held a 4–1 lead after two periods and dominated in shots, 24–15. Paul Shmyr closed the gap to 4–2 with a goal at 4:33 of the third period, but that was as close as the Seals got.

The following night the Seals moved on to St. Louis. If the Seals won, they would take sole possession of third place with 62 points, but a St. Louis win would give the Blues 63. After twenty minutes the game remained scoreless, but that would change just 5:35 into the second period when the Blues' Danny O'Shea scored. Gary Sabourin scored just two minutes later while Paul Shmyr was in the box to make it 2–0, St. Louis.

As the period wound down, there was a face-off in the Seals' zone. Garry Unger fired a shot at the goal as he was facing off against Craig Patrick, and because Kurt had his head down at the time, it gave Unger the break he needed to score. Stan Gilbertson made it 3–1 on a power-play at 6:22 of the final frame, but the Blues replied with a Brian Lavender goal shortly thereafter to win 4–1.

The Seals looked to avoid a three-game losing streak against Philadelphia on March 25. The Seals got a lucky break some five minutes into the game when the Flyers' Joe Watson had a goal disallowed due to a delayed penalty, but the Seals couldn't capitalize on the opportunity. The Seals paid for their impotent power play at 12:48 of the first period when Bobby Clarke redirected a shot by Rick Foley past Meloche. Bill Clement made it 2–0 when a shot by Ross Lonsberry landed in the goal crease. All Clement needed to do was tap it in. The Seals pressed in the third period, outshooting the Flyers 14–7, but goaltender Doug Favell kept the Seals off the scoreboard. When Bobby Clarke scored an empty-netter with just 31 seconds left to play, one could see the Seals' playoff hopes evaporate. While there was still a slim chance they could finish fourth, the Seals were definitely standing behind the eight ball.

The Seals concluded their road trip in Pittsburgh on March 29. Once again, the stars refused to align themselves for the now-desperate Seals. California built up a 3–0 lead in the second period on goals by Boldirev, Smith, and Leach, but at 12:59 former San Francisco Seal Ron Schock cut the lead to 2 goals while Smith sat in the penalty box. Gilbertson responded less than two minutes later with his 16th goal, but Syl Apps scored at 17:00 to make it 4–2, as the surging Pens started mounting a comeback. Greg Polis scored at 1:47 of the third, and Nick Harbaruk added another goal 2:28 later to pull the Penguins even. Pittsburgh allowed just 20 shots, and their big guns came alive when needed. Jean Pronovost drove a huge nail into the Seals' coffin when he scored with just over five minutes remaining, and the Penguins picked up the 2 points with a 5–4 win.

Both Philadelphia and Pittsburgh led the Seals by 3 points in the standings with just two games to play. In order for the Seals to make the playoffs, the Flyers and Penguins needed to tie in their head-to-head confrontation on April 1 and lose their remaining contests, which would both be played the next day. To make matters more interesting, the Seals needed to win both of their remaining games as well. As it turned out, the Flyers and Penguins tied 4–4, and the Flyers lost 3–2 to Buffalo on April 2, killing Philadelphia's playoff hopes. The Penguins demolished St. Louis 6–2 to secure fourth place, but it was a moot point since the Seals lost both of their remaining games, 2–1 to Minnesota on March 31 and 9–4 to LA on April 1.

Of the five NHL seasons under their belts, 1971–72 had been the most disheartening. From November to February all signs pointed to the Seals making a glorious return to the postseason. The Seals had fashioned a respectable 17-25-10 record in their first 52 games, but they then stumbled to a 4-14-8 finish, including an 8-game winless streak to close out the year. The Seals finished with 60 points, their highest total in three seasons, but one could only wonder what could have been if the Seals had done a few things differently. One flubbed shot, one missed check, one bad pass could have made the difference, but in reality, two games stand out as the season killers: the 8-6 debacle against Boston where the Seals blew a 6-1 lead, and the devastating 5-4 meltdown to Pittsburgh in the stretch drive. If the Seals had picked up a few points in these games, and if they had converted a few of their 18 ties into wins, it would have been enough to finish fourth, maybe even third.

The individual performances of several players reflected the team's end result. While the Seals were young and talented, they lacked consistency. Gerry Pinder, for instance, led the team in scoring with 23 goals and 54 points, but he was kept goalless the last 6 games of the year when the Seals badly needed a win. Bobby Sheehan also started the season on a tear, scoring 17 goals in the first 38 games, but scored only 3 goals the rest of the way. Sportswriter Bill Verigan, who followed Sheehan closely while the former played for the WHA's New York Raiders, explained: "He would burn himself out completely by the second half of a season. And he could be the leading scorer in the league for the first half of a season, which he was, on occasions, right up among those guys, both in the NHL and in the WHA. But by the end of the season, he'd be down in the middle of the pack." Sheehan had talent in abundance, but his career quickly fizzled, and within a few years he could barely hold onto a roster spot anywhere. "But he was just a loveable, likeable guy," continued Verigan. "He was at the bars every night in Manhattan. And I mean every night. And would be hung-over for many games. But he was the image of the [WHA] Raiders in that first year. Camille Henry, the coach, was just at wits end."[59]

One player who didn't have consistency issues was Gilles Meloche. Despite the catastrophic conclusion to the season, Meloche won the *Sporting News* West Division Rookie of the Year award thanks to his 16-25-13 record, 4 shutouts, and 3.33 goals-against average, none of which truly measured his contribution to the club. Meloche had inherited a tough job after coming over from Chicago, becoming the number one goalie on a team sorely lacking experience.

Dick Redmond led the defense corps with 35 assists and 45 points, both franchise records. Stan Gilbertson and Ivan Boldirev each scored 16 goals while Joey Johnston potted 15. After his trade from Boston, Reggie Leach scored 13 points in 17 games, a sign of things to come for the young sniper. The future looked bright indeed. With an average of 24.6 years, the Seals were the youngest team in NHL history and had clearly taken a huge step in the right direction.

Garry Young had done a masterful job putting this team together. The *Toronto Star*'s Jim Proudfoot, in his 1972–73 edition of *Pro Hockey*, wrote that "never had an NHL general manager done so much with so little in such a short space of time." Despite the heavy odds against him, Young had come up with a combination of players that worked. The new blood brought in to replace the aging veterans had exceeded all expectations, but Young's reasons for going with youth were simple. "We were stuck with a lot of older players who didn't have much future in hockey and for that reason," he said, "the team didn't have much of a future, either. My idea was that it would be better to lose with youngsters because then at least we'd have a chance to improve." His scouting experience with the Bruins helped him tremendously. "I had a pretty thorough knowledge of just about every player in the game," said Young. "That enabled me to get people who could help us in almost every deal we made."[60] Moreover, one should not forget the coup he pulled in getting Meloche from Chicago. Young played the whole situation like a world-class poker player at a table full of chumps. "We'll take a chance on him," the Seals GM said to the Hawks at the time of the trade, "but of course, you'll have to add another player [Paul Shmyr]."

Young was able to improve team spirit, something that had been lacking for a while. "I decided a key thing was to develop a sense of togetherness," he explained. "What you have here is a group of men playing a strange game in strange surroundings. Moreover, they are forced to overcome a lot of disadvantages which don't normally face NHL teams. They don't get to practise much and they're on the road a lot. So I worked hard to develop esprit de corps. The club did

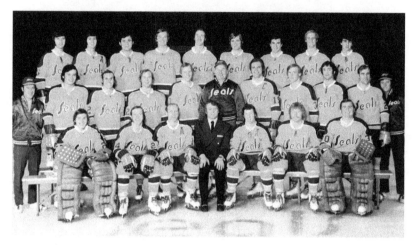

FIG. 8. The 1971–72 Seals in their bright white skates. Photo by J. D. McCarthy, from the collection of Doug McLatchy.

everything as a unit—travelled to games, went to movies, ate, went out after a game. This brought them together and resulted, I think, in a better overall effort."[61]

Despite the sixth-place finish, Young looked back at his first season as general manager with pride. "On the plane to the West Coast from training camp, one of the players showed me an article in a Toronto newspaper saying we should get a gold medal if we won 11 games this season," he said. "Well, we tied 18 and won 21, so we must have been doing something right."[62] No word on whether anyone on the Seals ever got those medals.

Unfortunately, the development of this talented Seals squad would run into another huge road block. A new menace lurked over the horizon, three words that would spell fear for the NHL for the next seven years: World Hockey Association. The NHL would never be the same after the emergence of hockey's second professional league, but no team suffered more as a result of the WHA than the California Golden Seals.

7

GOODBYE, OAKLAND, 1972–1973

The fall of 1972 signaled the beginning of the Dark Ages for Bay Area hockey: two years of defections, finger-pointing, childish name-calling, and abject failure that put the California Golden Seals on the fast track to oblivion. The catalyst of the Seals' disintegration was the founding of North America's second professional hockey league. The World Hockey Association quickly invaded NHL and minor-league rosters, signing anyone they could, from journeymen to all-stars. Finley, like most NHL owners, believed the upstart league posed no threat.

The decades-old "reserve clause" in all NHL contracts prevented players from becoming free agents, and its validity had never been seriously challenged. The league naively believed the reserve clause legally bound players to their current teams in perpetuity. In other words, if a player signed with the Bruins at age sixteen, he was their property until his rights were traded or sold to another team. Until that time the Bruins could do as they pleased with the player, even demote him to the minors if he refused to sign a contract for the amount that was offered. The player could hold out if he wanted, but in the end it did little good since the team could let him sit at home until he caved. "If anybody wants to challenge our contract," Clarence Campbell said, "we are prepared to defend it in court. I think it is reasonable to expert [*sic*] [the WHA] will sign somebody who is under NHL contract. Our course of action likely would be an injunction, together with a writ for damages. I have no desire to forecast what the decision of a court might be. Our contract is in harmony with those which have existed, over the years, in hockey and in other sports. I would expect it to be honored."[1]

Little did the NHL realize that many players saw hockey as a means to an end and sought financial security rather than a chance for the Stanley Cup. With the creation of the WHA, the players would control their destinies and play wherever they chose when their contracts expired. When former Black Hawk Bryan Campbell was asked how he could break NHL rules, sign with the WHA's Philadelphia Blazers, and suffer no consequences, he said, "It didn't matter. It was a renegade league.... I could have been on a five-year contract with Chicago; I could have gone, nobody could have stopped me. There was no rules or regulations saying that you can't leave the NHL to go to the WHA."

The contracts NHL hockey players had always signed were worth less than the paper they were written on. In Gare Joyce's *The Devil and Bobby Hull*, lawyer Don Regan, who defended the WHA in the landmark trial against the NHL, explained why, at the time, professional hockey contracts were not legally binding. A standard NHL contract "had all the things you've seen in a player's contract," he said, "but at the very end it said that—in this case, 'Bobby Hull agrees to play for the Black Hawks next year on the same terms as this year's contract except for the salary which is to be negotiated.' In any legal sense everything in a contract has to be definite and certain. So the part [pertaining to] this year is valid but next year is invalid."[2]

WHA clubs began offering ridiculous contracts to anyone who had worn so much as a jockstrap. Some players had apprehensions about jumping ship, but once a few brave souls took the plunge, dozens more followed. Bryan Campbell was among the many NHL players who signed with the WHA in 1972, and like many of those players, he jumped because he was assured there was very little risk involved, and that one way or another, he would receive the money he was promised. "Every NHL player that jumped, they said everything is the same," he said. "The meal money is the same, the travel is the same, the hotels are the same; everything was first class. The difference is the money is in escrow. That was put there because if the league folded, you'd still get your money.... So I'm thinking to myself, if I play in Chicago, I'm playing for half the money. If I blow out a knee and I can't play anymore, I'm fucked.... We're playing hockey for the love of the game, but we're also playing for a living."

Toronto goaltender Bernie Parent became the first star player to sign with the WHA, a $750,000 contract with the Miami Screaming Eagles (soon to be Philadelphia Blazers). As much as that figure frightened NHL teams, it paled in comparison to what came next. Bobby Hull accepted an outrageous ten-year $2.75 million offer from the Winnipeg Jets, including a $1 million signing bonus pooled together by all twelve WHA teams. Hull was the WHA's prize catch; he brought the fledgling league credibility. Furthermore, if the WHA could convince a star of Hull's stature to defect, it could convince anyone. Boston's Derek Sanderson soon signed a fat ten-year $2.35 million contract with the Philadelphia Blazers, followed shortly thereafter by teammate John McKenzie. Montreal's J. C. Tremblay then signed with Quebec, while Boston's Gerry Cheevers took off for Cleveland.

To the NHL's dismay, the courts gave the WHA its blessing to sign anyone it wanted. "Judge [Leon] Higginbotham [of the U.S. District Court for Eastern Pennsylvania] basically ruled that the days of slavery in pro sports were over," said "Wild" Bill Hunter, owner of the Alberta Oilers. "By ruling that Bobby [Hull] could suit up for Winnipeg, Higginbotham had effectively struck down the reserve clause and proclaimed that, from that day forth, professional athletes had won their freedom. This move sent a message to the owners in every league to start treating their players with respect."[3] Professional hockey would never be the same again.

Players on *successful* NHL teams were more than willing to accept huge WHA contracts, so it did not take much persuasion to get members of the Golden Seals to skip town. It was no secret the players were loyal to Garry Young, but players also had to think about their long-term future, and Finley balked at the notion of throwing extra money at his players to make the WHA go away. Besides, there was no guarantee Young was going to be general manager come October. "How many of us do you think will stay if Garry isn't here next season?" said one anonymous player at the end of the 1971–72 season. "We didn't make the playoffs. Garry will be blamed and you know how many managers Finley fired in baseball."[4] Knowing Young's position within the organization was tenuous at best, many players jumped ship. Young scrambled to re-sign his numerous free agents during the summer, but it would not be easy. He had assembled a fine team that had exceeded expectations, but he had built it on the cheap, which pleased Finley immensely. The owner, however, believed the WHA was doomed to fail, and he was not fond of giving players big raises no matter how well they played. That was bad news for Seals fans. The radical WHA owners did not care who could survive a bidding war and forced NHL clubs to raise their salaries to prevent players from defecting. In the WHA's first year of operation, the average NHL player salary jumped from $28,500 a year to $44,000, and it would continue to skyrocket.[5]

Negotiating a new contract with NHL general managers was about as much fun as going to the dentist. Dealings with WHA clubs were more personal and friendly; players of all skill levels were coddled and catered to, which meant a great deal to guys who had been treated like cattle for far too long. Seals leading scorer Gerry Pinder said playing in the WHA was a happy experience. "I looked at the new league as an opportunity to participate as more than just a spear-carrier, and that's exactly how it turned out," he said. "I wasn't a star player by any means, but I'd been in the NHL for a few years and spent some time with the Olympic team. When the management and scouts in Cleveland began asking my opinion on whether to sign certain guys or how to play certain teams, it really made me feel good. That kind of cooperation between players and management was unheard of in the National Hockey League."[6]

For a hockey player, the WHA was revolutionary. For anyone playing for the California Golden Seals, always on the brink of extinction, always having to beg for even the smallest pay raise, the risks of playing in the WHA were minimal. Pinder explained to WHA historian Murray Greig, "Many of us were interested right away because of the way . . . Charlie Finley treated us. He was a very nice man, charming and genuinely likeable, but he was a real tightwad when it came to paying his players." The Cleveland Crusaders offered Pinder about three times what the Seals had, but Pinder gave Finley plenty of opportunity to make him a suitable offer. "I think I was making $28,000 with the Seals," he recalled, "and I knew damn well that Finley wasn't going to come close to Cleveland's money, but I didn't sign right away."[7] Finley offered Pinder a small raise, but the Seals' star forward could not turn down the Cleveland offer:

I was playing in a golf tournament a week or so later, and had just finished my putt on the 18th green when a guy came running out of the clubhouse and said there was a phone call for me. It was Finley. He said "I'll give you a $500 raise over last year. Not only that, but we'll pay all your legal bills to get out of that contract with the WHA." He had no clue what I'd been offered. And when I told him, I don't think he believed me. He told me to wait a day or two, and he'd call again. When he did, it was the same thing. He just didn't believe the WHA was going to get off the ground, and he never, ever believed that any of his players were serious about jumping.[8]

In September, the Crusaders acquired the rights to Paul Shmyr from the Philadelphia Blazers and immediately negotiated a contract with the young defenseman. "My financial adviser . . . contacted me early on," Shmyr said, "and told me not to sign anything with the Seals until he had a chance to talk dollars with the Crusaders. We came to terms almost right away. Cleveland offered more than twice as much as I was making in California, along with a nice bonus. All the money was put in escrow, and the contract was guaranteed, with a no-trade clause." Nevertheless, Shmyr still entertained thoughts of staying in Oakland: "I flew into Cleveland, and at the hotel the night before I was going to sign I got a phone call from Charlie Finley. . . . A month or two before, they had offered me a two-year deal for half of what the Crusaders were going to pay me, but now Finley said he would match Cleveland's offer, no matter what. I thought it was a nice gesture on his part but he was too late. I'm a man of my word, and I had given the Crusaders my word."[9]

Wayne Carleton had been acquired a year earlier to provide the Seals with an offensive boost, but he scored just 17 goals. Carleton admitted years later: "Hockey was just a means to an end. I didn't really want to be in Oakland from the start."[10] He signed a deal with the Ottawa Nationals. "I wasn't very happy in Oakland with Charlie Finley and the white skates, even though we had a pretty good team . . . as the season wore on things seemed as if they were really coming to fruition with the new league. And a lot of guys were looking for an opportunity to make a move."[11]

The Seals had high hopes of reaching the 1972–73 playoffs with the help of a healthy Tom Webster, but the former 30-goal scorer received a $50,000-a-year offer from the New England Whalers. Finley, on the other hand, offered Webster nowhere near that much. By the time October rolled around, the WHA had lured regulars Pinder, Sheehan, Carleton, Shmyr, Webster, and Kurt, as well as prospects Ken Baird and John French.

The numerous defections foreshadowed what would later happen to Finley's Oakland A's. To illustrate just how much players hated playing for Finley, when true free agency became a reality in Major League Baseball, most of the A's stars bolted and never looked back. In 1975 pitcher Jim "Catfish" Hunter signed a lucrative deal with the New York Yankees. The following year, there was a mass exodus as Gene Tenace and Rollie Fingers signed with San Diego, Sal Bando scooted off to Milwaukee, Bert Campaneris moved to Texas, and Joe Rudi and Don Baylor went to California. One would think, by this point, Finley would have learned his lesson about mistreating and underpaying his players, but he never did.

Making matters worse for the Seals, Gary Jarrett retired during the summer, leaving another void to fill, but he was coaxed into joining the Cleveland Crusaders. Norm Ferguson was picked up by the New York Islanders in the expansion draft, while Frank Hughes and Ernie Hicke were selected by the Atlanta Flames. Hicke had signed a new contract with Garry Young in 1971–72, but injuries reduced him to a paltry 23 points in 68 games, convincing the Seals he was not worth protecting. There was one other problem too. "He was always on for a party," said Ron Stackhouse. "He had flashes of brilliance and times when he struggled . . . were probably due to his off-ice activities."[12]

Of all NHL teams, the Seals were hit the hardest by the WHA raids. Including those taken in the expansion draft, eleven players from the 1971–72 squad would be playing elsewhere come October, without one bit of compensation for the Seals. Finley could have avoided the fallout had he understood why everyone wanted out of Oakland.

Unfortunately for those left behind, the Seals had been on the verge of achieving bigger and better things. "We had the start of something and they let it slip through their fingers," said Stan Gilbertson. "We had 12 to 15 guys on this club who were young, good players on the way up when last season ended. I thought we'd all be back to pick it up from there."[13] This group of players really believed in itself, and as Shmyr put it, "We had a contender and I could see the Seals being the Stanley Cup champion in the next three or four years because we were so young and aggressive."[14] Booster Club member Larry Schmidt looks back on that 1971–72 squad fondly as well. "They could have been a dynasty, I'm not kidding you," he said. "They had some great players. They had Bobby Sheehan, Gerry Pinder, Wayne Carleton, Tom Webster, Ron Stackhouse, Carol Vadnais. God, they were the team of the future!"

While players left because Finley was cheap, many front office people left because he had no grasp on human relations. He never understood why people rarely worked for him for more than a year or two. In 1972 Finley went looking for a new play-by-play man for the Seals' radio broadcasts. At the time, Joe Starkey was working as corporate vice president in charge of human resources for the Northern California offices of Union Bank. He also moonlighted as a play-by-play man for various minor-league and college basketball, baseball, and hockey teams. When Starkey found out the Seals were looking for a broadcaster, he booked an appointment for Finley to listen to his tape. Starkey recounted:

> So I went to Chicago and he listened to the tape, and surprisingly enough—this was in September of '72—he offered me the job immediately, which kind of blew me away, but then, strangely enough, within 15 minutes he cancelled the offer. So what happened was that because of my background, a Master's Degree in business and an emphasis in human resources, that meant hiring and firing, and how you deal with people and all that. His reputation was already pretty awful for that sort of thing and so I told him in effect that, "Not only can I broadcast your games," I said, "I might be able to

cut into some of your turnover problems and some of the issues that apparently you're having with your employees." And he got mad at that, decided I was insulting him and so he basically threw me out of the office.

Undeterred, Starkey presented himself to the radio station that broadcasted the Seals' games. Station manager Len Smith was impressed with Starkey's tape, but he had no idea Finley had already rejected the budding broadcaster. It was only after Smith offered Starkey the job that he came clean. Smith said he would smooth things over with Finley, so Starkey promptly quit his job at Union Bank. "This is kind of an amazing story," Starkey remembered.

The A's were very good at that point. That was when they had three straight World Series teams and so they were in the midst of the World Series when he had hired me to do the hockey. At that time, World Series started in early October so [Smith] actually brought the tape to one of the World Series games in Oakland against the Reds and played the tape for him and Finley said, "The guy's pretty good. I don't see any problem in hiring him. I just wish I could understand why I recognize that voice so much." And I guess at one point [Finley] actually stood up in the booth and said, in effect, "Is that that son-of-a-bitch banker?" [Smith] said, "Yeah." And Charlie said, "OK, what the heck. Hire him anyhow." So that's how I got started in broadcasting and out of the business world.

Finley was right to hire Starkey. He would quickly become as much a part of the Seals as the players themselves thanks to his popular catchphrase that was yelled out after every Seals goal. He and a friend named Mike used to go to USC and LA Rams football games, and Mike would often yell "What a bonanza!" when the home team did something amazing. Starkey happened to use the catchphrase in early-season Seals games, but when he thought it was too "canned," he stopped. When fans started requesting he use the line again, he did, and it became his trademark.

While the broadcasting situation was settled, the same could not be said about the front office. In an intriguing twist, Fred Glover made a triumphant return to Oakland in August and became the Seals' new executive vice president. Glover had been the Cleveland Crusaders' director of player personnel, but he resigned after less than a month. Finley gleefully boasted of his minor victory after Cleveland had poached Pinder, Shmyr, and Jarrett. "Here they get a fine man like Glover," Finley said, "and they couldn't keep him around for more than three weeks. That ought to give you an idea of what a league that is. They'll be hearing from us, I'll guarantee you that much."[15] In the end, Cleveland heard diddly-squat from blowhard Finley.

Glover had always gotten along well with Finley. It was Garry Young who had reportedly fired Glover a year earlier. At the time of Glover's rehiring, Young lay in an intensive care unit recovering from a lung operation, but when he returned to work, Glover had already been installed as his new boss, making for a very awkward situation at the office. "I returned for personal reasons," was how Glover described his decision to come back to Oakland.[16] He also claimed there were no hard feelings. "When [Young's] back," Glover said, "he and I and Mr. Finley will sit down and decide on a new coach."[17]

Vic Stasiuk had done a more-than-respectable job motivating his young collection of players, and he had been promised his one-year contract would be extended at the end of the season, but no offer was ever made. "He felt that if we got one point for each game we played, we'd make the playoffs," believed Gary Croteau. "So he was always playing for the tie. He was basically just opening the gate and saying, 'Go get them guys.' He was old school. Even with a lead, he would just send one guy in on the forecheck. We could be winning 4–0 and he'd still be playing for the tie."[18] Like many of the players he had coached the previous year, Stasiuk became a free agent. He later signed a contract with the Vancouver Canucks.

According to Glover, "Finley was not too happy with what went on the year before. He told me that Garry Young told him to get rid of Vic Stasiuk, so Charlie said to him, 'You want to get rid of him; you're the coach.'"[19] So Young started the season wearing two hats.

How long he would be wearing them was anybody's guess, but he seemed upbeat considering the sudden turn of events. "I was very happy to accept the job," he said. "We'll work as a team. We want to bring a Stanley Cup playoff team [to] the Bay Area."[20] In September, Glover took over as general manager, pushing Young further down the organizational ladder.

To make up for the loss of players, the Seals were forced to promote many youngsters from the minors. Hilliard "Boot Hill" Graves performed well in training camp and showed an aggressive attitude that earned him a reputation as one of the fiercest and dirtiest hitters in the game. Graves's linemates that season, Pete Laframboise and Stan Weir, also became key contributors. Laframboise, the talented junior star from the Ottawa 67's of the Ontario Hockey Association, had been drafted by the Seals in the second round of the 1970 amateur draft, while Weir was drafted in the most recent junior draft.

Morris Mott was also given a chance because of the WHA defections and later earned the distinction of having his very own fan club. "There was a guy in New York who was in charge of the marquee at Madison Square Garden," Mott explained. "He decided to publicize the least known figure on each team that came in. So instead of 'Bill Walton and the Portland Trail Blazers' it was somebody else. So he picked my name from the Seals. So up on the marquee was 'Morris Mott and the California Golden Seals.' The next thing I know, this group of teenagers from Long Island formed this fan club around this guy that nobody had heard of. They would even toast their hero by drinking Mott's apple juice!"[21]

With the departure of Gary Kurt it was expected Lyle Carter would back up incumbent Gilles Meloche. Carter had briefly been the Seals' number one goaltender when Kurt proved to be a little shaky, but when Meloche stole the show in his shutout debut, Carter's ice time decreased. He also ran into injury problems in November, which had a profound effect on his career:

I'd made a save in Buffalo. We were leading the game 2–1. I'm going to say we were in the second period, I'm pretty sure, and the rebound went back to [Richard] Martin. He didn't even stop it; he blasted, and they tell me it was 90 miles per hour or more, and I was using a belly pad that shouldn't have been used in peewee hockey that they had come up with for me to use in that game. . . . I never thought of it at the time, I admit it, but why didn't somebody think of me using Meloche's belly pad? . . . [The belly pad Carter used] was not well-padded . . . and that's why I was injured . . . [The puck] hit me just in the bare skin you might say. It cut me for about a five-inch gash, it tore the rib cartilage, and actually knocked me out; I never knew what happened until I looked up and the players were all around me. I was laying on my back on the ice, and they took me off on a stretcher and so on. . . . [The injury] pretty much ruined my debut in the National Hockey League and ruined my season.

In January 1972 Kurt was recalled to back up Meloche, but Kurt failed to impress. Carter seemed assured a spot in Oakland now that his injuries were healed, but the WHA's Chicago Cougars came knocking with a three-year contract. Young countered with a two-year deal for two thirds the money Chicago offered and a promise Carter would remain in Oakland if he earned himself a spot in training camp. Carter chose Oakland.

Young ran into big trouble from the get go. "Things were so bad in training camp," Young said, "that one day a player skated into me, knocked me down, cracked one of my ribs and shattered my watch."[22] At camp, Carter outplayed both Meloche and recent acquisition Marv Edwards to earn one of the two roster spots, or so he thought. "Garry Young told me that I'd made the team," Carter recalled, "but he said they had a problem, and I said, 'Well, what's the problem, Garry? You told me in the summer who won the job in Oakland would be there, and apparently you're telling me Meloche and I won the job.' 'Well,' he said, 'we'd like Marv Edwards to tutor Meloche, and we'd like you to play every day in the minors.' And that's when the physical eruption happened." Carter made a strong case. His preseason numbers were far superior to those of Meloche and Edwards, but given what had transpired between the coach and goaltender, Carter was banished to Salt Lake City and would never play major-league hockey again. "Garry Young is deceased, he can't defend himself," Carter said, "and I wouldn't say anything against him that would hurt him other than it was a pretty tough blow to me to be sent to Salt Lake City when I felt I'd kept my word, I'd won the job, and I was being asked to go back to the minors while a veteran goaltender, and probably a good guy and everything . . . was going to tutor Gilles Meloche."

The season started on Saturday, October 7, against Vancouver. The Canucks defeated California 3–2 with Meloche taking the loss, and things just got worse from there. With just a win and a tie in their first eight games, the Seals sat dead last in the West. Even more unpleasant for team management was the pathetic Coliseum crowd of 1,998 that had witnessed a 4–3 California loss to the expansion Atlanta Flames on October 25. That entire first month was a very depressing time for the Seals' players. The team was a shell, fans weren't buying tickets, and everyone was miserable. After a 4–2 loss to Chicago on October 22, Walt McKechnie found out the Oakland A's had beaten Cincinnati in game seven of the World Series. The young Seal exclaimed, "Fantastic, just great!" *Oakland Tribune* reporter John Porter's description of what happened next illustrates the depressing atmosphere surrounding the team: "A couple of Oakland Seals jerked their heads in surprise as if that sort of thing shouldn't be said in the dressing room."[23]

Things looked much better versus Pittsburgh on October 27. Just 4:37 after the opening face-off McKechnie feathered a pass through two defensemen that Joey Johnston, just to the left of goalie Denis Herron, redirected into the net for a 1–0 lead. The Penguins outshot the Seals 11–5 in the period, but the Seals had a 2–1 lead after twenty minutes.

Four goals were scored in the second period, but the Seals had a 4–3 lead. The game remained close for the first 14:40 of the third period until McKechnie scored to put the Seals up by 2. Just over a minute later, McKechnie tallied again, putting the final nail in the Penguins' coffin. Final score: Seals 6, Penguins 3.

One thing that had worked well since opening night was the top line of Craig Patrick, Walt McKechnie, and Joey Johnston. The trio had dominated Pittsburgh, scoring 3 goals and 4 assists. All three players had come to the Seals prior to the 1971–72 season, but none had really stood out since Pinder, Sheehan, Vadnais, and Meloche garnered most of the attention. For the most part, the trio was relegated to playing on checking lines and killing penalties, but the following year all three players earned promotions, and, in turn, they rewarded Young for his confidence in them.

Joey Johnston thought McKechnie got a bad rap in Oakland, and that people wrongfully believed he was lazy, when in reality he could really fly:

> On the whole, I'd say Walt McKechnie was, to me, a hell of a player. People used to complain or say he's lazy and that, but you know, the taller the guy is, the more he looks to be lazy, but he's not. Maybe because when you're skating beside the guy, you know he can motor too. So from the stands or whatnot, if they say he's lazy, try skating with him! And the thing about Walter, when I'd holler for the puck, I'd get it. He was very giving with the puck.

Seals Booster Club member Dick Pantages remembers McKechnie was "a good centerman on that line and really helped the two wingers, who were probably our best two scorers." Gary Croteau also had high praise for McKechnie. "Walt was a great centerman and one of the best puck handlers in the league at that time. He was doing things then—like passing the puck between the feet or off the skates—that guys wouldn't do for years."[24]

McKechnie may have possessed the most tantalizing skills on the line, but Johnston's star shined the brightest of anyone on the team, with the exception of Meloche. Many of the players interviewed for this book agreed that Johnston and Meloche were the two best players the Seals had at that time. When asked who he thought was the best player on the team, Wayne King, who played in Oakland from 1974 to 1976, said, "I think Joey Johnston was . . . He controlled the game when he was out there, I think anyway. He was on the power play all the time. He scored quite a few goals."

Seals fan Larry Leal remembers Johnston fondly, particularly for his offensive vision. "Joey Johnston played Gretzky-style hockey before Gretzky did," he said, "because the puck would be in the attacking zone, and [he] wouldn't skate over and try to dig the puck out. He'd be skating a circle trying to get the pass . . . and every time I ever saw

Gretzky play, that's all he ever did. He never got involved with the work around the puck; he'd stay out by the blue line and shovel the pass so he could skate in and score. . . . I'd already seen that style in the NHL from Joey Johnston." Despite the favorable comparison to the NHL's greatest player ever, not everyone was enamored with Johnston's style of play. "He was a fast skater, a lot of razzle-dazzle," recalled Booster Club member Dick Pantages. "He was exciting, but he didn't have follow-through. If he charged up the ice and he scored, that was great. If he didn't, he'd just, kinda, you know, circle around and wait at the blue line. He was, I think, the highest-paid player at one time on the Seals."

Compared to his more flamboyant linemates, Patrick was the Invisible Man, but his teammates never doubted his heart and desire. "He was outstanding," said defenseman Rick Smith. "Skillwise, he was more of a defensive player, but he added so much to the team. He added dependability and was a great leader. He brought as much to the dressing room as he did to the ice. He was the heart of the team, a central ingredient. He was unsung and he didn't get all the attention he deserved." McKechnie echoed the sentiments of his teammate. "Patty, what a great guy," he said. "He got 20 goals on a line with Joey Johnston and me. He was a serious guy and a hardworking guy, and he was really dedicated."[25]

The line continued to impress both the Seals' brass and the fans with yet another stellar performance on November 3. Johnston, the feisty left-winger, scored another 3 goals and added an assist, while McKechnie scored a goal and 2 assists. Patrick picked up 2 assists in leading the Seals to a 6–6 tie with Boston. The Seals had fallen behind early in the third period as Phil Esposito gave the Bruins a 6–3 lead. Johnston, McKechnie, and Redmond each scored in the final frame, and the 8,120 fans in attendance became more and more delirious. "At the beginning of the game the [Oakland] fans were cheering for the Bruins," said McKechnie. "Then as the game progressed they cheered for us. Maybe we changed some of them over tonight." The Seals had drawn even, but the Bruins were not going to let the Golden Ones steal a point from them that easily. Boston's Ace Bailey, who had already scored twice, had a breakaway in the dying minutes, but

Meloche turned him aside to preserve the tie. "He was tough on me all night," Meloche admitted after the game. "It was a wild game—up and down. It's always wide open against the Bruins, but coming back from three goals makes it easier to go on the road."[26]

No matter how well the Seals' top line played, it could not save Young's neck from the chopping block. With the club floundering near the bottom of the standings with a 2-8-3 record, Finley abruptly fired his coach and replaced him with Glover. According to Glover, "The owner requested I handle the job temporarily, whatever that means."[27] Glover told reporters the search for a permanent coach had already started, but he also added, "Where do you pick a coach out of a hat at this time of year?"[28] Translation: "don't expect anyone to relieve me of this coaching job anytime soon." Although Glover had been the most successful coach the Seals had ever had, his return to Oakland did not help early on. His Seals lost 5-2 to Minnesota in his first game back behind the bench.

While Young was a failure as coach, it was not the reason Finley fired him. Young had been a successful general manager under very trying circumstances, and he had been faced with the unenviable task of convincing his players it was better to stay in Oakland for less money than go to the WHA. Joe Starkey believes Garry Young was suited for the job, and that the former general manager did what he had to do to keep the Seals' roster together:

Garry Young got fired as general manager not because he couldn't handle the job, but because the World Hockey Association had come into business, and they were trying to steal players right and left out of the NHL, and Garry was desperate to try to sign players before they were stolen away by the other league, and Finley wanted him out of there because he knew that Garry was trying to save the team at Finley's expense. . . . I can remember Stan Gilbertson actually called me at home one time and said, "I need to get hold of Garry Young. Do you got any idea where I can find him?" And I said, "No . . . what's going on?" He says, "I gotta get a contract from him quick before Charlie fires him, otherwise I'll never get the money that I can get out of Garry." That's the way it was operated.

As a result of Finley's stinginess, Young had to use shady tactics to save the team, which ultimately doomed him. After watching player after player leave Oakland, Young focused his attention on Dick Redmond, who had tallied 45 points in his first full NHL season. Young offered Redmond a two-year contract that would pay him $80,000 the first year and $100,000 the second, but according to Glover, "Charlie Finley didn't authorize that."[29] Redmond's contract was fair considering the Rangers had signed their top defenseman, Brad Park, to a reported $250,000-a-year deal, but anyone familiar with Finley agreed there was no way Redmond was ever going make that kind of money in Oakland. To put Redmond's contract into perspective, *no one* on the Oakland A's World Series championship roster, including Hall-of-Famers Catfish Hunter ($75,000) and Reggie Jackson ($70,000) was making that kind of money. Finley never would have paid his hockey players more than his baseball stars, who, incidentally, were also grossly underpaid by the baseball standards of the time.[30]

Chuck Catto, the general manager of the Seals' farm club in Columbus, Ohio, believed Young was "a bright guy, a very good hockey scout, but a lousy general manager. He could never say no. He lied, man. He lied and really believed in what he was saying. Most of all, Garry wanted to be liked and respected by his peers." Desperate to keep at least one of his talented youngsters in Oakland, Young attempted to fool Finley into thinking Redmond had been re-signed to a bargain contract of $30,000 per year. In reality, Young and Redmond agreed to a two-year deal worth $80,000 the first year and $100,000 the second year, far more than Finley ever would have authorized, but Young had been given the responsibility to sign players as he saw fit. Young asked Redmond to sign several copies of the contract: one for Young, one for Redmond, one for the Seals' main office, and one for the league. According to Catto, "Garry then put in false figures, less then [*sic*] what he and the kid agreed upon. . . . Garry Young had hidden the contract with the figures on it that the kid [Redmond] and he had agreed upon."[31] Eventually, the truth came out, and league president Clarence Campbell told Finley about Redmond's inflated contract:

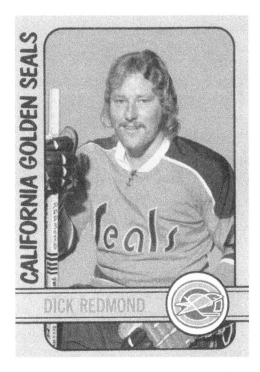

FIG. 9. Dick Redmond was embroiled in a contract controversy that eventually led to his trade to Chicago and the dismissal of Garry Young. Topps O-Pee-Chee trading cards used courtesy of The Topps Company, Inc.

Campbell was as petrified as I was. I had asked to see the contracts and Young told us they had been sent to the NHL registry (at league headquarters). In reality he didn't send them until three weeks later, on Nov. 4.

Campbell kept calling, asking where the contracts were. Young said they'd been mailed, then claimed maybe they had been lost in the mail.

When they finally arrived, Campbell called me and asked if I wanted to know what my hockey players really made. That's when I found out.[32]

When Redmond started receiving paychecks that only added up to a salary of $30,000 he lodged a complaint with the NHL Players' Association. Redmond's days in Oakland were numbered, but he felt no ill will toward Young. "Garry Young was trying to keep the nucleus of the team together," Redmond said. "There was a rumor that my contract was never registered with the league, but I don't think that's possible."[33]

Redmond, who had recorded 16 points in 24 games, was traded to Chicago in early December along with the rights to Bobby Sheehan, in exchange for defenseman Darryl Maggs and cash. "Dick was in the top five or six in the talent pool," said Rick Smith of the departed Redmond. "Some games he was like the Bobby Orr of the Seals; he quarterbacked the power play and had tremendous skill. The contract hassle he had with Garry Young and Charlie was a real distraction to the team. It made us feel like ownership was not in our corner."[34]

Glover told the media Redmond was traded because the defenseman wasn't producing. "It's as simple as that," he said, but the media wasn't buying it.[35] Why would the Seals trade away a young defenseman, who one year earlier had set a club record for points, for a player who, according to the *San Mateo Times*'s Hugh McDonald, "in 17 games with the Hawks had seen only about 20 minutes of ice time this season"?[36] The Bay Area media, looking for answers, hounded Maggs after his first game with the Seals, asking him to reveal his salary, but Maggs hesitated. When asked if it was $20,000, Maggs answered, "It was less than that. I'd say I was one of the lowest paid players in the National Hockey League."[37] Nevertheless, Maggs had serious talent, and he scored 3 goals and 11 assists his first 11 games with California.

In January, with the Seals all but out of the playoff picture, Finley, dedicated owner that he was, attended his *first* game of the season. He used the opportunity to hop onto his soapbox and clear the air on the still-hazy Redmond contract squabble. "I'll tell you what's wrong with this team," he said. "And it's not Charles Finley and it's not Fred Glover."[38] He also played the victim card, like he had so many times in the past. "I was conned," Finley said. "Not being a hockey expert I turned the operation over to Young, who I had faith and confidence in. Unfortunately, that confidence was, you might say, betrayed."[39] Finley also called Young "a sick man."[40] He believed Young had signed players to "inflated contracts without [his] knowledge" and claimed the Seals' freefall was all the former general manager's fault.[41] The beleaguered owner claimed, "What he did is going to cost me at least

$1 million this season." Then, in yet another classic Finley moment he stormed, "I lose $1.2 million, then have some bleep of a bleep pull the rug from under us and it's not fun."[42]

The whole Finley-Young-Redmond soap opera was yet another blemish on the Seals' sorry history. Old Charlie had been crying foul over this or that for years, and both fans and media were getting sick and tired of his bullshit. Over a year after Young's dismissal *Hockey News* columnist Geoffrey Fisher questioned Finley's conclusions concerning the former general manager's handling of free agents: "The fact is there is good reason to question Finley's charges against Young. If, in fact, Young had signed players to inflated contracts, it seems highly questionable that so many of the Seals would have defected to the WHA when they did."[43] Legendary hockey writer Stan Fischler declared, "The Oakland, California Golden Seals are an embarrassment to the National Hockey League; a festering sore on an otherwise rosy NHL financial complexion that bothers Clarence Campbell and his governors more than they dare admit."[44]

As 1972 came to a close, the "Case of the Million Dollar Deception" became more and more strange. Never one to let someone sully his (ahem) sparkling reputation, Finley revealed he had a notarized affidavit signed by Young in which the former general manager admitted he "lied to Mr. Finley and deceived him."[45] According to the January 13, 1973, edition of the *Winnipeg Free Press*, the affidavit stated it was Young's "responsibility to reach binding agreement only after approval from Charlie Finley."[46]

This legal document led to more questions than answers. Young explained he had signed the affidavit only because he had been under pressure to do so. In what could have been a scene from a Hollywood movie, Young explained: "When I got to Finley's office, Finley introduced me to a man who, he said, was a police sergeant. Two other men, he said, were police officers. They were not introduced."[47]

After talking for several hours, Finley asked Young to go with the three officers and take a lie detector test. "I still don't know where we went," Young recalled. "It wasn't a police station. The test took two, maybe three hours. It must have been four o'clock when we got back to the hotel. I couldn't sleep. That night, we tied the Hawks 3–3, but I still had a hunch something would happen."[48] Two days later, Finley asked Young to sign the affidavit and resign.

Young sought legal advice from lawyer and player agent Alan Eagleson, who discovered that Young was within his rights to sign players without Finley's consent: "Young shall also negotiate the contracts of the players of the parent NHL team," the 1971 contract stated. "Young will direct and assist the coach of the parent club and will recommend and make changes from time to time subject to Finley's approval."[49] In no way was Young required to get Finley's approval to negotiate a contract. Finley never did take Young to court, for the simple reason he had no case: Finley had *authorized* Young to spend his money on player contracts.

"I'm not going to knock him," Young said two months after losing his job.

> That would only be more publicity and the man loves publicity.
> My life has been hurt by this thing, but when things go bad everybody has to share responsibility, and I don't think this thing was all my fault. I'm not going to pass the buck but that seems to be the way Charley Finley operates—passing the buck.[50]

The scandal made Finley consider selling the franchise. He was looking for something in the range of $6 million dollars for a team he had acquired for $4.5 million in 1970. The players, on the other hand, just wanted some stability at the top. "We just never see Mr. Finley," said one player, "and it's not good for the morale of a club to have such a lack of interest shown by the owner."[51] At the time, it was believed at least six players, including Meloche, had been approached by WHA clubs.[52]

Finley may have been generous doling out the hat trick and shutout bonuses and buying players Gucci shoes, green luggage, and sports jackets, but his players were becoming disenchanted. "Everything that was good about playing for this team was due to Garry," one anonymous player declared. "Our loyalty was to him."[53]

Morris Mott explains why he thinks many players felt so loyal toward Young:

He was very loyal to some of the players; he would defend them. We had a losing record all the time, and he wouldn't let the people run the players down. . . . I can see why a lot of players liked him. He was very loyal to the guys that he thought were going to help him. . . . He had been in the Boston organization, and a lot of the players that he either had in California or traded for in California . . . had been with the Boston farm teams, and Garry knew them pretty well so he was kind of a Boston guy . . . that's my impression, anyhow.

Even players in the WHA sympathized with Young. Gerry Pinder and Paul Shmyr, getting ready to participate in the WHA's first All-Star Game, placed the blame for the Seals' misfortunes squarely on Finley. "If Garry wasn't there, none of us would have been back," Pinder said. "I think Finley was lucky to get back the players he did." Shmyr added, "If Finley said he wouldn't have lost a single player, it's unbelievable. I'll tell you one thing—he would have lost the whole team without Garry. . . . Maybe Young did some of those things we read about in the newspaper, but under Finley it's the only way to operate. I'm glad I'm not there."[54]

While Young may have occasionally bent the rules to survive in Oakland, he was not a bad person. In fact, in an interview for this book, former Seal Howie Menard told the story of how Young was responsible for him qualifying for his NHL pension. Menard recalled how he was about to sign a three-year contract with the Los Angeles Sharks of the WHA but was hesitant because of the potential consequences to his hockey career. "All kinds of things went through your head," he remembered, "so there were a lot of guys who didn't want to make the move the first year, the first two years, because the guys were afraid of getting stuck there . . . if they folded or something. So I called up Garry anyway, and I said, 'I just need a few games to get my NHL pension.' He said, 'Listen, I'll guarantee you 70 games.' . . . He put me on the protected list, and I qualified for the full season that year, believe it or not." Menard, however, was not in the Seals' plans. He ended up spending the entire season in Salt Lake City, but Menard was not heartbroken. "I was on the protected list," he explained, "so that qualified me for 70 games, or whatever the schedule was, so a lot of people don't know that. You're the first guy I ever told that to, but that qualified me for my National Hockey League pension."

Not many people sided with Finley in the "Case of the Million Dollar Deception." Fans had grown weary of Finley. Former Seals Booster Club member John Bonasera had had high hopes when Finley bought the club in 1970, but his optimism soon turned to despair:

When Finley got his hands on the Seals, my thought was, this might be a good thing. . . . Of course, Finley, in retrospect, in hindsight, from someone not on the inside, from all appearances, was doing everything he could to derail the franchise. His interest wasn't really in building a winning team or winning a Stanley Cup. It was our perception that he was more into just having tax write-offs for his other more lucrative businesses. . . . I literally had, in my bedroom, his picture tacked up to a corkboard, and I used to throw darts at that thing on a regular basis, so that was the impression that I had of the guy.

Over time, the team played slightly better for Glover than it had for Young and picked up a few points. Goalies Marv Edwards and Roger Crozier stole the spotlight from their teammates on November 9 as the Seals and Sabres battled to a scoreless stalemate. Edwards, in particular, was brilliant. In the third period he handled 15 Buffalo shots while Crozier had to face only 4. Not everyone was convinced Edwards had been spectacular. "The score should have been about 10-0," said Buffalo coach Joe Crozier. "We were hitting goal posts, hitting sticks, hitting legs. We just weren't putting the puck on the net. The Perrault [sic] line had only five shots on goal. That's not enough." Glover was quick to praise his own players for their outstanding night: "McKechnie did a great job. . . . And Edwards came up with the big saves in the final period. He's a cool one, experienced."[55] Edwards was quickly proving to be a reliable backup to Meloche, even though neither was winning a lot of games.

Eight days later only 4,272 fans showed up for a return match against the Sabres in Oakland. Buffalo came out strong, outshooting California 15-8 in the opening period, but once again the Sabres could not get anything past Edwards. In the meantime Joey Johnston gave the Seals a 1–0 lead at 14:40, and they never looked back. Reggie Leach scored 2 goals to give California a 3–0 lead in the second, and Johnston scored early in the third period. To add salt to the wound, Stan Gilbertson, who was mired in a season-long slump, scored his second of the campaign at 14:49 to make it 5–0.

Edwards had a shutout going into the third period, but Gerry Meehan stole the $300 shutout bonus from him with three minutes left when he fired one in from the left wing. "It was my fault all the way," the goalie admitted after the game. "Bert [Marshall] played it the way he was supposed to. It's the way we do it in practice—any 2-on-1 situation the defenseman stays in the middle and I take the shot." When asked by a reporter if he would accept a $275 bonus for the near-shutout, Edwards responded, "I'd go for that. Tell Freddie. Where's Freddie?" Unfortunately it was not Glover's money to give away. "I'm afraid I can't but I wouldn't mind doing it," he answered.[56]

In late November, when the Seals were beginning to close in on seventh-place St. Louis, the Golden Ones seemed to throw in the towel and lost three games in a row, a couple of which were doozies. Losing to the hapless New York Islanders 4–2 on November 21 certainly did not help the team's morale either, but at least the game was close. That was not the case on November 25, when the Seals traveled to Toronto. The line of Darryl Sittler, Rick Kehoe, and Denis Dupere scored 5 goals and 9 assists en route to an 11–0 annihilation of the Golden Seals. Joe Starkey recalled that the game was "so bad that Jacques Plante, who at that point was now near the end of his career . . . told the coach he was sick because he was so bored with the game after two periods; he didn't even want to finish it and keep the shutout."

The club was in the midst of its worst season ever, so much so that even when someone played beyond his abilities, the game's result was still horrendous. On December 10, 1972, light-scoring defenseman Marshall Johnston, playing as a forward this night, scored the first and only hat trick of his NHL career. "There was a friend of mine that was at the game," he remembered, "and he was sitting next to a guy that didn't know much about hockey. So this guy was telling him about how I wasn't that big a scorer and I was more of a defensive player and so on, so forth, and he supposedly knew something about the game, and then I ended up scoring a hat trick." Johnston also assisted on the Seals' only other goal that night, giving him a career-high 4 points. "The other thing I remember is after I got the third goal I was facing off, and [Wayne] Cashman skated by and said, 'Hey, Rocket, slow it down!'" Johnston still laughs at that one, but despite his exploits that night, Ken Hodge scored 3 goals of his own for Boston and led the Bruins to a lopsided 8–4 win. On the flight back to Oakland, the players decided to have a little fun, Boston-style. "We had a long flight back from Boston," remembered Gary Croteau. "The guys bought lobsters and had lobster races in the aisles of the plane."[57]

Bright spots were few and far between the first thirty games of the season. Joey Johnston had 16 goals and was on pace for 42, but no other Seal had hit double digits in goals; most teams had at least four or five such players. At the midseason mark, the Johnston-McKechnie-Patrick line was still the club's biggest threat. Despite the emergence of rookies Pete Laframboise, Stan Weir, and Hil Graves, the three members of the JJ-M-P Line were the only players with more than 20 points. *Hockey News* columnist Geoffrey Fisher said it best in his January 1973 description of the team: "There has never been in the modern history of the National Hockey League a team that was both so pathetic in its rating and so promising in its future as the current edition of the California Golden Seals. . . . The Seals are diamond-studded with young players who have outstanding potential for the future."[58]

As time went on, the pressure of working in such a caustic environment took its toll on Glover. Joe Starkey said Glover "was a very heavy drinker. He sobered up later and he was a good guy, but there's no question that the way he got through a lot of stuff was by late nights in the bar." Glover may have had his problems, but the media and other people in the Seals organization thought he was friendly, dedicated, and suited to his positions as coach and general manager. "Freddie was really a good hockey guy overall, there's no question about it," explained Starkey. "He was a great player who never made it into the NHL . . . and he did the best he could under very difficult circumstances in Oakland. He just didn't have many resources and didn't have much freedom to get anything accomplished."

With the playoffs all but unreachable, Glover found it difficult to manage and motivate his players. There were, of course, the usual practices where Glover felt the urge to put on his equipment and scrimmage with the boys, but there were also problems getting the players to the rink on time. On January 2, nine players were late for practice because they believed Glover had scheduled it for 12:45, but it was really at 10:45. Glover was none too impressed. "They said it was a misunderstanding in times," he said. "It's a funny thing. Some of them found out the right time." Glover said he had repeated three times when the practice would take place, but still some players misheard. As practice concluded, Glover made it clear, "There will be a skate for everybody at 11:30 tomorrow." Glover then glanced at the clock on the wall, bashed his stick against the ice and stormed into the dressing room to take off his equipment. No one dared follow him, but one observer commented, "You would think that the Seals would feel guilty enough to make sure they win tomorrow night."[59] Little did anyone know how prophetic those words would be.

Only 2,702 fans were in attendance January 3, and they witnessed the Seals take a 5–3 lead on Vancouver into the third period. Craig Patrick scored his ninth of the season just 1:35 in, and Darryl Maggs scored two minutes later, followed by Pete Laframboise's ninth, and third of the night, 30 seconds after that. Laframboise then scored a fourth goal at 9:15 to put the Seals up 9–3. Patrick scored another goal at 13:14 to give the Seals their first-ever 10-goal game, and Stan Gilbertson scored 1:01 later to make it 11–3. Several club records were set that night. Laframboise scored 3 goals in 14:39 to establish a team mark for fastest trio of goals. Hil Graves equaled both team and rookie records by recording 4 assists. Team records were also set for goals in one game (11), goals in one period (6), points in one game (29), points in one period (16), fastest five Seals goals (11:39), fastest six Seals goals (12:40), and largest margin of victory (8 goals).

What did Finley do during the Seals' moment of triumph? "Finley happened to sit right down below where our broadcast booth was," recalled Joe Starkey, "and he virtually paid no attention to what was going on in the game, didn't react to Pete's terrific night or any of that sort of thing, so I just never could quite understand why he wanted a hockey team to begin with."

Former Booster Club member John Bonasera still has fond memories of the Seals' triumphant moment:

A great moment was their 11–3 win over Vancouver. . . . I was home listening to the game on the radio and couldn't believe it. And one of the unique things about that game, aside from the fact that the Seals won, and aside from the fact that the Seals got 11 goals, and aside from the fact that Pete Laframboise had 4 goals, which were all kind of exciting and all that, but guess who was in attendance that night? Charles O. Finley! . . .

Interestingly enough, [sportscaster] Mike Forrest, after one of the goals, you know, like the eighth, or ninth, or tenth goal, or whatever . . . he's like, "Charlie Finley, on his feet yelling and cheering," and then a little later, "He must be thinking, Hey, what's all the fuss about? These guys are great!" The one game he goes to they get 11 goals!

The Vancouver game was an anomaly, but for a short time the team did play better, even though it was on pace to finish with its worst record ever. On January 10 the Seals defeated St. Louis 6–5, and then they tied their next three games, the first of which was a 3–3 draw against the Montreal Canadiens. Hil Graves continued his fine rookie season, scoring 2 more goals, his 11th and 12th, and also got an assist on Joey Johnston's 19th. California had a 3–2 lead until Claude Larose knotted it up with an early third-period marker. On the upside for California, the tie extended their home unbeaten streak to five games. Even more impressive than holding the storied Habs to a tie was the Oakland crowd of 12,033 that witnessed the match. Having a full house cheering "Go Seals Go" energized the club. "What a difference," said Patrick. "When we went out for the first faceoff, what a feeling! It shouldn't make any difference, but it does."[60] There is a logical explanation for the shocking turnout: not only was Montreal a good draw in Oakland, but Finley also cut ticket prices in half for the final twenty games of the season. "If I'm going to go broke I'd rather do it with a full house at half the price than 2,500 at full price," he declared.[61] During the first half of the season, the Seals had been averaging about 3,700 fans per home game, compared to over 6,000 the year before.

No matter what the poor Californians did, they could not string together a couple of wins. There were lots of ties, but wins were rare. On January 19, 1973, the Rangers peppered poor Meloche with 47 shots in an easy 6–0 win. In the second period alone the Rangers fired 22 shots his way; the Seals managed 2. McKechnie recalled in Ross Brewitt's *Into the Empty Net*, "Gilles Meloche is standing on his head in goal for us, we're down 1–0 and it should have been 10–0. . . . In the dressing room [in between periods] Stan Gilbertson gets up and asks, 'Who are the two wise guys?'"[62]

Not only did the Seals lose many games by very wide margins, but they also lost plenty against clubs that had no business pushing anyone around. For instance, on January 23 the hapless New York Islanders, who had scored all of 91 goals in 47 games, managed *8* goals against the Seals. The truly pathetic part was the fact the Isles had only six wins going into February, yet this was the *third* time they had beaten the Seals! Without California, whom they managed to beat a fourth time in March, the Islanders would not have won even ten games their inaugural season.

The frequent losses that had been a concern at the start of the season were now the norm. In fact, the Seals lost a team-record nine in a row between January 28 and February 11, a streak that was itself part of a fourteen-game winless streak, another dubious club mark. Over the course of the streak, California scored more than 3 goals just once, in a 6–4 *loss* to Detroit on February 1.

On February 23 the New York Rangers visited the Coliseum looking to grab an easy 2 points from the Seals, who, with a 9-38-14 record, were at their nadir. Unfortunately for the Rangers, Gilles Villemure was ineffective most of the game, stopping just 18 of 23 shots. The first period ended with the score tied 1-1, but McKechnie put the Seals up

by a goal in the first minute of the second period, but Glen Sather tied
the score some five minutes later. The oft-injured Ivan Boldirev struck
at 12:29 with his second goal, and Morris Mott opened up a 2-goal lead
three minutes later. The Seals had but 5 shots in the second period,
yet they managed to score three times, and put the Rangers in a 4-2
hole. The Rangers' Jean Ratelle closed the gap to 4-3 at 11:09 of the
third, but Craig Patrick scored the game's fifth goal on a breakaway
set up by McKechnie and Joey Johnston with less than two minutes
to go. Meloche was at his best in the California goal, blocking all but
3 of the Rangers' 37 shots. The Seals ended a few lengthy droughts
that night: a first win in fifteen games, and a first goal for Boldirev in
the same stretch. "The last time I scored," Boldirev said, "was the
last time we won, in Atlanta." Gary Croteau, who was injured at the
time, joked, "You blew it."[63]

Even when the Seals managed to finally win a game, they were
unable to build upon it and gain any momentum. Just two nights later,
the Philadelphia Flyers humiliated the Seals 7-0 at the Coliseum.
With the season now a complete write-off, captain Bert Marshall was
traded to the New York Rangers for prospects Dave Hrechkosy, Gary
Coalter, and cash.

As March rolled around, it became clear Fred Glover and his players
were not seeing eye to eye. After a 5-2 loss to Vancouver that was so
sloppy Hugh McDonald of the *San Mateo Times* suggested "the three
stars should be the referee and two linesmen," Glover denied he was
having any problems with his players. One anonymous Seal, however,
admitted, "There sure are problems. We're just playing out the string.
It isn't right. Some of the fellows just don't bother going after the puck.
It isn't fair to Gilles. . . . When someone doesn't pick up the man or
the puck, there's another shot blasted at Meloche. And he's one guy
who hasn't quit."[64]

A few nights later, with just 1:20 left to play in a 5-5 tie with Pittsburgh, Hilliard Graves was caught with an illegal curve in his stick.
The Penguins did not score on the resulting power play, but the penalty took away the Seals' chance at scoring the game-winning goal.
Glover was none too impressed with Graves. "He's been warned,"

he said after the game. "So have the rest of them." Graves was fined $200 but nonchalantly responded, "It's deductible."[65]

By this point several players were ready to pack it in. Joe Starkey recalled an interesting interview he conducted with Walt McKechnie that rendered the broadcaster speechless:

I was a rookie broadcaster. It was near the end of the first season. The Seals were in total chaos; they were a horrible team. Everybody hated Finley. Nobody knew what was going to happen next, and the night in St. Louis for the pregame show, live, when I asked Walt McKechnie how does he get through the last few weeks of the season when the team has been eliminated from the playoffs, he simply said, "Why would I even want to do that?" He said, "If I even had a choice, I would go home tomorrow. I would just as soon the season ended, I'm fed up, and I would just as soon get out of here." So, where do you go from there, folks?

As the season wound down, another anonymous Seal went on a venomous rant when interviewed by the *Oakland Tribune*'s Ed Levitt:

This is the worst run club in hockey. We've had it. . . .

It sort of makes you wonder what's the use of it all. Why am I here? What did I get myself in for?

Hell, even the owner of the club, Charlie Finley, doesn't seem to be interested in what's happening to us. . . .

We haven't heard from him in months. It would have helped if he came to us and told us what the heck is going on.

The way it is now, we don't know if the club will be sold or the league will take over the franchise. It'll be great if the league does take over and runs Finley out.[66]

The journalist barely got in two sentences of his own in the entire article, but he managed to explain that half a dozen players vowed to sign with WHA clubs unless the Seals got a new owner, a new coach, and some new talent. The player's rant did not end there either:

Everybody on the team is hoping Finley gets the hell out of hockey. I think that's the prime thing. . . .

Hockey used to be fun for us. Now it's miserable. Some of the guys enjoy playing on the road better than in Oakland. This is what bugs me.

I know there are loyal hockey fans here. But they need a winning team. And they would have had one if Finley had taken the time and made the effort to try and persuade those 11 players from jumping to the other league.

But Finley is too busy with other things. That's why he's so resented on our club. We all feel he pays more attention to baseball than hockey.[67]

The player then turned his attention to Glover:

We definitely don't want Glover back lousing up things again. Fred works hard. But he's just not a good coach. He doesn't know how to coach a team.

His methods are outdated. He doesn't know how to control the club. He has yet to learn how to get the players up for a game. He can't talk to us. He finds it too tough communicating with us. And we find it too tough communicating with him. . . .

The way things are now, we go home and take out our frustration on our wives. And they're getting fed up hearing us complain.[68]

The player admitted the rest of the team had felt optimistic about the 1972–73 season despite the WHA defections. By the end of the season, however, the anonymous player had become so disenchanted he gave Glover and Finley a sort of ultimatum on behalf of his teammates.

If conditions remain as they are, anywhere from six to eight players will leave the Seals and join the new league. . . .

I don't want to see it happen. But this is our life. We've got to be practical . . . It's like falling overboard. We want somebody to rescue us.[69]

With the season all but over, the NHL announced it had offered Finley the opportunity to sell them the Seals. "It was the confrontation that had to come," said an anonymous source to the *Oakland Tribune.* "Finley was given the chance to bow out gracefully on any reasonable terms." Another highly placed league source explained, "If Charlie wants out of the league, the board is prepared to provide the way out—quietly, peacefully. It may not be to his liking, but it will be fair. If he doesn't take the offer, he faces the disastrous situation with the Seals. He can hurt himself by falling into a bad commercial position or to the point where the league will have to take action."[70]

Of course, grace was never one of Finley's best qualities, and as always, he had to make negotiations difficult. "They [the board] were even willing to listen to what he wanted," said the anonymous source, "but Charlie wouldn't commit himself. The meeting ran two hours until 10:30 when the rest of the governors came in. Finley left a half hour later." This source indicated, "When Finley told them the sale was contingent on being able to move the hockey team out of the Bay Area, that was the end of that talk."[71] The NHL had no intention of letting the Seals leave California. The league also had no intention of simply stripping Finley of his franchise. Anyone who has followed the NHL closely knows the league has rarely played hardball with misbehaving owners. Sure enough, come opening night in October 1973, Finley was still the Seals' owner. There was no "disastrous situation" to face, and the league never did "take action" against Finley. If the players had expected the league to rescue them from Finley's clutches, they were terribly disappointed.

Despite the turmoil surrounding the struggling Seals, the club finally strung together a decent stretch of games, not that it mattered much. First, Meloche recorded a 2–0 shutout against a tough Minnesota squad in the Seals' 72nd game, and then the Seals won four in a row against Toronto, Detroit, and Los Angeles (twice) to close out the schedule.

As usual, the average person had enough fingers and toes to count the Seals' total wins. The club slumped to 16-46-16 and finished last in the West. The Seals' putridness even seeped down to their minor-league affiliate; the Columbus Golden Seals finished with a 10-62-2 record, dead last in the International Hockey League, and scored just 177 goals, which was 80 fewer than the next most impotent team. Their goals against average was a gaudy 5.31. The Seals' cupboard was completely bare, since most of the players who should have played in Columbus were playing in Oakland due to the WHA raids.

Although the Seals regressed badly in their quest to become a Stanley Cup contender, there were still a few bright spots. The Johnston-McKechnie-Patrick line led the club in most offensive categories. McKechnie led everyone with a career-high 54 points, while Johnston scored 28 goals to lead the Seals and established himself as one of the premier left wings in the league. At one time, Johnston was on pace for over 40 goals, but he slipped in the second half due in part to a broken jaw he suffered in January. He missed a few games as a result, was forced to wear a protective mask over the damaged area, and ended up having to suck his meals through a straw, causing his body to weaken considerably. Patrick earned the Seals' Unsung Hero award at the end of the schedule. The right winger contributed 20 goals and finished fourth in team scoring with 42 points. Reggie Leach also potted 23 goals to give the team's second line a spark. "Kids like Leach, who's only 23, give us good reason to feel optimistic about the future," said Glover, "and I might add that getting him makes up for at least one of the draft choices this club dealt away in the past."[72]

To fill out the roster, the Seals had to play rookies who normally would have spent time in the minors. Playing on a line with Pete Laframboise (16 goals, 25 assists) and Stan Weir (15 goals, 24 assists), Hil Graves led all Seals rookies with 27 goals and 52 points and was the club's candidate for the Calder Trophy. Graves quickly became known around the league as a pugnacious, irritating little punk.

The talent was there; it was the team's depth that was atrocious. Glover commented:

We think we can do a lot better up front in 1973–74. And we expect we'll be free of the injuries which kept such players as Ivan Boldirev,

Gary Croteau, Stan Gilbertson and Bob Stewart out of the lineup for extended periods. . . .

Beyond that we're a young club. Kids like Hilliard Graves and Stan Weir are sure to improve now that they've been around for a while.[73]

Glover was quick to note: "Our problem is still on defence. We gave up 323 goals [this] season, which is far too many, and you can't fault our goalkeeping. Gilles Meloche is outstanding."[74] Meloche was so outstanding he won the Larriburu Brothers Trophy as team MVP despite a 12-32-14 record and just one shutout. Meloche faced far more shots than should have been legally allowed. During one personal six-game stretch in January and February, Meloche faced totals of 42, 58, 51, 39, and 54 shots. Overall, he faced 40 or more shots fourteen times. With the departures of Bert Marshall and Dick Redmond, the only defenseman with more than three full seasons of NHL experience was Rick Smith. Darryl Maggs and Bobby Stewart had but two. Ted McAneeley had an adequate offensive touch, but he had just this one season under his belt. Terry Murray, the number six defenseman, had only twenty-three games of experience. Marshall Johnston also had experience and played well defensively, finishing with a plus/minus of -2 (most of his teammates finished -20 or worse), but since the club often found itself with holes at certain forward positions, Johnston was busy up front. If Meloche could see a light at the end of the tunnel, he must have been looking through a telescope. It was going to be a rough go if the Seals didn't do something soon to save him from his nightly trips in front of the firing squads.

Just one year earlier, experts exclaimed the Seals were the future of the NHL. Although it would have been impossible to shield all Seals players from the WHA's offers, the team's complete dismantling could have been avoided. Stan Gilbertson wondered how many defectors the Seals could have signed. "I understand it was a matter of only a few thousand dollars in some cases," he said in December 1972 and then suggested he "could go around the locker room and collect a few thousand from our players now if we knew it would mean having a good team."[75] Now it was too late; the damage was done. With no first-round picks at the amateur draft once again, and not enough talent on the roster to make a big splash in the summer trade market, the Seals would have no choice but to continue aboard their sinking ship.

8 BIG HATS, NO CATTLE, 1973–1974

When Fred Glover first arrived in Oakland in 1968, he led the Seals to a second-place finish and a playoff appearance. He was even named the *Hockey News* Coach of the Year. Glover's second go-around was not nearly as successful. When Glover returned to the Seals' bench in 1972, it seemed as though the game had passed him by. Players had once let slide the fact that Glover liked to scrimmage with them during practices, but this was no longer acceptable. By the end of the 1972–73 season, there were rumblings players were not happy with Glover's coaching methods. When Glover was asked if it was true some of his players were displeased with him, the still-interim coach said it was "all a lot of bunk."[1]

The following season, the dressing room environment became so sour that players barely paid any attention to Glover. In midseason, Joey Johnston dropped a bomb on a Montreal writer, in what was thought to be an off-the-record chat: "Glover doesn't say anything to a lot of the younger guys who need coaching. They're probably sailing along thinking they're doing everything right." Glover was unquestionably the busiest man in the NHL, holding down the positions of coach, general manager, and executive vice president, but Walt McKechnie put it simply: "It's [Glover's] fault for letting it happen. That's the way everyone on the team feels."[2] According to McKechnie, several players "were not pleased" with the coaching staff: "We had a team meeting and Charlie Finley flew in from Chicago. One player spoke up and voiced the opinion of the team. Charlie Finley listened carefully and then politely responded, 'If you don't like my fuckin' coach, you can get off my fuckin' team.'"[3]

Everything came to a head in December 1973 when Glover had a disagreement with some of his players at a Long Island hotel. A midnight curfew had been set for the entire team. One night Walt McKechnie, Rick Kessell, and Stan Gilbertson decided to have a drink at the hotel bar around midnight, which they believed was within their rights. After all, they had been at a restaurant just across the street earlier in the evening but had been responsible enough to get back to the hotel before curfew. Glover, however, was not impressed by his players' attempts at punctuality, and he got into a physical altercation with McKechnie.

"I think we were making fools of ourselves rolling around on the floor," Gilbertson said of the incident. "I tried to talk to Fred afterwards and he said to tell Walt 'Next time I'll put the boots to him.'" Kessell said he "didn't contribute much to what happened. I just stayed with the crew. I've seen stranger things happen . . . but not on this team. . . . It's the exception, not the rule when the executive vice-president, general manager, coach and whatever other titles he has rolls around the floor with a player. It was a stupid dispute: we thought it was one time and it was another." Gilbertson had a simple explanation for the entire incident: "When you're losing games like we do, the tension builds up. These things are bound to happen."[4]

Most owners faced with such an embarrassing situation would probably turn a cartoonish red and angrily smack the sports section of their morning paper against the desk, but not Finley, because by this point he had lost all interest in the Seals. Glover had a frank take on the rumor that he and Finley frequently kept in contact: "That's a bunch of baloney," Glover retorted. "He doesn't call me all the time. Maybe he calls his baseball men, but he doesn't call me."[5] As a result, players became even more disillusioned. "The way Finley has run this club," said an anonymous player, "you would think he didn't care what happened to the franchise or the players."[6]

Several players declared their intentions to jump to the WHA if something wasn't done to make the Seals competitive. Over the summer, Meloche weighed his options: "It's been a long year. I've missed all the good players and friends who left. I don't get down about defeats to the degree I'm not willing to work toward helping them develop a winner here, but I have to have hope and I have to be treated right. . . . I've been offered more from teams like Minnesota and Alberta and I'm tempted." Meloche was not alone in considering defecting. "It's tough to get up for games when you have little hope of winning," said Hil Graves. "A young player has to look for a secure future and things are unhappy and uncertain around here. The WHA's Winnipeg team made me a good offer and I'm interested."[7] Faced with the possibility of another mass exodus, Finley did something he had never done as Seals owner: he located a crowbar and pried open his wallet. Gilles Meloche, Reggie Leach, Walt McKechnie, Joey Johnston, Bobby Stewart, and Craig Patrick were all signed to lucrative contracts assuring their stay in Oakland for years to come.

While the Seals' forward lines and goaltending looked solid, the defense, which had allowed a whopping 323 goals, was a mess. It became even more frightening once the WHA signed Rick Smith and Darryl Maggs. "I could see the direction the club was heading in—and it was not up," Smith explained. "The WHA offered me $100,000. Charlie Finley's offer was $60,000. The year before, I had made $50,000."[8] According to fan John Bonasera, Smith was not particularly happy in Oakland:

Rick Smith was never a popular player, he was never a much-liked player where the fans are concerned. He went about and did his work, but he was not colorful, he wasn't very good, and he wasn't happy to be in Oakland and didn't mind telling people that, and so it got to the point where people didn't like Rick Smith. . . . One day, after a particularly small crowd was yelling at him—and he could obviously hear what they were saying—I've never seen a player turn to the crowd and flip 'em the bird . . . but Rick Smith has that distinction.

While Maggs was more offensively gifted than Smith, he did not mesh well with his teammates. "He had all kinds of talent but no work ethic," said Graves. "It was hard, mentally, to play for the Seals. He played some great games but he made a lot of mistakes, too. I think he gave up at the end of his time here." Some players believed Maggs was more interested in extracurricular activities than goals and assists. "Darryl was a good player and he could carry the puck, but he was a playboy," recalled Glover. "I think he slept in his van for months." Some players claimed Maggs used to practice his golf swing in the dressing room.[9]

Ray McKay was acquired from Buffalo at the intra-league draft to help replace Smith and Maggs. "We're mighty fortunate that McKay happened to be available," said Glover. "Not only is he perhaps the best defenceman outside the NHL. He's also got a lot of NHL experience, because he'd seen a lot of action with Chicago."[10] One would think that "a lot of NHL experience" meant a few hundred games, but apparently it meant sixty-eight games spread out over five seasons. McKay was a solid stay-at-home defenseman, but his offensive prowess was nothing to write home about. Just to give an idea of how pitiful the Seals' defense was in the offensive zone, McKay wound up tied for second with just 2 goals while the leader, Ted McAneeley, scored a whopping four times. In all, the Seals' defensemen would score a grand total of 12 goals.

To help fill out the blue line, Brent Meeke, Barry Cummins, and Paul Shakes, none of whom were household names, were added to the roster. Add these guys to the already unspectacular cast of McKay, McAneeley, Stewart, Johnston, and Murray, and you had the California Golden Seals' next-to-last line of defense. It seemed the only qualification a Seals defenseman needed at the time was a last name that started with *S* or *M*. For poor Gilles Meloche and Marv Edwards it was more than a coincidence that California's *S&M* defense would cause them much pain and suffering throughout the season.

The focus of the California offense sat squarely on the shoulders of the Johnston-McKechnie-Patrick line, which had contributed 64 goals and 145 points in 1972–73. "We are confident that the three of them will make significant contributions to the club," Glover said. "There's no doubt in my mind that they will improve on their 1972–73 records and that they will make a big difference in our playing record this season." Before getting into that physical altercation with Glover later in the season, McKechnie had made a great impression on his coach. "He's shooting more this year," the coach beamed. "Walt is an excellent playmaker and at training camp he showed a very strong improvement and much more mature attitude. I expect him to be a solid team leader."[11]

Big things were also expected of Joey Johnston, the team's 5'10", 180-pound sparkplug. He came to training camp fully recovered from his broken jaw and had every intention of cracking the 30-goal barrier this time around. In an interview with the *Hockey News* in October 1973 Johnston said he believed he and his teammates would exceed expectations: "All together it might appear to be a very gloomy scene for us, but I wouldn't be surprised to see our club in the playoffs." Johnston believed the problems that had plagued the club a year ago were a thing of the past. "We never really had a chance to put ourselves in the race after nine of our players jumped to the WHA a year ago. This time it's different. We have most of the same players back and they seem to be quite satisfied with their contracts. We've got the players who can score enough goals to win games in the NHL but we will have to work at playing the game much tighter than we did last season."[12]

Although youngsters like Johnston, Graves, McKechnie, and Leach had shown promise, most fans and hockey experts figured there was little chance the club would be playing meaningful hockey come April. Thirteen of eighteen *Hockey News* contributors predicted California would finish last in the West. Four others predicted they would finish seventh, while one writer generously predicted a sixth-place finish. The *Toronto Star*'s Jim Proudfoot summed it up best in his annual *Pro Hockey* publication. Proudfoot used only one word to describe the team's weaknesses: "everywhere." By comparison, the New York Islanders, the sad-sack expansionists who had won all of twelve games the previous year, received a more uplifting comment: "need help at all positions." "Help" sounded optimistic; "everywhere" just sounded hopeless. Furthermore, Proudfoot predicted the Seals would finish "last again," as though the "loser" label had become tattooed to the foreheads of the California players. The Islanders, on the other hand, were simply expected to finish "last."[13]

The gloomy forecasts did not concern Glover. "We have a fine group of young players who are capable of playing winning hockey," he said. "All we have to do is get the players thinking on the right track and get them obsessed with a winning complex."[14] If one believed Glover, the 16-win Seals were as good as guaranteed to be a contender. He also felt confident a permanent coach would be in place by September, but when training camp rolled around, the three-headed hydra was still calling the shots behind the bench.

In the preseason, the Seals finished with a solid 2-2-2 record, including an impressive 8-2 drubbing of the Pittsburgh Penguins. Following the big win, one Seal jubilantly exclaimed, "That was a hell of a season we had tonight."[15] For once the players were starting the season on a positive note.

The regular season started on Wednesday, October 10, 1973, with the St. Louis Blues paying a visit to the Coliseum. Just twenty seconds into the game, it looked like 1972–73 was going to repeat itself. Lou Angotti put the Blues up 1-0, but thanks to goals by Joey Johnston and Gary Croteau in the final two periods, the Seals managed to come away with a 2-1 victory. "There wasn't anything specific about our game that I liked, we just played an overall good game," said Glover. "For a change, we didn't let the other team push us around."[16]

It was extremely important to the players to get off to a good start. The previous year, the club had dug itself into a deep hole early on and was never able to pull itself out. How important was it to get off to a fast start this time? "It really feels like winning the Stanley Cup," said Croteau. "I don't think it's a carry over from last year's team. I think it's the feeling that we had in training camp because everyone worked so hard. It was much different than last year."[17] Two nights later, the Chicago Black Hawks came to town, and Joey Johnston picked up another goal and 2 assists, leading California to a 3-2 win. After this match the Seals vaulted into first place in the West for the first time in four years. "Everyone brought a new attitude to training camp this year," said Patrick. "Our team was a real joke last year and all the players knew it. We are determined not to let the same thing happen to us this season. We all came here to win."[18]

The 1972–73 season had been an unmitigated disaster from all perspectives. The constant bickering and childish name-calling between Finley and Young had been a huge distraction, and it showed in the standings. The Seals' new plan was to stay positive on and off the ice and to establish a winning attitude, but those were both Herculean tasks. Most players on the roster had not experienced winning since their junior days.

For years, the Seals had been a fountain of negativity, but in 1973 a number of players took matters into their own hands and joined a positive-thinking program designed to turn losers into contenders. The sessions were given by instructors (and Seals fans) Gary Gates and Ron Noble of the San Francisco chapter of a company called Mind Dynamics, Inc. Gates summarized his philosophy this way: "We become what we think about. Before a person can do anything physically, that person has to see it being done in his mind." Gates believed that 80 percent of a player's performance was based on his mental attitude: "It has to do with concentrating and can also be used to heal the body. A person can help heal his body by instructing his mind to help do it." Gary Croteau wholeheartedly agreed with Gates. He had suffered a leg injury the year before and started attending sessions around that time: "That's when I started in Mind Dynamics and it was a big help to me and still is."[19] Croteau was joined at sessions by Craig Patrick, Ivan Boldirev, Morris Mott, and Ted McAneeley.

Mind Dynamics became necessary for players like Boldirev, who was so despondent he started to question his career choice. "I was very depressed and everything was getting under my skin," Boldirev said later in the season. "It was about the second week of the season and it really was tough playing all the time and losing. Everywhere we went, we would always get rapped by the newspapers. I really thought about quitting the game. I think a lot of us on the team did."[20]

For a while, the negative attitude that had once poisoned the Seals' dressing room disappeared as the club reeled off impressive wins over St. Louis and Chicago to start the season. Unfortunately, Cinderella's carriage transformed back into a pumpkin before long. The Seals lost their next three games, including an 11–2 thrashing at the hands of the Detroit Red Wings. "The closest word to how we felt is embarrassed," said Joey Johnston.[21]

The Seals got their revenge the following game in Oakland, outshooting the Wings 40–19 and outscoring them, 7–3. Croteau scored a hat trick in this, his two hundredth game with the club. His linemates, Boldirev and Graves, each had a goal and 2 assists. "I don't think I've ever seen Boldirev skate like that since he came here," said Glover.

Boldirev later remarked, "You ain't seen nothing, yet."[22] Joey Johnston also scored, raising his season total to 6 and becoming the first Seal to score a goal in six consecutive games. The streak ended two days later against Atlanta when Johnston picked up only an assist, which still extended his points streak to seven games, a run that would come to an end in game number eight.

With 3 wins and 3 losses in their first 6 games, the Seals seemed to be turning a corner and developing a bit of a winning attitude. After 18 games, the Seals' record stood at 5-12-1, which was not great, but the previous year they hadn't won their fifth until game number 32. Excluding the 11–2 loss to Detroit, the rickety defense had held up well. Furthermore, Johnston, Croteau, McKechnie, and Boldirev had all looked good to that point, but the Seals were dealt a major blow in a late November practice when Reggie Leach accidentally skated over Gilles Meloche's hand. Explained the *Oakland Tribune*'s John Porter:

> Leach made one last wheelie and came zooming down left wing with the puck. He made a fake, then cut in front of the goal mouth as Meloche stepped full-length to stop the shot.
>
> Gilles' glove on the stick hand slid off and Reggie's left skate zipped across the back of the goalie's hand. The tendon in the baby finger was cut cleanly and the one next to it partially.[23]

Meloche, of course, being the affable team player he was, never blamed Leach for what happened. "Gilles told me after it happened that it was his fault," Leach said, "[but] I know it wasn't. It was a freak thing to happen. I heard the whistle, but I made just one more turn. The next thing I know, Gilles is bleeding."[24]

When Marv Edwards was told he would be the Seals' new number one goaltender for at least the next two months, he took it in stride. "I went home right away," he said. "It may affect some goalies differently to find out they must start in a situation like that, but for a number of years I used to be the No. 1 guy and I was ready."[25]

The Seals won their first game without Meloche, but things would get much tougher afterward. The one thing the Seals definitely did not need was a meeting with the Philadelphia Flyers. Over the last few years the Flyers had developed into the most fearsome team in professional sports. Their roster was loaded with wrestling monikers like Dave "The Hammer" Schultz, Don "The Bird" Saleski, Bob "Mad Dog/Hound Dog/Kamikaze" Kelly, and Andre "Moose" Dupont. Even the team's nickname, The Broad Street Bullies, sounded like a sadistic stable conjured up by Vince McMahon. To add even more legend to the Flyers, the dreaded "Philadelphia Flu" had started making the rounds in various NHL cities around this time. Perfectly healthy players often claimed to be feeling ill the day of a game with the Flyers, especially those played in Philadelphia, hoping they could delay their next meeting with the Bullies by a few more weeks.

During the 1973–74 season, an intense animosity evolved between the Seals and Flyers even though, from that moment on, the two clubs would always sit at polar opposites of the standings. Less likely enemies you could not find; the Flyers averaged over 20 penalty minutes per game, while the Seals averaged about 8 or 9 minutes. According to the *Drop Your Gloves* website, the Flyers were involved in 108 fights in 1973–74, and the Seals just 25, but every now and then someone in the California dressing room would poke the Bullies in the chest. One Seal who was never afraid of the Flyers was Hilliard Graves. He and the notorious Dave Schultz developed a heated feud, but surprisingly it was Graves who used to come out on top when they went toe-to-toe. "He had a hip check that would just send people flying," remembered fan Dick Pantages, "and he was feisty. . . . I think he gave [Schultz] the good old hip check once, and [he] never forgot about it." Graves was never one to rack up tons of penalties, but "he fought Dave Schultz every time we played Philadelphia," said Stan Weir. "He always held his own." Fred Glover believed Graves "could beat up Dave Schultz any day of the week. . . . They started Schultz so I started Graves and Graves would go out and beat the shit out of [Schultz]. There were fights galore and we needed a police escort to get to our hotel. I told the linesman and the referee, 'Thank God you were here.'"[26]

On January 24, a day before the Seals' final game with Philadelphia that season, Graves told the Flyers it was on! "I'm not afraid of him," he said, referring to Dave Schultz, "I beat him twice before and I'm ready to do it again if I have to." Them's fightin' words, all right, but

Graves didn't stop there. "Philadelphia likes to run around against us, but they don't play that way against Boston," he claimed. "We've beaten the Bruins more than they have in the last four years."[27] Graves clearly did his homework. From October 1969 to January 1974 the Flyers went a dismal 0-21-4 versus Boston, but the Seals were surprisingly better at 3-21-2 over that span.

McKechnie recalled his reaction to Graves's quotes for Ross Brewitt's book *Into the Empty Net*:

> Hell, they were the tough guys, we were just the punching bags. At practice one of the boys said let's just play the game, don't start any shit, and get it over with. Next day Hilliard Graves was quoted in the paper saying something like, "If they wanna get tough, they know where they can find me."
>
> That night, before the game, in comes Laframboise . . . big afro hair cut, big moustache, big trenchcoat, he really looked like a tough guy should, you know, 6'2", rangy, walked like a goddamn farmer. At the time he was on a line with Graves and Stan Weir. You could see he was pissed off, never even took off his coat, just sat down, took out the paper, already turned to the offending article, smacked it with a backhand, and said, "Can you fuckin' believe this shit? They got the Hound, the Bird, and the Hammer." . . . Glancing up he pointed at himself and his linemates. "And whatta we got? We got Big Mouth and the Two Chickens."[28]

When Graves threw down the gauntlet on January 24, it was the culmination of a very nasty season series between the two clubs. On December 2 the Flyers led 2–1 in the second period when the Seals' Barry Cummins, who, in just his fifth NHL game, blew his stack while subbing for an injured Terry Murray. Pugnacious Flyer captain Bobby Clarke accidentally struck Cummins under the eye with his stick, and the rookie snapped. He followed Clarke to the Philly bench and swung his stick at the Flyer's head, creating an eighteen-stitch gash. "I never saw the stick coming," said Clarke. "When it hit, I could see the blood and felt dizzy, but I didn't think I was hurt bad."[29]

Bill Flett immediately charged at Cummins. "The law, according to the Flyers," explained Dave Schultz, "was that anyone who hit Clarkie paid for it—no ifs, ands, or buts."[30] Before long Bob Kelly joined the ruckus, and so did the entire Seals bench. Cummins was submerged under a pile of Flyers. He eventually reappeared bloodied and was taken to the dressing room for repairs. Cummins received a game misconduct, a $300 fine, and a three-game suspension, while Kelly and Flett also got misconducts for leaving the bench. Graves and Schultz needled each other for ten minutes following Cummins's infraction. The violence did not abate, so the referee ejected Graves and Schultz, as well as the Flyers' Don Saleski and Ed Van Impe. Each was fined $100 afterward.

Clarke, the catalyst of the brouhaha, was not badly hurt and returned to lead his team to a 5–1 victory. Cummins was quick to apologize for his actions: "Clarke had cut me under the eye with his stick. I was mad and didn't have time to think. It was an impulse action that I regretted a second after it happened. I'm sorry—you always are when you hurt somebody." The next day, Cummins called Clarke from Oakland, having got his phone number from the *Philadelphia Daily News.* "He was really sick about what happened," said Clarke. "It takes a little courage to make a call like that."[31] Clarke accepted Cummins's apology, but the other Flyers involved in the brawl were not in a particularly forgiving mood. "I don't care what happened," exclaimed Flett, "you don't hit a guy over the head with a two-hander. . . . It's too easy to kill somebody." Kelly also added after the game: "It's an unwritten rule you don't hit anybody over the head. . . . If they use him against us again, you can bet there will be a repeat."[32] Brawls between the Seals and Flyers became the norm over the next few years.

More bad news occurred on December 5 when Marv Edwards twisted his left knee in a 3–3 tie with Atlanta. After a Chuck Arnason goal in the latter stages of the second period, the California goaltender appeared shaken, but he finished the period. Rookie Ted Tucker replaced Edwards at the start of the third period, finished the game, and earned the tie after Joey Johnston scored his 11th goal at 11:58. Tucker started in goal for the Seals on December 7, a 4–3 victory over

Pittsburgh, but he was replaced during the contest by journeyman Bob Champoux, who would take over as the Seals' number one goalie until Meloche returned. Edwards would be out three months.

With the Seals sitting at 7-16-2, and just 4 points out of fifth place, the wheels finally fell completely off the wagon. Both the New York Rangers and the New York Islanders took turns beating up on the depleted Seals before Pittsburgh blew them out 9-1 on December 12. Champoux could not stop the surging Pens, as they fired 5 goals past him in the second period alone.

Another blowout was expected when the Montreal Canadiens visited Oakland on December 14. A season-high 7,676 fans watched Montreal build a 2-0 lead in the second period, but the Seals refused to give up. McKechnie and Leach each picked up a goal and an assist to tie the game. Despite the forecast of failure, the Californians surprised the Habs with a 2-2 tie with practically the same lineup as in the Pittsburgh debacle. Glover was as baffled as anyone about his Seals' surprising effort: "If I could explain it, I'd bottle it," he said.[33]

As New Year's Day came and went, it became obvious the efforts to instill a positive attitude in the Seals' players had been for naught. The team lacked passion and aggression, and it showed in the standings. The *San Mateo Times*'s Hugh McDonald mused that the team Glover believed "was a bunch of tigers at the first of the season" had become "a pretty tame bunch of pussycats whom other teams scorned for their lack of hitting." Glover believed modern hockey players had become so spoiled and lazy that the sport was going to enter a very dark period within five years. He also boasted he could produce a better result than many of his players, who he believed "only use[d] their heads to grow long hair."[34]

Barry Cummins remembered how most of his new teammates had seemingly given up, but he had a theory that explained why the Seals, despite all their talent, kept losing. "It was a defeatist attitude," he said. "Everybody was trying but the difference between a winning team and a losing team is mostly attitude. You get on a roll when you are winning and everything works. The opposite is also true—when you start losing, nothing works. It's a snowball effect. It wears on you subconsciously. You're afraid to do something because you're afraid it will work out wrong. Hockey is a fast game—you have to anticipate or cheat a little. When you're losing, you're afraid to take that chance."[35]

Walt McKechnie, for one, had reached the end of his rope. A year earlier, with the Seals sitting in last place, McKechnie had let loose on rookie broadcaster Joe Starkey, stating he was sick and tired of losing. Fast forward to an early 1974 road trip when McKechnie suffered a pulled groin muscle that was expected to keep him out of action five weeks. McKechnie shot down the prognosis and predicted, "I won't be playing again this year." Even though he had scored 13 goals and 17 assists at that point, which put him among the team leaders in both categories, he was openly critical of himself. "I feel I can play for other teams in the league and that I can make the Seals," he admitted, "But I don't feel I have had a good year. I just haven't felt like playing," he said.[36]

Leach also made it clear he was hoping for a one-way ticket out of town. "I wouldn't mind going," he said. "If I got a phone call this afternoon I'd be packed and gone tonight." There were whispers the Flyers wanted to reunite Leach with Bobby Clarke, his old junior linemate in Flin Flon, Manitoba. In 1967–68 the duo had scored a whopping 137 goals between them. "With Leach on my line," Clarke said, "we'd really go. Just watch us." Leach was playing his cards close to his vest, not wanting to seem too eager about going to Philadelphia. "It doesn't make any difference to me which way I go," he said. Like McKechnie, he just wanted out, but so did the rest of the team. "I don't know," Leach said. "This is the way I feel. What else can I say?"[37] Over the last two months of the season McKechnie and Leach seemed to try making themselves look as attractive as possible to other teams; both stars finished the year on torrid scoring streaks.

Even Glover seemed to have thrown in the towel. As the Seals were preparing for a game against the Rangers, a reporter asked the coach what his game plan was. "We plan to show up," Glover replied.[38] The frustration of wearing multiple hats on a team going nowhere was taking its toll on Glover, and people around the league could see it. In February, sad-sack Vancouver was visiting Oakland when Glover spoke with newly appointed Canucks coach and general manager Phil

Maloney. "Congratulations, Phil. I think—or condolences," Glover said wryly. "I know what you mean, Fred," Maloney replied, sympathizing with his counterpart. "Maybe we should both take poison."[39] Just a year earlier, after the Seals had been routed 7-0 by the Philadelphia Flyers, Glover joked, "I think I'll take a run in my car at a bridge. If I survive that, I'll know it's all right to take this team on the road."[40] Glover needn't consider suicide; his time with the Seals was drawing to a close.

The Seals ended 1973 on an eleven-game winless streak. After 52 games, the team was a horrible 9-36-8 and a hopeless mess from top to bottom. January was a difficult month, even by Seals standards. There was a 9-4 loss to Chicago on January 6, a game in which Reggie Leach's hat trick was overshadowed by Dennis Hull's own 3 goals. Hull's comments after the game summed up the Seals perfectly. "That's a team that has problems," he said. "It's no big deal to score three against them. Anybody could do it. Their goalie gets no help at all." Poor Bob Champoux, who tried his best to hold down the crumbling fort while Meloche and Edwards nursed their injuries, was not accustomed to such a heavy workload. "They were playing loose, just looking for the breaks," Hull continued. "Their defensemen weren't taking anybody out. After about the middle of the second period that became contagious and we found ourselves playing that way too."[41]

On January 13 the Seals held a 2-1 lead over the New York Rangers after two periods, but in the last fifteen minutes of the game the Rangers scored five times and won, 7-2. The ice at the Coliseum was in poor condition due to the fact the thermostat on the automatic equipment was set ten degrees higher than normal, and no maintenance person was around to fix the issue. The Zamboni was brought out in the third period to mop up the puddles and shave the ice, but in the end the Seals would have been as successful had they just used galoshes to get around. Champoux was given no help at all as the Rangers outshot the sluggish Seals 15-3 in the third period, and 36-18 overall. Glover blamed the officials, but according to an LA Kings scout sitting in the stands, "That Seals' defense is slow and awful."[42]

FIG. 30. LA's Leo Labine is thwarted by Seals goalie Jim McLeod as Moe Mantha (8) and Jean-Marc Picard (6) come in to help. Photo by Bob Warren, courtesy of San Francisco History Center, San Francisco Public Library.

FIG. 31. The Seals celebrate their 1964 Patrick Cup championship at City Hall with Mayor John Shelley (left). Photo by Eddie Murphy, courtesy of San Francisco History Center, San Francisco Public Library.

FIG. 32. The 1968–69 Seals, the best team in franchise history. Photo by J. D. McCarthy, courtesy of Doug McLatchy.

FIG. 33. Gary Smith, circa 1969–70. "Suitcase" holds the franchise records for highest winning percentage (.382), highest save percentage (.900), and most wins in a season (22). He is the only Seals goaltender to finish a season with a winning record (22-20-7 in 1968–69) Photo by J. D. McCarthy, courtesy of Doug McLatchy.

FIG. 34. Hilliard Graves scored 27 goals and 52 points in his rookie season of 1972–73 and was the Seals' nominee for the Calder Trophy. Photo by J. D. McCarthy, courtesy of Doug McLatchy.

FIG. 35. When captain Joey Johnston was traded to Chicago in the summer of 1975, he was the franchise's all-time leader in goals (84) and points (185). Photo by J. D. McCarthy, courtesy of Doug McLatchy.

FIG. 36. As a rookie, Dave "The Wrecker" Hrechkosy led the Seals with 29 goals in 1974–75. Photo by J. D. McCarthy, courtesy of Doug McLatchy.

FIG. 37. Playing goal for the Seals sometimes felt like the loneliest job in the world. Photo by Elliot Lowe.

FIG. 38. Gilles Meloche dives on the puck as Chicago's Pit Martin and Dennis Hull go for the rebound. Jim Pappin tries to give his goalie a hand. Photo by Elliot Lowe.

FIG. 39. Ralph Klassen tries to stuff the puck past Boston's Gilles Gilbert. Photo by Elliot Lowe.

FIG. 40. Charlie Simmer (17) carries the puck out of the Seals' zone as Vancouver's Mike Walton (4) looks on in the Seals' penultimate game, a 5–0 loss, before moving to Cleveland. Photo by Elliot Lowe.

FIG. 41. J. P. Parise stretches in the dressing room. Behind him are Walt McKechnie (8) and Kris Manery (24). Photo source: Dennis Turchek.

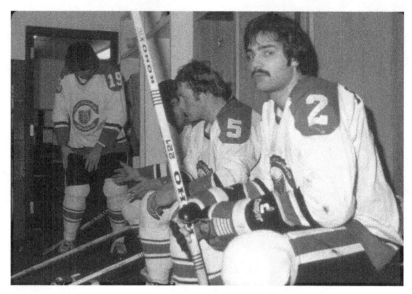

FIG. 42. Rick Hampton (2), Greg Smith (5), Jean Potvin, and John Baby (19) in the dressing room waiting to get back on the ice. Photo source: Dennis Turchek.

FIG. 43. Jeff Allan flashes the classic hockey player smile. He would play just four NHL games, all with Cleveland. Photo source: Dennis Turchek.

FIG. 44. The Holy Grail of Seals memorabilia: Scott Ruffell pilfered this Oakland Seals flag that once hung from the Coliseum's scoreboard by hiding it under his shirt. Photo courtesy of Rich Reilley.

FIG. 45. Seals vs. Minnesota North Stars, February 18, 1976. The Seals won, 6–3. Photo by Elliot Lowe.

FIG. 46. Seals puck, circa late 1960s. Photo courtesy of Peterborough Sports Hall of Fame.

As the season progressed, the team's sad situation became more and more laughable. The *Oakland Tribune* hinted that several players may not have been ready to play one night in St. Louis. "Are we all here?" asked one player as the bus was rolling up to the hotel to take the Seals to the arena. "You'd better check the bar. It's last call of [*sic*] alcohol," responded another player. The Seals ended up losing the contest 6–4, their 22nd loss (and 18th straight) in 23 road games. "It's the first time in my life that I'm happy to sit on the bench. I'd rather do that than go out and embarrass myself," said Pete Laframboise, who had seen his numbers and ice time dwindle since October. "You can go on all day knocking this team. It's just unbelievable," Laframboise continued. "You have lines and pairs of defensemen going out saying 'Let's play our best,' but as far as playing as a team . . ." Laframboise gave up in midsentence and simply shook his head.[43]

The Seals' poor goaltenders could have applied for sainthood or martyrdom, so thankless was their lot in life. "Playing goal for the Seals must hold all the fascination of walking across Niagara Falls blindfolded on a wire," wrote Geoffrey Fisher in the *Hockey News*. "The goaltender who gets the assignment to play for the Seals must feel about the same as the condemned man shuffling off to the firing squad."[44]

The team lacked passion and aggression. "Watch how many times we get beat one-on-one coming out of the corner," said McKechnie. "This is a different team on the road." The Blues' Barclay Plager believed he understood why the Seals were so bad. "Their problems obviously go deeper than the ownership," he said. "They have little enough to play for at home and nothing to play for on the road. Why should they play rough and get hurt?"[45] How bad were the Seals on the road? "The best thing that could happen to the Seals is that the fuel shortage would become so severe they would be forced to cancel the remainder of their road schedule," mused Geoffrey Fisher.[46]

Players had finally had enough of living under Finley's tight fists and putting up with Glover's increasingly sour demeanor. Fisher painted a depressing picture in an early February *Hockey News* article: "[Glover's] teams play now as if they were not taught a system. The players play individually. They pay no attention to the owner. They laugh bitter little laughs when you ask them about their owner. 'Yeah, I've met him,' Ivan Boldirev laughs bitterly. . . . 'I was told we'd have a new owner who cared about the club and we'd build up to a big league level. It hasn't happened. I don't know if I made a mistake [refusing offers from the WHA]. I've learned a lot playing against the top players. There's still hope the team will be sold and straightened out. Hope for tomorrow is all we have left now. We don't have much of anything today.'"[47]

As the Seals slowly trudged through the roughest patch in their history, the NHL stepped in and bought the decimated franchise from Finley. He had wanted to move the team to Indianapolis in June 1973, but the league kiboshed his plan. The fact Finley had suffered a serious heart attack in August helped speed negotiations along. Doctors strongly advised him to sell all his franchises.

Seals Booster Cathy White believes "it was the best news we had ever had. It didn't matter who bought it just so Finley was out." Finley had done irreparable damage to the franchise and had reduced it to a laughing stock. "He made us resent hockey," White said. According to the *Hockey News*, after the announcement of the club's imminent sale, "it was like the Fourth of July in January. Fans snake-danced around the building, inside and out, brandishing the newspaper headline stating 'Finley Agrees to Sell Seals.' . . . For weeks there had been signs hung from the balconies reading 'Sell Finley, Sell' and 'Sell Finley Or Else' and 'Finley, Take You'r [sic] Pucks And Go Home.'"[48]

Finley sold the team to the NHL for $6.5 million, thus ending his colorful tenure as owner of the California Golden Seals. "[It] was like Lincoln had freed the slaves. . . . If they could have voted to impeach Finley, they would have," wrote Geoffrey Fisher in the *Hockey News*.[49] Each team had contributed about $400,000 just to get rid of Finley. "Now that all the necessary paperwork has been completed," said Clarence Campbell, "our first order of business will be to screen the various applicants and to accept as soon as possible an appropriate purchaser."[50] Though attendance had dwindled in Oakland, Finley admitted he still made a profit selling the franchise. "I'm most satisfied with the price," he said, "and any time Finley can sell something and say he's satisfied, that speaks for itself."[51]

While Finley's personal and professional relationships were often strained, his hockey players, for the most part, did not dislike him personally. Then again, it's not as though he spent much time socializing with them, so it was difficult for them to develop any sort of opinion about him. Marshall Johnston, for one, never felt any ill-will toward Finley:

I've got nothing detrimental to say about Mr. Finley. We never missed a paycheck. He paid his bills. He ran his hockey team much the same as he ran the baseball team. I remember, those were the years when Oakland was winning [the] World Series, and we got prime seats for the World Series right behind the A's dugout.

He wasn't a big spender when it came to promotion, even in baseball. I mean, he had the smallest staff when it came to public relations and promotions and tickets and all. . . . And of course, hockey in California needed to be promoted. . . . I know a lot of players would disagree because when the WHA came in they wanted more money, and he wouldn't pay them, and that's why they went, but I personally don't have anything negative to say about Charlie Finley.

Despite occasional kind gestures like flying his players first class, buying players new suits, and handing out bonuses for shutouts and hat tricks, Finley will always be remembered for his role in destroying the California Golden Seals.

With Finley gone, the Seals underwent many changes. The team discarded the green-and-gold uniforms at the end of the season. There were plans to bring back radio and TV coverage, which the Seals had dropped after the 1972–73 season. Play-by-play man Joe Starkey had accepted an offer to call games for the Pittsburgh Penguins, but he would return to Oakland the following season. More importantly, the white skates were heading off to that big rink in the sky.

On a side note, while doing research for this book, I stumbled upon an old Seals Booster Club pin that someone had been trying to sell on eBay. The time to purchase the pin had expired, but I decided to email its owner anyway, thinking I had perhaps located another Booster.

Instead, I found New Yorker Greg Lamont, who, in February 1974, was on a California trip with his wife to watch the Rangers play. The Oakland game they watched was significant in Seals history in that it was the first home game after Finley had sold the club.

Lamont remembered the friendly atmosphere of the Oakland Coliseum and the warmth of the Bay Area fans. He and his wife still have fond memories of hanging out with the Booster Club, or as he called them, "real fans," as in those who sit high up in the arena and attend almost every game no matter what team comes to town. "It was a unique experience," he recalled, "because it was just a different environment. It was the exact same game, but it was sort of like you'd almost died and went to heaven, because all these people are nice and no one is like, 'Kill the bastard!' because that's the environment you grow up in [in] New York." The Booster Club made him and his wife honorary members and gave them the pin to *seal* the deal, so to speak. As a long-time Rangers fan, he explained the difference between attending a game at Madison Square Garden and attending a game at the Coliseum:

> A Ranger would hit a Seal, and it wasn't like, 'We'll kill you! We'll get you in the parking lot!' I mean, there was none of that. It was like, "Oh, okay . . ." So it was a totally friendly, very friendly crowd. That, to us, was kind of shocking. . . . Even though they lost the game, [it was] "Oh, okay, it was fun." . . . If the Rangers lost a game, the people would be piling outside, "Hey, the coach should be fired. He didn't do this . . ." Maybe because the game we went to, because Finley sold the team, they were all just happy about it, and win or lose, they were just happy that they had new ownership.

While Oakland fans may have been in the mood to party, lame duck Fred Glover probably felt relieved more than anything else that his time with the Seals was coming to an end. Fan John Bonasera attended one of Glover's last home games as coach of the Seals: "I remember being at a game, and the crowd, probably four thousand people, chanting, 'Bye bye, Freddie, bye bye, Freddie, we're glad to see you go!' Everybody was chanting and singing and telling him adios, and then literally within a day or two he resigned." In fact, the Seals' executive vice president, general manager, and coach resigned from all his positions, ridding himself of a tremendous burden. "I met with league officials yesterday afternoon and I was given the opportunity to stay with the organization," said Glover. "But I feel for the betterment of all concerned that I should bow out. The National Hockey League has given me a contractual settlement that I'm very happy with."[52]

Dependable stay-at-home defenseman Marshall Johnston retired from active duty and became the new coach. "I was tired of playing," Johnston admitted. "I was thirty-four years old . . . to be successful, I had to be prepared every game, mentally. . . . I was just a borderline player. . . . I played for some good coaches, and they approached me about coaching the team, and so I said, 'Well, why not?'" Johnston explained why, in his opinion, he was chosen to coach the Seals, rather than someone with more experience. "I think, probably, a lot of it had to do financially. . . . I was already under contract, and so I just went from a playing contract to coaching, so they didn't have to hire anybody else, there was no additional financial outlay necessary."

Make no mistake about it, the lack of money in the Seals' coffers was, as always, a huge concern. No matter who was at the top, the situation never improved. Leonard Shapiro, perhaps more than anyone else on the planet, knows firsthand what it is like doing promotions while hampered by a shoestring budget; he did so for two years in Oakland. Around January 1974 he was hired as assistant director of public relations, but he didn't start at the position until that summer. Today he is a walking, talking Seals' encyclopedia. His hands were continually tied due to the Seals' financial constraints. The Seals needed fans to make money, but it was impossible to draw fans with so little money for promotions. "My last year budget was $5,000 for advertising . . . and I blew that almost immediately in the first month of the season to try to get season ticket sales," Shapiro said, "and we very rarely had money to spend on the rest of the year to promote the team."

Shapiro and the Seals had to find more creative ways to get the word out that there was NHL hockey in the Bay Area. "We did a lot of nonprofits. . . . We were probably one of the first, if not *the* first team to do fund-raisers after our games. . . . We would sell tickets to organizations like the fire department, police department, and they would do hockey games, broomball games after the Sunday night, Sunday afternoon games, and they had to sell a hundred tickets and that brought a few dollars."

Shapiro was asked what he would have liked to do as far as promotions were concerned, and his answer explained perfectly how far behind other professional teams the Seals found themselves, mostly due to a lack of funds:

> Well, obviously stick nights, puck nights. They had done some of them in the early years when Trans-National had [the Seals]. . . . But after the WHA . . . it was mainly ticket price promotions. The second half, I believe, of the '72–'73 season, all the games were half price. . . . I wish we could have done T-shirt nights, put merchandise in the hands of the fans that would have promoted the Seals. We didn't really have the money to do that. . . . We couldn't go out and sell it to sponsors, because we didn't have enough people on the streets to sell it. I think what we're getting right down to the brass tacks of it . . . was most of the time the Seals were undercapitalized, bottom line. That is the root of all evil. You know, big hats, no cattle. That was one of Finley's lines for somebody else, but it fit our category too. We tried to wear big hats, but we had no cattle.

With Finley out of the picture the league appointed Munson Campbell as the club's new president. Former general manager Garry Young was named the Seals' new director of player personnel. He had the authority to make trades and acquire free agents, but he needed the approval of an NHL committee first. Of course, any decision Young made was influenced by how much money it would cost the Seals, and thus the league. The fact the league rehired Young lends credence to the notion he had done a good job as general manager his first time around, despite the negative publicity the Dick Redmond contract fiasco had created.

FIG. 10. Ivan "Ike" Boldirev scored 361 goals in his NHL career, including five 30-goal seasons. Topps O-Pee-Chee trading cards used courtesy of The Topps Company, Inc.

Although Young's new club had been floundering at the bottom of the West Division since November, he still saw great potential. The Seals needed, above all, players who could deliver a solid body check and occasionally drop the gloves. "We'll be putting a high priority on size and the ability to hit," Young admitted. "We've got a lot of talent on the club and a lot more on the farm club, but the road record of the Seals is a clear indication that there has been a lack of brawn to back up the play of the club."[53]

Aside from the Seals' top line, there was a decided lack of scoring everywhere else. After 55 games, All-Star Joey Johnston still led the team with an impressive 51 points, followed by Walt McKechnie's 43 and Ivan Boldirev's 39. Boldirev also scored 4 goals in an 8–6 win over St. Louis on January 9, equaling Laframboise's record set a year earlier. While Boldirev had already set career highs in goals and points, players such as Pete Laframboise, Stan Weir, and Hilliard Graves had seen decreases in production. Reggie Leach was also suffering through a season-long slump, scoring but five goals by New Year's Day.

While Leach partly blamed himself for his lack of production, he also believed Finley's lack of interest in the club had something to do with it. "I have not had the motivation I need to be at my best," he said. "If we had an owner who cared and some help at a few positions, I'm sure we would be a good hockey club. There are a lot of good hockey players with the Seals who have not played up to their ability."[54] Leach could make plays only an elite few around the league could, and yet he often found himself in slumps and lacking motivation. He could score a hat trick one night and then completely disappear the next. Joey Johnston remembers Leach as one of the best players on the Seals. "I liked him, tried to get him the puck because I know he could fire it," he said, "and if he came to play, he was dynamite." Leach wrote candidly about his time in Oakland in his 2015 autobiography, *The Riverton Rifle*:

> I have to accept some of the blame for the team's failure. In my last season there, my plus-minus record was -61. To compare, Orr led the league that season with +84. Also, I knew how to be a leader but I didn't step up. [Bobby Clarke] later told a reporter for the Montreal Gazette, "The Seals were never going anywhere and Reggie played like he was going nowhere." I'm not sure why I dropped the ball. Maybe I had lost some of my passion for the game after my experience in Boston. But that's no excuse. If I had chosen to make more of a contribution, Oakland might have been a better team. Instead, I was probably part of the problem.[55]

After Marshall Johnston took over behind the bench, Leach went on a blistering tear and finished the season with 22 goals and a career-high 46 points, giving fans a preview of what kind of special player he would soon become.

With Glover and Finley out of the picture, everyone seemed a lot happier, but that did not mean everyone was satisfied with the state of Seals' affairs. It would take years to clean up Finley's mess. Johnston, Leach, and McKechnie were all open to being traded, although none of them put a gun to Young's head. "If this club is to get out of the mess it's in, there will be some changes," McKechnie admitted. "If I was to be traded I wouldn't complain. That's part of the business we are in and there is no other way to remedy what's wrong with this club than to make changes."[56]

Fortunately, the Seals showed some improvement in Marshall Johnston's first five games behind the bench, despite a rash of injuries to many key players. Overall the players looked more confident and disciplined, but more importantly they had a game plan. Team meetings would now be held before games and practices. Players would wear team-issued sweat suits during practice instead of the assorted attire they had worn under Glover. Unlike his predecessor, Johnston would not partake in scrimmages with his players.

The first three games under Johnston were all losses: 7–3 to Pittsburgh, 7–1 to Minnesota, and 3–0 to Chicago. The fourth game, played in traditional black skates, was a close 4–3 defeat to the New York Rangers. The following game was a 2–2 tie against St. Louis. The team's attitude had begun to change since Johnston had taken over. The fundamentals, and the closer checking, would come later.

Despite baby steps in the right direction, few people expected much of a contest on March 2 between Montreal and California when the Seals ventured east to face the defending Stanley Cup champions. The Seals' record away from home at that point was 1-31-0, and Montreal rarely lost on home ice, especially to the weaker West Division clubs. But this year was different. Ken Dryden had refused to sign a new contract for that season, so he took a year off to practice law, leaving Michel Plasse, Wayne Thomas, and Michel Larocque to carry on.

Games against Montreal had always meant a great deal to Seals players, not only because several of them had grown up cheering for the Habs, but because no one expected the Seals to come out with a win. "When we went out there," remembered Bob Stewart about the March 2, 1974, game, "the comments in the paper were something like, 'We're on a winning streak and Oakland's coming to town.' They figured we were an easy win and it pumped us up real good."[57]

The Habs dominated the early part of the game, as always. Montreal had four breakaways in the first period alone, but Meloche shut the door. Just past the halfway mark of the period the Seals lost a face-off in their own end, giving Montreal control of the puck. Claude Larose scored on a rebound just in front of Meloche, aided by Ray McKay providing an unintentional screen. McKay made up for his blunder just thirty seconds later as he and Joey Johnston sent crisp passes in Reggie Leach's direction. Leach was free and clear to take a good, hard shot from the lip of the right face-off circle and tied the game 1–1.

The Canadiens quickly reminded the league's bottom feeders who they were playing by taking a 3–1 lead in the second period. Montreal dominated the Seals in every way until Hil Graves passed the puck to Boldirev standing near the Canadiens' crease, but the puck ricocheted off defenseman Guy Lapointe and dribbled past Michel Plasse for the Seals' second goal.

With California still down a goal, Graves unleashed a slap shot that hit Plasse in the face and sliced him open for twelve stitches. Plasse fell to the ice, and Weir poked in the rebound. The California goal stood despite the Habs' heavy protest. Debris rained down upon the ice, including six galoshes projected toward referee Dave Shewchyk's head, but he had made the right call. According to NHL rule 19(f), "When a player is injured so that he cannot continue play or go to his bench, the play shall not be stopped until the injured player's team has secured possession of the puck," meaning Weir's goal was perfectly legal.[58] The ghosts of the Forum must have been lingering a little too long at the concession stand after the Weir goal, because Gary Croteau beat Michel Larocque at 12:15 to put the Seals ahead by one, and the Seals accomplished something they likely never dreamed possible: a victory over the legendary Canadiens at the Montreal Forum to put an end to the twenty-four-game road losing streak. The hockey gods gave even the California Golden Seals a cookie once in a while.

Pete Manzolillo remembers how, as a teenager, he got so excited to learn the Seals had beaten the fabled Canadiens. "During the dismal 73–74 season," he said, "the Seals had a Saturday night game in Montreal. I had to go to bed early because I had a hockey game at 5:00 AM the next morning . . . so I didn't get the game result at 10:30–11:00 that night from the all-news radio station. Woke up at 3:30 the next morning and heard the unbelievable result on the news, 'California

4, Montreal 3.' I let out a whoop that woke my parents. Well, my dad had to get up anyway to drive me to the game!"[59]

The shocking victory could be described as the Seals' "Miracle on Ice," some six years before the U.S. Olympic Team laid claim to the term. To commemorate one of the greatest victories in the young franchise's history, the players surprised Marshall Johnston with a plaque, which he still has to this day. When he was interviewed for this book in 2009, Johnston looked over at the plaque in his home and proudly read out the inscription: "To Marshall Johnston, to his first coaching victory in the National Hockey League, March 2nd, '74, Montreal Forum, California 4, Montreal 3." When asked how it felt beating the Canadiens in the hallowed Forum, Johnston chuckled thinking about how Meloche had stood on his head, and how his guys managed to hang on for the win. "It's not much different today," he said. "When teams go in to play in Montreal, and to some certain respect, Toronto, there's always a special feeling about playing in those buildings." Ray McKay summed it up best when he said, "Beating Montreal in Montreal: that was our Stanley Cup right there."[60] The shocking defeat had no real effect on the Seals' season, but it may have destabilized a team that was a genuine Cup threat. Montreal was outscored 15-2 in its next two games, played to a 8-7-1 record the rest of the way, and was knocked out in the first playoff round.

The Seals may not have won a lot of games after Marsh Johnston took over behind the bench, but both times they did, it was at the expense of some mighty opposition. On March 10 Reggie Leach scored a hat trick in the Seals' 6-2 thrashing of red-hot Boston. The Bruins' thirty-six-year-old rookie Ross Brooks had begun his NHL career with a league-record fourteen straight wins, but on this night, the 12-44-9 Seals shockingly toppled the 43-12-9 Bostonians.

The Seals had little reason to celebrate the rest of the season, but there was one last interesting moment worth mentioning. During the second intermission of the Seals' final regular-season game at the Coliseum, a 4–2 loss to the Atlanta Flames, a beautiful twenty-four-year-old woman named Kathy McDonald engaged in one of the early 1970s most popular fads. "There was an old girlfriend of Bobby Sheehan," remembers Seals fan Larry Schmidt. "Between periods one night, you know what she did? She streaked on the ice nude. . . . She was a good looking blonde." She wasn't *completely* nude, however; she wore a pair of black skates and a gold necklace onto the ice with a sticker featuring the team's Carol Vadnais–inspired logo over her pubic area, and the word *Seals* painted in green on her body. According to the *San Rafael Independent-Journal*, "Miss McDonald later took a seat in the stands and was besieged with autograph-seekers from the crowd of 4,917. She said she was studying to be an assistant veterinarian. She also revealed she had skated only four times previously, and was a little worried about a chill spill."[61]

"None of the Seals officials would admit that it was a put-up job," wrote Hugh McDonald of the *San Mateo Times*, "but when the lady streaker did her thing the cameramen were all alerted. Fran Tuckwiler of the *San Jose Mercury*, who was selecting the three stars, wanted to give her the No. 1 star so she would come back into the spotlight. When they wouldn't go for that, Tuckwiler settled for Joey Johnston, Tom Lysiak and Ivan Boldirev."[62]

Despite streaking's often-spontaneous nature, several people were actually in on the young woman's plan. Former Coliseum stick boy Scott Ruffell explains how the streaker got onto the ice. "[We] helped the girl come out from underneath the bench, and she had like a big fur coat on. . . . I was about fifteen or sixteen then," Ruffell explained. "The guy that ran the Coliseum, the operations manager, he kind of set it up, and he got this chick all drunk and told her to do it, and she was only on the ice for maybe five or six seconds; she went right to the corner, and then she was gone. If you didn't know what was happening, you would have missed it. . . . It was in between periods, so none of the players got to see it. . . . A lot of the people at the arena didn't even see it; it happened so fast."

Like many tales that have found their place in hockey lore, there are conflicting details in the streaker story. "I knew that there was going to be streaker that night at the game," remembers Larry Leal, "because the arena manager told me that. And so, I was waiting for when the streaker was gonna show up, and being eighteen, it was real cool, you know. She came out of where the visitors used to come out onto the ice with a full body suit and white skates. And I'm going, 'Is this their idea of a streaker?' So she must have peeled off that body suit when she skated down to the other end of the ice. . . . I was let down when she came out with this body suit. I'm going, 'What the hell? I waited to see this?'" Since Leal was not standing up high in the crowd when she skated out, his field of vision may have been obscured as she skated from the north end to the south end of the rink, because as recently discovered photos of Miss McDonald reveal, she was most definitely naked.

Legendary Seals' cheerleader Krazy George Henderson was expected to take a perfect photo of the streaker, but he misfired: "This cute young girl had this outrageous plan. . . . I was supposed to take her picture. . . . As the players were introduced, she skated out from between the Seals players. The crowd was screaming, but I didn't see her until she was near the tunnel when she was skating off the ice. I snapped a picture of her head just then, right before two of her girl-friends were waiting for her with a coat in the tunnel. They weren't very pleased with my picture taking skills."[63]

As I concluded my interview with Ruffell, he explained to me one intriguing detail of a photo I had seen of the streaker: her knees. "So you know why her knees are all dirty? Cause she had to crawl out from where all the players were blowing their nose, and the snot, and Gatorade, and everything else, water, and skate crap all over the bench and the rubber mats. That's why her knees were all so screwed up."

The last twelve games of the season exemplified the struggle that had been the Seals' 1973-74 season: 11 losses and a tie. During that stretch the Seals allowed 5 or more goals seven times. The folks at the top could only shudder as they studied the brutal mess: a 13-55-10 record, 342 goals against, two twelve-game winless streaks, and an average attendance of less than 5,000 per game. "We're going to surprise a lot of people this season," Joey Johnston had said back in October.[64] He was right. It seems unlikely anyone would have pre-dicted the team could be any worse than it had been the year before.

Joey Johnston was invited to play in his second consecutive All-Star Game in January, finished the season with 27 goals, 40 assists, and 67 points, all of which led the team, and he won the Larriburu Brothers Trophy as team MVP. He was also elected team captain on February 15, shortly after Finley sold the team. "I was surprised to be named captain," Johnston admitted, "because my thing was my on ice performance not lecturing guys, and maybe some guys didn't like the way I acted off the ice."[65]

The Seals' anemic offense managed only 195 goals. Ivan Boldirev scored a career-high 25 goals and 31 assists, Walt McKechnie had 52 points in 63 games, and Reggie Leach had a career-high 46 points thanks to a late-season surge. The rest of the team was a different story. Pete Laframboise, Hil Graves, and Stan Weir had been expected to match their impressive rookie campaigns, but Graves finished with a paltry 11 goals and 29 points, while Laframboise and Weir scored only 16 times between them.

All the while the Seals' long-standing tradition of abandoning their goaltenders in a hail of pucks continued. Overall the team's four goaltenders recorded an atrocious 4.38 goals against average with Meloche registering the Seals' only shutout. The defense certainly made life interesting, due in part to the fact they just weren't aggressive enough. Bobby Stewart led the team with just 69 penalty minutes, but he only got into 47 games. Stewart had been hurting all season long with an injured shoulder and thigh. He was in no position to play it tough, but no one else on the roster picked up the slack.

Rich Gohlke of the *Fremont Argus* summed up the Seals' season aptly: "Every league has to have a last place team, but no team should be as far in last as the poor Seals. . . . The Seals operate in a type of perpetual shock. Usually they are shell-shocked after a devastating defeat. . . . I have never had the pleasure of seeing the Seals win a match this season . . . but our regular beat man tells me the team is more shocked when they win than after they get routed."[66]

The 1973–74 season was supposed to be about developing a positive, winning attitude in the players, but by February this goal had not been achieved. In fact, the positive thinking sessions given by Mind Dynamics turned out to be a load of hooey: the seminar company was shut down in December 1973 for making fraudulent claims and practicing medicine without a license. What actually turned the tide for the Seals was putting Marshall Johnston behind the bench and rehiring Garry Young. The Seals may have won just two games under the new regime, but overall they played much better. "Under

FIG. 11. Joey "The Jet" Johnston, Walt McKechnie, and Reggie "The Riverton Rifle" Leach combined for 72 goals and 169 points in 1973–74. Topps O-Pee-Chee trading cards used courtesy of The Topps Company, Inc.

the old management it was much different," said Walt McKechnie in late March. "For three years we had a habit of losing games. We just accepted defeat. Now it is a big deal. When we lose, you know somebody is going to get mad. Marsh and Garry get upset. There is more discipline on the team now and we have a lot to look forward too [*sic*] for next year."[67]

Despite the late-season change in attitude, the Seals were teetering on the brink of extinction once again. Three and a half years under Finley's watch had caused irreparable damage, reducing the Seals to a second-rate, almost minor-league hockey club. There was no miracle cure available to fix what ailed the Seals, and the only way they could be dragged out of the mire was by entirely dismantling the roster and starting over yet again. Costs would have to be reduced; the NHL had little interest in keeping the Bay Area's red-ink machine alive much longer, and trading away expensive veterans for prospects was the best way to make the Seals attractive to a new owner. The larger issue, however, was finding someone ready and willing to take a huge financial hit to keep the Seals afloat.

9

In October 1974 Gilles Meloche was entering his fourth season with the California Golden Seals. He had already played for four different coaches, two different general managers, and one director of hockey operations, had accumulated a career record of 37 wins, 90 losses, and 32 ties, and had seen more turnovers than a pastry chef. Just twenty-four years old, he had been in Oakland longer than anyone else with the exception of Joey Johnston, Craig Patrick, Stan Gilbertson, and Marshall Johnston, who had all been acquired just prior to Meloche's rookie season. Within a year, Meloche would be the only remaining member of that star-crossed 1971–72 squad.

Meloche was one of the few cornerstones around which the Seals could build. He had earned a great deal of respect from his teammates due to his strong work ethic and positive attitude in the face of overwhelming adversity. "There's not enough adjectives for me to describe him," said Marshall Johnston. "Obviously very talented, had an inward competitiveness that was admirable. Never, never—even though it was obvious where the goal wasn't his fault—but never, ever any indication of a dirty look at the defenseman or forward who made the mistake to really cause the goal."

Joey Johnston had high praise for Meloche, even comparing him to a present-day NHL star. "I'd say, you know that [Jonathan] Quick with L.A. nowadays, I'd rate him something like that. He had a hell of a lot of shots, way too much for anybody, and he'd play back-to-back games the majority of seasons. He was always able, willing. He didn't get frustrated. He always came to play. I mean, you could count on Gilles."

Larry Patey, a rookie who joined the Seals full time in 1974, had nothing but good things to say about Meloche: "Great guy. Good goaltender and a guy I looked up to when I got there. I spent quite a bit of time with Gilles. He was one of the . . . upper players in the league because we knew he was good, and I think they knew he was a good goaltender, and they tried to build a team around him."

FIG. 12. Gilles Meloche crouches in anticipation of another shot. Photo by Elliot Lowe.

Playing the toughest position on some of the worst teams in hockey history was a trying experience. Goaltenders around the league looked at the Seals' unfortunate brethren as being extremely perseverant. Gary Simmons joined the Seals before the 1974–75 campaign and recalls a chat he had with Ken Dryden. "We were talking before a game one time at center ice and Kenny said to me . . . 'Cobra, I think that if I got traded to the Seals, I think perhaps I'd retire.'" Even the very best cowered in fear at the thought of putting on a Seals jersey. Simmons took the extra work in stride. It took a special person to put up with the insanity. "Well, Kenny," Simmons responded, "you know it's true, Gilles and I get 44, 45 shots a game, but look at you . . . you might get 17 or 18 shots a game, but if your team's not scoring you have to stand there and try to remain in concentration all night, and you can let in one goal and lose. And you got the pressure to win, which is far greater than the pressure of getting a lot of shots like Gilles and I do."

The Seals put the most disastrous season in franchise history behind them. Charlie Finley was gone, and so were the white skates. Garry Young was back making the roster decisions, and the idealistic and popular Marshall Johnston had settled behind the bench. The franchise, however, was for all intents and purposes an orphan, and if it lost too much money, it was just a matter of time before the league moved or contracted the Seals. On February 2, 1975, the *Hayward Daily Review* published some of the letters they had received from readers who had responded to the question, "How would you feel if the California Seals moved out of the Bay Area?" Fans were far from unanimous in their appraisal of the Golden Ones.

Ruth Driscoll of Fremont weighed in: "[The Seals] have a good young team this year and you can't expect them to be number one ... with so many rookies on the team. Just give them time and they will be one of the best teams in the NHL." Eleanor Harris of Castro Valley was especially distraught by the thought of seeing the Seals leave: "I'd be heart-broken with a feeling of deep personal loss."[1]

On the other hand, if one letter summed up the club's first seven and a half years perfectly, it was from Ralph L. Williams of San Leandro:

From its very inception, the NHL Seals have to be the most poorly run sports franchise of all time. Every facet of the operation from the various owners, league officials, to and including the commissioner, Mr. Clarence Campbell, have done everything to alienate the fans and little to really promote attendance....

Another slap in the face to local fans is the inability of all concerned to call this team the Oakland Seals. They have been called almost everything apparently to hide the fact the games are played in Oakland....

Perhaps the most distressing thing of all is ... when I invariably see a star player on another team who was a former Seal.... The people in charge have consistently sold the fans down the river by disposing [of] the best and most popular players....

As far as moving the Seals to another city—I would be delighted. I feel sure the Coast hockey league would move back into this area. As a hockey fan of many years, I know there is not that much difference between the two leagues from an entertainment standpoint. In fact, I think some Coast teams of past years could have defeated the present Seals in a series of games.[2]

That was harsh, but nothing could possibly beat Jim Hausel of Castro Valley's quip: "Would I miss the Seals? Would Nixon miss

Watergate? Would a chicken miss lips? Would a bear miss the woods? . . . The Seals are acupuncture to my posterior given by a sadist. Thanks, but I'd rather be in Philadelphia."[3]

Garry Young faced a situation similar to the one he inherited his first time around: a team that had finished dead last and badly needed a major facelift. While not technically the Seals' general manager, Young still had the authority to make trades and clean up the mess Hurricane Finley had left in its wake, but since the Seals were owned by the NHL, Young needed the league's approval before making any roster moves. For the most part Young avoided one-for-one trades and struck deals that netted the club several young players or draft picks. This achieved two purposes: restocking the Seals' bare cupboards and getting rid of expensive contracts.

On May 23 Young sent Ivan Boldirev to Chicago for defensemen Mike Christie and Len Frig. Christie was a heart-and-soul player everyone appreciated and respected. Born in Big Spring, Texas, but raised in Canada, Christie picked up 5 goals, 37 assists, and 110 penalty minutes with Dallas of the Central Hockey League. "What Mike lacked in ability he made up for in desire," said Gary Simmons. "If somebody was in a fight and getting ganged up upon, he'd step in. He did a good job and was a good guy off the ice."[4] Joey Johnston remembers Christie as "a pretty solid dude and pretty quiet most of the time. He didn't go looking for trouble, but he was able to handle himself real well."

Frig was selected the CHL's top defenseman in 1973 and, like Christie, he could tango with the best of them. He racked up 224 penalty minutes in 1971–72 with Dallas and another 105 minutes the following year. While Christie was honing his game in the minors in 1973–74, Frig saw plenty of action with Chicago that year. The Lethbridge, Alberta, native's NHL rookie season included a +16 mark and 14 points in 66 games. Frig's offensive skills were a big part of the reason he was so coveted by the Seals' general manager. "He's the kind of puck-carrying, playmaking defenceman a team must have," Young said, "and you must remember he didn't get a lot of ice time in the 66 games he dressed for."[5]

The following day, Reggie Leach was dealt to Philadelphia in exchange for forwards Al MacAdam and Larry Wright, as well as the

Flyers' first-round pick in the upcoming amateur draft. "Reggie Leach, we had him for, I think, two years," remembers Seals fan Cathy White, "and Bobby Clarke wanted him, and Bobby Clarke did everything to get him, and of course, he did, and it set up Philadelphia; they were unbeatable. And I think Reggie was happier playing with Bobby." The defending Stanley Cup champs would not be disappointed, as Leach went on to record 306 goals in 606 games with the Flyers.

As for MacAdam, he turned into a heck of a hockey player himself. He became not only one of the Seals' most dependable players, but also one of the NHL's best two-way forwards and penalty killers and a two-time All-Star. The wiry, mustachioed, Prince Edward Island native would finish the 1974–75 campaign tied for second in Seals scoring, and he would be named the club's Unsung Hero for the season. "Our favorite was Al MacAdam," said Booster Club member Sandi Pantages, speaking for both herself and her husband, Dick. "Just a very gracious, nice person, and he didn't mind talking to someone, and none of the players seemed to mind that at the time. They were just very warm to the fans; they kind of had to be because there weren't a lot of them."

Over the next four years, MacAdam never missed a game, and he eventually became the franchise's all-time leading scorer with 217 points. MacAdam could throw 'em too! Despite his reputation as one of the nicest people in the organization, one did not want to piss him off. One time, according to Gary Simmons, New York Islanders legend Denis Potvin picked a fight with MacAdam, and "Big Al just cleaned his clock. I mean, it was pathetic. He just walked all over him." Several other people interviewed for this book confirmed this. "He was kind of a quiet, solid player," remembers Dick Pantages. "Every once in a while one of the opposing team decided he looked kind of meek and mild, and tried to fight him; Al would just clean their plow." Nevertheless, MacAdam, a practicing Catholic even in his playing days, wasn't boastful of his on-ice talents. "I'm the type of player that nobody notices," he said. "I just want to be known as a quiet individual on and off the ice. I'm not as flamboyant as some of the other players on our team"[6]

FIG. 13. Al MacAdam, the franchise's all-time leading scorer with 217 points, never missed a game in four seasons with the club. Photo courtesy of Elliot Lowe.

Before the dust had settled on the Leach trade, Walt McKechnie was shipped to the Rangers in a three-way deal that also involved the Bruins. It had been prearranged that the Seals would select veteran defenseman Jim Neilson from the Rangers in the intra-league draft in exchange for the right to select McKechnie. The Rangers would then trade McKechnie to Boston in exchange for Derek Sanderson. "In effect," said Young, "it was a trade of McKechnie for Neilson, made possible because [New York] wanted Sanderson, and we needed a strong leader on defence."[7]

Neilson had been a Second Team All-Star in 1968 and an All-Star Game participant on two other occasions. Although Neilson had never been flashy and had scored more than 40 points in a season just once, his plus/minus figures remained above zero from 1968 to 1973. "Neilson is a very underrated player, one of the best defencemen in the league," said Rangers GM Emile Francis. "He's a defensive man mostly, who takes his man out, keeps the puck cleared out of his zone and doesn't hesitate to block shots. I think he's a big loss, but obviously we had to give up a lot to get Sanderson."[8]

The Seals hoped Neilson could mentor eighteen-year old Rick Hampton, selected third overall in the 1974 amateur draft. Hampton signed a huge three-year $500,000 ($245,000 plus bonuses) pact. "I'm sure he's the highest paid 18-year-old in sports," said Hampton's agent, Alan Eagleson, "except for maybe Bjorn Borg, but he's not contract."[9] The Seals put a lot of faith in their young draftee, but according to many, including Joe Starkey, the team put far too much pressure on Hampton's shoulders. "Munson Campbell and the league were determined to create some interest around the team," Starkey said, "so they made a big splash with Hampton, tried to set him up as the new superstar, and clearly he wasn't ready for it. Would he have been if he had a year or two more in the minors, who knows? But he certainly wasn't ready for the kind of pressure he was under on a bad hockey team in an area that hardly cared about the sport."

The Seals organization did all it could to promote Rick Hampton, which did him no service. "If Rick played for New York or Boston or Montreal," declared Neilson in a *Sports Illustrated* article later in the season, "they'd be talking about him as the second coming of Bobby Orr."[10] In July 1974 Young did just that, claiming Hampton was "one of the finest junior hockey players I've seen since a fellow who wears a sweater in Boston."[11] Starkey recalled that when Hampton arrived in Oakland, "even most of the league thought that this guy had the potential to be a Bobby Orr type, which is pretty tough to live up to, but he looked like he had that combination of being able to score, great slap shot, play good defense. . . . Rick Hampton had everything but the right personality. I thought he had great skills, but he didn't have the drive. . . . Nice young man, but that didn't help much on the ice."

Seals fan John Bonasera remembers the hype surrounding Hampton and how his skills seemed tailor-made for the NHL:

This is a guy that, again, high hopes, high draft choice. This is going to be our Bobby Orr. . . . Looked the part, young, good-looking, fast-skating, but . . . I'd say he underachieved his whole career. His contribution to the Seals was brief. . . . Never would have thought that. Again, what do we know? We're in the Bay Area. . . . You're reading clips out of the *Hockey News* to get your information. There was nothing on television about this stuff back then, but here's this guy that's fairly highly rated and considered a top-notch prospect, and then you see him on the ice and he looks the part. . . . He wasn't much of a defensive player per se, but he was certainly a puck-carrying offensive threat, and he could skate like the wind and was fun to watch.

Hampton could hardly be blamed for the situation he was thrust into. He was not the first, nor would he be the last first-round pick burdened with the unenviable task of saving a bottom-feeding franchise from extinction. Gary Simmons believed the negativity and poor attitude that permeated throughout the club played a role in hurting Hampton's development:

Some of the veterans that had been there a few years didn't have a good attitude . . . after a while it gets to you, and young guys . . . particularly Ricky Hampton, the kid had a lot of talent, but he didn't have the maturity. He was eighteen years old . . . and to come in there and listen to these guys talking and that. He should have been in the minors playing a couple of years and getting his maturity. He sure had the talent; the kid was a good hockey player, but he got ruined by the management, and they ruined his career, in my opinion.

Garry Young had the unwelcome task of getting rid of the cancerous attitude that had seeped into the Seals' dressing room in 1972 when half the team defected to the WHA. The players had simply accepted losing as something that came with playing for the Seals, and they had gotten pushed around far too much, but that was going to change, according to management. "We won't be intimidated by Philadelphia this year," promised Munson Campbell. "We told the Boosters club when we took over that if they'd bear with us we'd give them a team that won't quit. And we're ahead of schedule on our commitment."[12] Campbell wanted a Seals ticket to mean something. There would be no more half-price games and ticket giveaways.

In other moves Hilliard Graves was dealt to Atlanta after a disappointing sophomore campaign for twenty-four-year-old John Stewart, an original Flame from 1972, who had scored 35 goals over the previous two seasons.

The Seals also acquired veteran Brian Lavender in exchange for prospect Hartland Monahan. Lavender's scoring exploits were never going to set the league on fire, but he excelled at cutting up his teammates. "Brian Lavender was a cool customer," remembered Simmons. "We were in Philadelphia one night. You start off with twelve, fifteen pucks, and I was playing that night so they're warming me up. Well, pretty soon there's no pucks left, and Lavender is passing them out to the guys to come in and shoot on me. And I said, 'Hey Lavy, where's the pucks?' He said, 'They're down the other end. The guys are too scared to go get 'em.' Great sense of humor."

Gary Croteau, while respected and hard-working, had suffered from several injuries since his sophomore season and was picked up by the Kansas City Scouts in the NHL's latest expansion draft. Pete Laframboise was picked up by the new Washington Capitals. With these two forwards gone, roster spots became available for rookies such as Larry Patey, Dave Hrechkosy, and Charlie Simmer, the very player who would become the trigger man on the LA Kings' famed Triple Crown Line in the 1980s.

As Joe Starkey put it bluntly, the Seals "completely wasted Charlie Simmer." Larry Patey said he owed much of the success of his rookie season to Simmer: "My 25 goals, I got to say half of them were, thank you, Charlie Simmer, for making it happen. But he was just that talented of a player that he could move the puck. . . . He would not make a mistake with it, that's for sure." For a while that season, Simmer showed he had all the skills to be a big-time star, but before long he was forgotten in the shuffle, and the Seals allowed him to drift away.

With both Gilles Meloche and Marv Edwards healthy, it seemed as though the Seals were set in goal. Edwards signed a new contract during the summer and even posed for the annual team picture in full gear, but he changed his mind and retired to become the Seals' assistant coach. The Seals dug deep into their pockets and handed coveted free agent minor-league goaltender Gary Simmons a three-year, $150,000 contract.

"Cobra," as Simmons was known, was one of a kind. Legend has it that while living in Arizona he earned his nickname by killing a rattlesnake with his bare hands and making a belt out of its skin. In reality, he got the nickname because of the way he would wriggle and slide in his crease, and the nickname has always been a great source of pride for him. Simmons took a long time getting to the bigs, and although he never became a star, he left a lasting impression on everyone he met. "Got to love the guy," said Larry Patey. "Guy comes into the dressing room with two Doberman Pinschers. I thought the world of him. . . . He did his own thing, but I had a lot of respect for him, and I like him a lot."

Simmons became a media darling in the Bay Area. He was loquacious, funny, and intelligent, and he had a wicked sense of humor. Simmons is still one of Joe Starkey's favorites. "If all else failed," Starkey said, "you could always talk to Gary Simmons and make a good interview out of it." One time Starkey was faced with the uncomfortable situation of hosting a two-hour radio talk show on a night the Golden State Warriors were playing in the NBA Finals. "I knew I wasn't going to get a call," he said. "Everybody was into the game on a different station. So I just called Gary Simmons. I said, 'I need you,' and so he and I basically chatted for two hours on the air."

Simmons' greatest claim to fame is undoubtedly his mask. For this book, when he was asked if it was true his mask was in the Hall of Fame, he humbly pointed out that "it is; I'm not." The mask was all black with a huge green cobra slithering between the eye holes and menacingly staring down shooters. Simmons explained there was one small problem with the design, something most fans have probably never noticed. Greg Harrison of Toronto was well known for making masks. "I told him I wanted a cobra on it, and whether I gave him a picture to put on it, I don't remember, it was too long ago, but I remember it came back with rattles. . . . I said at the time in many articles, 'typical easterner, he puts rattles on a cobra' . . . but he did a good job on it."

Simmons also loved to chew tobacco when he was backing up Meloche. At the time the Flyers' Bernie Parent would stall for time

FIG. 14. Gary Simmons defends his crease wearing his
legendary cobra mask. Photo by Elliot Lowe.

by going to the bench for a quick drink, but when referees caught
on to the ruse, goaltenders were left looking for other ways to stay
hydrated. Simmons recalled one incident:

> They didn't have those bottles on the back of the nets like they do
> now. And I played professional softball too in the summer up in
> Canada and I used to chew tobacco when I played softball, and
> I found it kept me much more refreshed than what gum did. . . .
>
> I remember one night, Dunc Wilson and I were sitting in Pitts-
> burgh at the old Igloo and all they had was either glass or chicken
> wire, I forget, at the time, between the two benches. And I said,
> "Hey, you wanna try some of this?" So we were both spitting it
> over there, and the funny thing was the puck got stopped there,
> and the linesman didn't want to pick it up. The referee said, "Pick
> it up," you know, there was swearing involved. He ended up having
> to pick it up with all this chew all over it. It was rather humorous,
> Dunc and I thought.

Simmons was a tattooed teetotaler who wore Native American
jewelry, a cowboy hat, and boots. The man also made it a point to
get the right to dress *his* way in writing. When it became time to sign a

contract with the Seals, Simmons met with Garry Young at the Phoenix airport hotel:

> I met him there, and we talked over things, and when we got to the final thing . . . I said, "Well, what's your policy on wearing neckties?" He said, "Because it's a California team, we don't need to do it at home, but when we go on the road from the hotel to the rink or from the rink to the hotel." And I said, "I don't wear ties." And he said, "Well, it's a team policy; you're gonna have to." And I said, "Well, I just don't wear neckties, and I want that in my contract." And he says, "Well, I don't know. What am I gonna tell the other eighteen guys?" And I said, "Tell 'em I got it in my contract." And he said, "Ah, the hell with it," he says, "OK."

Simmons's stellar play forced Marshall Johnston to use him almost as frequently as Meloche, but according to Simmons, there was little, if any, jealousy between him and Meloche:

> I had a habit of staying up all night watching TV, and Gilles was like a normal person; he slept at night, and so he'd always get me up for the games, and when I was playing he'd like kick the end of the bed, "Hey Cobra, get up, time to go!" and if he hit my foot I'd say, "Oh geez, I can't play tonight! I think you broke my foot!" "Ah," he said, "you're playing." One time we're in Buffalo, and he went over to lower the blind, and he burned his foot on those old-time heaters that they used to have in the room. He burned his foot on that, and the thing came down and hit him on the head, and he jumped on the floor and he said, "Oh, Cobra, I can't play tonight! I can't play tonight!" I said, "Yeah, you're playing." But we used to tease each other and pretend we were hurt, and we got good laughs out of it.

After the train-wreck 1973–74 season the club needed to exorcise itself of all the demons it had accumulated since its birth. One particular visitor strolled through the Seals' offices in the summer of 1974 and remarked: "The difference here is like night and day. The way they're working around here you'd think they were getting ready for the playoffs. And you know what? The way they've been shoring up, I wouldn't be surprised if they did."[13]

The players had an overall better attitude as well. They knew they were going to have to earn their place on the roster. One of the few returning veterans explained: "Before, once I made the team in September, I knew that there was no one on the team, or for that matter, in the whole organization, who could take my job. We just weren't that deep in quality players. This is probably the first year that I feel I really have to go out and win my position—to prove that I'm the best. I like that kind of challenge."[14]

According to a Seals spokesman, the team was doing as much as possible to break away from its past and improve its image:

We're into many different things this year. We're going to offer group rates, have promotion nights, advertise—we had a budget of zero for that last year—and form a speaker's bureau.

In addition, we have a radio contract.

Overall, we want to change the image of the California Golden Seals. Before, no one in the San Francisco Bay Area felt any connection with the team. We want to change that. We want to know how we can make a viable contribution to the community.[15]

There was a certain enthusiasm that permeated throughout the Seals' dressing room that season. These young bucks were proud to be playing in the NHL. Hall-of-Famer Jean Beliveau once scolded a young player for having thrown Montreal's sacred *bleu-blanc-rouge* jersey on the dressing room floor, but according to rookie Larry Patey, tossing the Seals' less-than-legendary sweater to the ground was equally sinful. "Your sweater, when you took it off, it never hit the floor," he said. "In other words, if you're upset, you made a mistake, you lost the game, whatever the story is, you never take your sweater off and throw it on the floor. You take it off and you hang it up." Patey, for one, was proud as hell to play for the Seals. So were most of the other young guys coming in. Patey remarked: "I think if you look at players that had been there for a long time, maybe they had their doubts, but then the players, like myself, that were coming in, we had a goal . . . a renewed goal. I think the older players, when they saw the newer crew coming in and starting to achieve and be positive, they fell into place as well."

To officially make the Finley era a distant memory, the Seals did away with their eccentric former owner's penchant for garish green-and-yellow attire. Instead the Seals would sport traditional white home sweaters and Pacific blue pants with California gold trim. The away uniforms would be Pacific blue from top to bottom. The uniforms were met with mixed reviews. Len Shapiro believed the road uniforms "looked like pajamas," but the "home uniform was very sufficient and everybody liked it. I liked the fact it was white, and that the people could read the names on the back of the jerseys easily."

Before the dust had settled on the changes made to the California Golden Seals, Garry Young left the club, saying he planned on entering private business. Others believed he resigned for health reasons. Whatever the reason, in November 1974 Young was back in the NHL coaching the St. Louis Blues. In August thirty-nine-year-old former Blues left wing Bill McCreary was named the Seals' new director of hockey operations. He had also been executive vice president of the Blues as well as their director of computer scouting.

While Young avoided the annoying micromanaging that had been Finley's trademark, McCreary liked to spread his influence to all aspects of the team. Many believed McCreary wanted to coach the Seals, but Marshall Johnston stood in his way. McCreary eventually forced Johnston to wear an earpiece to help out the coach during games. "Sometimes we can see things up in the press box that are hard to see from behind the bench," said McCreary. "After all, Marsh has the worst seat in the house." McCreary's plan was a disaster. During one home game against Boston, a former Seals defenseman noticed the earpiece and asked his old friend Johnston, "What are you doing, Marsh listening to the game?" At one point, instead of hearing McCreary's voice coming from a walkie-talkie up in the press box, Johnston heard someone's taxi request: "Go to 66th and Seminary."[16]

Initially Johnston had no negative feelings toward McCreary, and he worked as best he could with the players he had inherited from the previous regime, but McCreary was not happy with the way Johnston coached his players. "There's a guy that was scouting for the Seals at the time, and we were at training camp in Kingston," recounted Johnston, "and I was walking back to him after one of the practices and he said to me . . . 'You better watch it.'" During that training camp Johnston had cones out on the ice, which apparently bothered the general manager. "I had different drills where the players had to skate around the cones, pass between the cones, do this and do that, which obviously is a lot of things that go on in hockey school, and I guess Bill took exception to that and that wasn't what he had expected, but I was the coach and I was running the practices." According to Johnston, during one meeting McCreary told him, "We're running a pro camp here, we're not running a hockey school."

As the season wore on, McCreary continued to stick his nose in his coach's business. "Gary Simmons was our goalie," Johnston recalled, "and he had an asthmatic problem, and when there was a stoppage of play, he would come to the bench, and he had [an inhaler]. So McCreary had said to me one time, 'You know, you're gonna get a penalty for delay of game' . . . and I said, 'Well, this was a medical thing. . . . [Simmons] just comes over five seconds, doesn't take any time at all, and there was no problem.' So there were little things like that that led me to believe that he maybe wanted to be the coach."

It was going to be a rough ride for Johnston. There were going to be many new faces in the lineup, and most of them were not terribly familiar to the average NHL fan. The team could have been called the California Golden *Eagles*, considering how many members of the 1973–74 Salt Lake City farm team were called up to play major roles that season. Dave Hrechkosy, Ron Huston, Wayne King, Jim Moxey, and Larry Patey all played at least twenty-five games, while Bruce Greig, Gary Holt, and Brent Meeke saw spot duty for the Seals. Throughout the season a total of *eighteen* rookies found their way onto the roster at one time or another. "We have real talent here now," Johnston boasted to *Sports Illustrated*. "My job is to keep the kids—we are the youngest team in hockey—from getting down on themselves."[17]

The NHL made the Seals' already difficult situation even worse. For the 1974–75 season the NHL realigned its eighteen clubs into two conferences and four divisions, but this realignment made little geographic sense. The Seals, for example, were placed in the Adams Division with Boston, Buffalo, and Toronto, while the Smythe Division, consisting of Vancouver, Minnesota, St. Louis, Chicago, and Kansas City, would have been, geographically speaking, more logical. "We were the low man on the totem pole," explained Len Shapiro, "and Finley didn't care, and maybe he could have fought to get the team in another division, but there was nobody fighting for it. Again, it was just kind of a fait accompli we ended up in the division, and we had to go to Toronto and Boston. It made no sense whatsoever."

The division realignment posed two major problems for the Seals. The Boston Bruins were a league power, while the Buffalo Sabres and Toronto Maple Leafs were up and coming clubs, meaning the Seals were almost guaranteed to finish last. The Seals would also be stuck going on ridiculously long road trips to play games against their division rivals. Shapiro recalls traveling with the Seals on one road trip in 1974 that was "just amazing," for all the wrong reasons: "It was just like, go to a game, get on the plane, go to the next stop, play the game, go take one night off. . . . I'm not a player and I was exhausted. . . . There were no charters; we were flying commercial. . . . I really don't understand how [some of the players] made it sometimes after those rough games in Philly and on the Island, and Buffalo, where we got slaughtered, how they kept themselves up to get on the bus, get on the plane, and go to the next city." To save money, Shapiro explained, the Seals had to fly on game days, against NHL rules.

Exhausting road trips often meant there were sometimes extended home stands to balance out the schedule, but according to Gary Simmons, these were often just as brutal for a West Coast team:

These two-, three-week road trips, it pretty well crushed your chances. . . . I remember we came home one time, we had the whole month of December [1976] at home. The whole month we played nine or ten games at home, and it starts off really good, but then you get used to being around the house and that, and the last four, five games we got clobbered. . . . Being home too long is not good, and being on the road for two, three weeks is not good either. . . .

You did a lot more traveling than what the other teams did. Teams in the East would go on the road, play a game, and then they'd go back home right after the game. Well, we'd go there, sometimes we'd have two, three days between games and . . . you know, you got guys in a strange town, and towns got bars . . . they got nothing else to do.

Needless to say, the cards were stacked against the Seals, and it would not be easy getting into the postseason. *Sports Illustrated* slotted the Seals seventeenth out of eighteen clubs in overall team strength, ahead of only the expansion Washington Capitals. Even the Caps' expansion cousins from Kansas City were expected to fare better than the Seals. But what could you expect from a club that had just discarded its most talented players for a bunch of rookies and draft picks? They looked like another faceless expansion team. The roster looked as thin as, if not thinner than, the one that had been assembled at the June 1967 expansion draft. The Seals' only star players were Gilles Meloche and Joey Johnston. If the 1973–74 Seals could muster only 13 wins, this new bunch would be lucky to bag half that.

The Seals finished the preseason with 4 wins and 3 losses versus NHL and WHA competition, and that momentum carried into the regular season opener on October 9 as California tied St. Louis, 4–4. Stan Weir and Len Frig each scored twice for California, and Bobby Stewart dropped the gloves six seconds in to set the tone for the rest of the year. If the Seals were going to lose a lot of games, they were going to make their opponents earn every point. "There's no comparison between this year's team and last year's," Stewart exclaimed later in the season. "Our game plan this season is geared toward heavy physical contact. The whole team has to be aggressive. The forwards, as well as the defence, have to hit. We won't be pushed around."[18] As a team the Seals would increase their penalty minute total from 651 in 1973–74 to 1,101 in 1974–75.

Two nights later Simmons, in his first NHL start, blocked 24 shots in a 3–0 shutout over Atlanta. The shutout was the launching point of another classic Cobra story: "I remember going after my first year to speak to the Alameda California Rotary Club. They asked the usual questions, 'Why are the Seals so bad?' Etc. I told them, tongue in cheek, that I had a shutout my first game and was called into the GMs office and told, 'You do not get another shutout or win too many games. We like to be out of the playoffs by Christmas.' They roared with laughter. Except one guy who came up after and asked if I was really told to lose games. Then it was my turn to roar."[19]

"It was a close game," Simmons recalled. "I didn't have many shots, I think maybe 24-25, something like that. It was a great way to start . . . somebody came in after the game, and said, 'Nothin' to this league, huh?'" Simmons started to laugh right away. When talking to Simmons you get the feeling every one of his stories has a punch line to it. "The next game I played was in Buffalo," he said, "and we got clobbered like 6-1."

The Seals did not manage to win another game until the notorious Philadelphia Flyers came to town on October 25. The Broad Street Bullies were greeted by a Seals squad full of rookies and youngsters who had never experienced a team quite like this one. The result was not pretty. "I went to one of the biggest Seals-Flyers fights of all time," remembers Seals fan Larry Schmidt. "The game started at 7 o'clock or 7:30. It didn't get over until 11:30 or 12. . . . There was more food on the ice that night being thrown from the fans than I think they sold in the stands that night. It was unbelievable. . . . My scorecard was so filled up because there was so many penalty minutes."

It's the aftermath of a third-period fight between the Seals' Mike Christie and Philly's Orest Kindrachuk that people remember about this game nearly forty years later. At the 8:20 mark of the period, with California leading 4-0, Kindrachuk and Christie dropped the gloves, but referee Bryan Lewis gave Kindrachuk an extra minor penalty. Eyewitnesses claimed Don Saleski tried to goad Christie into jumping back onto the ice, which would have cost him two more minutes in the box, but Christie was smarter than that. Instead of accepting his minor penalty, Kindrachuk skated past Saleski to the Seals' penalty box to have a few words with Christie. Bob Kelly joined Kindrachuk and Saleski, and together the trio savagely beat Christie while other Flyers kept the Seals players away.

In the end Christie was left with an eight-stitch gash below his left eye, a four-stitch cut above it, and a two-stitch cut under his right eye.

"He was such a handsome young man, and they pummeled him," lamented Seals fan Cathy White. Bill McCreary was completely disgusted by what he had seen. "Christie's eyes were shut in the dressing room," he remembered. "Two guys held Christie and one guy punched him. They should have been banned for life. It was a cowardly act."[20] Munson Campbell was absolutely livid following the game. "We'll bring up the butchers," he said. "We'll meet them in the alley or on the ice. We have the big, tough players in our farm system who can come up here and take care of the Flyers."[21] The entire brouhaha lasted almost forty minutes. "I've seen bloodier battles and I've seen fights that came nearer to being riots," said one Seals official, "but this was probably the most prolonged and hardest to break up I ever saw."[22]

In an interview for this book Simmons told the story in a very serious manner. For a gregarious storyteller like him, the tone in his voice seemed to indicate the incident still bothered him. "Yeah, I remember it well," he said. "It was awful. It was just awful. It was embarrassing." At this point, his voice became much more solemn. "It was embarrassing that it happened, but you know we always used to have trouble with Philadelphia. We always used to have skirmishes and fights. Poor Mike, he really got waylaid that night, and I don't remember him getting much help." The Flyers' Tom Bladon, who was a close friend of Christie, agreed. "It wouldn't have looked so bad if some of the Seals would have come to help him out," he said. "But none seemed too interested in helping him. It's pretty sad when Jim Neilson—what is he, 36 years old?—is the first to get there to help."[23] Even Dave Schultz, the man who still holds the league record of 472 penalty minutes in one season, says he was turned off by the entire incident. In his book *The Hammer: Confessions of a Hockey Enforcer*, Schultz wrote, "It so happens I didn't hit a soul—I just don't like brawls that are one sided. I never did. I felt sorry for Christie. This was a side that I rarely showed on the ice—until later—and I'm sure few people noticed it."[24]

If there was one consistency in interviews conducted with Seals players for this book, it was their undying respect for Christie. Marshall Johnston said Christie was not "a heavyweight, but he was an honestly tough, physical player." Talking about the brawl against Philadelphia, Johnston admitted, "We couldn't match them when it came to physical

FIG. 15. Heart-and-soul defenseman Mike Christie was the
victim of a brutal penalty-box attack by the Philadelphia
Flyers. Photo by Elliot Lowe.

toughness and stuff. I mean, we just didn't have the personnel, but the
one thing that stands out in my memory was Mike Christie and the
way he stood up to them, Schultz, and the whole crew." Simmons said
Christie "had the heart of a lion," was "three quarters of our team's
guts," and "tried so hard every shift. . . . He just worked his butt off.
He was the enforcer, he was the guy that always was the third man in
when one of our guys was getting beat up. . . . If everybody had Mike
Christie's heart, we would have done a heck of a lot better."

In the end the Seals won the game 4–1, but eight players—the Flyers'
Kindrachuk, Kelly, Saleski, Schultz, and Dupont, as well as the Seals'
Christie, Frig, and Neilson—were all ejected. Overall, the Seals and
Flyers racked up a single-game NHL record 232 penalty minutes (144
for Philadelphia, 88 for California). Less than a week after the brawl
Saleski and Kelly were each handed six-game suspensions for their
part in the violent melee. Kindrachuk was not suspended but the
league handed him a $300 fine.

This new edition of the California Golden Seals was very green and
took its fair share of beatings in the first third of the season. Some days,
as the saying goes, "it just doesn't pay to come to the office." The Seals
found this out when they took on the New York Islanders on October
28. Joe Starkey recalled how, during this stinker of a game, even he got

fed up. "[Gary Simmons] got beat 10–1 by the New York Islanders," he said, "and in fact, on that magic night, which was a Monday night, because I remember it so vividly . . . it became so awful, I became like an irate fan, and I actually told the audience—I kid you not—I said, 'You know what? Tonight, it's a big night on TV, folks. Rhoda is getting married on the *Mary Tyler Moore Show*. You might want to go watch.'"

After the Islanders debacle, five more games followed without a win, and after sixteen games, the Seals' overall record stood at a woeful 2–10–4. Amazingly, only 3 points separated them from the third-place Maple Leafs.

Sensing a need for change, Bill McCreary traded Craig Patrick and Stan Gilbertson, who at the time had recorded only 8 points between them, to St. Louis for a pair of twenty-two-year-old forwards, Dave Gardner and Warren "Butch" Williams. Although both Patrick and Gilbertson had been with the Seals since 1971, neither shed any tears when they were told to pack their bags. In fact, after McCreary told them they had been traded, they went out and celebrated. Marshall Johnston, however, was sad to see them leave. "I just thanked them for the job they had done for us," he said. "They were a credit to this organization and I wanted them to know it."[25]

Williams and Gardner became key contributors to the team, but the trade did little to turn the tide in the short term. Meloche finally delivered his long-awaited first win of the season on November 13, a 2–0 shutout over Chicago at the Coliseum, but the Seals lost their next six games, dropping their record to 3–16–4. The most embarrassing defeat in that stretch was at the hands of the Washington Capitals, who had a 1–15–2 record. Losing to an expansion club is always tough, but when the expansion team is coming into the game riding a fourteen-game winless skid, it becomes downright humiliating. Seals' assistant director of public relations, Len Shapiro, was quoted as saying, "The Capitals are about 18, 19 players away from being a good team," a statement that was more true than funny.[26] Regardless, the Seals struggled against Washington all season. This time, the score was 3–3 entering the third period. Denis Dupere gave the Caps the lead at the 8:29 mark, and then just 51 seconds later rookie Mike Marson scored his first NHL goal to put Washington up by 2. Marson scored again about seven minutes later, putting the final nail in the Seals' coffin. Al MacAdam made it 6-4 at 19:04, but it was too little, too late.

The Seals' season couldn't have gone worse over the first quarter. Even poor Joe Starkey became the victim of embarrassment. On the night of November 23 Starkey was told, while on the air, that Joey Johnston had been traded to the New York Rangers and Marshall Johnston had been fired, but in fact, it turned out to be a hoax:

> We played Minnesota and at the end of the game when I end up doing the postgame show, you have . . . a private phone that would be connected, and if it rang, it was directed to the PR director of the home team. There would be no way, you would think, that it could be anything else calling you on that number. So while I'm finishing up the postgame show and there are no more commercials left, the phone rings, and my engineer is writing me a note, and the note says that Marshall Johnston has been fired and that Joey Johnston has been traded to the [New York Rangers]. So I have no way of checking this. Today, I would never say it because I would know better, but at that point, as a young broadcaster . . . the story came across, [and] there was no way to take another timeout, so I went with the story and proceeded to explain probably why it happened, which was part two of a mistake. . . .
>
> I got downstairs, and I'm going to commiserate with the two people involved, and they don't know what I'm talking about, and I think, "Oh my God, what happened here?" And so I've gone on the air, I've told the Bay Area audience that this has happened, and it turns out not to be the case, and what's really classic about it is this was a Saturday night game, the Sunday morning *San Francisco Chronicle* had a story that basically said what I did. They had taken it off the air and said 'Joey traded, Marshall fired.' On Monday, they blamed it all on me, of course. They said on Monday, "We've learned that none of the stuff we told you yesterday was true, and it was a mistake by the announcer," and all that sort of thing. Never happened again, I guarantee you.

To cope with the insanity of working for the California Golden Seals more than a few people turned to alcohol. Fred Glover was a heavy drinker for a while. Joey Johnston also downed more than a few shots while playing in Oakland. Dave Hrechkosy sometimes partied a little too hard. They all eventually got over their addictions, but it wasn't easy. Addiction counselors say that an alcoholic cannot begin the road to recovery until he or she has hit rock bottom. It is the same case for any struggling hockey club. With the earlier Washington loss, the Seals hit rock bottom, but they dusted themselves off and worked their way out of their hole.

Beginning with a hard-fought 3–3 tie with the Islanders on November 29, the Seals strung together a respectable 8-7-4 record, putting some heat on third-place Toronto. The Capitals fell 5–2 in Washington on December 1, and then the Seals beat both Atlanta and Minnesota soon afterward. California then outshot Washington 44–23 on December 20, in a second convincing 5–2 victory over the Caps. Though the Caps were no world-beaters, the Seals proved they could also beat Stanley Cup contenders. On December 27 the Seals traveled to Boston and beat the Bruins 5–2. "I've never seen them make a better effort," said a jubilant Marshall Johnston. "They showed a lot of grit. Everybody was helping each other and they were practically eating the puck."[27] The night following the outstanding effort in Boston, the Seals beat the much-improved LA Kings 3–2.

The real test, however, came on New Year's Day when the Seals ventured east to play the Leafs. At that point the Seals sat just 4 points back of Toronto. The Seals took a 2–0 lead on goals by John Stewart and Dave Hrechkosy before ten minutes had elapsed, but the Leafs evened the count before retiring to their dressing room. Charlie Simmer gave the Seals a 3–2 lead in the second, but Errol Thompson erased it with just over a minute left in the period. The Leafs continued to pressure the Seals' defense, but Meloche withstood eighteen drives in the final frame to preserve the 3–3 draw. Though the Seals did not get the result they were hoping for, they still felt good about their chances. After the game Hrechkosy expressed his opinions with an air of confidence that had neither been seen nor heard in the Seals' environment in years: "Don't be surprised if Toronto finishes out of the playoffs. They got a lot of great talent on that team but they just don't seem to hustle like the Leaf clubs I used to know and admire."[28]

Back in Oakland on January 3 versus Buffalo, the Seals were looking to gain a measure of revenge on the Sabres, who had outshot California 87–28 in their two previous meetings. The Sabres opened the scoring on a goal by Gilbert Perreault, but less than two minutes later Butch Williams tied the game at 1–1 while the Sabres had two men in the penalty box. At 9:41 of the second period Hrechkosy gave the Seals a 2–1 lead, but the talented Sabres were not to be outdone. Midway through the final period Jocelyn Guevremont scored the game-tying goal while Meloche's view was obscured. Unlike the two previous tilts, the game was not so one-sided, and the Seals came out with a 2–2 draw.

The schedule was not getting any easier for the Seals, but it was obvious they were not going to let the league's big boys push them around. Case in point: the Seals' next game, against Philadelphia on January 5. As always the Flyers drew a large crowd (11,157) to the Coliseum. The young Seals had clearly grown over the first half of the season. The Flyers suffered a shocking 5–1 drubbing. *Oakland Tribune* sports writer John Porter put it best when he said, "The fuzzy-cheeked kids that the local hockey fans were supposed to suffer with this season have begun to play as if they were scar-faced veterans."[29]

Even the Oakland fans got to the Flyers. During the game a fan threw beer onto Dave Schultz, and the "Hammer" tried to climb over the boards to get at the offender, who was quickly escorted out of the arena. The Flyers were at wits' end. "[The Seals] were all over the place. They never stopped forechecking," said Flyers goalie Bernie Parent. "Those guys skate harder than the Canadiens," said Joe Watson, who was unable to thwart a two-on-one by MacAdam and Gardner. "Zing, and they're by you." Flyers coach Fred Shero was gracious in defeat, pointing out the difference between this edition of the Seals and the one that had sputtered to 13 wins just a year earlier: "Give the Seals and their coach credit," he said. "We've had Stanley Cup experience two years in a row now, but they're a new team and beat us again. The Seals have made a few changes and they have players happy to be here like George Pesut and Al MacAdam. Some of the players with the Seals last year acted as if they were here for life."[30]

The Seals' 11–23–8 record was far from impressive, but there were plenty of reasons for optimism. The team was playing its best hockey in years, the Leafs were still within striking distance, and the Seals were showcasing a bumper crop of rookies. Dave Hrechkosy, who had been acquired from the New York Rangers for Bert Marshall in 1973, had scored 16 goals at that point and was tied for first among all NHL rookies even though he had cracked the Seals' line-up in only the sixth game of the season.

Hrechkosy certainly had a lot of flair. "He had quite an impression on the fans," remembers fan Cathy White. "He was sadly missed when he left, because he was a player that played with abandon. He just went out and hit everybody, and we called him the Wrecker." Hrechkosy had a few other nicknames too. His pointy mushroom-like haircut earned him the nickname "Flintstone," and he was also dubbed "Crazy Legs" because of his unusual skating style.

In an interview for this book Wayne King recalled a game in which Bobby Orr took the young Hrechkosy to school. "Orr was gonna take a shot from the point, give 'er one of those fake shots, and turn around backwards," King recalled. "Hrechkosy came right to the bench, and our captain Joey said, 'Wreck, you want a drink?' He stood straight up to block a shot, but Orr just went around him."

Between November 27 and January 24, Hrechkosy scored 17 goals, and the Seals started winning. Credit was partly due to the synergy Hrechkosy developed with "Spike" Huston and "Butch" Williams, who played on what was named the Wrecking Crew Line. John Bonasera has many fond memories of the Wrecker: "Who knew that he could score as many goals as he did? This was a guy who looked like anything but a person who could function on ice skates. He didn't look the part, kind of on the big, pudgy side, big curly hair. Just didn't really think much of him, and all of a sudden he's playing with Ron Huston and Butch Williams, and for some reason the line clicked."

Marshall Johnston had put the three players together for the first time on December 3, 1974, and in its first six games together, the line counted 11 goals. "Maybe we've jelled because we're three of the same type of hockey players," Hrechkosy said. "We think alike, do things alike. We're all mild mannered guys; we don't get down on ourselves or each other." The three players meshed well because, according to Huston, each player had a defined role. "'Wrecker' was up and down his wing and Butch mucked in the corners," Huston recalled. "I was the playmaker."[31] After 35 games, Huston had 9 goals and 23 points to his credit, and he would have contended for the team's overall scoring lead had it not been for a number of health issues he encountered throughout the season.

Larry Patey was also carrying a hot stick during a similar stretch. By the end of 1975, he had counted 10 goals and 8 assists and had become a real asset on the power play. Although he had been drafted in the ninth round of the 1973 entry draft, the red-headed Patey blossomed in Salt Lake City on a line with Wayne King and Del Hall, scoring 40 goals and 83 points and winning the WHL's Rookie of the Year award. When he arrived in Oakland, he brought with him an infectious, positive attitude, something the Seals needed if they were going to develop into contenders. "Personally, I was just charged to be there, you know, be in the league," he said, "and I think a lot of guys felt the same way. I think there was maybe several players that had been there previous years, that maybe you'd almost say they'd had enough. They were in a position where they were wanting to go forward, but were struggling to go forward, and [a lot of the younger guys] hadn't run into that wall yet."

Although the Seals had kept pace with the rest of the league most of the season, the clock eventually struck midnight, and Cinderella was left at the side of the road with just a pumpkin in her hands. Sitting just a few points behind third-place Toronto, the Seals lost six of seven games in mid-January. Someone had to take the blame for the collapse, and as is usually the case, the coach became the fall guy. The popular Marsh Johnston got the axe prior to the Seals' January 22 game in Pittsburgh, and general manager Bill McCreary took over the coaching reins for the rest of the season. It had been a tough season for a young, inexperienced coach like Johnston, but he had done a commendable job motivating his players and establishing a system that reduced the number of shots against Meloche and Simmons. "Marshall was very instrumental in developing players," remembers Cathy White. "He understood the game, he understood the people, the players, and he worked with them individually. I respected him." Joey Johnston appreciated what Marsh Johnston had brought to the table because, he believed, "There just wasn't enough coaching in those days." Joey the Jet believed the Seals played much better under their young coach than they had under Fred Glover. "I thought Marshall Johnston, he tried to work on things we needed to work on and to have us more defensive," he said, "which it showed by the scores." Patey believed "everybody really liked Marshall Johnston, including myself." Nevertheless, he also admitted he didn't think Johnston was "what we really needed to go forward. He was certainly a great guy to get us together and keep us moving."

Although Johnston was disappointed to be fired, he was not surprised: "I feel all right," he said at the time. "It is just an occupational hazard. I could be going to my own funeral, but I'm not," he reflected. "In this occupation, you have to accept the good and the bad. In the end, I think what cost me my job was that I stood up for what I believed in. You have to live with yourself and suffer the consequences."[32] In another interview he explained: "We had lost our last six games or something like that, and they felt there was more talent on the team than I was getting out of it. . . . I went into the job knowing the security of pro coaches is not the best, but I've been doing the best I could, and I haven't anything to hang my head for."[33]

McCreary denied a rift existed between himself and Johnston, but in reality they had rarely seen eye to eye, and it was just a matter of time before Johnston was replaced. The team had begun to play better in December so Johnston remained behind the bench, but once the Seals faded down the stretch, the heat was back on. "Sometimes there was a difference of opinion, but he was the general manager and I was the coach," Johnston said at the time. "I'm not going to get in a stinking contest with a skunk."[34]

McCreary told the media he made the change because he felt it would benefit the club. "I'm in the business to win," he said. "Hurting someone's feelings doesn't bother me. I am not here to lose. We have a chance for the playoffs, and I don't think we would have made the coaching change if we didn't."[35] In McCreary's two previous stints behind the

Blues' and Canucks' benches his record was a sorry 15-39-11, so the coaching change was not greeted with enthusiasm. Johnston was gregarious and friendly; the players, fans, and media loved him. "As usual, the affable Johnston, who lives in Hayward with his family, was eager to talk. It is too bad that the rest of the Seals' management doesn't always feel that way," lamented the *Hayward Daily Review*'s Joe DeLoach.[36]

Making matters worse for McCreary was the fact he butted heads with several players partly due to the fact they never forgave him for firing Johnston. "Johnston's firing was not popular with the Seals' players," said DeLoach. "Though they don't want to be quoted by name, the players on the Seals are not exactly overjoyed with McCreary as coach." That didn't stop Ron Huston from publicly stating his displeasure. "I can't say anymore about that guy," he said of McCreary, coming off a 4–1 loss to Pittsburgh on February 7. "We're [2-6] since he took over as coach. You know what I think of him."[37]

Johnston had earned the respect of his players. He was a teacher and a mentor to the many rookies who were forced to shoulder big responsibilities with the club. The veterans thought he was a thinking man's coach. The knock on McCreary was that he didn't seem to have the coaching skills or the right personality to stand behind an NHL bench, although as general manager he was knowledgeable and made some good moves. When Joe Starkey was asked to rate the various coaches he met during his time in Oakland he admitted, "It's hard to either flatter [McCreary] or insult him just because [he was] in such a difficult situation. I thought that McCreary, when he stepped in as coach, was the poorest. I thought he was completely miscast. I thought he was a prickly pear type of personality. Not easy to get along with anyhow. He was OK as a general manager, but when he fired Marshall and took over on the ice, I thought that the temporary position he was in was not good." Larry Patey admitted, "I don't think he was a coach. . . . I think when Bill took over, he probably did the right thing, made a change to see if he could try to stir things up, but he wasn't . . . one of these types of guys that motivated or got in your face if he had to and got you ready to play." Gary Simmons, as always, was blunt in his assessment of McCreary: "The only guy in the whole works that needs to be crucified is McCreary. I didn't like the guy, and despite what anybody tells you, they didn't like the guy either."

While Johnston was the quintessential player's coach, McCreary was a strict taskmaster. It did not take long for the players to draw a line between themselves and their new coach. Simmons recalled the Seals' first game with McCreary behind the bench, against Pittsburgh:

> In the first meeting, he said, "My method of coaching is going to be more defensive. We're not going to get near the shots on goal we've been getting, but neither is the opposition." . . . I played that game in Pittsburgh. I'm skating off the ice after the first period and the announcer says, "The Pittsburgh Penguins have set a new team record for shots on goal in one period: 26 shots."
>
> So they had two rooms in Pittsburgh, and the guys that smoked used to go in one room, and we're sitting there, and McCreary walks in, and I remember saying to him, "Bill, hey, let's cut out this defensive style. I can't take it." But I thought it was rather humorous. From what I heard from the players and from what I thought, I know I didn't like him. He didn't like me either, and that was fine.

While Simmons was also disappointed to see Johnston leave, he was not at all surprised:

> I have a theory. McCreary had coached in Vancouver and not done well. We were right in the playoffs, like 3-4 points behind the Leafs, from making the playoffs, and my theory is that we had like 25 games left, and about 21 of them were at home, and I think he thought, "Man, I can really look good if I take over coaching. We got all these home games." . . . We did pretty well at home. We didn't do well on the road, and I just saw it as a way of looking good. I mean, we're 4 points out of the playoffs. Marshall, with what we had, was doing a wonderful job, I thought, and to me, McCreary did that to make himself look good, and it didn't work out.

Simmons makes a good point about the cushy schedule. Throughout the team's history the Seals were frequently victims of unfortunate first-half scheduling. The previous year, 19 of the Seals' first 32 games had been on the road. Result: 7-22-3 record. Even worse, in 1975–76, the Seals would play 17 of their first 24 games on the road. The 1974–75 schedule was just as tough. That the young Seals were within striking distance of a playoff spot was nothing short of amazing. When Johnston was fired after 48 games, 28 of them had been on the road. At that point, the Seals' home record was 8-6-6, while their road record was 3-22-3. Of the final 27 games of the season, only 8 were on the road. If McCreary had been looking for an opportune moment to look like a genius, this was definitely it.

As January drew to a close, Clarence Campbell admitted during a league meeting in Montreal that because of the rising costs of owning the Seals the league was considering offers from potential buyers outside the Bay Area. "It is true that Denver and Salt Lake have shown a very strong interest in the purchase of the Seals,"[38] Munson Campbell confirmed at the time, but just over a week later, he revealed there were two prospective local groups hoping to keep the Seals in Oakland. He claimed to have met with each group at least once despite the fact Clarence Campbell said there were "no immediate prospects of anyone buying the Seals."[39] Munson claimed he had encouraged the two bidders to combine their resources and make an offer.

Clarence Campbell admitted the Seals had lost approximately $1.8 million in the first four months of the season, a staggering figure at the time. "The league [cannot] stand these losses," he said. "It's altogether unreasonable. The Seals' operation is draining our financial position at a very rapid rate."[40] He had more sobering statistics to share: "We are losing $10,000 a day operating the Seals despite a careful operation and we cannot continue this indefinitely. The cost of operating an NHL team today is about $3 million [a year]. It was only one million when the Seals came into the NHL at the time of the original expansion."[41]

Despite the Seals' admission that local suitors had shown some interest in buying the team, the relocation gossip persisted for months. Bill Cunningham, the general manager of the Oakland Coliseum, tried to squash the rumors by pointing out that the Coliseum had a binding contract with the Seals "for three more seasons after this one.

And we will do everything possible to see that the contract terms are upheld.... The contracts are made to be lived up to. We live up to our terms and we expect our tenants to do the same." Not everyone, however, agreed with Cunningham's statement. One anonymous Seals official retorted by saying, "Contracts can always be purchased."[42] Newspapers continued to report the Seals were on their way out of Oakland.

To further threaten the Seals, Clarence Campbell announced that the league had finally settled a $3 million lawsuit brought on by Barry Van Gerbig. Van Gerbig, as you may remember, wanted to move the Seals to Vancouver many years earlier, but the NHL nixed that plan, so Van Gerbig sued the league. In December the clearly exasperated Campbell claimed, "In the past two years, we've spent $4,000 per day on our own litigation. We're in this trouble because we were stupid enough to give a franchise to a schoolboy who played good golf and wore a Princeton tie."[43]

The courts ruled in favor of the NHL because it was determined the league was a "single entity" and therefore was "not in violation of antitrust law since a firm cannot conspire with itself." The Seals were not in competition with the NHL, but rather a partner with the NHL. In his ruling Judge Curtis explained, "As a member team, [the Seals] will continue cooperating with the defendants in pursuit of [the league's] main purpose, i.e. producing sporting, events of uniformly high quality appropriately scheduled as to both time and location so as to assure all members of the league the best financial return. In this respect, the plaintiff and defendants are acting together as one single business enterprise, competing against other similarly organized professional leagues."[44] In early February Van Gerbig and the league finally came to an agreement. "The matter with Van Gerbig is completely resolved," Campbell said. "He signed the papers and took the money. There were no damages involved, simply a matter of legal fees."[45] The threat of moving had always hung over the Seals like the sword of Damocles, but legally it was not going to happen until the lawsuit was settled. That was no longer the case. Unless the Seals turned things around immediately, it was just a matter of time before the team headed for greener pastures.

In the meantime, in the weeks following Johnston's firing the Seals seemed to turn a corner, compiling a 6-6-3 record during one stretch, including a spectacular 6-1 win over Toronto on January 24. It didn't matter much since the Leafs still had an 8-point lead over California in the standings, a point spread that only grew in the following weeks. By March 1 the Leafs had climbed to 23-29-11, while the Seals lagged 14 points behind at 16-37-11.

There was not much left worth playing for at that point, but Simmons turned in his second shutout of the season against the troubled Kansas City Scouts on February 15. Six days later the Californians tripped up the Boston Bruins 6-4 at the sold-out Coliseum, the first such occasion of the season, and just the eleventh time in eight years. This game happened to be the first time the Seals actually won in front of a sold-out Coliseum. Dave Hrechkosy scored 2 more goals to bring his total to 25, which easily put him on pace to pass the 30-goal mark.

On March 14, Wrecker scored his 28th goal and sixth game winner, a team record, in a 4-2 win over Detroit. Hrechkosy credited Marshall Johnston's faith in him as the reason for his successful rookie season. "I wasn't doing well early in the season and I was a little discouraged about not playing more," Wrecker admitted. "The coach told me to keep working hard and not to worry. Then I was put into a game by surprise, got a shorthanded goal—that's really a lift—and that was it. I was a regular. Like the coach said, all I had to do was keep plugging away."[46] Wrecker seemed in perfect position to break Norm Ferguson's team record of 34 goals, but with ten games left in the schedule, Hrechkosy was only able to score once more, finishing the year with 29 goals.

With the season all but over, the Seals won their last game of the season on March 21 against St. Louis, 7-4. The Seals then went winless in their next 8 games to close out the schedule. During this final stretch the Seals experienced the ultimate embarrassment: losing at home to the woeful Washington Capitals. Since the beginning of the season the Caps had won only 6 games—all on Washington ice. To that point they had lost every one of their 37 road games to tie the Seals' dubious record from 1973-74. How bad were the Capitals that season? For one thing, they were outscored 446-181. Back-up goaltender Michel

Belhumeur finished the season with *zero* wins in 35 games, which is no surprise considering the Caps gave up 10 or more goals in a game *seven* times! To this day players from the 1974–75 Capitals still hold, in whole or in part, the five worst single-season plus/minus marks in NHL history. Bill Mikkelson finished the year a horrific -82 despite playing in only 59 games! Coming into their March 28 game with the Seals, the Caps were riding a 17-game winless streak.

Washington got out in front 3–1, and the Seals barely noticed, putting up just 9 shots in the first period. In the second period the Seals reduced the Caps' lead to 1 on a goal by Charlie Simmer, and Dave Gardner made it 3–3 five minutes into the third period. The world was right again, and it was just a matter of time before the Seals pulled off win number twenty, or so it seemed. Washington stormed back less than two minutes later on a goal by Nelson Pyatt, but the Seals could not get the tie and salvage their pride. Pyatt scored an empty netter at 19:28 to seal the deal, and Washington skated away with a shocking 5–3 win.

Needless to say, McCreary was none too impressed by the end result. "With the good weather, [the players'] minds seem to be on golf and tennis," he said after the game. For Stan Gilbertson, the former Seal who had found his way to Washington by way of a trade with St. Louis, it had been strange going to a city where losing was even more common than in Oakland. But for one brief, shining moment he could savor a sweet victory. "When we got those two quick first period goals, we thought we had a chance to win," he said. "We've been beaten so often, it's really good to win. I spent enough time with the Seals and we always seemed to be setting negative records."[47]

It was a bittersweet night for Butch Williams, who, personally, had played a great game. "I got to play against the Capitals, my brother's team," he recalled. "I ended up with a few points (one goal and two assists). I was the first star and Tommy (two assists) was the second star. They beat us. Our dad was listening to the game over his short wave and that made it special. The game was in Oakland and the Capitals won. Tommy marched a garbage can around their dressing room like it was the Stanley Cup."[48] Gary Simmons also remembered the game. "I, fortunately, was not playing in it," he explained. "It was damn embarrassing."

The story of the Stanley Cup garbage can has been told count-less times, but former Cap Ron Lalonde shed some new light on the famous postgame celebration. "We came in the dressing room, and we were quite happy, and one thing led to another," he said. "We all signed—it was a plastic green garbage can—and then somebody sug-gested taking it out, and they actually took it out back into the arena and skated around the ice with it. There was nobody left in the rink, but we made a big deal of this garbage can. I think [the Seals] were in the league for the next year, and that garbage can was still there with all our names on it." Defenseman Jack Lynch remembers that night fondly. "We got back to the hotel," he wrote in an email message, "and partied like hell until the wee hours!! I don't recall if the can was still there the next year but I do remember someone from another team saying that they had seen the can in the visitors' dressing room."[49]

California finished the season with 19 wins, 48 losses, and 13 ties, by far its best performance since 1971-72. The Seals' many youngsters gave every indication the club was headed in the right direction. Larry Patey led the team with 25 goals and 45 points. Stan Weir also had 45 points, while Al MacAdam and Dave Hrechkosy each had 43. The seventeen rookies who suited up for the Seals over the course of the season accounted for 114 of the team's 212 goals.

The additions of Jim Neilson, Len Frig, Mike Christie, and Rick Hampton helped whittle the Seals' 342 goals against average in 1973-74 down to a more respectable 316, but the defense corps was still a work in progress, as evidenced by the occasional 10-0 blowout that befell the Seals. Hampton in particular "had a lot to learn about playing defence," said coach McCreary, "but you could see him improving, game by game."[50] The young defenseman also made a good impres-sion on the fans, winning the Booster Club's Most Popular Player award.

The Seals were far from being Cup contenders, but the club had improved by leaps and bounds. "It really wasn't that bad of a season for us," said Gilles Meloche. "All I have ever wanted to do was to have something to play for. We had a shot at the playoffs and that made the season worth it all. As long as I have ever been here, I have never experienced that feeling." Spike Huston, who scored 33 points in just 56 games, was also quick to point out the Seals' overall improvement. "You can't really judge this team by the number of games that we won and lost," he said. "We're a young team that needs experience and consistency. Lots of our losses were due to stupid mistakes, but just because we didn't make the playoffs doesn't mean the season wasn't a success."[51]

While the Seals had improved on the ice, the club's financial outlook was not so promising. At the start of the 1974–75 season the Seals had sold only 600 season tickets.[52] Although by the end of the season the club averaged more than 6,000 fans per game for the first time in three years, even the moribund expansionists from Kansas City (average attendance of 7,356) and Washington (an even more remarkable average of 10,004) fared better despite their cumulative 23-121-16 record.

The NHL was sick and tired of babysitting the orphaned Seals and was desperate to find a responsible owner with deep pockets. When the NHL took control of the Seals in 1974, fifteen other teams had shares in the club, and they were losing tons of money because no one came to the Coliseum. Making matter worse, the Seals also attracted small crowds on the road, unlike the Philadelphia Flyers or Boston Bruins, so keeping the Seals in the league made everyone a loser in the end. "We spent an enormous amount of money supporting that team," said an exasperated Clarence Campbell. "The league will absorb a very substantial amount of losses." According to Campbell, the NHL had spent $11 million running the Seals, a figure which included the $6.5 million owed to Charlie Finley, as well as other operating losses and legal fees. "It was a grievous experience," Campbell continued. "I will never consider the NHL purchasing a franchise to try to bail it out of financial difficulties."[53]

There was speculation the Seals would move to Denver and the bankrupt Pittsburgh Penguins to Seattle. Both western cities desperately wanted franchises in the NHL's next expansion phase, but they were more than ready to put up an orphaned franchise right away.

Ivan Mullenix, president of the Denver Spurs of the Central Hockey League (CHL), showed great interest in purchasing the Seals. There was only one obstacle in his way: a certain Melvin M. Swig, whose family owned the ritzy Fairmont Hotel in San Francisco, and who had been one of the WHL Seals' original owners back in 1961.

New York Rangers president William Jennings approached the fifty-nine-year-old Swig in February 1975 about the possibility of taking the Seals off the league's hands. Swig had always had a soft spot for hockey, so he and a friend met with Jim Cullen, the NHL's legal adviser and agent responsible for ownership of the Seals. "We talked details," Swig said, "started to bring interested parties together and got quite a little support. I told Jennings and Cullen we were interested." Nevertheless, despite Swig's sincere interest in making the Seals a success once again, he also knew that buying the club was a huge gamble. He told Cullen and Detroit Red Wings owner Bruce Norris, another curious party, "It would be more difficult to make the Seals a going concern now than it would be starting from scratch." Swig said, "I would expect they would take this into consideration."[54]

Swig talked about using the team's first-round pick to select a big young defenseman to shore up the blue line. He also pondered acquiring the flashy, but troubled, Derek Sanderson. Listening to Swig, it was obvious he knew his hockey, unlike the blustery Finley, who simply liked to see his name in the papers. Swig spoke like he knew how to build and grow a business: "I think that with an interested local group, working at promoting hockey and using their influence in such fields as sale of season tickets, it could be done."[55] Swig was the Seals' white knight, the one man who could save and, more importantly, who *wanted* to save the franchise from certain doom. "Swig should have got the team in the first place," said George Black, then-president of the Seals Booster Club, numbering 760 members at the time. "He's a hockey man who will build this club. I'm even willing to go to San Francisco to watch them." Former Booster Club president Ty Toki had met Swig when the hotelier was still owner of the San Francisco Seals: "I saw Mel Swig out on the ice with the team one day and wondered who it was because I didn't know him at the time. I met him and he turned to be a regular guy. I'm optimistic for the team now."[56]

Seals fan Elwood Strelo felt equally enthusiastic about Swig. "He knows what he's doing," he said. "He knows the secret is entertainment and identity and he's got the industrial swack that will mean five times more season tickets. The Seals' biggest problem was in the front office, not on the ice. What a mish-mash of problems. If they had been a public entity, they would've been voted out of office."[57] Gary Simmons was also very impressed by what he saw from Swig: "I have already met Mel and he is a real super guy," he said at the time. "I have talked to some of the old Seals' players who played for Mel when he owned the team in San Francisco and they tell me that he is is [*sic*] a real prince. He is the type of person who cares. Someone who takes the players' interests at heart."[58]

Players, journalists, and fans suddenly felt optimistic about the team's future, but as always that optimism was dished out with a side order of skepticism. Len Frig may have said it best when he explained, "It wouldn't take very much to turn around this team.... A couple of more veterans with our young talent could put us in the playoffs next year.... It could happen next year, and maybe, it will never happen."[59] If that wasn't the Seals' spirit, alive and kicking.

This time around, the hockey gods finally gave the Seals a break. On July 28 the white knight rode in on his trusty steed and rescued the troubled franchise, even though he was somewhere between $400,000 and $600,000 short of the league's target price. Two of his financial supporters had just turned their backs on him due to recently modified tax laws in the United States, but Swig promised he would soon have all of the necessary funds, and that was good enough for the league. The NHL had no intention of keeping the team on life support another season. League owners were so glad to be dusting their hands of the Seals they provided Swig with the missing funds, because that was actually cheaper than having the Seals on their books another year. Swig could only smile at the turn of events. In the event the Seals continued to lose money, Swig had the option of moving the club to a location of his choosing as long as the league received notice by May 15. Satisfied with the terms of his sweetheart deal, Swig assumed all of the $4.5 million still owed to Finley by the NHL, to be paid off over a period of five years.

Swig also expressed an interest in building a large new stadium for the Seals, and in July the San Francisco Redevelopment Agency approved a plan to build an 18,000–20,000-seat arena in the Yerba Buena Center. "With the size of the present arena, it is impossible to make money," Swig said. "We can't make a profit in Oakland. We'll have to take losses, but that's part of the purchase price." Despite the obvious financial issues Swig would be facing, he had no intention of being tight-fisted. "We do not plan any cost-cutting," announced Swig. "We won't be extravagant, but we'll maintain the staff we have and do everything first class all the way. Our player salaries will be higher than last year."[60] The Seals were not out of the woods yet, but if they could hang on for just two or three more years, the club would have a brand new rink to call home.

The California Golden Seals were finally turning the corner and putting the darkest period of their history behind them. It had been five long years since anyone in a Seals uniform had seen the playoffs. It had been even longer since the top of the organization had seen any kind of stability. If the Seals were ever going to establish themselves as a lasting Bay Area entity, the time was upon them.

10 SWIG VS. MOSCONE, 1975–1976

The Seals' eighth NHL season had seen the club dismantled in order to bring in a cheaper, defense-oriented group of players into the fold. Even though the club had finished in the division cellar a third straight year, the club had improved itself exponentially.

The hot button issue over the summer, other than the ownership situation, was the status of captain Joey Johnston, the longest-serving and unhappiest of all Seals players. "I just worked hard and hoped somebody noticed so I could get a job outside this organization," he admitted. "The city was great, the people were nice but I hated playing with a loser." At the start of the 1974–75 campaign, the twenty-five-year-old Johnston seemed poised to lead the team in scoring once again, and he picked up exactly where he had left off the year before, scoring 17 points in the Seals' first 20 games. On April 5 Johnston scored the 84th goal and 185th point of his Seals career, supplanting Ted Hampson as the franchise's all-time leading scorer. Despite the accomplishment, Johnston's season had been a struggle, amounting to just 14 goals and 23 assists in 62 games. He broke his wrist in a game versus Kansas City in December, but he continued to play and struggled to keep up the pace he had established early on. "I played 21 games with it," Johnston recalled. "The swelling caused it not to show up on the x-rays. It was very frustrating. My wrist hurt with every pass."[1] A fight with Montreal's Doug Risebrough on February 2 caused further damage to the wrist, forcing the captain to undergo a second x-ray that revealed the cause of his pain.

The wrist injury aside, Johnston was also fed up with losing and was ready to move on. Commenting on the November trade that had sent Craig Patrick and Stan Gilbertson to St. Louis, Johnston said, "It was an act of God, a miracle for them. Why not trade me and get something for me? Look, I'm just sick of losing all the time. My wife's sick of it, too. This is my fourth year with this team. I've served my time."[2] He even vowed to leave Oakland at the end of the season once his contract expired. He admitted talking to several WHA teams about jumping leagues. Johnston asked Bill McCreary to hand the captain's C over to a more experienced player like Jim Neilson, but in the end Johnston remained captain.

Knowing full well the free-agent left winger was never going to stay in the Bay Area, McCreary completed a blockbuster deal that sent Johnston to Chicago for 36-goal man Jim Pappin. Johnston himself, however, was the true catalyst of the deal. His contract had expired on May 30, and he then signed a free agent contract with the Black Hawks. Under league rules the Hawks were forced to compensate the Seals for their loss, hence the reason Pappin was sent to Oakland. "Johnston was unhappy in Oakland," said McCreary, "and Pappin, I understand, was being given a hard time by the Chicago fans. Sometimes when that happens, a trade is the best thing."[3] The good news was Pappin had scored 270 career goals; the second-highest scorer on the Seals' roster was Jim Neilson, with 63 goals in 13 seasons!

Johnston, however, was ten years Pappin's junior, meaning, in all likelihood, Pappin's skills would only decline while Johnston's hadn't yet peaked. "I couldn't believe I was traded," Pappin remarked years later. "I was all done. I was 36-years-old and I think I had only one year left on my contract.... I was so used to being in Chicago, I was never going to play again but the Seals kept calling. I had a bad back and skated with the local junior team to get into shape."[4] Pappin also wanted to play closer to his family, who lived in Sudbury, Ontario. "I have nothing against Oakland," he admitted in September. "It's just a family situation for me. I have three kids . . . to consider and told them I wanted to play for a club an hour's travel from home."[5] Pappin announced his retirement during training camp, leaving the Seals with a huge void at right wing, but he returned ten games into the season. His return was brief, however, as he soon developed Bell's palsy, causing him to miss a good chunk of the season.

Former Seals Booster Club member John Bonasera had season tickets at the Coliseum for the 1975–76 season. He remembers how his initial excitement over the Johnston-Pappin trade quickly faded:

I'll never forget the morning when I got up to go to school and I looked at the sports page, and one of the smaller headlines in the sports section was that the Seals have acquired Jim Pappin for Joey Johnston. . . . He was their leading scorer, but geez, we traded him, and we're getting Jim Pappin! Oh my God! This is tremendous. I was beside myself. He was one of my favorite players in the league. . . .

Jim Pappin's career as a Seal was far from successful. In hindsight, he didn't play a whole lot of games, he didn't last very long, he just wasn't very successful, and so for me, personally, it was a very disappointing thing . . . it was pretty apparent once we saw him that he was past his prime.

Johnston's career also took a turn for the worse during the summer. One month after the trade, a terrible car accident left Johnston with a broken wrist and serious head injuries. He was transferred to a Toronto hospital immediately. Doctors thought he was goner, but Johnston survived the ordeal, and fought his way back into the Chicago lineup. Unfortunately the accident had caused a balance problem. He even had difficulty jogging, because his head would spin constantly. Johnston went scoreless in thirty-two games with the Hawks, so they sent him down to Dallas to help him get his game back, but it was a frustrating experience. After just one game, Johnston left some of his teammates a note explaining that he just couldn't handle the rigors of playing professional hockey. Just twenty-seven, Johnston called it a career and returned home to Peterborough. Retirement was not easy for Johnston. He admits to a lot of drinking in the 1970s, but he is proud to point out now that he hasn't had a drink in thirty years.

Had McCreary known that trading a rising star like Johnston for a fading veteran would cause more harm than good, he probably wouldn't have sent twenty-two-year-old Stan Weir, the Seals' second-leading scorer, to Toronto for thirty-one-year-old Gary Sabourin. "I got Sabby for a purpose," explained McCreary. "He is a hard-working, sincere type of athlete and I knew he'd be a tremendous influence on the young group of players we were putting together."[6] Simmons did not often see eye to eye with McCreary, but their opinions of Sabourin were almost identical. "Gary Sabourin was a guy that had been around a long time," Simmons remembered. "He was very helpful when he came, with the younger players, because he talked to them, and he counseled a few of the younger guys. He did a good job." Rookie Dennis Maruk spent much time with Sabourin and appreciated having the veteran player mentor him. "I roomed with Gary Sabourin, pretty much all my first year," said Maruk. "I was able to get a lot of information, a lot of direction from Gary Sabourin, which was nice because I was really young. . . . I asked a lot of questions, and he was real cordial about everything." While Sabourin would prove to be a useful asset in the short term, Weir would continue to play good hockey long after Sabourin retired.

At the amateur draft the Seals selected Ralph Klassen third overall. Klassen had accumulated 68 points in 41 games with Saskatoon of the Western Canada Hockey League (WCHL) and had picked up an impressive 28 points in the 1974–75 playoffs. Eighteen picks later, the Seals chose Dennis "Pee Wee" Maruk, a speedy, creative forward from the London Knights of the Ontario Major Junior Hockey League (OMJHL). At nineteen Maruk broke Marcel Dionne's league scoring records by racking up 66 goals and 145 points. The 5'8" Maruk was small by NHL standards, so every team, including California, passed him over in the first round, which was a huge mistake. "He was a total competitor," said Klassen. "We got along very well. He had a lot of fire in his eyes and was very self motivated. He wanted to prove he belonged because of his size. He was electrifying to watch, a real crowd pleaser and very confident." According to his future linemate Al MacAdam, Maruk "was one of the fastest four or five players in the league, no one could accelerate like he could. He was loaded with guts and determination."[7] Wayne King remembers that Maruk "had a little showmanship, he could skate fast. . . . He was sort of cocky himself when he was playing."

John Bonasera remembers Maruk's visits to Booster Club meetings as being particularly special because the brash young rookie was gregarious and comfortable in front of the fans:

There was a particular Booster Club event that I remember going to where the guest speakers were Ralph Klassen and Dennis Maruk. . . . The funny, interesting part to me was Ralph Klassen was shy, and you could tell he was uncomfortable in that situation, standing at a dais with a microphone, and if he had his choice he wouldn't be there at all, and Dennis Maruk was the complete opposite. Dennis Maruk was happy-go-lucky, and, you know, give me that microphone, and I'm gonna shine, and you people are gonna love me, and I love you. It was so funny. Maruk kept picking on Klassen, and poor Ralph had nothing to fight back with. He just wanted to get the heck out of there, and I remember just sitting there and laughing.

Maruk had grown up a Toronto Maple Leafs fan and had hoped to be drafted by his hometown team, but he was nevertheless happy to be in Oakland because he knew he had a good chance of cracking the lineup. "When I went to camp, they said I was going to play in the minors, and I had not signed a contract and all that," Maruk remembered. "My agent at the time was 'Boom Boom' Geoffrion, and he told them that I was going to score them a lot of goals, and what happened was the first preseason game, I was in LA against the Los Angeles Kings. . . . [I] ended up having a good game—I think I scored a couple goals—and bussed back to Oakland and signed a contract right there."

Geoffrion's prediction turned out to be true. Maruk scored lots of goals for the Seals. Before long he started hearing strange chants at the Coliseum whenever he touched the puck. "Oakland fan support was really good," Maruk remembers. "I mean, they were awesome to me. They started that 'Marooook!' chant every time I touched the puck. . . . I thought they were booing me, and so it made me work harder, but no, it was the chant they'd started, and I really appreciated it." John Bonasera became a huge Dennis Maruk fan. "Me and my buddies just adored Dennis Maruk," he said. "I mean, he was clearly our best player the last year, and toward the end of the season we hand-painted a big sign and hung it at the south end of the arena for a few games, and it simply was 'Marookie of the Year,' and I can take credit for that; I know people have told me they remember that, but me and my buddies were the ones who made that sign and loved the guy."

Obviously any team with such great young talent in need of guidance requires a responsible coach to lead them in the right direction. The *Hayward Daily Review*'s Joe DeLoach expressed what everyone was thinking: that Bill McCreary was not the right person to coach the team. "The Seals' management made a glaring mistake late in January," he opined, "when first-year coach Marshall Johnston was fired and replaced by general manager McCreary. The players respected Johnston greatly as a coach and resented McCreary.... McCreary is not a good coach: he has indelibly proven that in three unsuccessful jobs with the Seals, St. Louis and Vancouver. McCreary, however, has strong qualities as a general manager. His place is in the front office and not behind the bench."[8]

McCreary got the message. Immediately after the Seals' final regular season game McCreary announced, "I won't be back next year as coach of the Seals."[9] Jack "Tex" Evans of the Salt Lake City Golden Eagles was promoted to the Seals during the summer, and he was more than qualified for the job. Evans had played for the WHL Seals back in 1966–67, and he later guided the Eagles to the CHL championship in 1975. He was named the CHL's Coach of the Year that same season, and in the *Hockey News*'s fiftieth anniversary issue, he was named the best coach in that league's history.

Born in Morriston, England, in 1928, Evans had to work hard to stretch out a pedestrian fourteen-year NHL career. The only thing that stood out on his résumé was the Stanley Cup he won with Chicago in 1961. Evans was a no-nonsense, pipe-smoking toughie who promised to whip the Seals into shape. "I didn't get to know Jack very much 'cause I was playing on the third, fourth line," remembers Wayne King, "and he didn't really talk too much to the guys on the third and fourth line. He didn't play them a lot. He was a tough old coach though.... Looked like a gangster."

"I really liked Tex because I played with him in San Diego," remembered Simmons. "Tex was old school. When I played with him in San Diego he was forty-four years old. He was the assistant coach and still playing defense.... Nobody stood in front of that net when Tex was on the ice. I mean, he was a tough old bird, and he played the way they played back then. If you stood there, if you had the balls to stand there, you were going to pay the price." Simmons enjoyed playing for Evans but believes it was difficult for him to coach a team that didn't always project a macho image: "We didn't have a lot of players like [him] on the Seals, and I used to see Tex get so red behind the bench. He was more, 'let's go, come on, we gotta win.' . . . He had the reputation . . . he used to get so red and mad when we'd have somebody do something that was a little less manly on the ice."

One of the biggest knocks against players from the Finley era was that many lacked drive and discipline. Some players simply accepted losing, gave up easily, and cashed their paychecks. This attitude disturbed many players when they first arrived in Oakland. "The team did not have a winning attitude but they changed it around," remembered Mike Christie. "The leadership on the club was not conducive to winning. I remember my first game in Oakland. After the first period, were [*sic*] getting beat pretty badly. Our captain, Joey Johnston said, 'Well boys, only 239 more periods to go.'"[10]

Another reason for the blasé attitude was the fact the Seals' roster had been razor thin for years, so the team's best players were guaranteed to make the team, which created a lack of motivation. "I always played well enough to make the team, but I think it was only at about 80 percent of my capacity," Reggie Leach admitted years later. "I played well enough to get my bonus. It was an easy attitude to get into—to not care if you win or lose. I had to change my attitude when I was traded to the Flyers." The Seals' lackadaisical attitude disappeared under Evans. "I loved the guy," said rookie forward Bob Murdoch. "I could always count on him being the same every day regardless of the situation. He was a hard nosed guy. If you worked hard for him, there were no problems. If you didn't, you disappeared."[11] Jack Evans was not going to allow a defeatist attitude to poison his locker room. Everyone was going to work hard now that he was in charge because he knew the Seals had talent in Salt Lake City, having coached there previously.

Evans had his work cut out for him. "The opening of our training camp last summer was a terrifying thing for a coach," Evans admitted in midseason. "We had 21 days to pick the team and get some kind of system going, and more than half the players were strangers to each other and, of course, to their coach."[12] It was a similar situation to a year earlier when the coaching staff had found itself with a bunch of rookies who were somehow supposed to make the Seals competitive. This time around recent draftees Klassen and Maruk were joined by new regulars Fred Ahern, Bob Murdoch, Bob Girard, Gary Holt, George Pesut, and Tim Jacobs. That's *eight* rookies who would play at least half the season in Oakland. The young players would be all right under Evans, but that didn't mean rookie mistakes would be tolerated. One time Maruk was supposed to hop on the ice for his shift, but because he was so mesmerized watching his idol Phil Esposito play, the Seals' rookie forgot to jump over the boards. Evans went up to Maruk and told him, "Well, you're gonna be sitting there for a few more." Maruk laughed about it inside, "but I was mad and upset," he admitted.

There was a new enthusiasm in the Bay Area that summer, and it showed on the ice. In the Seals' season opener in Atlanta, the Flames took a 3–1 lead in the second frame, but the Seals stormed back to win 4–3. Dave Gardner scored a goal, as did Bob Murdoch and Ralph Klassen, who were both playing in their first NHL game. The Seals also won their second game three nights later, a 2–1 decision over the Detroit Red Wings. By the time the Seals played their home opener against Washington, they carried a respectable 2–2 record in four road games. Before an Oakland crowd of 7,996, the Seals fought the Capitals to a 3–3 draw.

A late-October swoon dropped the Seals' record to 3-9-2, but they rebounded nicely. Gary Sabourin scored 4 goals in a 7–5 win over the Rangers in Oakland on November 7, giving him the overall team lead with 8 goals. A few nights later versus the Islanders Maruk set a league rookie record by scoring his third consecutive short-handed goal—smashing the old mark of two held by five players.

By the end of November the Seals were off to their best start since 1971–72: a 8-14-2 record after 24 games. Even more surprising was the fact the Seals had played 17 of those 24 games on the road and had gone 5-11-1 away from home. The two previous seasons combined the Seals had gone an embarrassing 7-68-3 on the road. As a team the Seals sat 12th out of 18 clubs with a decent 3.33 goals against average.

On offense the 3-M Line of Maruk, MacAdam, and Murdoch became the team's focal point. The three players had great chemistry together from day one. "We were the young guys," Maruk explained, "and I think Jack Evans put us together, and we seemed to look pretty good, so he kept us together, and that's what it was for the first three years." Individually the members of the 3-M Line stood out. "Of course," explained Maruk, "I came from a scoring background. . . . MacAdam was more the physical, tough left winger, and Bobby Murdoch and I were guys that had some pretty good hands in scoring, and we just were able to complement each other."

Maruk and MacAdam became excellent penalty killers, scoring 9 shorthanded goals between them that season. Maruk's 5 goals set a new league mark for rookies. "I think we were able to create that excitement defensively as well as killing penalties," Maruk explained. "We were able to create some scoring chances because of our speed and our puck handling ability, especially Al MacAdam. . . . Al and I killed penalties a lot, and Al was a real strong, strong forward so I was able to cap off him, and we were able to create some two-on-ones and scoring chances . . . and when we had the opportunity we were able to try and create some scoring chances shorthanded." John Bonasera described Al MacAdam as a "great player . . . hard-nosed, and just a very talented player who wasn't a ginormous goal scorer, but he had some decent seasons. . . . Just a strong, solid kind of two-way forward back in the day."

According to Maruk, the often-forgotten third man on the line, Murdoch, "was really a gifted, great scorer, great shot player, and was able to make some pretty good plays. Of course, not as physical, he was more offensive-minded like his brother [New York Rangers star Don Murdoch], scoring goals. . . . I would think that he was a great team guy, liked everybody, came to practice, worked hard in games . . . and he was a big part of my success, because we were able to make some nice plays, and I got some goals but also got some nice assists." Maruk added that Murdoch had the ability to find open ice, making it easier to find him. "Bobby would always put himself in a good shooting position, whenever I would slide the puck to him . . . and he had a good chance to score all the time because he had a great

FIG. 16. The 3-M Line faces off against Boston. Photo by
Elliot Lowe.

shot." Bonasera described Murdoch as "a sharpshooter, a sniper that
had a little bit of talent. Of course, he never really realized anything
great, but that first year showed some flash."

According to Bonasera, the 3-M Line played an even greater role
than leading the Seals on offense; it gave the Seals the kind of league-
wide exposure that had always eluded them:

> That line was special. . . . In a kind of weird way it was kind of neat
> that we had a line that had a nickname, because in those days there
> was the G-A-G Line, and there were several popular line combina-
> tions and they all had nicknames of some sort, and the Seals had a
> mishmash of players that interspersed from game to game, and you
> never really had any solidarity, and then finally a line combination
> or two that might stick for a season, and then we came up with the
> M Squad, the 3-M Line, and that was kind of cool that around the
> league they were recognized.

At the opposite end of the scoring spectrum, last season's club
scoring champ Larry Patey was traded to St. Louis after scoring
only 8 points in 18 games. Patey's subpar performance could have
been attributed to an ankle injury he had battled all season long. In
exchange for Patey the Seals received Wayne "Bones" Merrick, a

twenty-three-year-old center coming off a solid 65-point season. He had also finished the campaign a respectable +29, proving he was an excellent two-way player. Not only was Merrick a former first-round pick, but he had also been one of the Blues' most popular players. In fact, Blues fans were outraged when they found out Bones was leaving. For several games afterward they would chant "We want Merrick!" at home games. Even though Merrick loved St. Louis, he was excited to be going to Oakland. "I think we're going to make the playoffs," he said. "In fact, I'm sure of it. The guys on this team want to play hockey. There's no fooling around."[13]

The Seals had also lost patience with Dave Hrechkosy. The two other members of the Wrecking Crew Line had already fallen out of favor with McCreary and were no longer with the team. Ron Huston, who never got along with McCreary, was traded before the season started, and Butch Williams was demoted after just fourteen games, leaving Hrechkosy to fend for himself. The former 29-goal scorer suffered through a terrible sophomore jinx and was sent to the minors to find his game. After scoring a baffling 14 points in 38 NHL games, he was also shipped to St. Louis for two draft picks. Simmons believed Hrechkosy's scoring suddenly dried up because he had to play without his trusty centerman, Huston:

Hrechkosy had a bonus for 30 goals. When Huston got hurt . . . [Hrechkosy] didn't get another goal the rest of the year. McCreary, in his infinite wisdom, the next year figured that "Spike" Huston was a bad influence on Hrechkosy so he traded Huston to Phoenix, and Wrecker got a few goals, but he ended up getting traded to St. Louis. I mean, what kind of thinking is that? It doesn't take a genius to figure out the guy's got 29 goals when Huston gets hurt, and he ends up 21 games later with 29 goals. It doesn't take a genius to figure out what the secret was. I mean, Wrecker was a good goal scorer, but Spike was a great passer, and Spike set him up all the time.

While it is a bit of an exaggeration to suggest Hrechkosy was completely shut down after Huston went down, Wrecker did score just 3 goals in the final 17 games of the season and didn't score once in the final 8 games. Hrechkosy had also scored 5 goals and 3 assists in the 11 games Huston missed between December 22 and January 16. It was well known, however, that Wrecker liked the occasional drink and often partied pretty hard off the ice. "His off-ice activities hurt him," MacAdam said. "It slowed him down. He was a big guy and he took the league by storm his first year and then he was out of the league two years later. A good time guy, but like a lot of the guys on our team, he didn't care where he was playing. He would play the same in California, Salt Lake or anywhere." Wayne King got to know Hrechkosy well in the years they played together. "We played in Salt Lake before we came up," King remembers. "He was a good goal scorer, when he came to Oakland anyway." King did not know why Hrechkosy was traded, but he also admitted, "I don't want to think about [the reasons]," and then laughed. "Gotta keep those secret." For his part Hrechkosy admitted responsibility for his difficult second season in the NHL. "I don't think I was mature enough to handle the press and outside interruptions that my success caused going into the 1975–76 season," he said.[14]

John Bonasera has fond memories of the line that took the Bay Area by storm in 1974–75. "For like half a season they were awesome," he remembered. "Butch Williams went to have basically no career. Spike Huston went on to have basically no career. . . . But for [those] magical few months, that was a fun group. . . . It was just a sort of a convergence of the planets and the stars or something, and everything aligned properly." In fact, the Wrecking Crew Line spent even less than half a season together, but their impact was huge. The line was formed on December 3 and stayed together until Huston went down with an injury on December 22. When he returned after eleven games out, the Crew was reunited until Huston went down again on February 21. In all, the trio played about thirty-one games together, but in that time Hrechkosy scored 12 goals and 9 assists, Huston had 8 goals and 10 assists, and Williams had 7 goals and 9 assists. The Seals went 8-19-4 during the Wrecking Crew's run, but only 11-29-9 the rest of the way.

The players who had helped the Seals on the road to recovery the previous year were now being cast aside in one way or another. New captain Jim Neilson injured his leg just twenty-six games into the season and would be out for months. It wouldn't be easy replacing the man who had been voted the Seals' best defenseman and Most Valuable Player the previous year. On December 3 Jack Evans handed the team captaincy over to rugged defenseman Bob Stewart, who was highly respected by everyone in the dressing room. At one time Stewart had been the club's policeman, but now he had greater responsibilities. "The day of the cheap penalty for me is over," he declared. "You learn over the years to play a smarter game if you expect to make it in the NHL. Now I try to play a thinking man's game. There's no sense taking a bad penalty that hurts your club."[15]

Soon after the announcement, Len Frig went down with an injury, leaving the club with only three experienced defensemen—Stewart, Hampton, and Christie—and between them only Stewart had more than two hundred games of NHL experience. Nevertheless, the defense tightened up, allowing just 3.33 goals per game in December, even though the Seals went a disappointing 3-6-1 during that time.

On January 2 the Seals began the New Year with a convincing 8–5 victory over Washington. Wayne Merrick tallied 3 goals and 3 assists for a team record 6 points. The Seals fired a club record 51 shots at Caps goalies Ron Low and Bernie Wolfe. A week later the Capitals suffered a 5–0 whitewashing at the hands of the Seals. Simmons notched his first shutout of the season, and Murdoch counted 3 assists for the winners, while MacAdam set a new team record by scoring the winning goal for the third consecutive game. One week after the second Washington blowout the Seals embarrassed the New York Rangers, 7–0, to give Simmons his second consecutive shutout.

At the All-Star break the Seals had amassed 38 points in 45 games, their highest total ever at that point, but division rivals Toronto, Buffalo, and Boston were all playing great hockey, keeping California in last place. The Seals' good fortune continued after the break. They scored a convincing 4-1 victory over Kansas City on January 23, followed by a 5-3 win over Toronto two days later. In the Toronto-California tilt Wayne Merrick scored another hat trick, giving him 8 goals in his last 5 games and leading the Seals to their fourth consecutive victory. "I think it's very realistic for us to think we can make the

FIG. 17. Rugged defenseman Bobby Stewart is the franchise's all-time leader in games played (414) and penalty minutes (691). Photo courtesy of Elliot Lowe.

playoffs," Merrick said after the contest.[16] About a week later Merrick was feeling even more confident in his new teammates and boldly predicted: "[The Seals] are going to make it this year. I see no reason why we can't catch Toronto."[17]

Jack Evans's troops rarely let any points get away without a fight. Black Hawks coach Billy Reay declared, "Nobody can take California lightly anymore. I think the Seals are the team of the future—the team that is going to shake up the National Hockey League. Their record doesn't show it, but they are a very underrated team."[18] No one was talking that way about the Seals two years earlier. *San Mateo Times* sports writer Dick Draper illustrated the changes the Seals had undergone up to that point in the season:

Time was when the California Seals were the turn-the-other-cheek team in the National Hockey League.

Give them a hard check or two, or three, and they would fold. Easy pickings. Give them an elbow in the gut and they were Charles Atlas rejects, 100-lb. weaklings being bullied, bothered and bewildered by NHL musclemen....

It is tooth for tooth now, an aggressive, tit-for-tat brand of hockey.[19]

During a nine-game stretch in January the Seals went 7-1-1, improving their overall record to 19-24-5. Gary Simmons even won six games in a row, a club record for goaltenders, and gave up just 12 goals in the process. The Seals looked for a team record fifth straight win on January 28, but they fell 4-2 to the Capitals. Bernie Wolfe was brilliant in goal for Washington, stopping Dennis Maruk on three separate breakaways. "Maruk is a super player, but tonight, Bernie was a little better," said Caps' coach Tom McVie. Normally the Seals would have staged a comeback and given the pathetic Capitals reason to shake, but when Merrick was ejected in the first period for having made an obscene gesture following a fight with Yvon Labre, the Seals were left without their top scorer. The win snapped the Caps' sixteen-game losing road losing streak. "We could have put the game away," said Jack Evans. "Then, we had three straight defensive lapses to allow them to score. We played well for 2½ periods, but that wasn't enough."[20]

Two days after the Washington debacle the Seals played host to the juggernaut Montreal Canadiens before 10,660 fans. Montreal, who had lost just one of its previous twenty-four games, had a 5-1 lead in the third period and looked to turn this one into a massacre. The Seals stormed back in the third period on goals by Dave Gardner, Bob Murdoch, and Gary Holt. The Seals lost 5-4, but the fact they gave the vaunted Canadiens all they could handle meant something to the players. "We're getting more and more confident the more we play," said Holt. "It showed how much more confident we are just by the way we came back. This team has a good future in front of it."[21]

The Washington and Montreal losses were just the beginning of a nine-game winless streak, but following 7-3 and 6-3 victories over Minnesota in mid-February, the Seals made a final push for a playoff spot. The Coliseum was rocking for the Seals' February 20 contest versus Philadelphia, but even though the Seals gave a spirited effort in front of their fans, the Flyers won 5-4.

The Seals gave the Flyers fits all night. The Seals' fans were displaying levels of passion that had never been seen at the Coliseum. The capacity crowd of 12,021 had the Flyers crying for mercy. "How can anyone control himself with those bleeping idiot fans," questioned

Flyers coach Fred Shero. "Just go to our bench and listen. No human has to take the bleep. Put a glass between the fans and the bench and it would be all right. If you had people this close in baseball and football, there'd be riots every day.

"We don't have to accept this bleeping abuse. We're not animals," continued Shero, although many players and coaches around the league probably snickered at the irony of the Broad Street Bullies coach's plea for peace and sanity.[22] The Seals had certainly come a long way since Finley ran the team into the ground. It had been unimaginable to think of Seals fans as passionate and animalistic, but now they were actually getting under the skin of the loathsome Flyers.

The Seals may have lost to the Flyers, but there was no way they were giving up on the playoffs yet. "We *have* to win," declared captain Bobby Stewart. "We're still in the playoffs until we're mathematically out. We have twenty games left, and we have to win on the road—that's all there is to it." The Seals' playoff hopes would all come down to a seven-game road trip. "I figure we can win four of those games," Stewart said. "We can beat Detroit, Toronto and Chicago—we usually play well against the Hawks and with a little luck we'll get something there. The Islanders are up and down." Of course, Stewart knew time was running out and even the slightest slip-up would be fatal: "If Toronto wins and we don't . . . well, it's all over."[23]

Gary Simmons had been on a hot streak since the start of the New Year, but Jack Evans gave Meloche an opportunity to prove himself against Chicago, and the young netminder was outstanding. Meloche even took a Dennis Hull slap shot to the head that knocked him to the ice, but Meloche stayed in the game. "If he hadn't had a mask on," admitted Evans, "it would have killed him."[24] In the meantime the Seals built a commanding 4–1 lead that stood until the third period. Ivan Boldirev made it 4–2 with just over 14 minutes to play, and Mike Christie scored an empty net goal to polish off the Hawks, 5–2, and cut the Leafs' lead in the standings to 10 points.

The Seals took their momentum to Madison Square Garden, where the Rangers would be the young club's latest victims. The Seals took a 4–1 lead thanks in part to Al MacAdam's second hat trick of the season. Ron Greschner scored a power play goal in the dying minutes of the second period, and then Carol Vadnais and Wayne Dillon scored 50 seconds apart early in the third to make it 4–4. With about three minutes to play, Jim Moxey stole the puck from Steve Vickers behind the Rangers' net and fed the puck to Dave Gardner, who then dished it to Fred Ahern, who tapped the puck into the cage. Bobby Stewart scored an empty-netter with just six seconds to play, giving California a 6–4 win.

The Seals had played inspired hockey for the better part of the season, gaining respect from players and coaches around the league. They had come a long way, but no matter how many club records they set, or how tough they played against the league's best teams, reality eventually set in. After huge wins over Chicago and New York, the Seals could not muster another win on the trip, effectively eliminating them from the playoffs.

By the time their sixty-eighth game rolled around, California was 19 points behind Toronto, but the Seals proved they could hold their own and kept the Leafs to a 7–7 draw in Oakland on March 7. The game itself was noteworthy for *Oakland Tribune* sports writer John Porter's assessment of the wide-open goal fest: "To the purist, the hockey game was like fumes that belch from a bus tailpipe." Gary Simmons was even more blunt in his postgame comments: "That was one of the worst displays of hockey I've ever seen. That's not National Hockey League hockey." And Simmons was the backup that night. Poor Gilles Meloche stopped just 18 of 25 shots and was bewildered by what had transpired in front of him. "A hockey game? A 7–7 score is more like a football game. This was stupid. I'd have nothing to do, and then they'd come down the ice and score." Meloche's counterpart Wayne Thomas faced a whopping 48 shots. While it was encouraging to see the Seals so offensive-minded for one of the rare times in their history, there was still much work to be done to be considered a genuine playoff threat.[25]

Two weeks later the Seals took on the St. Louis Blues, and this time, the Californians did not leave their goalie out to dry. After spotting the Blues the first goal, the Seals stormed back with seven of their own. The much-improved Rick Hampton scored the winner at 13:53 of the first period and in doing so broke Dick Redmond's club record for points by a defenseman. Just for good measure, Hampton scored again in the second period, giving him 14 goals on the year. Rookies also played a big part in California's big night. Maruk picked up 3 assists in the contest, Murdoch scored his 19th and 20th goals of the season, and Ahern picked one up as well.

You would have thought Jack Evans's team had actually won something of significance by the way he gushed over his boys. "I like to think we got a bunch of winners out here," he said. "You really have to hand it to this team. We could just as easily go through the motions out here, maybe trying to set some individual records. But we're still playing with the enthusiasm and special pride I like. We're beating some teams on our enthusiasm alone."[26]

In an act of team pride that would have been unheard of just a year earlier, Gary Sabourin dressed for what amounted to a nothing game against Los Angeles to close out the season. Sabourin had undergone an appendectomy just days earlier but took part in the pregame warm-up. "This club is going places next season," Sabourin said, "and I wanted the guys to know that I was with them even though I couldn't play."[27] Sabourin did not play that night, but his simple gesture did not go unnoticed. "The most significant thing we've accomplished this season is developing a pride in the uniform," said Bill McCreary. "Look at what Gary did. He didn't have to do that, but that's the kind of players we want."[28] The pride that had withered away during the Finley regime had finally been restored.

The Seals put on an outstanding show defeating the visiting Kings 5–2 in front of 6,442 fans. Maruk completed his fine rookie campaign by scoring his 29th and 30th goals of the season. The crowd chanted "Marooook! Marooook!" throughout the game, giving him a real lift. There may not have been many fans, but at least they were passionate. "These fans here are great," he said. "They're responsible for a lot of my play. When I hear the fans calling my name, it makes me want to play harder than I already do. The fans don't come to see me. They are here to see good hockey, so I just do everything in my power to give them that when I'm on the ice."[29] At the end-of-season awards banquet, the Seals' Booster Club named Maruk the team's most popular player.

The Seals finished the season with a respectable 27-42-13 season, and the team's annual yearbook proudly dubbed the 1975–76 season "the record-breaking year" and for good reason: 35 club records were either equaled or broken. Among the 16 team records broken during the 1975–76 season were most goals scored (250), most power play goals (71), highest power play conversion rate (18.6%), most shots on goal (2,297), most season series victories (7), most shorthanded goals (9), most assists (398), and most scoring points (648).

The 3-M Line set a club record for goals scored by a line (84)—MacAdam (32), Maruk (30), Murdoch (22). Maruk set an NHL rookie record for shorthanded goals in a season (5) and established new club marks for assists (32) and points (62) by a rookie and for goals by a center (30). Murdoch led the team with 9 power play goals and finished among the Seals' top five in goals, points, game-winning goals, and shots on goal. MacAdam led the team in goals (32), points (63), and game-winning goals (5). MacAdam was named the club's Most Valuable Player and was co-winner (with Wayne Merrick) of the Wralstad Memorial Award for sportsmanship. MacAdam led by example rather than by talking: "Wherever he showed up he committed to every shift he was out there," said Maruk. "Al MacAdam was more of our work horse who got the puck for us."

After the 3-M Line, the Seals boasted a fine supporting cast. Bones Merrick scored 25 goals and 27 assists in just 56 games en route to becoming one of the NHL's best second-line centers. Merrick scored 6 points against Washington on January 2 to set yet another club record. He was joined on the second line by Bob Girard and Gary Sabourin. Sabourin's career seemed to be in decline just a year earlier, but he scored 21 goals with the Seals. The twenty-six-year-old Girard enjoyed a solid 16-goal, 26-assist rookie season, which was respectable for a guy who had played defense most of his life. Girard was named the Seals' Unsung Hero for 1975–76. Evans was particularly happy with his decision to place the three together on one line: "I like a strong forechecking club and I wanted a line that could be used mainly for checking and penalty killing. The first night I put the Girard line together they scored six goals and Bob got a 'hat trick.'"[30]

FIG. 18. Dennis Maruk rips a shot during a warm-up. Photo
by Elliot Lowe.

On defense Rick Hampton emerged as the power play quarterback
the Seals had been lacking since the days of Carol Vadnais and Dick
Redmond. "Crow" set club records for assists (37), points (51), and
power play goals (8) by a defenseman. "If some of our other youngsters improve the way Rick has, we'll be in the Stanley Cup hunt pretty
soon," praised Evans. Overall, the Seals' top five defensemen had
become a very solid unit. Jim Neilson had been enjoying another fine
season until he injured his knee before Christmas. Bobby Stewart, Len
Frig, and Mike Christie brought plenty of grit to the table as usual,
keeping opponents honest. Evans was particularly impressed with
captain Stewart, despite his team-worst -34 rating. "We've always
been able to count on Stewie," he said. "He's consistently good and
commands a lot of respect because of his toughness. He's easily the
most physical of our defencemen."[31]

In the crease Meloche and Simmons gave Evans the opportunity
to rotate his goaltenders, knowing full well either man gave the Seals
a chance to win every night. They combined for a respectable 3.48
goals-against-average and 3 shutouts.

Behind the bench Evans was rewarded for his successful rookie
campaign. A new award—named in honor of Dr. Robert Willmott,
a man who had shown great loyalty to the club—was created by the
Seals' Booster Club to reward an individual who made a significant

contribution to the sport of hockey over the course of a season.[32] Jim
Moxey heaped much praise on his coach: "We have a very young and
inexperienced bunch of players and when the pressure gets heavy we
have a tendency to get rattled. . . . Evans is the kind of coach that will
take you off in a corner and explain what you are doing wrong and how
to correct it. He'll never criticize you with the other players around."[33]

With the team playing its best hockey ever, its players brimming
with confidence for the first time in years, and its owner resolved to
keep the team afloat, the Seals seemed destined to remain in the Bay
Area for years to come. To the surprise of many, the season-ending
victory over Los Angeles would be the last time the California Golden
Seals took the Coliseum ice.

An average of 6,944 fans turned out for each Seals home game. In
their last ten home games, the Seals had averaged 8,011 fans, which
was encouraging, but the Seals were still dead last in attendance for
the ninth straight year. Ironically, Seals attendance hit an all-time high
at a time when attendance figures in many other markets had begun
a sharp decline that would continue for the rest of the decade. Mel
Swig had started running into money trouble, due in part to the fact
the Seals' rink was too small and in the wrong location. He enlisted
the aid of Cleveland native George Gund III, who invested in the
Seals in midseason. "I was originally told I was going to have a very
small interest in the team, but it turned out to be much bigger," Gund
remembered. "Mel told me he had a lot of people ready to invest in the
team, including the Doobie Brothers. They never did get involved. I
was initially focusing on things in Sun Valley. Shortly after I invested
in the Seals, the cash calls started coming."[34] Swig had been assured a
new arena would be built in San Francisco, ensuring the Seals' would
remain in the Bay Area. The Seals' survival depended on this. In a
2011 interview for this book, Gary Simmons explained the version of
the story he had heard:

> [Swig] wanted to buy the team from the NHL, but he only wanted
> to buy it on the condition that it move from Oakland to San Fran-
> cisco. Now, the Swig family was the third most powerful family in
> San Francisco. The Aliotos, who Joe Alioto was the mayor, they

were the most powerful, and the Swigs and the Aliotos got along really, really great; they were tight. . . . Mel was trying to buy the site where the Moscone Center is now, he was trying to build his thing, and Alioto went in, they'd picked this select committee to decide whether to OK this thing or not.

So the way I heard it, Alioto went into this meeting with these fifteen people that were deciding whether to do this or not and he said, "Have you come to a decision?" And they said, "Well, we're going to take three weeks and we're going to think about it and then we're going to vote." And Alioto said, "The man needs to let know the NHL by tomorrow; that's the deadline. You're going to have the vote today and you're going to vote 'yes.'" So they voted "yes."

Swig had some grand plans for the California Golden Seals and the city of San Francisco. Simmons visited Swig's office one day and saw a big table with a scale model of the Yerba Buena Center. Swig told Simmons, "That's going to be your new office." Simmons was impressed. Swig explained that there would be high-rise apartments on one side, high-rise office buildings on the other side and a mini-mall with a few retail outlets. Simmons asked Swig whether there would be a restaurant there, and Swig told him there would be at least two or three. Simmons and Seals public relations man Len Shapiro had become business partners in the Round Table Pizza franchise, so Simmons asked Swig if one of the restaurants at the Yerba Buena Center could be a pizzeria. Swig thought it was a great idea. "He and Leonard went to the same synagogue, which didn't hurt," said Simmons. "And so he said, 'Look, if this thing goes through,' and he stuck out his hand and we shook on it, he said, 'you and Leonard have a deal.'" Simmons then asked Swig how many events were expected to take place at the arena, and Swig figured 285 the first year and 335 the second year. "Do you have any problem with a pizza parlor catering to all these events?" Simmons asked. "He said, 'No, I think it would be a good idea.' So we shook hands on it."

Although the arena project had been approved by city supervisors, Swig learned the hard way that in the world of politics, timing is everything. Joe Alioto lost the San Francisco mayoral election to George

Moscone, who decided to hold a new vote to decide the fate of the $20 million Yerba Buena Center Arena. On May 13 San Francisco city council voted 13–3 against the erection of the building. With the Seals' future hanging by a thread, Joe Starkey could not believe the San Francisco city council had voted against the arena plan. "It was a stunner," he said. "I didn't see it coming. . . . I kept thinking all along that they can't be this dumb, that they would not be bright enough to realize what a value it would be to have a major sports arena in downtown San Francisco." There was, however, more to the story than Moscone not showing any interest in a new home for the Seals. "He ran an investigation into the report and then said that the survey had to be resurveyed, so basically, it went nowhere," explained Len Shapiro. "Then there were plans to remodel the Cow Palace but that never happened either."[35]

To this day San Francisco is without a major-league hockey rink, and Starkey believes the city made a monumental error in rejecting Swig's arena plans. "The key to staying in the Bay Area was . . . the new building," he said. "They desperately needed the San Francisco arena, but San Francisco is no different today than it was then. They are one of the most inept run cities in America. They don't have any sense of futuristic thinking."

Years later the San Francisco Giants also needed a new stadium and received little help from the city. "The Giants," said Starkey, "who are now virtually anointed sainthood here from the World Series, and they sell out every game and all that, they went hat and hand over and over and over again to get the city to help them even a little bit with building a new stadium, and the San Francisco fathers never agreed to anything. When the Giants built their new ball park a decade ago they did it, literally, every penny on their own. And so, what did that do for San Francisco? It made the coffers burst with property tax improvements, all those kinds of things, but there wasn't a single leader in the city of San Francisco that had the foresight to say, 'You know what? If we build this new ball park for the Giants, this might revitalize the whole part of the town, which it did, but through no help from the city." The folks on city council may have changed, but their hard-line attitude has not.

The day after learning the Yerba Buena Center Arena proposal had been rejected, Swig informed the league he was going to exercise his option of transfer. At the Stanley Cup luncheon in Philadelphia, Clarence Campbell explained that when Swig bought the club from the NHL, he was given "the right to give . . . notice that he planned to dispose of the club to a place of his choice if the notice was given by May 15."[36] Franchise relocations are almost always fraught with whispers and controversy, and since this potential relocation involved the Seals, the NHL should have expected the worst. Campbell was livid when a two-page release from the Seals claimed the president had misinterpreted the letter Swig had sent him regarding the Seals' future. The Seals said Campbell's statement simply did not "reflect the true facts." Swig had no intention of pulling up stakes and whisking the Seals out of Oakland, but he was keeping his options open in case it became necessary to move. "It's stupid for them to say that. I have it right here in writing," Campbell exclaimed to the *Oakland Tribune* from Montreal on May 15. "I didn't make any announcement at all. I was asked (by a reporter): 'What about the situation in Oakland?' I don't want to hurt Mr. Swig, but I'm not going to stand there and cover up for him." And then, reiterating the fact that he had had just about enough with the California Golden Seals, Campbell said, "[I am] anxious for Mr. Swig to do whatever he wants to do."[37]

Once again Swig held the franchise's future in his hands, but he kept his cards close to his vest. "We have not made any decision as to what our move might be—if any—at present," Swig said. "Sometime early in June we'll have to know where we're going. We're taking a long, hard look at our alternatives. We want to make sure we're doing the right thing for everyone involved. We're going to have to make a cold, hard decision to keep the team in Oakland or move it, depending on what the situation looks like."[38] Upon hearing Swig's declaration, it is doubtful any Seals players spent much time checking out Bay Area real estate trends. They knew the score: the Seals were down by a goal, and there was about a minute left on the clock.

A week after Swig exercised his option of transfer, the *Oakland Tribune*'s Ed Schoenfeld revealed the Seals had yet to pay rent to the Coliseum for the last nine home games of the season, despite several notices asking them to fork over the money. "We ran out of funds," said Swig, even though the Seals had sold more tickets and grossed more money in admissions ($1,465,958) than they ever had. By comparison, the 1972–73 edition of the club had sold just $707,152 worth of tickets. Swig explained that the amount owed was "relatively small" and that they intended to "pay up within the next couple of weeks," but this was still bad news for Seals fans.[39] There was supposedly as much as $25,000 worth of bills to be paid, a sign that an owner plans on selling his franchise since the buyers can often be persuaded to pick up the tab. It was now 2–0 with thirty seconds left to play.

Seals' president Munson Campbell insisted Swig had not pushed the panic button but was merely protecting his interests. "By sending the letter (to the league), Mr. Swig was merely exercising his right to keep his options open. The letter has absolutely nothing to do with his intended direction for his franchise, and no intention to move the club was either suggested or implied."[40] That didn't stop Swig from listening to offers from Denver, San Diego, Seattle, and Miami.

What else could Swig do? The club needed a larger rink in a better location to attract more fans. "There was just no way that we could play in Oakland and make a living or break even," Swig said years later. "If we sold out every seat in the building every game, we still could not come out even."[41] Struggling franchises in Minnesota, Pittsburgh, and Washington were averaging about ten thousand fans a game, and those teams were drowning in red ink.

"This club is going places next season," said the injured but enthusiastic Gary Sabourin prior to the last game of the season.[42] Little did he know how prophetic he had been. According to Ed Schoenfeld, in the May 22nd edition of the *Oakland Tribune*, Swig and Clarence Campbell had been sniffing around Denver, the city that had eyed the Seals a year earlier. "When I visited Denver and inspected the new (McNichols) arena," said Swig, "I found it to be excellent. All facilities are first-class."[43] It certainly seemed as though Swig was doing much more than "exercising his right to keep his options open."

While the Seals were thinking of uprooting themselves, the American Basketball Association was teetering on the brink of extinction. Carl Scheer, the Denver Nuggets' president and general manager, was busy discussing a merger with the National Basketball Association, but he joined a group of investors planning to bring the Seals to Colorado. Broadcaster Bud Palmer was the spokesman for the group and did most of the negotiating with Swig. "I think you hit the nail on the head," he told a Denver reporter. "I feel very good about it, but nothing is consummated." He did indicate, however, that he would be visiting San Francisco the following week.[44]

Despite Palmer's best efforts, George Gund thwarted him. For several months he had discussed with Cleveland Crusaders owner Jay Moore the idea of moving the Seals to Ohio. The Crusaders had been a member of the WHA since the league's inception, but now the walls were crumbling all around them. The Crusaders couldn't attract flies at Richfield Coliseum, and the team was looking to close up shop. Gund convinced his brother Gordon and Swig to move the Seals to Cleveland. "Yes, I've heard some talk of it," said Swig. "He mentioned something to me about a month ago about it. We were just kicking around possible places, but we dismissed Cleveland because the Crusaders were there at the time."[45] They weren't there anymore. The California Golden Seals were now down 3–0 with two seconds left on the clock.

The choice between Denver or Cleveland was made much easier when Bud Palmer was forced to drop out of the running. Managers of McNichols Arena wanted to charge the new team a rental fee that would increase the overall cost of the franchise approximately 15 percent. "We figure now that we would need an average attendance of 13,200 to break even," said Palmer. "That's just too high. It's illogical.... We had projected costs down through 1983 and felt we might lose close to $1.5 million before breaking even. Now we're talking about an investment of $4 million to $6 million down the line to reach the break-even point."[46] In the meantime the Denver Nuggets were looking to join the NBA (at a cost of $4.5 million), so Scheer did not have the capital to also invest in a last-place hockey team; he pulled his 50 percent investment off the table. Swig was reportedly asking $7 million for the Seals, so Palmer settled for the much cheaper (somewhere between $5.8 and 6 million) but far less talented Kansas City Scouts, who were in such dire straits they were on the verge of being contracted.

Nevertheless, there were still a few people lining up to invest in the Seals' future. Jay Moore had lost an estimated $1.5 million in the fifteen months he had owned the Crusaders, but believe it or not, Moore was actually thinking of organizing a group of investors looking to bring the NHL to Cleveland. "As soon as the loose ends are tied up with the WHA," he revealed, "I'll then start to work harder to see what can be done about an NHL franchise for Cleveland."[47]

In the end it didn't matter what Moore planned on doing. Swig brought the Seals to Cleveland himself, although the transfer was the least of Swig's problems. For one thing, the Seals owed more than $500,000 to various people. Swig also needed to shell out between $300,000 and $400,000 to buy off the last two years of the team's lease with the Oakland Coliseum. Then there was the kicker: another $2.7 million to Charlie Finley, whose dark shadow continued to hover over the franchise. Once the Seals' debts were paid off, the team's Oakland office was closed for good. The league's Board of Governors gave conditional approval to move the franchise on June 30.

According to Len Shapiro, the Seals' assistant public relations director during that final season, the club had been prepping for the move for some time. One of his most famous stories is how he learned the Seals were moving to Cleveland:

> February 1st, 1976, I came to the office, and no one was there; it was just me and Loretta Marcus [the Seals' PR secretary] . . . and we were the only two in the office, and we were just saying that something just didn't feel right, and as good loyal employees we started to snoop around. . . . We went into Munson's office, lifted up his organizer, and right there in the front, big print, was, as luck intended to write, was "Book the Cleveland Hilton," and I knew at that point that this team was doomed, that finally after all those rumors of going to Vancouver, Denver, Seattle, Phoenix, it was moving to Cleveland.

Neither Shapiro nor Marcus made the move to Cleveland with the rest of the team. Munson Campbell, upset with Swig's handling of the relocation, defected to Bud Palmer's camp and became president of the new Colorado Rockies. Swig signed a lease with the Richfield Coliseum and had local investors contribute approximately $1.7 million. The chairman of the board couldn't have been happier with his decision. "I'm very pleased," Swig said, "and I think that the Cleveland area is going to be a great opportunity for us. . . . I think the fans already have shown great enthusiasm."[48]

The California Golden Seals' official date of death is July 14, 1976. The *Oakland Tribune* ran a small article announcing the bad news. Sports writer John Porter actually used the team's full name when he opened his article, something he almost never did. Above the headline read the words "Hockey Obituary." "The California Golden Seals are dead," the article began. "The end came in Chicago last night at 11 p.m. CDT when owner Mel Swig and the National Hockey League's finance committee reached an agreement for the transfer of the franchise to Cleveland. . . . The Seals had been sickly from birth when they joined the NHL nine years ago. They suffered with unstable management and last-place teams, but the terminal cancer proved to be the advent of the World Hockey Association in 1972." Swig expressed his deepest regrets about moving the franchise. He had once been the Seals' white knight, and now he was being vilified. "I had to do it," he explained. "There was no choice. . . . Some people will think I moved the Seals deliberately. They don't realize that I couldn't come out even in Oakland."[49]

The Seals won 5–2 over Los Angeles in the final regular-season game in Oakland. Ironically the club that had gained the reputation of perennial cellar dwellers became one of the few sports franchises to win both its first and last league games. Between those two dates, however, the Seals were not quite so lucky, going 180-401-115.

The announcement was a shock to many. Dennis Maruk, for one, had no idea the Seals' win over LA would be the team's last hurrah in Oakland: "I got a phone call saying that they [the San Francisco city council] voted against it," he said. "That was the late mayor Moscone. . . . So I was in shock really, especially when I was just twenty years old, in my first year." Fan John Bonasera remembers how the 1975–76 season had finished with such optimism and hope:

At the end of the very last season—it probably was in April of '76—the Booster Club held a barbecue picnic out in the Alameda County fairgrounds in Pleasanton, and so I went to that with a couple of friends, and at that time we did not know that we were toast. It wasn't until a few weeks later that the word started spreading that there was a good chance the team was moving. So we went to that event. Again, the last season was a very successful one; by comparison, things were looking up, people were excited, there was a big turnout at the fairgrounds. There was probably as many people at that damn picnic as there was at an average game, but again, that's where the loyalty comes into play. We had a ball.

Gary Simmons was not thrilled to hear the news the Seals could possibly be moving. He also had a premonition the Seals' new locale was not going to be pleasant: "I was doing a hockey school over on the peninsula, and I'm driving across the Hayward Bridge, and I hear, 'The California Seals announced today that they may be moving. Four sites have been named.' One was Denver. I remember thinking, that's an alright town. New Orleans—which I'd never been to New Orleans, I still haven't—Miami, and Cleveland. And I thought, 'It'll be Cleveland.' And I'd been to Cleveland in the American League, and the truck drivers called it 'Mistake on the Lake,' and they weren't lying. I just hated Cleveland."

The news of the team's transfer caused a flood of emotions: surprise, sadness, and anger, all in varying degrees. Though the club had never been successful, it seemed as though it would always remain in the Bay Area. After all, how many times had the local fans been threatened with relocation? For John Bonasera, the news of the Seals' departure was like getting stabbed in the heart:

[Wayne Walker] did a piece on the imminent sale and transfer of the Seals . . . and [I had] a portable reel-to-reel recorder. I used to like sticking the microphone up to the speaker of the TV set and make recordings. . . . I had the recorder ready to go for this report, so I have the audio of this last report. . . . He started mentioning

Bobby Orr, Bobby Hull, Phil Esposito . . . he just named some names [who] he says will no longer come visit the Bay Area. . . . It was very sad, very kind of maudlin music playing in the background, talking about the history. . . .

I cry listening to it now. I'm sure I was crying watching it then, and then at the very end, the last sentence is something like "The ice has melted at the Oakland Coliseum." . . . It's one of those little three-minute pieces just was like, that was the end, and sure enough, within a day or two came the formal announcement of the sale and subsequent moving of the team. . . . This was just a matter of a couple of weeks after the picnic that I had attended and thinking next year is gonna be even better and all that, and then poof, it's gone. . . . For me personally, that report was the one that drove it home, and like I said, I still have the original three-inch reel-to-reel tape of that, and every now and then, to torture myself, I'll pull it out and listen to it.

Looking back, Joe Starkey believes that had the arena been built, it would have created a snowball effect and would have led the Seals to future success:

I thought that if they had simply been told that a building was about to go up in San Francisco after the '75-'76 season ended, I think it would have changed everything. I think with that commitment, then the owner, Mel Swig, would have spent some money on getting better players, [the players] would have had a whole different attitude . . . toward being there, because they all liked living there; they just didn't like the fact that nobody came to the games. And so if you had that whole momentum factor built in of a team that was now gaining traction in the area, they're getting a new stadium, the players are clearly better than they've been in the past, I think it would have changed a lot of things. No question in my mind.

Gary Simmons, for one, adored playing in the Bay Area, and to this day he believes the Seals would have been successful had the city of

San Francisco built a new arena. "The Bay Area was just a wonderful place to play hockey," he said. "We had six thousand fans that made as much noise as fifteen thousand anywhere else. They were wonderful fans. . . . I think if we had stayed in Oakland or if Mel Swig would have gotten his building over in San Francisco, there'd be no Sharks now, it would still be the Seals, and they would be prospering like crazy in San Francisco."

11 MISTAKE ON THE LAKE, 1976-1977

"I remember Canada was playing Russia in some series in '76 there," recalled Gary Simmons, "and I remember they were showing the games in San Francisco, and this guy asked me to come over and do the color between periods . . . and I remember one of the questions he asked me. He said, 'Bill McCreary has gone on record as saying that it'll make a difference of 12, 14 points in the standings just being in Cleveland and less travel. Do you agree with that?' And I said, 'Which way in the standings did he say, up or down?'" Simmons laughed. "And he said, 'What do you mean by that?' 'Look,' I said, 'You're taking people . . . You're taking guys that used to finish practice in Berkeley or in Dublin and they would go out golfing or go and see some wonderful sights.' I said, 'What are they going to do twenty-six miles out of town in Cleveland? Throw snowballs. There will be nothing to do.' It was a complete waste of time in Cleveland. Terrible move."

Cleveland has always had a hard-working blue-collar reputation, but no one would ever consider the city one of the jewels of the eastern United States. "We're playing Boston," remembers Simmons, "and [Gerry Cheevers] had played three years in Cleveland. . . . We're skating around in warm-up, and 'Cheesy' says, 'Hey Cobra, how do you like Cleveland?' and I said, 'Screw you, Cheesy!' And he laughed, and he says, 'One thing about it, Cobra, the Russians will never drop a bomb on Cleveland!'"

Simmons has never hidden his feelings of disgust about leaving the comfy confines of the Bay Area to play in Ohio. "The first time I stepped on the ice I noticed a whole bunch of dead flies in the corner," he said to the *San Francisco Examiner*'s Ross McKeon in 1997. "I said, 'They committed suicide because they're in Cleveland.'"[1] Making matters worse, moving to Cleveland had put a wrinkle in Simmons's business plans. At the time he and Len Shapiro were partners in a successful Round Table Pizza restaurant, so the move to Cleveland hurt them in more ways than one. "Leonard had plans for getting a bus and having a pizza and beer thing and having the bus go to the game and then come back to the pizza parlor after," Simmons recalled. "We had big ideas." Simmons was driving home from a hockey school at which he was working when he heard the awful news the Seals were relocating. "That was devastating to Leonard and I. I mean, Leonard was out of a job." Despite the Seals' move, Simmons and Shapiro made it work and enjoyed a twenty-eight-year partnership in the pizza business.

Simmons had never wanted to leave the Bay Area. It had always been a great place to play, despite the ownership problems and financial constraints. "We didn't have solid ownership until it was too late," Simmons said. "It's too bad because we had the start of a good team. The fans that we did have here were awesome. You won't find any better fans anywhere. They just didn't have much of a product to come watch."[2]

Mel Swig and the Gunds were hoping Cleveland's proud hockey past would translate to a successful NHL future. In 1952 Cleveland had been considered for an expansion franchise thanks to the AHL Barons' overwhelming success on the ice and at the box office. The city was prepared to meet all of the NHL's membership requirements, "$425,000 to cover the franchise, league reserve fund and working capital and 60 per cent of the stock to be owned by Cleveland residents," but the league nixed the proposal.[3] In *Hockey! The Story of the World's Fastest Sport*, Dick Beddoes, Stan Fischler, and Ira Gitler offer one possible explanation for the NHL's decision: "From the past there were the spectres of all those failed franchises of the 1930s. In the present were new financial problems. Although there was no depression, the post-war prosperity was over and people were not going out to see losers."[4] The NHL already had two struggling franchises, the New York Rangers and the Chicago Black Hawks, and games involving these two clubs provided little excitement for fans; therefore, the league chose to remedy those two problems before looking toward expansion. Once the great expansion of 1967 was announced, however, Cleveland was rebuffed again.

The city was rejected a third time in 1971, but the WHA deemed Cleveland acceptable, and the Crusaders were born. Even though the

Crusaders boasted solid teams featuring players like Gerry Cheevers, Paul Shmyr, and Gerry Pinder, they never built a solid fan base and moved to Minnesota in 1976. The Crusaders' home rink, the cavernous 18,544-seat Richfield Coliseum, was situated in the middle of nowhere, smack dab in between Akron and Cleveland, so few fans were interested in trudging out there in the dead of winter just to watch a hockey game. "The rink in Cleveland was twenty-six miles out of town, a two-lane road to get there," said Gary Simmons. "It used to take me forty-five minutes just to get home after the game, and I lived eight miles away. . . . It was a beautiful rink, a state-of-the-art rink, but it was just way out in the middle of nowhere, and it was just brutal." The Coliseum was so far away that there was a time every year when the parking lot lights could not be turned on because they interfered with sheep breeding in the fields nearby.

One time, when the transplanted Seals showed up late for a meet-and-greet luncheon with over six hundred fans, the jokes flew fast and furious. The tables reserved for the players remained empty as management tried to explain the delay without actually knowing themselves what was going on. Harry Howell, who was general manager at the time, said he told his front office staff the team "had to be more visible this year," but joked that perhaps he had said "invisible." Someone in the crowd quipped: "They're probably lost. None of them have ever been to Cleveland before." In fact, they *were* lost. After more than two hours of wandering about, the angry and embarrassed team finally made it to the luncheon. "We had a bad bussie," explained Wayne Merrick. "He took us through every plant and steel mill in town. We couldn't believe it. He didn't even know where the freeway was."[5]

It was decided the former Seals would take on the name of Cleveland's old AHL team, the Barons, and the new team colors would be red, white, and black. On the now-defunct "Cleveland Barons Retrospective" website, the logo's design, created by Walter Lanci, was explained: "It was generally felt all along that we would work with a large 'C' that would be original and different. . . . We also wanted to work in the configuration of the state of Ohio, because the Barons are the sole representatives of the state in the NHL. This was to be a whole new thing, something with dignity that you would remember."

Lanci, who owned the Offset Color and Printing Company in Bedford Heights, explained the many meanings behind the beautiful and creative new logo. "We feel that the words Cleveland Barons within the 'C' have an elegant look, like an official seal. Also, the 'B' to represent Barons is not really gothic, but a modification of the old English. The Ohio map is, we think, a truer representation than most Ohio state configurations in use now." Lanci believed the new logo combined dignity and tradition. "It's something that will grow on you . . . you won't get tired of it as people tend to do with so-called 'modern' graphics."[6]

When the people of Cleveland finally received their long-awaited NHL franchise, there was a sense of disappointment. As Cleveland hockey historian Gene Kiczek so colorfully put it, "The California Seals were not exactly the Rolls Royce of hockey. They were more like an old clunker with a few shiny parts."[7] Cleveland fans were expected to pay higher prices to watch a team that had not reached the playoffs in seven years; the WHA Crusaders charged between $4.50 and $6.50 for tickets, but the Barons would charge between $5 and $10. Furthermore, an awful schedule did nothing to entice fans. Because of the team's last-minute move to Cleveland, the best arena dates had already been reserved for the NBA's Cavaliers. In the end, the Barons received only four Saturday home games and three on Sunday. The rest would be spread out from Monday to Friday, meaning people would have to rush home from work and then sit in an hour of two-lane traffic just to get to the game at 7:30.

Another issue that would plague the team had nothing to do with hockey. Basketball had always been popular in Ohio, but when the Cavaliers won the Central Division title and reached the conference finals in 1976, it stirred considerable interest in the once-laughable expansion team. The Barons would have a hard time knocking the Cavs off the first page of the sports section. The 1976–77 season was promoted as the "rebirth of hockey in Cleveland," but it would be a daunting task convincing fans to support a team that hadn't reached the playoffs since 1970.[8] The Barons' first preseason game, a 2–1 loss to Detroit, drew only 2,238 fans.

At the amateur draft the still Golden Seals had the fifth overall pick, but instead of selecting future NHL stars such as Bernie Federko, Paul Gardner (brother of Barons' Dave), Brian Sutter, or Randy Carlyle, the club chose Swedish defenseman Bjorn Johansson. "We're really pleased with this year's draft," chirped Bill McCreary. "In Johansson, we have an aggressive player, a very good skater with a fine shot. He is an excellent puck carrier and has an added dimension that's not always found: toughness."[9] Johansson was a bust. His NHL career: 15 games, 1 goal, and 1 assist. Third-rounder Mike Fidler from Boston would fare much better. In his senior year at Boston University, Fidler led his team to the Eastern College Athletic Conference (ECAC) championship and helped it qualify for the National Collegiate Athletic Association (NCAA) tournament. Following the draft, Fidler was sent down to Salt Lake City for more seasoning, but after scoring 12 goals in 10 games, he was called up to the Barons for the rest of the year.

On October 6, 1976, before a disappointing crowd of 8,899, the NHL officially arrived in Ohio as the Los Angeles Kings paid a visit to Richfield Coliseum. Despite lackluster attendance figures in the preseason, the meager opening night crowd still surprised some public relations officials who noted that phones had rung off the hook after the announcement of the franchise's move to Cleveland. It was expected about 7,500 season tickets would be sold. In reality the total fell well short of everyone's expectations.

The Barons' starting lineup that night included the 3-M Line of Maruk, Murdoch, and MacAdam. On the back end were Mike Christie and Rick Hampton, while Meloche started in goal. The Barons played their style of game, full of speed, but it was the Kings' Mike Murphy who drew first blood at 15:11 of the second period. Fred Ahern scored the first goal in the history of the NHL Barons at 8:41 of the third. "That's one of the best ovations I've ever heard," he said after the game. "They made enough noise to make the place sound like it was packed. Maybe someday that'll be my claim to fame but I hope it isn't."[10]

Maruk scored with 8:21 remaining to put the Barons up 2–1, and before long the "Marooook! Marooook!" chants began. The Kings were aggressive, however, and pushed the Barons around as much as they could. It took just two minutes for Tom Williams to put a backhand shot past Meloche and even the score at 2-2, which is how the game ended.

The Barons made a good impression in their first outing, despite the fact they did not win. *Elyria Chronicle-Telegram* sports editor Jerry Rombach seemed excited about the prospects of such a young, fast club in Cleveland: "With the speed of the Barons, they should be a fairly entertaining team to watch this season. And, they have an honest-to-goodness colorful player [Maruk] who the fans will be loving before it's all over."[11]

Win number one, a 6-3 thrashing of the Washington Capitals, came three days later, but the novelty of opening night had worn off, and only 5,208 fans showed up. After a one-game road trip, fewer than 4,000 showed up for the Barons' 4-2 loss to Atlanta. Despite two more wins at home, a 3-0 shutout by Meloche over Chicago and a 6-2 win over St. Louis that brought the Barons' record to 3-2-2, few fans made the trek from Cleveland or Akron. A paltry crowd of 5,653 showed up for the Chicago game, and fewer than 3,500 attended the St. Louis game.

Thankfully the vicious Philadelphia Flyers always drew large crowds. On November 5 a crowd of 10,297 fans made the long trip to Richfield Coliseum, hoping the Broad Street Bullies would get involved in a tussle or two with Cleveland's more physical customers. In this game, however, it was the Barons who dished out the punishment. The 3-M Line came to life with 2 goals from Murdoch and another from Maruk. Rick Hampton tied a team record with 4 assists, and the Flyers staggered out of the Coliseum with a 6-4 defeat under their belts. With the 3-M Line on a hot streak, the Barons went on a team-record seven-game unbeaten streak.

Two wins and four ties later, the Cleveland Barons' 6-7-6 record, representing their best-ever start, put them in a third-place tie with Toronto. In the first twenty games of the season, the 3-M Line had performed well, but a lack of production from the second and third lines was distressing. Losses began to mount as the injury bug took its toll on the young Barons. Both Charlie Simmer and Dave Gardner suffered knee injuries in late November, and soon after Mike Fidler and Gary Sabourin were sidelined with various health problems. No matter

DENNIS MARUK • CENTER

FIG. 19. Dennis Maruk is the franchise's all-time leader in goals (94) and is second all-time in points (211). Topps O-Pee-Chee trading cards used courtesy of The Topps Company, Inc.

how bad things got, however, the rock-solid goaltending tandem of Meloche and Simmons continued to shine and kept the Barons in the game when key scorers played poorly.

On December 6 the Canadiens played host to the injury-riddled Barons, who entered the contest riding a nine-game winless streak. The Habs, on the other hand, had lost only four games since the start of the season, and they had not lost to the Barons or Seals since 1974. The odds were definitely against the Barons, but they pushed the Canadiens to the limit. Guy Lafleur gave the Habs a 1–0 lead at the 8:57 mark of the opening period, and it looked as though the onslaught had begun, but instead the Barons fought back. In the first period Hampton and Merrick had excellent scoring chances on separate breakaways, but Ken Dryden managed to thwart both shooters.

With the score still 1–0 in the second period, controversy entered the contest. It appeared as though Bob Gainey had made the score 2–0, but the goal was called back by referee Bob Kilger, who believed the puck had been kicked in. According to Montreal coach Scotty

Bowman, the Barons "put it in themselves. . . . Gainey didn't touch it. [Kilger] must have seen it in his sleep."[12] The score remained 1-0 as time wound down. Rookie defenseman Greg Smith nearly tied the game with less than two minutes remaining, but Dryden managed to kick out his right leg and keep the puck out of the net. It was yet another loss, but keeping the score close against Montreal was still an amazing accomplishment.

The Barons' winless skid reached eleven games after a lopsided 5-1 loss to Buffalo in Cleveland. The Barons managed but 4 shots in the first period as Meloche began losing his mind. Sabres players were clogging Meloche's crease, but referee Alf Lejeune did the Barons no favors. In fact, he handed Meloche three penalties, all of which put the Barons down two men. Meloche was incensed. "He's the worst ref in the league," he said. "On the first call, two of their guys were in the crease poking [me]. They scored and I told him about it. He turned away and I told him he was a jerk."[13]

The winless streak was starting to grate on the Cleveland players. "You don't score goals and you become frustrated," said Jack Evans. "It's really getting to the guys. I've run out of reasons why one night we play well and the next we don't," Evans continued. "I don't know why we don't start games in this building with intensity when we do elsewhere. We just don't play the same here."[14]

Things started looking up on December 10 when the Washington Capitals came to town for the first game of a home-and-home series. Gary Sabourin, now fully recovered from his injury, opened the scoring just 26 seconds into the game. Washington goalie Ron Low gave way to back-up Bernie Wolfe at 13:10 of the first period, after allowing 4 goals on 14 shots, but the goaltending change did little to improve the Caps' fortunes. Scorers for Cleveland, in what became a 7-1 romp, included Sabourin, MacAdam, Christie, Murdoch, Hampton, Neilson, and Fidler. At long last, all of the club's gunners were healthy and heating up.

In game two of the home-and-home series Cleveland dumped Washington 4-2 in DC. Returning to Richfield on December 15, the Barons shellacked the Red Wings 7-3, for the club's first three-game

FIG. 20. Square-jawed coach Jack Evans observes his troops from the bench.
Photo source: Dennis Turchek.

win streak since moving east. The Barons then won two of their next four, bringing their overall record to 11–17–7, their best thirty-five-game start since 1971–72. Unfortunately the Barons' inconsistency allowed the Leafs to stay ahead in the overall standings.

On Boxing Day against Boston, Cleveland was looking for its twelfth win. The Bruins built up a commanding 4–1 lead in the first period only to watch it disintegrate in the second. Cleveland outshot the B's 9–3 in the second and whittled the gap to 4–3, thanks to goals by Dave Gardner and Wayne Merrick. Not to be outdone, the Bruins mounted an offensive attack of their own and fired home 2 goals in the final few minutes of the game to ice the 6–3 win.

Versus Montreal the following night the Barons' impotent offense managed only 19 shots at Ken Dryden. In the next game against Toronto the Barons had many more scoring chances, but the defense loosened up and allowed 6 goals. The Barons followed this inconsistent trend the next three outings, and not once during these contests did they manage to score more than twice. In the midst of a stretch against some of the league's top teams, the Barons embarked upon another one of their patented losing streaks, this time six games long. "If you look hard at the league, you'll find that the teams that play in streaks are a notch below the top teams," Evans said a few days after a 7–2 beating by Philadelphia. "We fall into that group, and until we can beat the other teams at our level with regularity that's where we'll stay." Evans continued, "It used to be difficult to score three goals against us. This whole thing is frustrating. During one stretch, we couldn't score. Then we went a stretch when we averaged five goals a game."[15] The 3-M Line had gone into a funk, and whenever that happened, the Barons usually lost. Dennis Maruk had been slashed just above the wrist in a game with the New York Rangers on December 19, and he had played with the pain for two weeks.

When the Vancouver Canucks came to Cleveland on January 7, the Barons were looking to reestablish themselves as a playoff contender. The Canucks led 2–1 after the first period, but something during the intermission must have sparked the Cleveland players. The Barons' Phil Roberto scored just 30 seconds into the second period. Two minutes later Ralph Klassen scored the club's first short-handed marker of the season to give the Barons a 1-goal edge. Wayne Merrick scored at 4:04 to make it 4–2, Cleveland. The Canucks tried to mount a comeback after the Merrick goal, reducing the gap to a single goal, but Dave Gardner scored Cleveland's fifth goal less than two minutes after the Canucks had made it 4–3. The Barons went on to win 8–4.

As had been the trend all season long, the Barons once again strung together a few good games after a lengthy winless streak, but Mel Swig decided to give general manager Bill McCreary the axe anyway. "We probably overestimated his business ability," Swig said about McCreary. "He was trying to combine business and hockey ability and it was probably just too much. I'm not saying anything bad about his hockey ability."[16] Assistant general manager Harry Howell assumed the position of acting general manager. Howell then traded Gary Simmons and Jim Moxey to Los Angeles for goaltender Gary Edwards and veteran center Juha "Whitey" Widing. "We've been talking trades all season, but nothing much was happening until this finally came up," said Jack Evans. "We felt we could improve ourselves a slight bit with this trade."[17]

Edwards was a quick, agile goalie who modelled himself after the legendary Glenn Hall. Edwards was the Kings' Rookie of the Year for 1972 and won the club's Unsung Hero award in 1975. In the latter season he had a stellar 2.35 average and 3 shutouts, helping the Kings to a surprise 105-point season. Widing, on the other hand, was on the downside of a productive career that had seen him net 138 NHL goals since 1970-71. He was only twenty-nine, but two years removed from the last of five consecutive seasons of 50 or more points.

Ironically it was not Simmons who asked to be traded out of Cleveland, but Meloche. According to Simmons, the trade came as a shock to both of them:

I had heard rumors that I was going to New York. I heard rumors I was going to Boston. Gilles had asked to be traded. We played a game on Friday night against Boston in Cleveland, and Gilles had played an awesome game. We were ahead about 3–1 . . . They scored [4] goals in the last [11:46] of the game; second, third rebounds, Gilles didn't have a chance. He comes into the dressing room, he throws down his gloves, he throws down his mask and, "*Tabarnak!*" You know; he was pretty upset.

So Harry Howell, who was the acting GM [said] . . . "Cobra, can I see you in Tex's office?' So I walked in there and he said, "We've got to make some changes here, and I just want you to know you've been traded." And I don't say anything outside because inside I'm thinking "Yahoo!" I shook his hand and shook Tex's hand, and thanked them very much, and I walked out the door, and I thought, "Wait a minute." I went back in, I said, "Where'd I get traded to?" And he said, "LA."

So I walked out, and Gilles is just picking up his stuff. He's just picking up his gloves, his stick, and mask that he'd thrown, and I said, "Hey Gilles." He says, "Yeah." And I said, "I just got traded." "*Tabarnak de câlisse!*" He throws his stuff down again. He says, "I ask to get trade, they trade you! What's up wit' dat?" And I said, "Gilles, I talk English better than you."

The Barons were coming off that 5–2 loss to Boston when Edwards made his debut. On January 23 Edwards shut out the Buffalo Sabres and the mighty French Connection Line of Rick Martin, Gilbert Per-reault, and Rene Robert, 3–0. After a six-day layoff the Barons were a little rusty and lost their next game, 4–3 to Detroit, with Meloche in goal. Meloche started the next two games as well, but Cleveland was outscored by Chicago and Montreal by a combined score of 16–6. Evans went with Edwards against Pittsburgh on February 3, and Edwards recorded his second shutout in three games, but the Barons managed just 22 shots in a scoreless draw.

In the meantime the Barons' principal owner weighed the damages caused by the club's pathetic attendance record, and the diagnosis was not pretty. The franchise was hemorrhaging money due to the fact that after twenty-five home games, it was only averaging about 5,200 fans per game. Swig estimated he had poured about $4 million into the club since purchasing it less than two years earlier. Cleveland suffered through terrible winters in both 1977 and 1978, no doubt con-tributing to the Barons' horrible attendance record. In his 1996 book *High Sticks and Hat-Tricks*, the 6'3" Gene Kiczek recalled: "Snow [was] piled well over my head alongside my driveway. This city has seen nothing like that winter since."[18] Even the NBA Cavaliers experienced a sharp decrease in attendance. If people refused to risk their lives driving some forty-five minutes or more to watch a winning basketball team, what chance did the Barons have when they were already far down the list of priorities for Cleveland sports fans?

The media accused Swig of using scare tactics to get fans to come to the Coliseum. He had told reporters he could not guarantee the Barons would remain in Cleveland unless attendance improved. The Barons were dead last in attendance, perpetuating a dubious team tradition. Swig explained he was not trying to scare anyone but was "attempting to point out the problems [were] serious" and that the Barons needed to "make a serious effort to solve them." Swig later added that he was "at least 90 percent sure" the Barons would be in Cleveland for the 1977–78 season. In mid-January, Swig admitted he needed help: "We do have a lease at the Coliseum that runs for four more years. And I intend to talk to Sandy Greenberg (owner of the building) about some help, perhaps financial . . . but right now fans are what we need. Just a show of interest from them. And we're not begging. We just want to see if the interest is really here. We'll do everything we can to find out."[19]

The fans weren't buying any of that, especially after Swig made some inappropriate comments in an interview with the *Cleveland Press*'s Bob Schlesinger on January 11. "We want to do what's necessary to make the thing go," he said. "But if it seems we're just pouring money down a rat hole, then we'll have to sell or fold the franchise." Like Oakland, Cleveland has never had a sterling reputation, but citizens will certainly defend their city's honor. "The city had been the brunt of bad jokes because the Cuyahoga River had caught on fire, and the Mayor once set his hair ablaze," said Gene Kiczek. "The list seemed endless. Now the hockey team's owner referred to the city as a 'rat hole.' It was a huge insult."[20]

At the league's annual meeting in Vancouver at the end of January 1977, Swig appealed to the board of governors to lend him some $500,000 to ensure the Barons would finish the season. Clarence Campbell made it clear the league was not about to hand over such a large sum without thinking things through first. "The league has made an offer and it is his choice whether to accept it or not," the president said. It was believed the league offered Swig $250,000, but considering the Barons' enormous attendance problems, a quarter-million dollars was peanuts. "It will depend on what alternatives, if any, Mr. Swig has," Campbell continued. "I can't believe he is entirely without resources. It now is a question of his capabilities to meet his current situation with some assistance." In his defense Swig explained that his ownership partner George Gund III had tried to raise "something like $4 million in new capital" but failed, forcing Swig "to pull everything back together again after not being fully prepared to do so."[21]

The NHL was left scrambling; there was no action plan outlined in the league bylaws to tackle the unlikely event of a sudden franchise failure. "There could be a draft of players, or an auction sale, I would assume," Campbell said, less than reassuringly.[22] The NHL had grown tired of propping up the ailing Barons, but folding a franchise in midseason would have been downright embarrassing. What unfolded over the course of three weeks in February 1977 would become one of the most controversial, most incomprehensible series of meetings and deals in sports history.

When the Barons' financial plight became public, it was believed the NHL would donate an equal amount of money as the Barons themselves managed to collect. As in 1974, when the Seals were bailed out by the league, the other clubs again balked at the idea of using their money to support a team perennially on the verge of collapse. The league claimed to have spent in the neighborhood of $8 million keeping the franchise alive over the years, but if the NHL stopped giving the Barons money, the league faced the possibility of dealing with three major issues. For one thing, if the Barons folded, two dozen players would be out of a job. Furthermore, owners would also lose revenue as a result of canceled games. Finally, if the Barons went belly up, NHL owners would be responsible for paying Charlie Finley the rest of the money owed to him when he sold the Seals to the league.

The expansion frenzy of the last decade had come to an abrupt and brutal end. The only profitable teams in the NHL were, of course, old reliables like Montreal, Toronto, Philadelphia, and the New York Rangers, as well as Vancouver and Buffalo, both born just seven years earlier. Not even the Boston Bruins were immune to the reality of the situation. When Bobby Orr was patrolling the blue line in Boston, the Bruins had enjoyed 117 consecutive sellouts. In 1976–77 the Bruins sold out only 2 games. The Penguins had already declared bankruptcy, the Scouts had moved to Colorado, and the Flames eventually asked their own players to purchase tickets just to stay afloat. Likewise, the WHA was a wasteland of dead or dying teams. A year earlier, the expansion Denver Spurs became the Ottawa Civics, but after just 7 games in Canada the team disbanded. That same year the Minnesota Fighting Saints folded after 59 games. The Cleveland Crusaders then moved to Minnesota to become the new Fighting Saints for the 1976–77 season, but that franchise went belly-up after 42 games. The Houston Aeros had been one of the WHA's flagship franchises, winning championships in 1974 and 1975, but by 1977 they were struggling to pay their players. The Indianapolis Racers, who were one of the best-attended teams in the WHA, asked their players to defer salary payments.

In 1976–77 there were eighteen teams in the NHL and another twelve in the WHA. The two leagues had become greedy and had expanded so quickly that there were not enough quality players to go around, creating a great disparity between the best and worst clubs. Games had become lopsided and boring. The most unstable franchises were located in nontraditional markets, and for the most part their teams had no chance of winning a championship, so few fans bought tickets. Hockey franchises had become money pits, but the U.S. government was also partially responsible for that problem. As lawyer and player agent Bob Woolf revealed to *Time* magazine in 1977, the IRS "took a good tax-shelter deal away" the year before, and without that break, no one was looking to invest in a sports team. As Woolf put it, "There isn't fresh money around."[23] Rich businessmen had gotten into the hockey business in the hopes of cashing in on the NHL's successful expansion project. By 1977 everyone wanted out.

The Cleveland Barons became the poster child for professional hockey's greed and poor planning. Pro hockey players had rarely been concerned about bounced checks and deferred payments, but this was now the norm, and Cleveland would be no exception. "I had never imagined this happening until the day they told us we weren't being paid," said team captain and player representative Bobby Stewart. "I just didn't think the National Hockey League would come to that point."[24] Even the *Washington Post* was cracking jokes at the Barons' expense: "Do you know the Cleveland Barons are going to bounce back in the National Hockey League? Owner Mel Swig is planning to tie each of his players to his check."[25]

At the All-Star break Swig asked the league for approximately $600,000 just to get through the season, but the league cringed at the thought of spending more money just to keep this dying team on life support another few months. Swig then met with National Hockey League Players' Association (NHLPA) executive director and player agent Alan Eagleson and John Ziegler, chairman of the NHL's Board of Governors, for six hours trying to find a way to get the Barons through the season. A meeting with the Cleveland players would take place February 2. "I really wasn't surprised about this," said Stewart. "I was up in Vancouver and saw what was going on last week. Everything will depend on what comes out of tomorrow's meeting. I suppose they will ask us to take a pay cut like Atlanta did, but if it's a real big one I don't know how many players will go along with it. Some of the guys may figure it would be better to be free agents and hope to get picked up by somebody else."[26]

On the day of the meeting the players were asked to defer 27 percent of their salary, retroactive to January 1, until May 15. Swig swore he would have enough money to pay everyone if they agreed to the deferment plan. Swig would have until February 17 (fourteen days) to pay the players, and if they were not paid within those two weeks, every single Baron could become a free agent. Free agency was not necessarily a desirable option for some players, as Eagleson explained: "Of the 25 players involved, I would say 10 or 12 of them could get jobs immediately with other teams in the NHL. There's some who simply won't get employment." Even if a few players became free agents and signed with other clubs, it would spell disaster for the Barons. Imagine the Barons without Gilles Meloche or the 3-M Line. "It's my feelings," said Eagleson, "that if the top players, they have the right to do it, decide to leave the club then the Cleveland franchise will probably terminate."[27]

The players accepted the salary deferment, but it was difficult for many to live on a fixed income. Stewart admitted, "It's been a trying experience." Stewart had signed a five-year contract before the season had started, but he was facing the possibility of watching it all go up in smoke. "Instead of going to a restaurant now after games, I go home and have a sandwich. I don't go out after practice. I told my wife the other day that we're really going to have to watch our budget. Until we find out what the situation is, we're not going to spend any money unless we have to."[28]

Alan Eagleson and John Ziegler hoped Swig could find the necessary funds. "Mr. Swig has asked the owners and players for help," Eagleson explained, "and to date the owners have rejected his requests."[29] By February 4, however, it seemed as though the Barons had found themselves a savior. In a conversation with Gary Sabourin, Swig mentioned that a potential new backer had been found. The details of the deal were hazy, but Sabourin passed the news on to Stewart. Sabourin told him Sanford "Sandy" Greenberg, a Washington businessman and owner of the Richfield Coliseum, was interested in helping the Barons. According to Richfield Coliseum president Peter Larsen, "The offer included $1 million in new money to finance the operation for the rest of the year plus a personal commitment to raise another $3–4 million to continue the team."[30] All seemed well in Cleveland, but just a few hours after the meeting between the parties took place, the deal vaporized.

Howard Nemerovski, Swig's attorney, revealed that Greenberg's offer "was for less than $1 million and did not have in it an unequiv-ocally firm commitment to raise additional money." Swig also com-mented on the disheartening turn of events: "The deal presented to us was best expressed as 'locked in concrete'—impossible to be changed in any way." There was simply no way the two sides could come to an agreement. "With the rejection, it absolutely ends any hope of keeping the team alive—at least from Sandy's view," Larsen sourly added. "Our indication is that with the rejection of the offer, the team is finished. The only person who could have saved it was Sandy. It is finished, to his horror."[31]

Swig refused to give up. He told his players they would receive their February 1 paychecks before the February 17 deadline. How-ever, their February 15 paychecks would have to be delayed a few days in order to meet the upcoming midnight deadline. By delaying the players' February 15 payroll, Swig now faced another two-week period to reorganize himself, and another deadline fast approaching. Another problem was that the league gave Swig only enough money to pay twenty-seven of the team's forty-six contracted players toiling in Cleveland and Salt Lake City of the CHL—because that was the number of contracts Greenberg was going to assume at the time of the proposed agreement to buy the team. The nineteen who were not paid, including NHLers Phil Roberto, Glenn Patrick, and Frank Spring—who happened to be enjoying the most productive season of his NHL career with 21 points in 26 games—and sixteen other players toiling in the Central League, became free agents at midnight. The three discarded Barons were given the back pay they were owed from the NHLPA's emergency fund, and a cold pat on the back as the door closed behind them. Patrick was not very impressed by the way the situation was handled: "I don't have too many good things to say about Mr. Swig," he said. "He never faced us. The organization's very poorly run, not first class at all."[32]

Months later Dick Rosetta of the *Salt Lake Tribune* explained how the entire Golden Eagles organization still had a bad taste in its mouth as the Barons came to town for an October preseason game:

> It would be easy to pass off Saturday's game as just another scrimmage where no ones [sic] wants to get hurt, but there are a few sour memories which will be revived even though most of the folks who were involved with Cleveland last year during the mid-winter "shaft" of the Eagles are no longer around.
>
> Salt Lake fans, most of them anyway, have not forgotten that former Cleveland owner Mel Swig released over a dozen players last year in mid-February—cut them off completely, threw away contractual obligations and said, in effect, make your own soup.
>
> Well, Lyle Bradley, Gary Holt, Tom Sundberg and later on, Brent Meeke, remember Swig's antics and Cleveland is Cleveland to them . . . whomever is at the controls.[33]

With the Barons' tank running on empty, Stewart organized a team meeting at his home on February 17 for all the Barons who were left. The players took an informal vote to decide whether or not to boycott their February 18 game against Colorado. Fourteen of the twenty players voted in favor of the boycott. Stewart told the media what the players' plans were concerning their immediate future: "Right now the majority of players have decided that they will not dress for tomorrow night. That is not definite. I still have to communicate with Eagleson and Swig about this. We hope some type of agreement can be reached." He added, "We just want some type of guarantee because when we go out on the ice to play we are putting ourselves in jeopardy. As representative for the players, right now it doesn't look very good."[34]

Cooler heads prevailed as the fateful team practice came to an end, and the Barons, just nineteen strong, played the Rockies to a sloppy 3–3 tie. Instead of boycotting, they gave Swig an ultimatum: either hand over the late paychecks by February 22 or find a suitable owner who would. "Of course, we'd rather they pay us," said Bobby Stewart, "but if we don't have the checks by noon Tuesday we won't play Buffalo Wednesday night." To further emphasize the seriousness of the situation, Stewart candidly told reporters, "They can beg us all they want, but we won't play. It's as simple as that."[35] Stewart phoned Swig at his San Francisco residence to give him the news. "I don't give a damn," Swig shot back.[36] Stewart, Eagleson, and Campbell eventually came to an agreement. Stewart was told that in the event the players' demands were not met, the league would give them its blessing to boycott the Buffalo game. "If by noon Tuesday of next week this situation has not been rectified," revealed Stewart, "unless we are paid in full or Mr. Greenberg steps in, every team in the league will back our team in our decision not to continue playing."[37]

After ten years of dodging financial bullets like characters out of *The Matrix*, the Cleveland Barons were finally going to meet their maker. Or so it seemed. With professional hockey at its nadir, no one was interested in buying the worst-off of the NHL's sinking ships, and the league had absolutely no intention of taking over the club once again. "The players tried for three weeks to keep the franchise alive," explained Eagleson. "They played without pay and without contract protection. I can no longer persuade them to play, nor would I do so. They are risking their futures and their careers." With the Barons all but finished, the NHL was looking down the barrel of a loaded gun. As Eagleson put it, "I expect the Cleveland Barons' situation to be little more than the tip of the iceberg . . . All one has to do is look at the scores, not on the ice, but the attendance in the box scores. I told these players a little while ago not to be surprised if they are with another team next year and I wind up making this same talk to them."[38]

At noon on February 23, 1977, the Barons' players "retired" and officially became free agents, meaning they would not be playing the Buffalo Sabres that night. Players around the league stood behind their Cleveland brethren. "There's only so much a person can take," said Washington's Mike Lampman. "We're like any other employee. We're not charitable institutions. I would have done the same thing." Lampman's teammate Bernie Wolfe believed it was "just stupid" to let a team as troubled as the Barons even start the season and that someone should have done "a bit more thinking." Ed Westfall of the New York Islanders predicted doom if the Barons folded in midseason. "I'm certainly on the side of the players," he said. "The problems will be unreal if they fold now. We probably don't know the half of it. The scheduling problems would be unbelievable. What would happen to the players? There are, say, half a dozen that some teams would be interested in. Who would get them? Only the teams that can afford it." Westfall's teammate Denis Potvin said, "The players should be the first priority, not the franchise itself. I think the league should pick up their salaries through at least the end of the year. It hasn't been fair to the players. They're not the cause of this."[39]

In the end, after much haggling and persuasion, Swig, Eagleson, and the NHLPA were able to scrounge up the necessary funds. Swig himself contributed $350,000, and the league added another $350,000, while the NHLPA loaned the Barons $600,000, for a grand total of $1.3 million. The news of the Barons' resurrection was not received warmly by the players. "I don't mind staying, if we have good ownership," said Rick Hampton. "But I've been going through this kind of thing for three years now. If this is just a hold off until next year, and we're going to go through the same thing again, I would rather have left now."[40] Al MacAdam was also skeptical about his future in Cleveland: "I was really ticked off before the game when I heard the news. . . . It takes a lot to get my goat and my goat was got. I was upset when the decision was made for us to stay here. This is just like the first two weeks of February. There is no guarantee the team is going to be sold yet . . . 75% of the team is disappointed they are staying here." MacAdam even contemplated a real retirement. "I've thought about it quite seriously," he said. "It could still happen. Money doesn't mean that much to me."[41] Gilles Meloche did not exactly give the deal a ringing endorsement either. "I don't know," he said. "I definitely will talk to Harry, but I'm a little mixed up right now. At least now we know it's a settled thing until the end of the season. And that's good for the whole team because five or six guys were uncertain about their future in hockey if the team folded."[42]

Bob Stewart may have been exaggerating just a tad when he spoke at a team press conference on behalf of his teammates. "Needless to say there are a lot of happy players in there now," he said. One would guess he was either lying, or trying to put on a happy face for the media. "We thought it was hopeless yesterday," Stewart admitted. "We want to give our appreciation to Mel Swig and his family for donating $350,000 into the franchise. He's shown he has faith in us by putting up the money." Stewart was hoping to let bygones be bygones, and to get back to playing hockey. "He's said some things he shouldn't have and we've said some things we shouldn't have," Stewart said. "I've been annoyed with him at times and he's been annoyed with me. But now, it's all over. I hope all the pressure we've gone through this last month can be forgotten."[43]

Swig had been through hell in his two years of ownership. During the season, he became the franchise's second owner to suffer a heart attack, and like his predecessor Finley, Swig had also taken a beating in the press. After the dust settled, Swig took the opportunity to clear his name in the eyes of fans, players, and local media:

> I was the villain in the eyes of the press and players when, in fact, I felt I had done everything in my power to continue running the operation. I didn't have to. Then came the time when I said, "Hey, this is it." It was time to call a halt. I know young people well enough to know how upset and emotionally distraught they are. They are not considerate of my problems, but I can't blame them. They have built up animosity without knowing the facts. I'm sure if they knew the facts, they would not have that animosity.[44]

The Barons' resurrection shocked the Cleveland players, but no one was more shocked than the hundreds of NHL players who found out years later that they had unknowingly loaned the Barons the $600,000 donated by the NHLPA. The other seventeen teams sure as hell weren't going to give Cleveland any money. Former Bruins president Paul Mooney revealed that the teams "were arguing among themselves. We were talking $40,000 a team and no way some teams—Washington was one—were going to pitch in to save Cleveland. That's how the loan came about. Ziegler turned to Eagleson and said, 'Fork up the dough.'"⁴⁵

In Russ Conway's illuminating book, *Game Misconduct*, the author exposed Eagleson's questionable business practices. Eagleson was at his slimy best when it came to rescuing the Cleveland Barons. In 1977 Ed Westfall was the Islanders' player representative, and according to the minutes of several meetings between owners and players, Westfall was present when the loan was approved. Westfall was confused when he found out he had voted to approve such a large loan. "What Cleveland loan?" he wondered. "I don't remember anything about a loan to the Cleveland Barons." Boston's Terry O'Reilly also denied attending these meetings. "Those minutes say it was a unanimous vote to approve, but that's totally untrue!" he exclaimed. "I did not vote to approve any of that. As far as a loan to Cleveland, this is the first I've heard about $600,000 of Players' Association money going to Cleveland or the NHL. I didn't vote on any of this."⁴⁶

Another of Eagleson's schemes involved investing his clients' money in the Barons. For instance, Colorado star Wilf Paiement unknowingly had $20,000 invested in the Barons. Paiement even made a handsome profit on the deal: "When Paiement got his money back, early the next season, [Eagleson's Sports Management Limited] sent him a letter informing him that a check for $21,147.85 'which is repayment in full of your loan to the NHLPA' had been deposited in his account." Upon learning the details of the Barons loan, many players were upset they had never been consulted in the first place. "He never gave me the opportunity to be a part of that loan and make a profit on interest," revealed former NHLPA vice president Brad Park. "You'd think the responsibility of the Players' Association executive director would be to be fair to all players. Every player deserved the chance to decide whether or not he'd be a part of that loan individually." Ed Westfall was just as surprised when he learned how the Barons survived their financial scare. "I also never knew Alan Eagleson had mixed our Players' Association money into a loan with players he represented so his players could make money. This is all new to me."⁴⁷

Eagleson had a vested interest in keeping the Barons alive. He was not trying to save the players' jobs but rather had an ulterior motive. According to Russ Conway, "As the union director who also operated a player agency and management business, the loan put him in the position of giving players he represented an unfair advantage over players he didn't. And since Eagleson had many clients on the Cleveland team, it was in his interest to keep those players solvent so that they could continue to pay him."⁴⁸ Eagleson's schemes would eventually come to light, long after the Barons disappeared, but for the time being the team was safe.

On February 23 the Barons finally played the Buffalo game they had threatened to boycott, but only 3,185 fans hastily turned out to see the Sabres win 5-3. The score may have looked close, but according to Dennis Maruk, the game was a mighty struggle for many a Cleveland player:

Nobody wanted to play the game because [of] what was going to happen . . . and all of a sudden, the league took over the team, and we all had to go out and play the game. I know a couple of guys were still in a bar that day, so it was kind of cute, and they ended up having to play the game because the insurance was taken care of. . . . Regarding the situation, we didn't know if we were all going to be drafted by other teams, and so it was really kind of a lot of different things that were going on. As a professional athlete, it was kind of tough, but we still went to play because other teams are going to take a look at you. You had to go as an individual, you had to look at your own personal pride and say, "Look, no matter what, if the team's not going to be here, I've still got to perform and do my job because hopefully someone, a better team, whatever, were going to select me in the draft."

As the Barons' financial crisis died down, the club strung together a modest three-game win streak between February 28 and March 5, but in the end, for the seventh season in a row, the Barons would be looking at the Stanley Cup playoffs from the outside. The Barons finished 25–42–13, 18 points behind the Leafs and 43 behind the first-place Bruins. In the last month of the season, with the Barons out of the race, the fans actually started coming to the rink in larger numbers. The club's last six home dates drew an average of over 10,000 fans per game, coincidentally around the time the Barons reduced their $9 tickets to $7. Thanks to the late-season flurry, attendance swelled to an average of 6,194 per game by the end of the season, but that was still by far the worst mark in the league.

As for the 1976–77 campaign itself, it was actually better than it looked in the final standings. The players deserved a lot of credit for playing as well as they did considering the sword of Damocles hung over their head most of the season. Like the year before, several franchise records were either broken or tied. The 3-M Line set records for most assists (110 total) and most points (183 total) by a line in one season. Maruk set club marks for assists (50) and points (78) and was named the Most Valuable Player. MacAdam scored 22 goals and 41 assists to lead all Cleveland wingers and represented the Barons at the NHL All-Star Game. Murdoch endured an injury-riddled season but finished with 23 goals and 19 assists in just 57 games. Between December 10 and December 26, Murdoch was particularly deadly, scoring at least 1 goal in seven consecutive games and at least 1 point in eight straight games to set two more club marks. Gilles Meloche was outstanding as usual, putting together a respectable 3.47 goals-against average.

Despite some accolades for the Barons' best players, the season was also a massive disappointment. The club was expected to put its sorry history to rest, win new fans, and challenge for a playoff spot. In the end, attendance was lousy, and only Detroit, Colorado, and Washington finished with fewer points. The club's lackluster season can be attributed to a wide range of reasons. Though finances and poor attendance had been major concerns in Oakland for a number of years, no player can grow accustomed to these things, no matter how talented he may be. The club needed fan support in order for it to be successful on the ice. If the Barons truly were the "pride of Cleveland town," as the team's fight song claimed, the city certainly had a funny way of showing it.

Injuries also crippled the team's chances at making any upward moves in the standings. Fred Ahern fractured his arm, Bob Murdoch tore ligaments in his knee, and various health problems forced both Gary Sabourin and Jim Pappin to retire in midseason. Rick Hampton played only 57 games and was forced to play as a forward for 32 games due to the numerous injuries up front. Eleven of his 16 goals were scored as a forward. Jim Neilson played only 47 games, forcing Mike Christie and rookie Greg Smith to take their games up a notch, but they responded well. Christie and Smith scored 59 points between them, while Christie finished the year with a plus/minus mark of +18, a team record. That mark was equivalent to about +618 on a team like Montreal or Boston! Mike Fidler dazzled Barons fans in his first 46 games of the season before a broken leg killed his chances at winning the Calder Trophy. He finished with 17 goals and 16 assists, a pace that would have netted him 30 goals and 28 assists in a full schedule.

Despite the disappointing finish, good news loomed over the horizon. Starting in 1977-78, fourth-place clubs in strong divisions would be given a chance to qualify for the playoffs. Under the old playoff format, all clubs finishing first, second, or third received automatic berths. Under the modified system, only the top two teams in each division would receive an automatic pass into the postseason. Of the remaining ten clubs, the four with the highest point totals would also qualify for the playoffs. Therefore, no matter how well the Sabres, Bruins, and Leafs played, there was always a chance for Cleveland to get into the dance.

According to the 1978 edition of *The Complete Handbook of Pro Hockey*, "The big gap between the Barons and Toronto is deceptive because of Cleveland's internal situation. Man for man, the Barons aren't as bad as their record indicates, and given big performances from a half dozen key players and solid work from everyone else, could cut into that 18-point deficit."[49] The Barons had been lucky to survive the season, and maybe the franchise was turning a corner, but as the German proverb says, "Luck sometimes visits a fool, but it never sits down with him."

12

ONE LAST GASP, 1977-1978

The Barons may have survived their first season in Cleveland, but like a boxer scoring a lucky knockout after being manhandled the entire fight, the Barons didn't look good. It had been a decade since the California Seals played their first NHL game, and the franchise was shakier than ever. One more catastrophe would likely nudge the Barons into the abyss. It was widely believed the Barons had lost $2 to $3 million in 1976–77, reportedly more than any other team in the league, and there was no way the club could afford to go through the financial wringer one more time.

It was the same old story: the club needed to find a responsible owner with deep pockets, and the club needed to entice a good ten thousand people to games on a regular basis. That was easier said than done; hockey franchises were hardly a hot commodity in 1977. The NHL told Mel Swig he had to get his finances in order by June 1 or else the league would dissolve the franchise. Early on, Sandy Greenberg was the Barons' primary suitor. As owner of the Richfield Coliseum, Greenberg did not want to sit idly and watch a second hockey team desert his rink, leaving him with the NBA Cavaliers as his only tenants. Greenberg had offered to buy the Barons in February 1977, but Swig turned him down. By the end of April they signed a new deal that would give Greenberg the option of buying the club. Greenberg had until June 8 to prove to the NHL governors he had a suitable plan and enough money to ensure the Barons' survival for years to come. The financial target: $3 to $3.5 million. Greenberg thought it over and ultimately decided it was wise not to invest in the Barons. Instead, George Gund III and his brother Gordon, who were minority shareholders in the Barons, took the plunge.

It had originally been the Gunds' idea to move the Seals to Cleveland. Now they would get the chance to prove they had not made the mistake of a lifetime. The Gunds paid Swig over $5.3 million, including $500,000 cash, $3 million in notes to Swig, and $1.8 million in notes

338

to Charlie Finley, for full control of the Barons. "Hopefully, this will be an investment that will pay off in the long run," said George Gund.[1] According to the *New York Times*, Swig was so over the moon, "he burst out of the decisive meeting with the [NHL] board of governors and mistakenly walked straight into a ladies restroom."[2]

The Gunds had been fortunate enough to grow up in an affluent family. Their father George II had accumulated a net worth in the neighborhood of $600 million, and when he died in 1966, the brothers inherited a portion of his estate. Growing up in Cleveland, George III became a huge hockey fan, even organizing the first hockey team at Case Western Reserve University. He later moved to San Francisco, where he became an art collector, philanthropist, and importer and distributor of Eastern European films. Gordon, on the other hand, endured many health problems as an adult. He was diagnosed with retinitis pigmentosa and gradually started losing his vision at twenty-five. Long before he became involved with the Barons, he had gone completely blind.

In an effort to increase attendance at the Coliseum, the Barons announced they were reducing the price of the most expensive tickets from $10 to $8.50. During the summer, the Barons launched an aggressive new publicity and promotion plan in and around Cleveland and Akron. Peter Larsen was named president of Ohio Barons, Inc., the company created by George Gund to purchase and run the hockey club. Larsen would be responsible for ticket sales as well as promotions. The new owners were determined to keep the club in Cleveland and put lots of money toward promotions and other improvements. This was a far cry from the previous season, when the Barons had very little money to spend on advertising. "There were many requested dollars that never came," said former general manager Bill McCreary. "We had $17,000 in the bank account. It's difficult to start programs that undercapitalized."[3]

The Gunds also retained coach Jack Evans and appointed Harry Howell as permanent general manager. The new owners gave Howell carte blanche to acquire the players he felt were necessary to make the Barons a contender. If anything, the Gunds were not going to be stingy owners, a factor that had always hampered previous general managers' decisions. "So far," said Howell, "I've had no restrictions on signing players or trading players to strengthen the franchise. Our first goal is to sign our top draft choices, Mike Crombeen, a potential star, and Dan Chicoine, who also would be a great asset. The others would be invited to camp and signed if their play warrants it."[4]

Though the Barons of 1976–77 finished with only 63 points, if the players hadn't played the second half of the season worrying about whether they would get paid, the Barons could have fared much better. Only a few minor changes were made to the roster. The Barons signed twenty-three-year-old University of Michigan star Kris Manery, and he would see plenty of ice time in Cleveland. Bob Murdoch and Dave Gardner signed new contracts, but Juha Widing, who had scored only 14 points in 29 games with the Barons, accepted an offer to play for the WHA's Edmonton Oilers, while offensive-minded defenseman Brent Meeke took a year off before going to Europe to play out the rest of his career.

Charlie Simmer had become an afterthought after his solid rookie season in 1974-75, but the LA Kings signed him to a new contract and played him with veteran Marcel Dionne and budding star Dave Taylor on what would become known as the Triple Crown Line. Simmer would score 56 goals and 101 points in 1979–80, and 56 goals and 105 points in 1980–81, earning First All-Star Team berths both years. He scored another 44 goals in 1983–84, and 36 in 55 games two years later. Once again, the Barons had let an impact player slip through their fingers.

At the amateur draft none of the Barons' selections ended up making a significant impact. Fifth overall selection Mike Crombeen played forty-eight games but came nowhere near repeating the 42-goal performance he had enjoyed with the OHA's Kingston Canadians the previous year. Dan Chicoine (23rd overall), Reg Kerr (41st overall), John Baby (59th overall), and Jeff Allan (95th overall) all dented the Cleveland roster that season, but none made much of an impression.

The Barons started the 1977-78 schedule in Los Angeles. Backed by the stellar goaltending of Rogie Vachon, the Kings blanked Cleveland 2-0. Surprisingly, it turned out to be the Barons' last loss for a while. On

October 15 the Barons handed the Washington Capitals a 4–2 defeat before more than 10,000 Cleveland fans. Players and management must have been ecstatic to see so many fans at the Barons' home opener and absolutely crestfallen when only 3,252 fans showed up four nights later when the Kings visited. The Barons got to Vachon early as Fred Ahern scored at 8:56 of the first period, but former Seal Ernie Hicke responded a minute later. Maruk scored his first of the season in the opening minute of the second period, putting Cleveland up 2–1. Six minutes later, a shot from Bob Murdoch hit Vachon above his left eye, forcing him to yield the crease to Gary Simmons. Cobra played well in relief of Vachon, but Murdoch scored again before the period was over to give Cleveland a 3–1 lead. In the Barons' goal Meloche turned aside 27 shots. "He's just playing great," Evans declared. "I haven't seen him play this well this early in the three years I've been with this club."[5] The Barons came away with a 3–1 win, putting them a game above .500.

The Barons were fired up in the early days of the season. "The team and myself feel more secure and relaxed knowing that the franchise is stable," said Evans after a 7–4 thrashing of Minnesota on October 20.[6] That October it looked as though hell had shockingly frozen over as nothing could stop the Barons from winning, but the North Stars gave Cleveland a scare just 12 seconds into the contest when Roland Eriksson put one past Meloche. Wayne Merrick scored just 34 seconds later with his first of the season, followed by a goal by Dennis Maruk at 1:58. With the Barons up 4–3 in the third, Gardner waltzed into Minnesota territory with a defenseman on his tail, but he still managed to slip the puck past goalie Paul Harrison. Gardner and Ralph Klassen also scored goals in the final three minutes to put the game out of reach and give the Barons their third consecutive win.

Meloche stole the spotlight October 22 when the Barons faced the St. Louis Blues. The Blues had lost four in a row entering the game and had scored a measly 6 goals since the start of the season, but they fired 53 shots at Meloche. "The Robber Baron," as he came to be known, certainly could have been accused of larceny on more than one occasion. At the other end of the rink his teammates, possibly in awe of his heroics, managed only 17 shots, but the Barons came away

$2.00

CLEVELAND
BARONS

1977-78 MEDIA GUIDE

FIG. 21. Barons Media Guide. Clockwise from left: Gary Edwards, Gilles Meloche, Al MacAdam, Bob Murdoch, and Dennis Maruk. Author's collection.

with a 3–2 win, their fourth in a row, tying the franchise record. The Barons failed to prolong the streak, however, dropping a 3–2 decision to Pittsburgh on October 23. By the end of the month, the Barons were under .500 again.

A match with the 1-8-1 St. Louis Blues on November 2 seemed like a perfect opportunity to start the month on the right foot. Dennis Maruk scored twice in the first period and twice in the second to double his season total from 4 to 8, but each time the Barons found themselves ahead by a goal, they blew it. Final score: Blues 4, Maruk 4. A few nights later Meloche blocked 41 shots, and the Barons beat the Detroit Red Wings 4–3 to even their season record at 5-5-1, the farthest into the season they had ever carried a .500 record.

The following night against Detroit, Gary Edwards made his second start in three games, but the Barons' lack of offense did the club in. "You can't let Cleveland skate," said Detroit coach Bobby Kromm. "If you do, they'll catch you with your pants down. We took away their skating tonight and took away their efficiency."[7] In fact, only 1 shot out of their scanty 24 managed to break through the Wings' tight defense. The 4–1 loss was one of the Barons' brighter spots over the next few weeks. In their next five games the club went 0-4-1, and hell returned to its familiar blistering state.

With the Barons wilting and sitting last in the Adams Division with a 5-10-2 record, the two-time defending champion Montreal Canadiens strolled into Cleveland on November 23. A franchise record 12,859 fans turned out at the Coliseum, and they brought with them lots of enthusiasm and hope for an upset victory, even though the Barons had not beaten Montreal since 1974.

At this point in the season only the dazzling Maruk had displayed much offensive prowess; in 17 games, he had scored 12 goals, but the rest of the team had scored just 28. Fidler and Manery had scored 5 each on the second line, but Murdoch, MacAdam, Gardner, and Merrick had achieved underwhelming results since the second week of the season. Once again, against Montreal, the offensive load was put on the shoulders of buzz saw Maruk. He picked up an assist on Murdoch's first period goal, and in the second Maruk got a breakaway and scored to put the Barons up by 2.

The score remained 2-0 well into the third period until the Habs woke from their slumber and pounced on Gary Edwards. The Canadiens broke the shutout at 8:52 of the third on a goal by Pierre Mondou. Guy Lafleur, Yvan Cournoyer, Jacques Lemaire, and their friends continued to blitz Edwards, but the Barons' goaltender refused to give in. In the dying minutes the crowd began yelling "dee-fense . . . dee-fense" at the top of its lungs in support of the home team. When the clock ran out and the Barons had claimed a shocking 2-1 victory, fans erupted in excitement.

It was Cleveland's first win over Montreal since March 2, 1974, a stretch of fifteen games. The win also ended the Barons' six-game winless streak. "No doubt about it," said Maruk, "you beat the Canadiens and it's a big thrill. Never mind those eight-goal games. I'll take this anytime." Peter Larsen could barely contain his excitement: "When Maruk got that breakaway and scored, I went crazy. I even had tears in my eyes." It was believed that such a tremendous win would be a huge morale booster for the club. "This is going to bring everyone closer," said Dave Gardner. "We just beat the best hockey team in the world. And if we beat them, we can beat anybody."[8]

Two nights later the Philadelphia Flyers played host to the Barons. The Barons beefed up their forward lines just a few days before the game, acquiring defenseman Randy Holt, one of the toughest competitors in the league. Although the twenty-four-year-old Holt had only 42 games experience at the NHL level, he proved he could hold his own; he would establish a Barons' record with 229 penalty minutes in just 48 games!

Only twenty-five seconds into the game Bobby Clarke scored on a shot that deflected off Edwards's right shoulder and into the net. Evans disagreed with the referee's decision to let the goal stand. "Clarke's goal shouldn't have been allowed," he said. "He had the stick over his head." Gardner responded for Cleveland, but afterward it was all Philly. The Flyers continued to get in Edwards's face, frustrating him to the point that he took a penalty for hitting Orest Kindrachuk, who was standing near the crease. "It's a cumulative thing that's been happening for about six years, not just with Kindrachuk but with all of them," said Edwards after the game. "They always come in on you and push you around."⁹ With the Flyers still buzzing midway through the first period, Reggie Leach snared the rebound off a Kevin McCarthy drive and deposited the puck past Edwards to give Philadelphia a 2–1 lead. Not long after, Maruk put the puck past his own goaltender and the Flyers were up 3–1.

During the last minute of the opening period the Flyers sparked yet another of their patented bench-clearing brawls. As a result Mike Christie, Randy Holt, and the Flyers' Andre Dupont and Rick Lapointe were thrown out of the contest. "I think the fight hurt them," said Bobby Clarke. "They lost two defencemen and it's tough to play that way."¹⁰ The Flyers peppered Gary Edwards with 48 shots and pasted the Barons, 7–2. It quickly became obvious that if the Barons were going to get into the playoffs, it would be by winning a wild-card berth because the third-place Maple Leafs were pulling away and only getting better. When Cleveland defeated Washington 3–2 on December 2, the Barons moved to within 2 points of the final playoff spot, held by the New York Rangers.

Mired in the lower reaches of the NHL's scoring parade, the Barons needed an offensive jolt in a hurry, so they traded slumping Bob Girard to Washington for former Seal Walt McKechnie, who had fallen out of favor with Caps coach Tommy McVie after producing only 4 goals in 16 games. After leaving California, "McKetch" had an unsuccessful 53-game stint in Boston but then found his groove in Detroit, scoring a career-high 82 points in 1975–76. The question was whether he could find his scoring touch again.

In the short term McKechnie's presence did little to help the Barons. The humiliation of losing to Philadelphia a few weeks earlier was nothing compared to the thrashing the Flyers would give the Barons on December 11, 1977. Things were all right for the first 10:45 until Reggie Leach opened the floodgates. Before the first intermission Philly scored three more times in a span of 44 seconds. Defenseman Tom Bladon scored on a 35-foot shot at 17:54 and then earned an assist on Don Saleski's goal at 18:13. Bladon then picked up a third point on Mel Bridgman's goal 25 seconds later.

The massacre continued in the second period. Rick MacLeish scored at 7:13, and Bladon notched his second and third goals before the buzzer sounded. Philadelphia led 8–0 after 40 minutes, but the Flyers had no intention of taking their foot off the gas. Just 2:47 into the third, Bladon scored again and then picked up assists on goals by MacLeish and Bill Barber later in the period, bringing the score to 11–0.

The Barons had absolutely nothing but pride left on the line. Bernie Parent was looking for his fourth shutout of the season, but Maruk stole Parent's shutout bonus by scoring on a 35-foot shot with just 1:06 left. "That hurt," Parent said. "I could have made more dollars tonight had it been a shutout." Maruk's goal was a small consolation for the Barons. When all was said and done, Bladon had scored 4 goals and 8 points in the game, a new NHL record for defensemen. The Flyers outshot Cleveland 52–18 en route to an easy 11–1 victory. "No comment," Jack Evans said when pressed by reporters after the debacle. "What can you say about a game like that?"[11]

The Barons continued to play inconsistently through to the end of the calendar year, putting their playoff hopes in jeopardy, but their fortunes changed when two Czechoslovakian hockey clubs from Kladno and Pardubice visited North America for an eight-game exhibition tour against NHL clubs. Heading into action against Cleveland on January 4, Kladno had not yet lost a contest. In front of a Cleveland crowd of 7,117, the Barons jumped out to a 3–1 lead in the second period. The Czechs clawed their way back and tied the game at 3–3 in the final period, but rookie Kris Manery scored with only 4:51 left on the clock to seal the win. Manery had scored 11 goals in his last 15 games. The Barons' defense held up for the final few minutes to preserve the surprising 4–3 victory. "We were over-confident and that is what beat us," admitted Kladno coach Bohuslav Prosek. "We were expecting an easy game after the Toronto game. We hadn't seen Cleveland play but we got a message that said they were not very good."[12] Although the upset over Kladno counted for nothing in the standings, it became a turning point for the Barons. The club regained its focus and started moving up in the standings.

On January 6 the Barons scored an impressive 6–1 win over Vancouver, giving Evans reason to praise his club: "It must of [*sic*] given them some confidence to play against one of the top teams in the world and beat them," Evans said about the Barons' earlier win over Kladno. "When you get six goals you have to be optimistic about things."[13] That night Maruk scored 2 goals, his 20th and 21st, to become the first player in franchise history to reach the 20-goal plateau three consecutive years.

A playoff spot was still within reach, so Harry Howell did something few, if any, other general managers in team history had done: he became a buyer. The Gunds had shown they were serious about winning when, just weeks earlier, they gave Howell permission to add a proven scorer like McKechnie to the lineup, but with the owners loosening the purse strings once again, the Barons' players must have thought the apocalypse was looming. Just one year earlier, the Barons had been on the verge of collapse. Now they were joining the NHL arms race.

Fred Ahern and Ralph Klassen were both struggling to score with any regularity, so they were shipped to Colorado for right wing Chuck Arnason and left wing Rick Jodzio. Arnason had scored just 4 times in 29 games, but he had broken the 20-goal barrier in three of his last four seasons. Arnason was a steal, scoring 21 goals in 40 games with Cleveland.

The Barons lost 5–3 to the Islanders on January 7, but Howell was more concerned about pulling off a major trade. Cleveland was 9 points behind the Penguins and Rangers for the final playoff spot, so three days after the Islanders game, Howell sent the slumping Wayne Merrick and future considerations (Darcy Regier) to Long Island for left wing (and original Seal) Jean-Paul Parise and defenseman Jean Potvin.

Merrick had struggled throughout an injury-ridden campaign that saw him score only 2 goals and 5 assists in 18 games. The previous year as well Merrick had had his fair share of problems. "Everything I did went wrong," he said. "It got to the point where I thought things couldn't get worse. But they did. All the little things added up. I worried about my game; when things were not working game in and game out, my game suffered. You can be in your best shape, but if you're not mentally ready, forget it."[14] Going to the Islanders was a blessing for Merrick. He regained his scoring touch, picking up 24 points in 37 games, and would remain with the team long enough to play a part in its four Stanley Cup championships in the early 1980s.

The gritty and respected Parise, on the other hand, had scored 12 goals and 16 assists in 39 games with the Islanders. He was a key player in the 1972 Summit Series, which saw the NHL-sponsored Canadian squad triumph over the Soviet Union. He was also a former two-time All-Star with the Minnesota North Stars and had totaled 216 goals to that point in his career.

Jean Potvin was the elder brother of Islanders' superstar Denis Potvin. Jean's forte was his defensive skills. Although he was not as flashy as Denis, Jean set career highs with 55 assists and 72 points in 1975–76. This season he had scored just 11 points in 34 games, but it was hoped his experience would help settle the Barons' shaky defense.

It didn't take long for the Barons to reap the benefits of their two most recent deals. The night following the Islanders' trade, the two teams met in Cleveland. The four newest Barons—Parise, Potvin, Arnason, and Jodzio—were all in the lineup, but it was the Islanders who led 1–0 after twenty minutes. The Barons came out strong in the second period on goals by Rick Shinske, Walt McKechnie, and Dennis Maruk to take a 3–2 lead. Kris Manery scored his 17th of the season in the final stanza to put the Barons up by 2, but the Isles' Mike Bossy scored with less than two minutes remaining to cut the lead to 4–3. The Islanders then pulled their goalie, hoping for the equalizer, but Al MacAdam hit the empty net and gave Cleveland a hard-earned 5–3 win.

Defeating the powerhouse Islanders for the first time in two years was a tremendous accomplishment for the Barons. Jim Neilson was quick to acknowledge the importance of his new teammates' roles. "We just did not have enough experience before," he admitted. "These guys help steady us down. Anytime you bring a guy with six or seven years experience who still has some legs left, he is going to help." Evans was particularly impressed by the attitude of his new players: "Before the game," he said, "the new players were talkative and very informative. They gave us leadership. There was confidence in the conversations and I felt good about it."[15]

FIG. 22. Three new Barons acquired during the 1977–78 season, J. P. Parise (23), Walt McKechnie (8), and Chuck Arnason (26), face off against Boston. Photo source: Dennis Turchek.

After defeating the Isles, the Barons made a habit of beating up the other top NHL clubs. What was most surprising about the Barons' sudden surge was that they were forced to play four games in four nights. The rough schedule was drawn up because the Barons were originally scheduled to play Buffalo on January 4, but the game was postponed until January 12 to allow the Barons to play Kladno. The Sabres came to Cleveland riding an eleven-game undefeated streak, but they were in for quite a surprise.

Gilbert Perreault scored just 2:17 into the game, the first of his 3 goals on the night, but the Barons did not fold. The Sabres' defense was sloppy, giving goaltender Don Edwards fits all night. Just a few minutes after Perreault's first goal, an errant MacAdam pass caromed off Jerry Korab's skate and bounced over the Sabres' goal line. Before the period ended, Jim Schoenfeld's clearing attempt bounced off Craig Ramsay's skate and found its way past Edwards. Despite the shoddy defense, Perreault's hat trick put Cleveland in a 3–2 hole entering the third period.

Brimming with their newfound confidence, the Barons fought back and overwhelmed the Sabres with 4 straight goals. Rick Hampton scored his second of the game two minutes into the frame, then at 5:46 Potvin launched a shot from the blue line that eluded Edwards and put Cleveland up 4–3. With less than six minutes to play, Dennis Maruk scored on a pass from Kris Manery. Not to be outdone, J. P. Parise scored his first goal for Cleveland with just 1:12 left to play. "The sign of a good club," Parise explained after the game, "is that nothing bothers you. You keep on plugging, play disciplined, patient hockey and learn to believe in yourselves." Evans agreed with Parise's assessment. "We aren't making the same mistakes that we have made in the past," he said. "The new players have improved our team. We aren't buckling under the pressure. It was good to see the other team get beat by its own mistakes."[16]

The infusion of new blood had brought immediate dividends to Cleveland, so the Barons and Rockies hooked up for another trade before the week of January 8 was up. In a purely defensive-minded transaction, Cleveland sent Mike Christie to Denver for fellow defender Dennis O'Brien. The night following the trade the Toronto Maple Leafs came to town looking to cool down the surging Barons. The score was tied at 2–2 early in the final period until the 1:08 mark, when Rick Jodzio scored his first NHL goal, the game winner in a 5–2 Barons' triumph. Once again the new Barons were the heroes. Earlier in the contest Chuck Arnason and Walt McKechnie had each scored goals of their own. "I'd have to say right now this is the best team I've coached," Evans exclaimed after the game. "It's got the ingredients on the ice to be a winner. We've got a little more talent now. Winning has made me smile for the first time in six months." Gary Edwards faced just 20 shots. "It's fun when you're winning," he said. "This is like when I was in L.A."[17]

Riding a three-game win streak into Pittsburgh, the Barons looked to match the franchise record for consecutive victories. Unfortunately the Barons were so exhausted from playing four games in four nights that the Penguins outshot them 31–18 in an easy 4–2 win. Nevertheless, the Barons' hot streak had helped them stay in the playoff picture. On January 17 the New York Rangers held down the final playoff position, but thanks to the league's new wild-card playoff format, the Barons were only 5 points out.

FIG. 23. Jim Neilson (5), Jean Potvin (6), and Walt McKechnie march onto the Richfield Coliseum ice. Photo source: Dennis Turchek.

The Barons continued to roll along despite a couple of one-sided losses to Montreal and Buffalo. First the Colorado Rockies made the trek to Cleveland hoping the Barons were still reeling from two pastings, but it was not to be. Dennis Maruk scored his 26th and 27th goals, and Kris Manery scored his 19th as the Barons blitzed the Rockies, 9–4. Maruk and Mike Fidler each picked up 3 points in the victory, but most importantly Maruk's second goal gave him 85 for his career, surpassing Joey Johnston for first place on the franchise's all-time list.

The following night the Barons visited Boston, and despite being outshot 29–15, it was the Barons who came out on top. Fidler broke a 1–1 tie with his 15th goal, and the struggling Bob Murdoch scored his 10th goal to put the Barons up by 2. The score remained 3–1 until Peter McNab responded for Boston with less than a minute to go, but it was too little, too late. The 3–2 win closed the Barons to within 4 points of the last playoff spot. Gary Edwards played an outstanding game, frustrating Boston coach Don Cherry to no end. "They had one thing going for them, their goaltender," he complained. "They should all get on their knees and thank him very much. They just dumped the puck out of their end, sat back and waited for the breaks. They certainly didn't outskate anybody."[18] The Barons may not have won all of their games with ease, but one thing was certain: the Barons were turning heads. They had beaten the Islanders, Sabres, Leafs, and Bruins, all Cup contenders, in the span of two weeks.

When the Atlanta Flames came to Cleveland on February 15, they knew they could not take the Barons lightly, and early on they didn't. Kris Manery scored his 20th goal in the first minute to put Cleveland up 1–0, but the Flames tied the game just 40 seconds later. The Barons then wilted badly, letting Atlanta take a 5–1 lead early in the second period. Walt McKechnie scored at 14:12 to make it 5–2, but it was in the third period that the Barons showed resilience they never knew they had. Randy Holt scored at 2:13, and Mike Fidler made it 5–4 just 9 seconds later. Fidler then scored another at 11:50 to make it an improbable 5–5 draw. The Barons outshot the flustered Flames 39–19 in what should have been a statement announcing the Barons were about to put an end to their eight-year playoff drought, but in reality the Barons' foundation was about to crumble once again.

Between January 6 and February 1, the Barons went 8-6-0 to inch closer to a playoff spot, but the 5–5 tie against Atlanta was the Barons' sixth straight game without a win. On February 17 the Barons beat Vancouver thanks to a last-minute goal from Dave Gardner to put an end to their six-game winless streak, and the players felt upbeat and optimistic. "I doubt if we could play a lot better," said Gardner. "We're at our peak right now."[19] The fact of the matter was the Barons had already peaked and were headed down a slippery slope. Some people around the NHL felt the Barons second-half resurgence was fleeting. In January, after the Barons had defeated the Maple Leafs, their coach, Roger Neilson, spoke some prophetic words. "Guys like Potvin and Parise have to have a steadying influence, and they're good, experienced hockey players," he said. "And guys that come in new always play their best, for a while at least."[20] That "while" had come to an end.

FIG. 24. An exhausted-looking Gilles Meloche leads the Barons out of the dressing room. Photo source: Dennis Turchek.

After the Vancouver win the Barons hit the road for games against Montreal and Toronto and came out on the losing end both times. Next up was the Sabres on February 25 at the Coliseum, and this affair was a real doozy! The goal judges could have used some sun screen to protect them from the goal light's constant red glow. The funny thing is the Barons actually had a 2–1 lead three quarters of the way through the first period, but then everything fell apart. Danny Gare scored at 15:36 to tie the game 2–2; then Rod Seiling put Buffalo up by 1 at 19:35. The Sabres scored five more times in the second period to go up 8–2 and chase Meloche from the game, but they were not about to ease up on the gas. Jerry Korab scored on the power play 37 seconds into the third period, followed by goals by Derek Smith and Fred Stanfield before the period was 1:50 old. Even though the game was a complete wash, the merciless Sabres launched 26 shots on Gary Edwards in the final period alone en route to a 13–3 humiliation.

The beating administered by the Sabres represented only the third time in the NHL's sixty-year history a club had scored that many goals in a game. Meloche was left with a bitter taste in his mouth. "They made me look like the fool in the last game," Meloche recalled later in the season. "For sure, it was the worst game I played all year. It was one of those games you wish you were 100 miles away. This team, they just want to kill you. They want to make you feel like fools." When Cleveland paid a visit to Buffalo in the dying days of the season, the Barons looked to defend their honor. "That was on everybody's mind," said Maruk. "We wanted to win badly tonight."[21]

The Sabres, already assured of a playoff spot, were on cruise control and started rookie goaltender Bob Sauve instead of All-Star Don Edwards. The Barons, on the other hand, had everyone ready to go and could not have been more prepared. "They come out and throw everything at you the first 10 minutes," said Bobby Stewart about the Sabres. "If you let them get a couple goals up, watch out—they'll blow you out."[22] The Barons made sure that didn't happen again.

While Maruk was enjoying another excellent season, Al MacAdam and Bob Murdoch had yet to find their scoring touch. Coach Evans decided it was time to reassemble the 3-M Line after having broken them up earlier in the season. Maruk opened the scoring just 1:33 into the game, and the Barons never looked back. In the end Cleveland walked away with a 5–3 win, and the 3-M Line scored four times. Maruk, for one, could not have been happier to be reunited with his wingers. "It just shows what putting the three of us together will do," he said. "For two years it was tic, tac, toe and everything worked well, but we only played together for about a month this season."[23]

In reality the game in Buffalo was nothing more than a moral victory. It was only the Barons' second win after a horrendous fifteen-game winless streak had mathematically eliminated them from the playoff picture. "If nothing else, the Barons were a good Christian team," wrote Gene Kiczek in *High Sticks and Hat-Tricks*. "They gave up winning for Lent!"[24] The Barons closed out the 1977–78 schedule with a 3–2 home-ice loss to the Pittsburgh Penguins, another golf-course bound team. The New York Rangers earned the final playoff spot, 14 points ahead of the Barons.

It was yet another disappointing finish for the hard-luck Barons. They had numerous chances to move up in the standings, but most of the time their hot streaks were followed by lengthy losing skids.

FIG. 25. Jim Neilson (15), John Baby (19), Walt McKechnie (8), and Gilles Meloche (27) try to contain the Bruins. Note the lack of fans in the stands. Photo source: Dennis Turchek.

Despite Dennis Maruk's club record 36 goals, the return of Walt McKechnie, and the solid play of Kris Manery, Mike Fidler, J. P. Parise, and Chuck Arnason, it was clear the Cleveland Barons still had a lot of work to do. MacAdam went from 63 points the previous year to just 48. Murdoch went from 42 points in 57 games to 40 points in 71 games. Many of Murdoch's teammates felt he could have had a much more successful career had he focused more on hockey. "He was a good scorer but he was a partier and it cut years off his career by drinking," explained Gary Simmons. "He was a good guy and a free spirit. He liked the outside stuff that went along with being in the NHL."[25]

The team averaged fewer than six thousand fans per game, the lowest attendance in the league for the eleventh year in a row, but as far as Harry Howell was concerned, it was business as usual as he prepared his team for the 1978–79 season. He signed a three-year contract extension to stay with the club, and he even chose some new uniforms and team colors, which were expected to be a big hit. "The jerseys were going to be like the New York Rangers," said Barons radio color man Bob Whidden. "They were beautiful and said 'Barons' down the front just like the Rangers. It was going to be great."[26] The club signed college star Mike Eaves to a contract and reacquired Fred Ahern, while Gary Sabourin, who had not played in over a year, planned a comeback.

The Gunds had had some big plans for the Barons, but those went out the window when attendance bottomed out. "While we knew that owning the Barons would require a major investment," admitted Gordon Gund, "we have discovered that the requirements in both money and time are far more enormous than we had anticipated."[27] The Gunds had supposedly lost in the neighborhood of $3.5 million since taking over from Mel Swig, forcing the brothers to reevaluate their investment.

At the June Board of Governors meeting, the fate of the Cleveland Barons was top of the agenda. One of the plans discussed was to have the Barons play the next two years somewhere near New York City until they could be formally moved to East Rutherford, New Jersey, when the Meadowlands Arena would be ready. The Gunds also had the option of selling the franchise to someone else, but with the state of professional hockey in shambles and with franchises folding left, right, and center, no one was going to invest in the deepest of hockey's money pits.

Gordon Gund called new NHL president John Ziegler and suggested the Barons merge with the struggling Washington Capitals. Ziegler thought merging the Barons and Minnesota North Stars would be a more enticing proposal. "Actually, we pursued them when we heard they might be interested," said Stars general manager Lou Nanne.[28] Times were definitely getting tougher in several NHL cities, and no team fell upon harder times quicker than the Minnesota North Stars. The North Stars had finished the 1977–78 season dead last and had missed the playoffs four of the last five seasons. Attendance at the Met Centre had hit nearly 600,000 fans between 1972 and 1974, but when the Stars missed the playoffs in 1974, attendance plummeted from over 15,000 per game to 13,587 in 1974–75 and all the way to 8,666 in 1977–78. "We were losing so much money, we had to make cash calls on the partners," said Stars' president Walter Bush. "It got so bad that one of our guys said, 'Why don't we just get rid of the team, buy a jet and we'll get four tickets for every building in the NHL? Whoever wants to go watch a game can go. It would be cheaper than what we're doing.' We just got tired of kicking a can down the road."[29]

While Dennis Maruk, Rick Hampton, Mike Fidler, and Harry Howell were in Prague representing their respective countries at the World Hockey Championship, the Gunds weighed their options. George Gund and Bush both happened to be in Prague when the subject of merging their teams came up. "We signed a deal on a napkin in the beer hall down in the basement of the Imperial Hotel," Bush remembered.[30] There could not have been a more fitting end to a franchise that had always given the impression it was anything but major league. There was no decorum, no fancy stationery with NHL club letterhead, not even an old, rusty typewriter to give the agreement's words a look of authenticity. Broadcaster Bob Whidden, for one, was shocked to learn the Barons would be no more. "You could have knocked me over with a feather," he said. "I could feel it in my gut. I was just sick to my stomach."[31]

The unusual concept of a merger was exactly what the Gunds were looking for. To make money, the Gunds needed to have a controlling interest in the arena where the Barons played. The extra money earned from parking, loge suites, and concessions would help cover the losses caused by poor attendance. The Gunds had tried to gain a controlling interest in the Richfield Coliseum in January 1978, but negotiations with Sandy Greenberg fell apart. When the North Stars came sniffing for a partner and offered the Gunds a majority ownership of the Metropolitan Center in Bloomington, the offer was too perfect to pass up.

The Gunds had grossly underestimated the financial woes that had already plagued the Barons as a result of the team's weak performance, impractical arena location, weather problems, and fan apathy. In folding the Barons, the Gunds did not feel they were letting the Barons' fans down; the brothers had sincerely hoped to make pro hockey successful in Cleveland, but no matter how deep their pockets, they could not continue losing millions of dollars. The Gunds had expected to turn the corner after three years, but after careful consideration they realized that goal was impossible. "That was our expectation," said Gordon Gund. "But we realized it would take more like five years. It's very difficult to build a winner. Our market study described an embryonic hockey situation. People were just fed up. Our credibility was very low." They also came to the conclusion that "Cleveland requires winning teams, perhaps more so than other cities."[32]

The Barons, and the Seals for that matter, had been on life support long enough. Most of the league governors agreed it was finally time to pull the plug on this failing operation. The Gunds arrived at the annual meeting in June 1978 hoping to have the unusual merger plan approved. The Barons' owners looked much like their franchise: ragged and beat-up. Gordon walked in with his white cane and pushing George, hampered by a bad back, in a wheelchair. In typical Seals/Barons fashion the merger itself was a series of odd occurrences. During one of the general managers' meetings at the amateur draft, Lou Nanne approached Gordon Gund, but twice when Gund tried to shake Nanne's hand, the Barons' owner missed. "Why is this guy playing with me?" Nanne asked himself, not knowing that Gund was blind. Not long afterward Nanne heard someone call his name, but Nanne could not understand where the voice was coming from. He eventually looked under a table only to see George Gund lying there smoking a cigar. Gund told him he needed to lie there because of his bad back. The Barons' lawyer, on the other hand, was in a nearby bathroom and talked to Nanne through a door because he could not stand cigar smoke. "What am I getting myself into here?" Nanne thought, with good reason.[33]

Awkward beginnings aside, the merger idea was warmly received. One wry general manager believed the merger would benefit the league. "If you mix one bag of shit with another bag of shit," he said, "all you've got is a bigger bag of shit. But at least we'd solve a problem."[34] The owners agreed, and the Gunds formally dissolved the Barons. The Gunds then bought the Stars for $10–12 million and assumed all of their debts. The merged franchise would continue to be known as the North Stars but would take the Barons' place in the Adams Division.

John Ziegler accomplished something his predecessor Clarence Campbell never could: fix the catastrophe that had originated in the Bay Area eleven years earlier. "We believe this transaction solves two significant problems we were having to deal with," Ziegler said. "It was clear that after work by people in Cleveland that the response was not sufficient, at least not encouraging enough to continue."[35] The contraction of the Barons, not to mention the folding of the WHA's Houston Aeros, would greatly strengthen the NHL as several new free agents would be looking for employment. The Gunds could also smile knowing the switchboard at North Stars headquarters "was overloaded with calls from across the state. . . . Not in five years had the public shown as much interest."[36]

As part of the merger agreement the new Minnesota team was allowed to protect two goaltenders and ten skaters from the Barons and the old North Stars. The remaining players were then subjected to a dispersal draft where the league's five weakest remaining teams (St. Louis, Washington, Vancouver, Pittsburgh, and Colorado) could select unprotected players for $30,000 each. Ziegler believed the merger "offered an opportunity to solve a financial problem for the league" and that the new North Stars would be a very strong team. Besides, the league's five weakest clubs would also have the opportunity to add a few quality players. The Barons' Dave Gardner was not among those ecstatic about the merger. "There's not much to say," he said in a telephone interview from his summer home in Port Perry, Ontario. "I don't know what to think. In a way, it's too bad we didn't all become free agents."[37]

The North Stars took full advantage of the bounty that had fallen into their lap. Nanne retained Gilles Meloche and Gary Edwards to give Minnesota's goaltending a significant boost. Al MacAdam, Greg Smith, Mike Fidler, Kris Manery, J. P. Parise, and Jean Potvin were also kept. Dennis Maruk was protected by the Stars in the draft but was traded to Washington for a first-round pick just two games into the 1978–79 season. Bob Murdoch and Bob Stewart were traded to St Louis, Chuck Arnason was dealt to Washington, Walt McKechnie went to Toronto, and Rick Hampton and Dave Gardner were sent to

Los Angeles as compensation for the Stars' signing of Gary Sargent. The North Stars, on the other hand, held on to their own star players Tim Young, Glen Sharpley, and Brad Maxwell, among others. All in all, the Stars came out of the merger looking very good.

After the merger the North Stars restructured their front office. Nanne handed the coaching reins to Harry Howell rather than Jack Evans, which was an ill-fated decision. Although Howell had once been an excellent player, he was not suited to be a coach. Former WHA bench boss Glen Sonmor replaced Howell after the Stars won just three of their first eleven games. Evans, on the other hand, was reportedly heading to either Los Angeles or Chicago for the new season, but neither deal materialized. He later found success coaching the Hartford Whalers to their first and only division title in 1987.

The Barons had only been in Cleveland for two years, but their sudden departure still stung. "When I heard the news, I just started crying and shaking for hours," lamented Barons Booster Club president Kathy Rafferty. "I couldn't believe it. They sent every season-ticket holder a letter last fall promising a three-year effort. They said they made their promise in good faith. What happened to their good faith?"[38]

Jerry Rombach, sports editor of the *Elyria Chronicle-Telegram*, lamented the loss of the Barons as a "knock" to city pride, but he also believed he understood why the Barons failed. "I am particularly upset with the Cleveland people," he said, "who last year bought the Barons and promised fans here a trial of at least two years before making any decision. People will support hockey, as well as baseball, football and basketball in this area. It's just that they are so hungry for a title contender they can't stomach anything less, which is (sic) been our steady diet for over 10 years except for one bright season for the Cavaliers a couple of years ago."[39]

The Gunds had surveyed to find out if there was a point in keeping the club in Cleveland, but according to the results, people just were not interested in supporting the Barons. "We're truly sorry that the situation in Cleveland was such that it was impossible to continue there," said Gordon Gund.[40] The brothers had little choice but to cut their losses. The franchise had been in terrible shape since day one.

Every time someone new bought the team, they had no choice but to take on all of the previous problems and debt their predecessors had left behind. Bob August said it best in his *Cleveland Press* column from April 3, 1978: "It is a malady the Barons share with the [baseball] Indians. Teams simply can't make it with constant fluctuation at the top, with a succession of leaders charting courses in different directions. The only hope . . . is ownership that will provide the stability under which progress is possible."[41]

In Minnesota the franchise had a chance to survive and thrive. Minnesotans' support for hockey was strong and went deep down to the grassroots level thanks to the area's cold climate and numerous lakes that had always created an ideal skating atmosphere during the winter months. The fact the Stars had once regularly attracted crowds of fifteen thousand proved this market had potential. Although the California Seals/Cleveland Barons franchise was officially dead, life went on for many of its players. Once the former Barons settled into their new home and the Stars started winning again, the fans came back in droves. Our heroes from California and Cleveland played a big part in the North Stars' future. Finally the on-ice success the California Seals had promised fans back in 1967 was going to become a reality.

13

THE ROAD HOME

The 1978–79 season allowed the former Cleveland Barons players to get accustomed to their new surroundings. Al MacAdam finished with 58 points, Mike Fidler scored 49 points in just 59 games, and Gilles Meloche won 20 games for the first time. Rookie Bobby Smith led the team with 30 goals and 74 points on the way to capturing the Calder Trophy. Thanks in part to the influx of talent from the Minnesota-Cleveland merger, the North Stars improved by 23 points in the standings, even though they still finished last in the Adams Division.

The Stars were well on their way back to being a significant team when the WHA finally perished. Following the Winnipeg Jets' 1979 Avco Cup victory, the NHL admitted four of the rebel league's clubs—the Jets, Edmonton Oilers, Hartford Whalers (née New England Whalers), and Quebec Nordiques—for the 1979–80 season. Former Seal Paul Shmyr moved to Minnesota because the Stars had acquired his playing rights in the merger. Some years later, in a retrospective issue of the *Hockey News*, Shmyr was recognized by a panel of former WHA members as the league's best-ever defenseman, beating out long-time NHL stars J. C. Tremblay and Pat Stapleton for the honor.[1] Shmyr became the Stars' captain in 1979.

The 1979–80 North Stars vaulted into third place in the Adams Division with a team-record 88 points thanks in part to the efforts of Masterton Trophy winner MacAdam and first-time All-Star Meloche. The top line of MacAdam, Smith, and Steve Payne accounted for 111 of the club's 311 goals, the fourth highest mark in the NHL. MacAdam was the team's high-scorer with 93 points, while he and Payne tied for the club lead with 42 goals. Although Shmyr had lost a step since returning to the NHL, he led a fine defense unit that also boasted Greg Smith, Gary Sargent, and the flashy Craig Hartsburg. Meloche and Gary Edwards held the opposition to just 253 goals against, the NHL's sixth-lowest mark. Another highlight that season occurred on

January 6, 1980, when the Stars beat Philadelphia 7-1, ending the Flyers' league-record thirty-five-game undefeated streak.

The high-flying Stars steamrolled past the Leafs in the preliminary playoff round and marched into Montreal to face the four-time defending champion Canadiens. The Stars opened the series with shocking 3-0 and 4-1 wins at the Montreal Forum, but the Habs bounced back with three straight wins. Trailing 3-2 in the series, the Stars rallied for a 5-2 win in game six. The Habs had been almost invincible at the Forum the last decade, but on the night of game seven Al MacAdam scored the winning goal, the biggest of his career, to end the Habs' hopes for a fifth consecutive championship. In the semifinals the Flyers humbled the Stars in five games, but considering everything the Stars had accomplished, no one had any reason to hang their head.

The following season the Stars finished third again with 87 points. New faces such as Neal Broten, Dino Ciccarelli, and goaltender Don Beaupre emerged as key players who would continue to shine throughout the decade. In the 1981 playoffs the Stars defeated Buffalo, Boston, and Calgary to reach the Stanley Cup finals, but the competition here would be far tougher. The defending champion New York Islanders had racked up 110 points during the regular season, and they were not about to let a bunch of kids run roughshod over them. Despite Ciccarelli's 14 playoff goals, and Meloche and Beaupre's hot goaltending, the Isles triumphed in five games.

For the 1981-82 season the Stars were moved to the Norris Division, where they won division titles in 1982 and 1984. In the latter season the Stars pushed themselves into the Campbell Conference finals, where they were swept by Wayne Gretzky and the Edmonton Oilers.

The mid-1980s signaled the changing of the guard in Minnesota. MacAdam, Smith, Meloche, and eventually Ciccarelli were all traded away. In their place emerged stalwarts Brian Bellows, Mike Modano, and Jon Casey, but the transition was difficult. Between 1986 and 1993 the Stars never finished higher than third and had a losing record every season. Attendance bottomed out around eight thousand a game in 1990-91. The only bright spot for the team was a surprise appearance in the 1991 Stanley Cup finals, where the Stars lost to Pittsburgh in six games.

The Gund brothers claimed to have lost about $16 million in Minnesota, so they considered moving the team to, of all places, San Francisco. "Minnesota does not want [the North Stars]," Gordon Gund told the other NHL governors. "The only way you'll get Minnesota to want it is to let us leave; then maybe two years later, they'll want an expansion franchise."[2] Although Gund turned out to be correct, the NHL refused the brothers because the league wanted to install an expansion team in San Jose instead.

The Gunds insisted on selling the Stars for no less than $50 million, the same amount as the expansion fee for the new San Jose franchise, hoping this would dissuade anyone from wanting to buy the Stars and forcing the league to let the Stars move to California. League governors were upset, but at the same time, they treaded lightly in their negotiations with the Gunds, because preventing the Stars from moving risked facing a lengthy and expensive lawsuit.

Norm Green, co-owner of the Calgary Flames, had an idea that he hoped would please all parties. He suggested the Gunds sell the Stars for $31 million to one of the San Jose franchise bidders, a group led by his childhood friend, former Budget Rent-A-Car CEO Morris Belzberg, and former Hartford Whalers owner Howard Baldwin. Then the Gunds could purchase the San Jose franchise for $50 million.

The Gunds were not enamored with the idea of trading their established NHL franchise for an expansion team chock full of retreads and minor leaguers, so the league sweetened the deal. The San Jose franchise would be permitted to select players from the Stars' roster via a special dispersal draft. In fact, it was a sort of *de*-merger of the Cleveland Barons and Minnesota North Stars, meaning that, technically, the old California Seals live to this day in the form of the San Jose Sharks. It was an offer the Gunds couldn't refuse.

As always, anything even slightly involving the Seals had to be a convoluted affair. The North Stars, in turn, would be allowed to participate in the expansion draft meant to stock the Sharks with the rest of their roster. The Sharks drafted twenty-four players from the Stars' roster, although only four of those players—Shane Churla, Brian

Hayward, Neil Wilkinson, and Rob Zettler—had spent any significant time in the NHL. The Sharks did grab a real gem, though, in the latter stages of the draft: Russian goaltender Arturs Irbe.

The North Stars, on the other hand, picked up useful veterans such as Jeff Hackett, Rob Ramage, Charlie Huddy, Tim Kerr, Kelly Kisio, Guy Lafleur, and Dave Babych, but they were all traded away before the 1991-92 season started. The expansion draft had little effect on the Stars' on-ice performance, but attendance improved slightly. Norm Green bought out Baldwin and Belzberg when the duo realized they could not cover the $31 million purchase price, but Green soon ran into problems of his own.

Green planned on developing the area around the Met Center in Bloomington and creating a skyway that would link the arena to the Mall of America. Green felt this would generate sufficient revenue to cover the losses the Stars incurred as a result of sagging attendance and rising player salaries. The Metropolitan Sports Facilities Commission owned the land around the arena and wanted $28 million for it. There were also reports that the commission favored Minneapolis, and that helping Green would take business away from Minnesota's most important city. Green thought about moving the team to the Target Center in Minneapolis or the St. Paul Civic Center, but in the end those deals both fell through. There was also a tempting local offer to buy the Stars for $55 million, but Green held out for $60 million.

The other dark cloud hanging over Green's head was a sexual harassment suit brought on by three women, including Karen Dziedzic, the daughter of a popular local politician, accusing Green of inappropriate behavior around the office. The press was merciless, and Green became annoyed by the finger-pointing, so he moved the team to Dallas even though the deal he signed was no better than anything he had been offered in Minnesota. Reunion Arena had no luxury boxes, and it would cost him $4 million of his own money just to renovate the building for hockey. Minnesotans would have to wait until 2000-2001 for NHL hockey to return when the Minnesota Wild set up shop in St. Paul.

Minnesota hockey fans went through the wringer in the 1990s, but those in San Jose experienced calm and stability. Well into the twenty-first century the game continues to thrive in the Bay Area thanks to the tremendous success of the Sharks. Not only did their stunning teal blue uniforms and vicious stick-biting shark logo earn them millions of dollars in merchandise revenue, but they have also found fortune on the ice.

In the first two years attendance at the tiny Cow Palace was impressive: 10,888 the first year and 11,045 the second, despite a cumulative record of 28-129-7. This time the NHL gave the venerable rink its seal of approval. Apparently, like fine wine, the Cow Palace had just gotten better with age. The Sharks regularly sell out their current home rink, HP Pavilion. Many of those old Booster Club members who had wept when the Seals moved to Cleveland were more than willing to listen when the NHL knocked on their door once again. John Bonasera worked as a freelance statistician for the Sharks from 1991 to 2013. Joe Starkey became the Sharks' first play-by-play man.

The Sharks have had their fair share of success. In 1993–94 and 1994–95 the team advanced to the second round of the playoffs, something the Seals had never done. Savvy veterans such as Bernie Nicholls, Kelly Hrudey, and Tony Granato were then brought in to compliment youngsters Jeff Friesen and Owen Nolan, but the team simply hovered around .500 for a few years. In the first round of the 1999–2000 playoffs the Sharks gave their deriders reason for optimism when they shocked the 117-point St. Louis Blues with a seven-game upset. As with their two previous playoff successes earlier in the decade, the Sharks were dismissed in the second round, this time by Dallas. The Sharks have won their division six times, and they have reached the Western Conference final four times, most recently in 2016 when the team went one round better to face Sidney Crosby's Pittsburgh Penguins in a Stanley Cup final that harkened back to the 1970 West Division semifinal between Oakland and Pittsburgh. This time too, with much more at stake, the Penguins would end up on top. At the close of the 2016–17 season the Sharks had put together an all-time record of 929 wins, 802 losses, and 253 ties/overtime losses.

California's support for hockey has grown by leaps and bounds since the Seals left Oakland. "To be here tonight and see the crowd, it all demonstrates that hockey is thriving in California. And that's great to see," said NHL Commissioner Gary Bettman to the *Los Angeles Times* as 18,593 fans watched the Sharks and Kings do battle in game seven of the 2013 Western Conference semifinals. He added, "If we were trying to be a little trite, we could say we've gone from the Golden Seals to a Golden Era."[3] In keeping with Seals tradition, the Sharks lost that night.

During the interviews conducted for this book, I often asked the following question: "If you could describe the California Seals in one sentence, what would it be?" The responses were incredibly diverse, often reflecting the period in time my interview subject was involved with the Seals. Lyle Carter, who was part of the star-crossed 1971–72 team that challenged for a playoff spot, described the Seals as a "young and exciting hockey club." Tim Ryan, who was with the team in its early years, summed up the team as "a talented bunch of hockey players who gave their very best, and many of them felt that the biggest achievement in those first couple of years was being part of NHL history." Joe Starkey broadcast Seals games at the nadir of the Charlie Finley era, so he described the Seals as "turmoil from the day I arrived till the day I left." Joey Johnston said, "I think it all starts from the top down, and we just didn't have it at the top." Jim Lingel had always regretted not selling enough tickets to make the Seals successful during their inaugural campaign, so he described the team as "good players, dumbbells in the office."

Gary Simmons and Larry Patey had more philosophical views. Simmons described the Seals as "a bunch of guys on a ship to nowhere," while Patey saw the Seals as "a team looking for a place to go, which was obviously up." Booster Club member Sandi Pantages believed the Seals were "a team with a great deal of promise without time given to it to act it out," while husband Dick said they were "a sometimes exciting team on the verge of greatness, and then they disappeared." Booster Larry Schmidt remembers the Seals thusly: "They tried the best they could with what talent they had." Fan John Bonasera summed the team up as "one of the most lovable yet dysfunctional franchises in hockey history." Cathy White, who followed the team throughout its entire history, may have summed up the Seals best, simply calling them "entertaining." That they were!

The question I hoped to have answered when I started doing research for this book was, "Why do people still care about this team?" That is, without a doubt, a big question. The team may be long gone, but it has definitely not been forgotten. Former Seal Morris Mott is now a history professor at Brandon University in Manitoba, and he believes he knows why the team has become a fascinating part of hockey lore:

> I forget who it was who said this, "Everybody wants to find out about the history of the world and what was going on when they were about 10 or 12 years old." . . . When you get to a certain age you become interested in what was happening when you were a kid, so it makes some sense for these teams, these defunct teams, or abandoned teams, to have some fascination for people, whereas the teams from an earlier generation, the teams that I was once interested in like the New York Americans or the Montreal Maroons, nobody gives a damn anymore, but that's because all the people have gone who can even remember it.

John Bonasera has difficulty explaining why he remains fond of the team that broke his heart so many years ago. His rapport with the Seals evokes images of an ill-fated relationship between two people who have no business being together:

> I have a love affair with the Seals yet it was a total—and I can't use the word, but it starts with "cluster." . . . They were constantly in a state of chaos, confusion, and dysfunction. . . . And the fact that anybody, let alone me, found something to latch onto and to enjoy, and not just at the moment, but sort of as a lifelong thing. . . . The fact that it's sort of a love affair in a totally dysfunctional way, which makes it very kind of human. . . . There was no legitimate reason to be interested in this team, to follow this team, to care about this team, and yet here it is forty, fifty years later if you go back to the San Francisco days, and there's still people out there who have fond, fond memories of this, and it doesn't necessarily make sense. If we could figure out what it is and bottle that, that would be awesome. Either that, or we just have several loose screws.

FIG. 26. Calm before the storm. Krazy George Henderson
sits quietly with his drum, waiting for another opportunity
to work the crowd into a frenzy. Photo by Elliot Lowe.

Bonasera may not fully understand the reason for his passion, but
many Booster Club members stuck by the Seals for reasons that are
quite clear. "I think the fans were passionate," said Sandi Pantages.
She believes the Seals "were an underdog, and I don't know if it was
[feeling] sorry for the underdog, or [you] always thought, 'Well, they'll
get better, something will happen.'" There may not have been many
Seals fans, but "our fan support was very vocal," remembers Cathy
White. One of the reasons Seals fans were so rowdy was because of
their one-man cheerleading squad, Krazy George Henderson. "That
SOB. I wanted to grab him," said Philadelphia's Dave Schultz. "He
was a piece of work. He was good and did a great job."[4] Krazy George
was a high school electronics teacher when he started coming to Seals
games in 1971. Fans immediately noticed the weirdo in Levi's, battered
tennis shoes, and yellow Sparky the Seal T-shirt banging his drum
and running up and down the aisles of the half-empty arena. "He was
from San Jose, and he'd come up and just run down the empty aisle
when they were on the face off . . . getting ready to drop the puck,"
remembers former stick boy Scott Ruffell, "and he would go 'BANG!
BANG! BANG! BANG! BANG!' . . . and the players would go 'What the
fuck?' and turn around and almost . . . hit him in the head with a stick,
because he scared the shit out of them. But he was real mellow; he

never swore or nothing, so he'd go, 'You turkey!' or something. We used to laugh at him; he was crazy."

George became an immediate hit, leading the crowd in cheers of "Go Seals, Go" and "Seals, ooh, ooh."[5] Before long, the Seals offered him free tickets to games, free food in the press box, and a few bucks for gas if he became their official cheerleader. Eventually, the Seals would pay him $25 a game. "I remember once we took Krazy George to Vancouver on one of our trips," remembers Cathy White, "and I had one of the fans come up to me and say that they would be willing to pay him to come out there, go north, and lead the audience in response to the team, because [Seals fans] were so noisy. . . . I think eighty-one of us went up to Vancouver, and we made more noise than the rest of the arena." Sandi Pantages remembers that same trip: "what struck us so much was how quiet the audiences were. . . . Krazy George did go on that trip to Vancouver and somewhat stunned the people in that crowd."

Long-time Booster Club members would argue that spending the last few decades pining over a sad-sack defunct team has not been a waste of time. The Booster Club has become an almost mythic organization in the hockey world. At its peak in the 1970s it boasted between four hundred and a thousand members, depending on the source. Due to the ravages of time there are now only about thirty members. The club has no website and does very little promotion, in part because there would be too many people asking for Seals merchandise, which the club simply does not have. Len Shapiro manages a Seals Facebook page, and since 2016 I have managed a website, GoldenSealsHockey .com, that keeps the team's spirit alive, but that's about it as far as Booster Club advertising goes.

When I interviewed eighty-nine-year-old Cathy White for this book at her retirement home in Ottawa, Ontario, she talked to me in great detail about her beloved Seals and the friendships the hard-luck franchise forged. "I guess it's a sense of loyalty," she says. "I can't think of any other reason. I knew you were going to ask me the question, and I've pondered this because I'm still a Booster Club member. One of the reasons was because we, as a Booster Club, went on a trip at least every year, and the fellow who arranged the trips [George Black] just died. . . . We used to be the 'Black and White Committee.' I think, as long as George was getting the group together, we all were anxious to go. . . . We saw Edmonton play before they ever won the Cup, and we were so impressed with them. Gretzky, of course, was just outstanding. We did a lot of traveling, and I think if George hadn't died, probably we would still be traveling."

In the Seals' NHL days, the Booster Club, led by their long-time president Ty Toki, was very busy organizing social activities. There were barbecues, trips, monthly meetings, and guest speakers, which included several players over the years. Many Boosters would get together to have a few pints at the Edgewater Hyatt House in Oakland partly because one of their members worked there.

There were also awards banquets for the Seals family at the end of the last two seasons. The Seals may not have been good enough to win many NHL awards, but Bay Area fans believed their heroes deserved some sort of recognition. "We didn't have people that were competitive in the trophy area," remembers White. "Montreal got named, and Toronto got named, and probably Detroit, but nobody from the California Seals ever got named. . . . Because of the fact we didn't participate in any of the awards, we had our own set of awards, and we gave them to the people that we felt deserved them for whatever reason, like the best defenseman, the best centerman, that kind of thing, and they were on display in a cabinet in the hotel where [other teams] stayed."

Those trophies are long lost now. Perhaps they are buried in a closet somewhere with that plaque the players once planned on presenting Charlie Finley but decided to scrap instead. Like those old trophies, the Seals will one day be no more than a memory, nothing more than a few printed words or a couple of photos of the team's more famous players. Memories will fade, and all those associated with the Seals will pass away like the last members of an ancient tribe. "Now the membership is about thirty," remembers Sandi Pantages, "and we're now having some third generation, and another family, there are little kids, and by then we're getting into people that have never been to a Seals hockey game or hardly even heard of the Seals, but they're family and friends who have come into the club for one reason or another. And we have maybe fifteen to twenty people who will come to a meeting—we meet once a month at Ricky's Sports Bar in San Leandro." The Boosters are still a very tight bunch. The club is "like extended family," as Pantages put it. Eventually, there won't be any more Booster Club members who have any recollection of the California Golden Seals, but the club itself will survive.

It wasn't easy being a Seals fan. Not only did the team rarely win, but it was barely noticed even when it lost. Look for pictures of the Seals in hockey books, and you'll surely notice the dearth of green and gold uniforms. It was as though the team never existed aside from a few shots of white skates coupled with snide quips about Finley's eccentric behavior. Finley almost never attended games; he was more interested in his baseball team, so the Seals became almost invisible. In 1973-74 the Seals didn't even have radio or television coverage, because Finley didn't think it was much of a priority. The NHL did little to promote the fact there was a team in the Bay Area, even though they steadfastly refused to let it relocate. "We could listen to [games] on the radio," remembered Cathy White, "but the NHL televised very few California games. Now they might have covered the Los Angeles Kings because it was a bigger market there, but they didn't cover the Bay Area at all. Well, they made a token offering; maybe one or two games a year, that's all." It really was a shame to ignore the Bay Area, a market with passionate fans who loved hockey. "I used to work at my computer and listen to the game at the same time," White continued, "and when something exciting was happening the computer waited."

Hockey fan Pete Manzolillo grew up on Long Island but became a huge Seals' fan in the early 1970s. Seeing the Seals on TV was a rarity, so the team's East Coast fans could not afford to miss out on such an event.

> I also remember that game against the Rangers in Oakland where they wore the standard skates for the first time. It was televised here on Long Island on a NY city station. I had a high school hockey game that night at 11:00 pm, same starting time as the Seals game. No way was I missing it. I was one of 3 goalies on the team but since it was more of a "rec" league that year, each goalie played a

FIG. 27. Filmmaker Mark Greczmiel in his Golden Seals jersey getting ready to watch the Anaheim Ducks. Photo courtesy of Mark Greczmiel.

period each instead of a whole game. I never told anyone I wasn't going to the game but at 10:30 I get a frantic call from one of the players, "WHERE ARE YOU?! THE BUS IS GETTING READY TO LEAVE!" I mumbled, "ahh, I'm sick . . ." The answer: "BULLS*** PETE, YOU'RE STAYING HOME TO WATCH THE SEALS!!"[6]

The Seals may not have gotten much screen time in the 1970s, but Mark Greczmiel is hoping that will no longer be the case in the twenty-first century. Greczmiel moved from Canada to California as a child and attended several games with his father and brothers, and he quickly became a fan of the much-maligned franchise. He then became a television producer and worked on television shows such as *E!'s True Hollywood Story*. He raised nearly $31,000 from friends, family, and fans to help with the completion of his excellent documentary on the history of the Seals, which was released in January 2017 and can be downloaded from iTunes. The film will hopefully turn a few younger fans on to California's white-skated warriors.

The reasons Mark Greczmiel, Cathy White, John Bonasera, and Dick and Sandi Pantages still love the Seals are obvious: they went through hard times with their hockey heroes and always held out hope tomorrow would be a better day. They enjoyed deep personal connections with the players and remember the sights and sounds of the Coliseum. Speaking for myself, after years of research and contemplation, I still don't know why I love the Seals. For me, being born in 1979, the Seals are nothing but a series of photos, numbers, and names. I know by looking through books and studying the backs of hockey cards that Norm Ferguson scored 34 goals in his rookie season, and that Joey Johnston was a three-time All-Star, but I don't have any fond memories of the Seals. I don't have any emotional attachment to the team. I never saw them play. I never felt the sting of all those losses. I never felt the need to throw darts at a picture of Charlie Finley. I never felt the need to slap coats of white house paint on my own skates or buy Kelly green luggage just to show my support. I never had my heart ripped out of my chest when the team moved to Cleveland.

I do, however, remember the pain of watching the Calgary Flames hoist the 1989 Stanley Cup at the Montreal Forum. I also have fond memories of my beloved Canadiens winning the Cup four years later. I remember thumbing my nose at all those smug, bandwagon-jumping Leaf fans who had suddenly become passionate about Doug Gilmour and Felix Potvin because they had finally led Toronto to a half-decent season. It felt good telling them to stick it after my Habs pulled off the impossible and won Lord Stanley's mug, and the Leafs, well . . . they're still crying about Gretzky's high stick on Gilmour.

I have my reasons for loving the Canadiens. My father and my grandfather both followed the Habs, so my brother and I did too. We both worshipped Patrick Roy. As kids growing up in Cornwall, Ontario, it was natural for us to be Montreal fans in the 1980s. The Toronto Maple Leafs and Quebec Nordiques both sucked, the Ottawa Senators hadn't yet come into existence, and the other Canadian teams were so far away I was lucky to see them on TV more than once a month. It's easy to understand why I still support the Habs; they've given me great pleasure (and some heartache) over the years. I've seen them win, I've seen them lose, I've seen them trade the best goaltender in

NHL history for peanuts, and I've seen them build themselves back up again. I stand by my team for better, for worse.

Frank Selke couldn't understand why I would write a book about the Seals. After all, he had been through hell in Oakland. I, however, as a simple observer of the Seals' madness, could never truly feel his pain. For Selke, working for the Seals was a nightmare; for me, the Seals were just an interesting topic to research. Perhaps, like John Bonasera, I too have a few screws loose.

In evaluating the overall impact of the California Seals on the NHL, one more question needs to be asked: Could the California Golden Seals have won the Stanley Cup if the club had had a few breaks following their breakthrough 1971–72 season? Some more optimistic fans would be tempted to say "yes," or at least lean toward the "yes" side of the debate rather than the "no," but the fact is that the Seals were never destined to win hockey's Holy Grail, despite their potential for greatness. Considering they would have had to go through either Montreal, Boston, or Philadelphia on the road to the Stanley Cup, their chances were slim at best no matter how stellar Gilles Meloche or Dennis Maruk might have been. However, had Tom Webster, Paul Shmyr, Wayne Carleton, Bobby Sheehan, and Gerry Pinder not defected to the WHA, the Seals could have been a playoff contender for years.

No single be-all-end-all answer exists to explain the team's excruciatingly difficult eleven-year struggle. The Seals' penchant for trading away first-round draft picks proved costly. Had the Seals retained their first overall pick in 1971 and selected either Guy Lafleur, Marcel Dionne, or Rick Martin, who knows what would have happened? Would Lafleur have soared in Oakland with Joey Johnston or Walt McKechnie on his line rather than Lemaire and Shutt? Who knows? Then there was 1973, when the Seals traded their second overall pick to Montreal, who then traded it to Atlanta. The Flames happily selected Tom Lysiak, a three-time All-Star who produced 843 points in 919 career games. The Seals could have used a player of Lysiak's ilk, or Lanny McDonald, Bob Gainey, or Rick Middleton, for that matter, all of whom were chosen later in the first round. By 1974, even when the Seals had learned their error of their ways, they still wasted their high draft picks. For every Dennis Maruk there were three or four Ken Bairds. Even though third-overall pick Rick Hampton set a franchise record for points by a defenseman in 1976, he never duplicated that success. Ralph Klassen was a decent player, but not the superstar Seals management thought he would become. Things became worse in 1976, when the Seals drafted Bjorn Johansson fifth overall (15 career games) instead of Bernie Federko (1,130 career points). In 1977 the Barons selected Mike Crombeen over defenseman Doug Wilson (827 career points, seven All-Star Game selections, one Norris Trophy) and Mike Bossy (nine 50-goal seasons).

If poor drafts had been the Seals' only problem, they probably would have survived, but their failure was a result of so much more. Bottom line, most of the Bay Area hockey fans lived far from the Coliseum and did not relish the thought of crossing the bridge to Oakland. "There's a famous line," explained Len Shapiro. "The San Francisco Bay Bridge is ten miles from Oakland to San Francisco and from San Francisco to Oakland it's a thousand miles." Morris Mott believes it was the distance between the Coliseum and the hockey fans, not Oakland's bad reputation, that was the reason people stayed away from the rink: "I think if people from San Francisco didn't come to Oakland to see the games, it probably had to do with [how] it took forty minutes to get there . . . than with any kind of alienation towards Oakland. . . . Probably, if the people from San Francisco didn't show up it was because they just weren't that interested in hockey. . . . The general point is that if you have to drive a long way, forty-five minutes or whatever, that puts an obstacle in the way of going to a hockey game."

Another major problem for the Seals was related to the media technology of the time. Shapiro explained that getting game film to the TV studios in time for the 11 o'clock news was a huge problem that would not have existed had the team been located in San Francisco:

We were on Hegenberger Road in Oakland. We were forty-five minutes away from [TV] studios in San Francisco. . . . We couldn't break away to the city, bring players in, film, and stations couldn't come out to the arena. They had to leave after the first period . . . to get back and develop the film so we even had highlights on. So in San Francisco they might have been able to stay for the second period and leave early in the third period, and their studios would have been ten minutes away. . . . And also, the *Chronicle* was right down the street from the proposed location, the *Examiner* was right down the street so the major media markets would have been there too. . . . [San Francisco] was also the advertising headquarters of the West Coast at that point. You still had major advertising agencies that handled major accounts, were right there in San Francisco, and we could have made presentations to them a lot easier.

And then there was Charlie Finley. He could have retained most of the WHA defectors had he just offered them a bit more money. In fact, most players liked the Bay Area and would have stayed if Finley had offered them a reasonable raise that showed he respected them, but instead he lowballed them. The players just wanted to feel appreciated, but Finley, being the cheapskate he was, allowed half his team to walk away.

The players tried their best to make the game work in the Bay Area. In some ways they succeeded. The fact people were so enthused to reminisce with a first-time writer from Ottawa about a bottom-feeding hockey team that had packed up some forty years earlier tells you something about the indelible mark the Seals left on their fans. Larry Leal remembers playing pickup hockey as a teenager with Walt McKechnie, Joey Johnston, Gary Croteau, and Ivan Boldirev: "You want to talk about an eighteen-year-old kid being on a high. Hey, I'm playing with NHL guys here! . . . [One time] McKechnie passes the puck and passes it behind me, and then actually skates up after the play is over and apologizes to me, that he didn't hit me with the puck. I say, 'Don't worry about it!' and he goes, 'No, no, training camp is coming up, and I should be better than that.'"

These summer scrimmages also gave Leal a permanent reminder of how hard professional players can shoot the puck:

[Boldirev] was skating down the boards on me. I'm playing left defense, and he winds up and takes a slap shot. I never even saw the puck. All I know is that my left leg hurt . . . he had cracked my

FIG. 28. Seals equipment repairman Joe Serratore, working on a pair of the infamous white skates. Photo courtesy of Rich Reilley.

FIG. 29. California Seals ring given to Joe Serratore in the 1970s. Photo courtesy of Rich Reilley.

shin guard, and I still have a bump there. So that was on a Monday night. On Thursday night, exactly the same play setup, and Ivan Boldirev's got this big shit-eating grin on his face as he's skating in on me, 'cause he knows the same thing was happening again, and he winds up to take a slap shot. I side stepped it, and the goalie is yelling, "Man, what are you doing?"

[Leal answered,] "It was a clear shot on goal, buddy." Boldirev skated up to me and said, "You're supposed to block that with your body," and I go, "Hey, I ain't being paid to play this game!"

Another time, Cathy White received a sweet thank-you note from Joey Johnston and his wife. Sandi Pantages read it to me over the phone: "Dear Cathy. Please express our thanks to the Seals Booster Club for the lovely Christmas party. We loved Santa's Village, and Jody had her first look at Santa Claus. Sorry we didn't get to see all of you more, but with a spoiled eighteen-month-old, one doesn't tend to stay around too long. Thanks so much. Joey and Pat Johnston." Personal touches like that are not often seen nowadays. When Howie Menard was interviewed for this book, he said, "Remember, all the guys are a good bunch of guys. A good bunch of people, believe me. Loyal bunch of guys, that's the main thing." He was right.

When discussing the deep, personal connections fans made with the Seals, it would be impossible not to mention the impact Joe Serratore had on everyone's lives. For decades he ran a shoe repair shop in San Leandro. He also repaired equipment and sharpened skates at the Coliseum from the Seals' first days to their very last. Sadly, Joe passed away at eighty-two on December 31, 2013. Lifelong friend Rich Reilley, who provided several photos for this book, took the time to write out his feelings about Joe and kindly asked me to include a short mention of Joe in this book. Here are some of Rich's thoughts:

I am 53 now and have been going to his shoe shop since I was around 8 or so. On any given day you could go in his shop and find a player, or trainer doing something with Joe to improve the performance and comfort of whatever the item he was working on. This expanded far past just the Seals as he would often have the opposing team trainers working right alongside of Joe in his shop or at the Coliseum. He also had very close ties with the Raiders and the A's personnel. Players would often sign photos to Joe in gratitude for something he did for them. I would go places with Joe in recent years and no matter where we went I heard from any direction . . . Hey, Joe!

For over forty years Joe kept a dear souvenir, a Jostens California Seals ring given to him by the team, in mint condition. "The only time Joe wore the ring out was to a special hockey event somewhere. He would present it to people with such pride," commented Reilley. Even after the Seals moved away, their fans kept the faith.

While the Booster Club remained loyal, and players loved their fans' enthusiasm, there were moments when the Seals had a somewhat strained relationship with the Bay Area. "Two to three days after he bought the team, Finley called a press conference," recalled ticket manager Sam Russo. "He said the team was so bad he was cutting the price of tickets in half. The season-ticket holders [who had already paid for their tickets] lit up the switchboard. They wanted a refund."[7] Of course, keeping with Finley's reputation, he had never even told his employees of the price reduction, so no one knew what to say to appease the angry ticket holders.

Another time, at the conclusion of the 1972–73 season, the San Mateo Junior Hockey Association held an awards dinner for almost four hundred people, including several youth hockey players. Joey Johnston was scheduled to present the California Golden Seals' "perpetual awards" to several children, but he never showed up. Needless to say, those in attendance were unimpressed, and in the next day's edition of the *San Mateo Times* the Seals were shown no mercy. Underneath a photo of some of the kids posing with their awards, a short write-up of the event lamented: "it was another example of the Seals' offhand, minor league attitude toward public relations."[8] The snub may have been low-key, but the Seals didn't have the fan support to be able to get away with that kind of blunder. For the most part, though, the Seals' most loyal fans, that core of two to three thousand fans who showed up every night, had strong personal connections to the players they admired. "We were all a family," said Larry Leal, "a family of 2,000 every game. . . . Now it's just a fond memory."

The Seals didn't exactly project the same image as the Montreal Canadiens on or off the ice, but individually many players stood out. Reggie Leach played a big part in Philadelphia's second Stanley Cup championship in 1974-75. He became a Second Team All-Star the next year, leading the league with 61 goals and scoring a league-record 19 goals in the playoffs en route to winning the Conn Smythe Trophy as playoff MVP, even though the Flyers lost the Cup to Montreal. He scored another 50 goals in 1979-80 and retired in 1984 with 381 goals to his credit. Carol Vadnais went on to play in three more All-Star Games, and he helped the Bruins win a Stanley Cup in 1972. He retired in 1983 with 587 points in 1,087 games. Following the Stars-Barons merger, Dennis Maruk found his way to Washington, where he scored 50 goals in 1980-81, and 60 goals and 136 points in 1981-82. He retired with 878 points in 888 career games. Al MacAdam scored 42 goals and 93 points with Minnesota in 1979-80 and won the Bill Masterton Trophy that same year. Charlie Simmer twice scored 50 goals for the LA Kings and became one of the premier snipers of the 1980s.

Brighter days also lay ahead for Gilles Meloche following the merger. "Almost without question, Meloche is the greatest goalie to have a sub-.500 record over such a lengthy career," said hockey historian Andrew Podnieks.[9] Meloche's years of suffering finally paid off when he was selected to play in the 1980 and 1982 All-Star Games. Between 1978 and 1985, Meloche strung together a respectable 141-117-52 record with Minnesota, before moving on to Pittsburgh for three more years. He became a scout and goaltending consultant for the Penguins, and he has had his name engraved on the Stanley Cup three times.

To date, seven former Seals—Bert Olmstead, Rudy Pilous, Harry Howell, Bud Poile, Seymour Knox III, Bill Torrey, and Craig Patrick—have been inducted into the Hockey Hall of Fame. Patrick, the most recent inductee, was the assistant coach and assistant general manager for the 1980 U.S. Olympic gold medal–winning "Miracle on Ice" hockey team. He then guided the Pittsburgh Penguins to Stanley Cups in 1991 and 1992 after drafting Jaromir Jagr and trading for Ron Francis and Tom Barrasso in separate smart moves.

Torrey was the architect of the New York Islanders dynasty of the 1980s. He shrewdly ignored the temptation to trade first-round draft picks for quick fixes. Torrey drafted little-known goaltender Billy Smith in the 1972 expansion draft. In ensuing years Torrey used the amateur draft to acquire Denis Potvin, Bryan Trottier, Clark Gillies, and Mike Bossy. Between these five players, they won three Calder Trophies, three Conn Smythes, three Norrises, three Lady Byngs, one Art Ross, one Hart, one Vezina, and one Jennings. All five are in the Hall of Fame, not to mention the Islanders coach, the late Al Arbour.

The United States Hockey Hall of Fame has also inducted several former Seals. Craig Patrick, Tommy Williams, and Jack McCartan have all been enshrined, while cartoonist (and Seals fan) Charles M. Schultz of *Peanuts* fame has also found his way in. Schultz, who often made long treks to Oakland just to see the Seals play, had been asked by Munson Campbell to create a mascot for the team. Schultz loved the idea, but unfortunately he had little time to dedicate to this endeavor. Therefore Paul Haubursin, an artist affiliated with Schultz, took on the task, and "Sparky" the seal, named after Schultz's moniker, was born. Dressed in full Seals uniform, including stick and strap-on skates, Sparky graced the team's media guides and publicity photos for several seasons.

In 1997 San Jose was chosen to host the NHL's All-Star weekend. During the festivities a game was scheduled between a team of NHL legends and a select group of retired players who had once played for the Sharks, Kings, and Seals. Of the eighteen players on the California side, nine had once played for the Seals: Al MacAdam, Dennis Maruk, Walt McKechnie, Craig Patrick, Charlie Simmer, Carol Vadnais, Gilles Meloche, Gary Simmons, and Rick Smith. Fred Glover coached the California squad.

More than seventeen thousand fans attended the reunion of the California Golden Seals. The California Heroes jumped out to a 2–0 lead in the first half—the game consisted of two 15-minute periods—on goals by Doug Wilson and Kelly Kisio. Meloche stopped all seven shots he faced in the period, while his counterpart, Darren Pang, stopped four of the six drives directed his way.

Gary Simmons took over for Meloche in the second period, but he was not greeted warmly by the NHL greats. Just forty-five seconds into the period, Lanny McDonald beat him for a goal. Before the ten-minute mark of the frame, the NHL legends scored three more times to take a 4–2 lead.

With time running out, California's Ron Duguay slipped one past Richard Brodeur—who had replaced Pang for the second period—to close the gap to 4–3, but that was as close as they would get. The only Seal to score any points was Maruk, who picked up two assists. It was somewhat sad, yet totally fitting, that the Seals would end up falling short on the scoreboard one last time.

There was one other Seals reunion at HP Pavilion nearly twenty years later. On January 7, 2017, as the San Jose Sharks were preparing to play the Detroit Red Wings, Bert Marshall, Gilles Meloche, Gary Simmons, Ernie Hicke, Norm Ferguson, and Dennis Maruk, wearing Sharks home jerseys, were in attendance in recognition of their work with the Bay Area's first NHL team. Fans who had never even seen the Seals play giddily picked up free green Oakland Seals throwback T-shirts, and many old-time hockey aficionados stood in line for autographs and handshakes with some long-overlooked heroes of hockey. The Seals hadn't been forgotten, and the fans knew why the Sharks were a successful NHL franchise. Although the Seals were not always as golden as their nickname advertised, they were the ones who laid the groundwork and gave Bay Area fans the bug that spread the game's popularity throughout Northern California.

Years ago the Seals' chances of winning hockey's ultimate prize were slim. They had to deal with two-week road trips, geographically baffling divisional alignments, little to no budget, and incompetent owners. The Sharks have none of these problems, so their chances of winning hockey's biggest prize are excellent. The Anaheim Ducks captured California's first Stanley Cup title in 2007, Los Angeles followed suit in 2012 and 2014, and the Sharks came oh so close in 2016, so the odds of a West Coast team capturing the sacred mug are not nearly as long as they used to be. If the Sharks do win the Stanley Cup in the near future, one can only wonder if the streaker will break out the body paint, slap on a pair of green-and-gold skates, and make an appearance at the parade.

SEALS / BARONS RECORD BOOK

WHL all-time season-by-season record

SEASON	GP	W	L	T	PTS	GF	GA	PIM	FINISHED	WIN. %
1961–62	70	29	39	2	60	229	270	580	3rd Southern	.429
1962–63[a]	70	44	25	1	89	288	219	806	2nd Southern	.636
1963–64[b]	70	32	35	3	67	228	262	758	4th	.479
1964–65	70	31	37	2	64	255	283	933	5th	.457
1965–66	72	32	36	4	68	243	248	888	4th	.472
1966–67	72	32	30	10	74	228	242	692	4th	.514
WHL Totals	424	200	202	22	422	1473	1524	4657		.498

[a]Won Lester Patrick Cup defeating Seattle
[b]Won Lester Patrick Cup defeating Los Angeles

NHL all-time season-by-season record

SEASON	GP	W	L	T	PTS	GF	GA	PIM	FINISHED	WIN. %
1967–68	74	15	42	17	47	153	219	785	6th West	.318
1968–69	76	29	36	11	69	219	251	809	2nd West	.454
1969–70	76	22	40	14	58	169	243	845	4th West	.382
1970–71	78	20	53	5	45	199	320	937	7th West	.288
1971–72	78	21	39	18	60	216	288	1009	6th West	.385
1972–73	78	16	46	16	48	213	323	840	8th West	.308
1973–74	78	13	55	10	36	195	342	651	8th West	.231
1974–75	80	19	48	13	51	212	316	1101	4th Adams	.319
1975–76	80	27	42	11	65	250	278	1058	4th Adams	.406
1976–77	80	25	42	13	63	240	292	1009	4th Adams	.394
1977–78	80	22	45	13	57	230	325	1010	4th Adams	.356
NHL Totals	858	229	488	141	599	2296	3197	10054		.349

WHL all-time season-by-season playoff record

SEASON	OPPONENT	GP	W	L	GF	GA	RESULTS
1961–62	Spokane	2	0	2	4	11	Lost quarterfinal
1962–63	Los Angeles	3	2	1	9	12	Won quarterfinal
	Portland	7	4	3	22	19	Won semifinal
	Seattle	7	4	3	25	25	Won Lester Patrick Cup
1963–64	Portland	5	4	1	23	18	Won semifinal
	Los Angeles	6	4	2	19	24	Won Lester Patrick Cup
1965–66	Victoria	7	3	4	21	28	Lost semifinal
1966–67	Seattle	6	2	4	10	18	Lost semifinal
5 seasons in WHL playoffs		43	23	20	133	155	

NHL all-time season-by-season playoff record

SEASON	OPPONENT	GP	W	L	GF	GA	RESULTS
1968–69	Los Angeles	7	3	4	25	23	Lost quarterfinal
1969–70	Pittsburgh	4	0	4	6	13	Lost quarterfinal
2 seasons in NHL playoffs		11	3	8	31	36	

WHL all-time home and away record

HOME

SEASON	GP	W	L	T	PTS	GF	GA
1961–62	35	21	12	2	44	127	101
1962–63	35	28	7	0	56	173	98
1963–64	35	22	12	1	45	139	117
1964–65	35	21	14	0	42	146	124
1965–66	36	21	14	1	43	147	110
1966–67	36	18	15	3	39	125	123
WHL home game totals	212	131	74	7	269	857	673

AWAY

SEASON	GP	W	L	T	PTS	GF	GA
1961–62	35	8	27	0	16	102	169
1962–63	35	16	18	1	33	115	121
1963–64	35	10	23	2	22	89	145
1964–65	35	10	23	2	22	109	159
1965–66	36	11	22	3	25	96	138
1966–67	36	14	15	7	35	103	119
WHL away game totals	212	69	128	15	153	614	851

NHL all-time home and away record

HOME

SEASON	GP	W	L	T	PTS	GF	GA
1967–68	37	12	16	9	33	86	84
1968–69	38	17	14	7	41	119	111
1969–70	38	15	16	7	37	94	112
1970–71	39	17	21	1	35	118	139
1971–72	39	14	12	13	41	129	125
1972–73	39	11	15	13	35	126	146
1973–74	39	11	18	10	32	112	143
1974–75	40	15	15	10	40	125	124
1975–76	40	16	19	5	37	136	136
1976–77	40	14	17	9	37	119	131
1977–78	40	14	17	9	37	128	146
NHL home game totals	429	156	180	93	405	1292	1397

AWAY

SEASON	GP	W	L	T	PTS	GF	GA
1967–68	37	3	26	8	14	67	135
1968–69	38	12	22	4	28	100	140
1969–70	38	7	24	7	21	75	131
1970–71	39	3	32	4	10	81	181

1971-72	39	7	27	5	19	87	163
1972-73	39	5	31	3	13	87	177
1973-74	39	2	37	0	4	83	199
1974-75	40	4	33	3	11	87	192
1975-76	40	11	23	6	28	114	142
1976-77	40	11	25	4	26	121	161
1977-78	40	8	28	4	20	102	179
NHL away game totals	429	73	308	48	194	1004	1800

WHL all-time season-by-season coaching record

SEASON	COACH	W	L	T	PTS	WIN. %
1961-62	Max McNab	29	39	2	60	.429
	Playoffs	0	2	0	0	.000
1962-63	Norman "Bud" Poile	44	25	1	89	.636
	Playoffs	10	7	0	20	.588
1963-64	Norman "Bud" Poile	23	30	2	48	.436
	Nick Mickoski	9	5	1	19	.633
	Playoffs	8	3	0	16	.727
1964-65	Nick Mickoski	2	7	0	4	.222
	Norman "Bud" Poile	29	30	2	60	.492
1965-66	Norman "Bud" Poile	4	5	2	10	.455
	Charlie Burns	28	31	2	58	.475
	Playoffs	3	4	0	6	.429
1966-67	Rudy Pilous	10	17	7	27	.397
	Charlie Burns	22	13	3	47	.618
	Playoffs	2	4	0	4	.333
WHL regular-season totals		200	202	22	422	.498
WHL playoff totals		23	20	0	46	.535

NHL all-time season-by-season coaching record

SEASON	COACH	W	L	T	PTS	WIN. %
1967–68	Bert Olmstead	10	32	11	31	.292
	Gordon Fashoway	5	10	6	16	.381
1968–69	Fred Glover	29	36	11	69	.454
	Playoffs	*7*	*3*	*4*	*6*	*.429*
1969–70	Fred Glover	22	40	14	58	.382
	Playoffs	*4*	*0*	*4*	*0*	*.000*
1970–71	Fred Glover	20	53	5	45	.288
1971–72	Fred Glover	0	1	2	2	.333
	Vic Stasiuk	21	38	16	58	.387
1972–73	Garry Young	2	8	3	7	.269
	Fred Glover	14	38	13	41	.315
1973–74	Fred Glover	11	38	7	29	.259
	Marshall Johnston	2	17	3	7	.159
1974–75	Marshall Johnston	11	28	9	31	.323
	Bill McCreary	8	20	4	20	.313
1975–76	Jack Evans	27	42	11	65	.406
1976–77	Jack Evans	25	42	13	63	.394
1977–78	Jack Evans	22	45	13	57	.356
NHL regular-season totals		229	488	141	599	.349
NHL playoff totals		11	3	8	6	.273

Note: According to NHL records, Olmstead's coaching record is 11-37-16, and Fashoway's record is 4-5-1, but the timeline of events in Olmstead's life contradicts league records. The March 11, 1968, *Oakland Tribune* states, "Olmstead's mother died in Saskatchewan. Olmstead has been back in Canada since learning his mother was gravely ill," meaning Fashoway was behind the bench during this time. Furthermore, the April 14, 1968, *Tribune* states, "With 21 games left, [Olmstead] turned over his coaching duties to aide Gordon Fashoway. The latter's record was five wins, 10 losses, and six ties."

WHL all-time coaching record

COACH	W	L	T	PTS	WIN. %
Norman "Bud" Poile	100	90	7	207	.525
Playoffs	10	7	0	20	.588
Charlie Burns	50	44	5	105	.530
Playoffs	5	8	0	10	.385
Max McNab	29	39	2	60	.429
Playoffs	0	2	0	0	.000
Nick Mickoski	11	12	1	23	.479
Playoffs	8	3	0	16	.727
Rudy Pilous	10	17	7	27	.397
WHL regular-season totals	200	202	22	422	.498
WHL playoff totals	23	20	0	46	.535

NHL all-time coaching record

COACH	W	L	T	PTS	WIN. %
Fred Glover	96	206	52	244	.345
Playoffs	3	8	0	6	.273
Jack Evans	74	129	37	185	.385
Vic Stasiuk	21	38	16	58	.387
Marshall Johnston	13	45	12	38	.271
Bert Olmstead	10	32	11	31	.292
Bill McCreary	8	20	4	20	.313
Gordon Fashoway	5	10	6	16	.381
Garry Young	2	8	3	7	.269
NHL regular-season totals	229	488	141	599	.349
NHL playoff totals	11	3	8	6	.273

WHL all-time season-by-season regular-season attendance

SEASON	ATT.	GP	AVG.
1961–62	194,530	35	5,558
1962–63	144,048	35	4,116
1963–64	132,762	35	3,793
1964–65	144,335	35	4,124
1965–66	100,224	36	2,784
1966–67	149,871	36	4,163
WHL totals	865,770	212	4,084

NHL all-time season-by-season regular-season attendance

SEASON	ATT.	GP	AVG.
1967–68	183,507	37	4,960
1968–69	172,481	38	4,584
1969–70	236,555	38	6,225
1970–71	208,953	39	5,358
1971–72	237,542	39	6,091
1972–73	208,803	39	5,354
1973–74	191,782	39	4,850
1974–75	246,897	40	6,172
1975–76	277,977	40	6,944
1976–77	247,758	40	6,194
1977–78	227,029	40	5,676
NHL totals	2,439,284	429	5,686

All-time NHL power play record

SEASON	GOALS / ATTEMPTS	SHG AGAINST	SCORING %
1967–68	41 / 259	6	15.83 (7th/12)
1968–69	44 / 286	5	15.38 (9th/12)
1969–70	45 / 324	12	13.89 (12th/12)
1970–71	39 / 316	7	12.34 (12th/14)
1971–72	44 / 278	6	15.83 (12th/14)
1972–73	41 / 250	4	16.40 (11th/16)
1973–74	34 / 268	14	12.69 (16th/16)
1974–75	48 / 359	13	13.37 (17th/18)
1975–76	71 / 382	10	18.59 (12th/18)
1976–77	59 / 298	12	19.80 (10th/18)
1977–78	42 / 275	8	15.27 (16th/18)
Totals	508 / 3295	97	15.42

All-time NHL penalty killing record

SEASON	GOALS / ATTEMPTS	SHG SCORED	KILLING %
1967–68	45 / 259	6	82.63 (9th/12)
1968–69	42 / 226	3	81.42 (9th/12)
1969–70	49 / 258	4	81.0 (6th/12)
1970–71	58 / 254	3	77.17 (11th/14)
1971–72	55 / 259	5	78.76 (9th/14)
1972–73	56 / 242	4	76.86 (tie 14th/16)
1973–74	46 / 221	6	79.19 (13th/16)
1974–75	67 / 267	5	74.91 (16th/18)
1975–76	52 / 262	9	80.15 (9th/18)
1976–77	52 / 237	2	78.06 (12th/18)
1977–78	61 / 235	3	74.04 (14th/18)
Totals	583 / 2720	50	78.57

Miscellaneous records

NHL Hat tricks: (29)

SEASON	PLAYER
1967–68	Gerry Ehman vs. Los Angeles, January 7, 1968
1968–69	Norm Ferguson at Detroit, January 25, 1969
	Brian Perry vs. Chicago, February 19, 1969
1969–70	Earl Ingarfield at Minnesota, December 27, 1969
	Earl Ingarfield vs. Toronto, January 23, 1970
	Mike Laughton at Minnesota, January 25, 1970
1970–71	Gary Croteau vs. Minnesota, January 27, 1971
1971–72	Norm Ferguson vs. Philadelphia, October 13, 1971
	Bobby Sheehan vs. Vancouver, October 15, 1971
	Gerry Pinder at Detroit, October 24, 1971
	Carol Vadnais vs. St. Louis, February 20, 1972
	Joey Johnston vs. Buffalo, March 8, 1972
1972–73	Joey Johnston vs. Boston, November 3, 1972
	Marshall Johnston at Boston, December 10, 1972
	Pete Laframboise (four goals) vs. Vancouver, January 3, 1973
1973–74	Gary Croteau vs. Detroit, October 24, 1973
	Reggie Leach at Chicago, January 6, 1974
	Ivan Boldirev (four goals) vs. St. Louis, January 9, 1974
1974–75	Larry Patey vs. New York Islanders, March 9, 1975
1975–76	Al MacAdam at Detroit, October 11, 1975
	Gary Sabourin (four goals) vs. New York Rangers, November 7, 1975
	Dennis Maruk (four goals) at Pittsburgh, November 18, 1975
	Wayne Merrick at Washington, January 2, 1976
	Wayne Merrick vs. Toronto, January 25, 1976
	Jim Moxey at Minnesota, February 15, 1976
	Al MacAdam at New York Rangers, February 25, 1976
1976–77	Robert Murdoch vs. Detroit, December 15, 1976
1977–78	Dennis Maruk (four goals) vs. St. Louis, November 2, 1977
	Chuck Arnason vs. New York Islanders, March 25, 1978

Appendix of Tables

Penalty shots for Seals/Barons:

PLAYER AND RESULT	GAME SCORE
Norm Ferguson successful vs. Ed Giacomin, November 24, 1968	(NYR 3, OAK 2 at NY)
Joey Johnston unsuccessful vs. Rogatien Vachon, January 2, 1974	(CAL 5, LA 2 at CAL)
Wayne King unsuccessful vs. Gilles Gilbert, January 10, 1976	(BOS 3, CAL 2 at BOS)
Dennis Maruk unsuccessful vs. Tony Esposito, January 14, 1976	(CAL 2, CHI 2 at CAL)
Al MacAdam successful vs. Denis Herron, December 16, 1976	(PIT 5, CLE 4 at PIT)

Penalty shots against Seals/Barons:

PLAYER AND RESULT	GAME SCORE
Chico Maki unsuccessful vs. Chris Worthy, December 15, 1968	(CHI 7, OAK 4 at CHI)
Fred Stanfield unsuccessful vs. Gilles Meloche, February 23, 1972	(BOS 8, CAL 6 at CAL)
Chuck Arnason unsuccessful vs. Gilles Meloche, February 16, 1974	(PIT 7, CAL 3 at PIT)
Bobby Schmautz unsuccessful vs. Gary Simmons, November 2, 1975	(BOS 5, CAL 0 at BOS)
Reed Larson unsuccessful vs. Gilles Meloche, November 5, 1977	(CLE 4, DET 3 at DET)

FRANCHISE RECORD AT THE NHL ALL-STAR GAME

1968-Bobby Baun; 1969-Ted Hampson, Bill Hicke, Carol Vadnais (2 PIM); 1970-Harry Howell, Carol Vadnais; 1971-Doug Roberts; 1972-Carol Vadnais; 1973-Joey Johnston; 1974-Joey Johnston; 1975-Joey Johnston (1 assist); 1976-Al MacAdam (1 goal, 1 assist); 1977-Al MacAdam; 1978-Dennis Maruk

TEAM CAPTAINS' HISTORY:

Harry Pidhirny, 1961-62; Eddie Panagabko, 1962-65; Al Nicholson and Charlie Burns, 1965-66; Charlie Burns, 1966-67 (WHL years); Bobby Baun, 1967-68; Ted Hampson, 1968-71; Carol Vadnais, 1971 to February 1972; Bert Marshall, February 1972 to March 1973; No Captain from March 1973 to February 1974; Joey Johnston, February 1974 to June 1975; Jim Neilson and Bob Stewart, 1975-76; Bob Stewart and Jim Neilson, 1976-77; Al MacAdam, 1977-78

ALTERNATE CAPTAINS' HISTORY:

Gary Edmundson, 1961-62; Nick Mickoski, 1962-63; Charlie Burns and Len Haley, 1963-64; Unknown, 1964-65 and 1965-66; Jack Evans and Gerry Odrowski, 1966-67; Billy Harris and Wally Boyer, 1967-68; Gerry Odrowski, Bert Marshall, Bryan Watson, and Gary Jarrett, 1968-69; Bill Hicke and Bert Marshall, 1969-70; Carol Vadnais and Bill Hicke, 1970-71; Bert Marshall, Wayne Carleton, and Tommy Williams, 1971-72; Ivan Boldirev, Rick Smith, Marshall Johnston, and Dick Redmond, 1972-73; Ivan Boldirev, Walt McKechnie, Marshall Johnston, Gary Croteau, and Joey Johnston, 1973-74; Len Frig, Stan Gilbertson, Jim Neilson, and Bob Stewart, 1974-75; No alternate captains after 1974-75.

GENERAL MANAGERS' HISTORY:

Joseph J. Allen, 1961-62; Norman "Bud" Poile, 1962-66; Rudy Pilous, 1966-67; Bert Olmstead, 1967-68; Frank Selke Jr., 1968-70; Bill Torrey, 1970; Fred Glover, 1970-71; Garry Young, 1971-72; Fred Glover, 1972-74; Garry Young, 1974; Bill McCreary, 1974-77; Harry Howell, 1977-78

Seals all-time WHL regular-season scoring

PLAYER	GP	G	A	PTS	PIM
Al Nicholson	349	127	158	285	103
Nick Mickoski	266	105	172	277	96
Ray Cyr	370	64	195	259	26
Charlie Burns	230	92	145	237	101
Len Haley	242	108	123	231	340
Wayne Connelly	175	93	95	188	75
Eddie Panagabko	207	67	119	186	136
Tom Thurlby	414	57	106	163	175
Gary Edmundson	167	62	84	146	204
George Swarbrick	212	73	65	138	230
Moe Mantha	204	40	86	126	160
Dan Belisle	125	54	63	117	36
Gerry Odrowski	250	27	83	110	350
Del Topoll	114	27	78	105	66

Wayne Maxner	127	45	55	100	104
Orland Kurtenbach	70	30	57	87	94
Bob Solinger	70	30	55	85	4
Gerry Brisson	122	41	41	82	40
Jean-Marc Picard	277	12	64	76	313
Forbes Kennedy	77	28	44	72	139
John Gravel	134	20	43	63	56
Harry Pidhirny	66	24	34	58	12
Carl Boone	62	30	27	57	22
Michel Harvey	61	23	34	57	24
Larry McNabb	200	5	41	46	403
Ron Harris	85	20	25	45	114
Rudy Panagabko	72	19	25	44	30
Camille Bedard	70	7	32	39	68
Gary Dornhoefer	37	10	25	35	58
Gord Redahl	51	16	17	33	10
Larry Lund	104	10	23	33	47
Ron Schock	43	11	21	32	28
Dallas Smith	70	14	16	30	79
Stan Gilbertson	102	7	19	26	57
Cliff Pennington	26	6	15	21	4
Doug Senior	48	5	16	21	30
Jack Evans	71	3	18	21	52
Paul Jackson	193	3	18	21	122
Ken Girard	31	9	11	20	2
Jim Hay	57	4	15	19	101
Keith Wright	36	2	17	19	19
Ed Hoekstra	31	11	7	18	4
Bob Kabel	47	9	9	18	20
Bob Bailey	23	2	12	14	26
Floyd Hillman	70	0	14	14	122

Marty Howe	36	2	10	12	28
Jim Wilcox	62	3	7	10	26
Bob Leiter	20	2	8	10	10
Jack Martin	28	3	6	9	12
Barney Krake	37	3	5	8	8
Yves Locas	12	1	2	3	0
Jim McCloskey	23	0	3	3	24
Don Bamburak	9	2	0	2	2
Real Chevrefils	6	1	1	2	0
Jack Price	2	0	2	2	0
Hugh Currie	7	0	2	2	4
Gary Collins	16	0	2	2	10
Bob Perreault (G)	140	0	2	2	60
Mike Draper	6	0	2	2	2
Jack McCartan (G)	114	0	2	2	40
Gerry Ouellette	7	1	0	1	0
Ray Dupont	1	0	1	1	2
Joe Daley (G)	7	0	1	1	0
Jim McLeod (G)	67	0	1	1	18
Harley Hodgson	n.a.	0	1	1	6
Pete Lambo	1	0	0	0	0
Bob Ames	1	0	0	0	0
Dale Guame (G)	1	0	0	0	0
Don Hogan	1	0	0	0	0
Tommy Green (G)	1	0	0	0	0
Ron Vermette	2	0	0	0	0
Doug Favell (G)	2	0	0	0	0
Owen Mailley	2	0	0	0	0
Henry Goy (G)	2	0	0	0	0
Guy Murphy	2	0	0	0	0
George Berube	3	0	0	0	0

John Henderson (G)	13	0	0	0	0
John Chasczewski	5	0	0	0	15
Nelson LeClair	5	0	0	0	0
John Annable	5	0	0	0	0
Jean-Guy Morissette (G)	7	0	0	0	2
George Wood (G)	10	0	0	0	0
Bev Bentley (G)	62	0	0	0	0
Robert Gray (G)	—	—	—	—	—
Marcel Pelletier (G)	—	—	—	—	—
Al Smith (G)	—	—	—	—	—
Totals	424	1470	2480	3950	4569

Seals all-time WHL playoff scoring

PLAYER	GP	G	A	PTS	PIM
Al Nicholson	37	13	18	31	10
Nick Mickoski	30	8	22	30	10
Ray Cyr	36	8	19	27	2
Charlie Burns	24	2	8	10	17
Len Haley	30	12	16	28	39
Wayne Connelly	18	6	7	13	10
Eddie Panagabko	28	11	20	31	8
Tom Thurlby	43	8	12	20	22
Gary Edmundson	19	5	3	8	12
George Swarbrick	13	4	5	9	24
Moe Mantha	30	8	16	24	40
Dan Belisle	18	8	7	15	2
Gerry Odrowski	24	0	4	4	44
Del Topoll	7	0	0	0	4
Wayne Maxner	11	1	3	4	0
Orland Kurtenbach	17	4	13	17	51
Bob Solinger	2	1	0	1	0

Gerry Brisson	14	6	2	8	4
Jean-Marc Picard	35	1	5	6	29
Forbes Kennedy	6	2	0	2	4
John Gravel	13	2	4	6	0
Harry Pidhirny	2	1	2	3	0
Carl Boone	2	0	0	0	0
Michel Harvey	7	2	1	3	2
Larry McNabb	35	6	10	16	57
Ron Harris	13	3	1	4	27
Rudy Panagabko	6	0	2	2	4
Camille Bedard	17	0	2	2	8
Gary Dornhoefer	—	—	—	—	—
Gord Redahl	—	—	—	—	—
Larry Lund	11	1	0	1	4
Ron Schock	7	1	5	6	6
Dallas Smith	—	—	—	—	—
Stan Gilbertson	13	4	2	6	6
Cliff Pennington	—	—	—	—	—
Doug Senior	4	2	0	2	0
Jack Evans	6	0	2	2	4
Paul Jackson	28	2	3	5	14
Ken Girard	2	0	0	0	0
Jim Hay	2	0	1	1	0
Keith Wright	5	0	1	1	0
Ed Hoekstra	6	1	3	4	2
Bob Kabel	4	0	0	0	2
Bob Bailey	2	0	0	0	16
Floyd Hillman	2	0	1	1	7
Marty Howe	2	0	0	0	0
Jim Wilcox	—	—	—	—	—
Bob Leiter	1	0	0	0	0

Jack Martin	—	—	—	—	—
Barney Krake	—	—	—	—	—
Yves Locas	—	—	—	—	—
Jim McCloskey	—	—	—	—	—
Don Bamburak	—	—	—	—	—
Real Chevrefils	—	—	—	—	—
Jack Price	—	—	—	—	—
Hugh Currie	—	—	—	—	—
Gary Collins	—	—	—	—	—
Bob Perreault (G)	11	0	0	0	10
Mike Draper	—	—	—	—	—
Jack McCartan (G)	5	0	0	0	0
Gerry Ouellette	—	—	—	—	—
Ray Dupont	—	—	—	—	—
Joe Daley (G)	—	—	—	—	—
Jim McLeod (G)	17	0	0	0	0
Harley Hodgson	—	—	—	—	—
Pete Lambo	—	—	—	—	—
Bob Ames	—	—	—	—	—
Dale Guame (G)	—	—	—	—	—
Don Hogan	—	—	—	—	—
Tommy Green (G)	—	—	—	—	—
Ron Vermette	—	—	—	—	—
Doug Favell (G)	2	0	0	0	0
Owen Mailley	—	—	—	—	—
Henry Goy (G)	—	—	—	—	—
Guy Murphy	—	—	—	—	—
George Berube	—	—	—	—	—
John Henderson (G)	—	—	—	—	—
John Chasczewski	—	—	—	—	—
Nelson LeClair	—	—	—	—	—

John Annable	—	—	—	—	—
Jean-Guy Morissette (G)	—	—	—	—	—
George Wood (G)	—	—	—	—	—
Bev Bentley (G)	2	0	0	0	0
Robert Gray (G)	3	0	0	0	0
Marcel Pelletier (G)	3	0	0	0	0
Al Smith (G)	1	0	0	0	0
Totals	43	133	220	353	504

Seals all-time WHL regular season goaltending

PLAYER	GP	MINS	W	L	T	GA	SO	GAA
Jean-Guy Morissette	7	438	5	1	1	17	1	2.33
Joe Daley	7	426	6	1	0	17	2	2.39
Doug Favell	2	120	1	1	0	6	0	3.00
Jim McLeod	67	4090	43	23	1	202	4	3.01
Jack McCartan	114	7013	48	54	12	383	3	3.28
George Wood	10	600	2	7	1	37	0	3.70
John Henderson	13	793	4	8	1	49	0	3.71
Bob Perreault	140	8394	62	71	5	525	0	3.75
Bev Bentley	62	3738	28	33	1	237	4	3.80
Henry Goy	2	97	1	1	0	10	0	6.19
Dale Guame	1	60	0	1	0	7	0	7.00
Tommy Green	1	60	0	1	0	11	0	11.00
Totals	424	25829	200	202	22	1524[a]	14	3.49

[a] 23 empty-net goals, not counted in individual statistics

Seals all-time WHL playoff goaltending

PLAYER	GP	MINS	W	L	T	GA	SO	GAA
Marcel Pelletier	3	183	2	1	0	7	0	2.30
Jack McCartan	5	300	2	3	0	13	0	2.60
Jim McLeod	17	1054	10	7	0	56	3	3.19

Bob Perreault	11	677	8	3	0	41	0	3.63
Al Smith	1	60	0	1	0	4	0	4.00
Robert Gray	3	140	1	1	0	11	0	4.71
Doug Favell	2	113	0	2	0	10	0	5.31
Bev Bentley	2	120	0	2	0	11	0	5.50
Totals	43	2647	23	20	0	155[a]	3	3.47

[a] 2 empty-net goals, not included in individual statistics

Seals / Barons all-time NHL regular-season scoring

PLAYER	GP	G	A	PTS	PIM	PPG	SHG	GWG	+ /-
Al MacAdam	320	88	129	217	214	19	4	10	-51
Dennis Maruk	236	94	117	211	162	15	7	8	-29
Joey Johnston	288	84	101	185	308	23	3	5	-117
Ted Hampson	246	61	123	184	37	19	2	4	-65
Bill Hicke[a]	262	79	101	180	155	26	0	10	-76
Walt McKechnie	250	62	109	171	124	12	4	2	-45
Dave Gardner	289	67	99	166	33	15	1	7	-58
Gerry Ehman	297	69	86	155	56	14	0	10	-85
Rick Hampton[b]	285	56	96	152	125	17	1	3	-88
Carol Vadnais	246	63	83	146	560	20	1	9	-71
Norm Ferguson	279	73	66	139	72	15	0	10	-57
Bob Murdoch	206	59	72	131	110	20	0	10	-35
Ivan Boldirev	191	52	77	129	134	9	2	7	-91
Gary Jarrett	268	54	71	125	111	10	0	7	-61
Gary Croteau	270	47	76	123	47	5	0	4	-105
Wayne Merrick	154	45	70	115	69	11	0	6	-34
Stan Weir	216	42	58	100	38	10	0	1	-86
Bobby Stewart	414	19	80	99	691	3	0	1	-208
Reggie Leach	171	51	43	94	86	7	0	8	-102
Stan Gilbertson	235	41	47	88	107	11	0	4	-90
Mike Laughton[a]	189	39	48	87	101	9	0	9	-60

Craig Patrick	203	40	46	86	35	4	1	1	-96
Mike Fidler	124	40	44	84	55	11	0	6	-17
Hilliard Graves	153	38	43	81	82	4	0	4	-46
Earl Ingarfield	129	34	47	81	22	12	0	3	-19
Mike Christie	225	10	65	75	356	0	0	2	-25
Ernie Hicke	146	33	37	70	117	10	0	3	-47
Jim Neilson	213	9	61	70	138	1	0	0	-82
Doug Roberts	230	11	57	68	280	3	0	1	-112
Bert Marshall	313	8	60	68	395	2	0	0	-107
Gary Sabourin	109	28	39	67	37	6	0	4	-13
Bob Girard	173	27	40	67	98	4	1	2	-33
Dick Redmond	109	15	52	67	110	4	0	0	-33
Greg Smith	155	16	48	64	159	6	0	2	-56
Marshall Johnston	202	14	47	61	42	4	1	0	-73
Dave Hrechkosy	112	38	19	57	39	12	2	7	-30
Ralph Klassen[b]	164	22	34	56	55	6	2	1	-53
Pete Laframboise	147	23	32	55	40	2	0	1	-56
Gerry Pinder	74	23	31	54	59	7	1	1	-18
Larry Patey	98	29	24	53	91	9	1	4	-28
Dennis Hextall	78	21	31	52	217	1	0	3	-21
Morris Mott	199	18	32	50	49	2	1	2	-49
Kris Manery	78	22	27	49	14	7	0	1	-15
Jim Moxey	126	22	27	49	57	4	0	0	-29
Bobby Sheehan	78	20	26	46	12	2	1	3	-16
Ron Huston	79	15	31	46	8	0	0	3	-27
Brian Perry	95	16	29	45	24	2	0	1	-8
Len Frig	208	8	36	44	395	4	0	0	-63
Fred Ahern	108	26	17	43	111	6	0	6	-31
Ted McAneeley	158	8	35	43	141	1	1	0	-64
John Stewart	76	19	19	38	55	2	0	2	-42
Rick Smith	81	10	28	38	103	3	0	0	-60

Warren Williams	77	11	25	36	125	2	0	0	-23
Ron Stackhouse	84	9	27	36	81	3	0	2	-31
Don O'Donoghue	125	18	17	35	35	3	1	1	-52
Charlie Burns	73	9	26	35	20	1	2	1	-15
Dick Mattiussi	156	8	27	35	92	1	0	1	-50
Chuck Arnason	40	21	13	34	8	5	0	2	-2
George Swarbrick	99	16	18	34	137	4	1	3	-30
Frank Spring	55	14	20	34	12	6	0	0	-6
Wally Boyer[a]	74	13	20	33	44	1	0	0	0
Billy Harris[a]	81	12	21	33	4	1	0	0	-7
Wayne Carleton	76	17	14	31	45	4	0	0	-27
Brent Meeke	75	9	22	31	8	1	0	0	-25
Bob Dillabough	100	12	17	29	20	1	1	3	-23
Tommy Williams	50	10	19	29	10	2	0	0	-29
Jim Pappin	56	8	21	29	20	2	0	1	-10
Harry Howell	83	4	25	29	66	3	0	3	-36
Paul Shmyr	69	6	21	27	156	0	0	0	-27
Charlie Simmer	80	11	14	25	64	4	0	0	-22
Joe Szura[a]	90	10	15	25	30	1	0	1	-10
George Pesut	92	3	22	25	130	2	0	0	-23
Larry Cahan[a]	74	9	15	24	80	5	0	1	-39
Joe Hardy	63	9	14	23	51	2	1	1	-22
Wayne King	73	5	18	23	34	2	0	0	-13
Johnny Muloin	135	3	20	23	85	1	1	0	-53
J. P. Parise[a]	40	9	13	22	27	1	0	0	-16
Alain Caron[a]	59	9	13	22	18	3	0	0	-23
Darryl Maggs	54	7	15	22	46	0	0	1	-22
John Brenneman	52	11	10	21	20	2	0	0	-13
Larry Popein	47	5	14	19	12	0	1	0	-17
François Lacombe	74	2	16	18	50	1	0	0	-8
Tony Featherstone[b]	76	8	9	17	61	1	0	1	-12

Rick Shinske	52	5	12	17	8	1	0	1	-16
Jean Potvin	40	3	14	17	30	0	0	1	-5
Terry Murray	91	0	17	17	60	0	0	0	-55
Gerry Odrowski	116	9	7	16	34	0	5	2	+4
Autry Erickson[a]	66	4	11	15	46	0	0	0	-19
Kent Douglas[a]	40	4	11	15	80	1	0	0	-18
Gilles Meloche	355	0	15	15	48	—	—	—	—
Juha Widing	28	6	8	14	10	1	0	1	-7
Ken Kuzyk	41	5	9	14	8	0	0	0	0
Ray McKay	72	2	12	14	49	1	0	0	-36
Gary Holt	52	6	7	13	52	1	0	0	-10
Gene Ubriaco	41	5	8	13	18	1	0	0	-5
Bobby Baun[a]	67	3	10	13	81	0	0	0	-18
Ron Harris[a]	54	4	6	10	60	1	0	1	-27
Brian Lavender	65	3	7	10	48	0	0	1	-10
Tim Jacobs	46	0	10	10	35	0	0	0	-3
John Baby	24	2	7	9	26	0	0	0	-10
Howie Menard	38	2	7	9	16	0	0	0	-5
Rick Kessell	51	2	6	8	4	1	0	0	-6
Phil Roberto	21	3	4	7	8	0	0	0	-7
Mike Crombeen[b]	48	3	4	7	13	2	0	0	-26
Glenn Patrick	37	2	3	5	70	0	0	0	-13
Rick Jodzio	38	2	3	5	43	0	0	1	-9
Bryan Watson	50	2	3	5	97	0	0	1	-17
Randy Holt	48	1	4	5	229	0	0	0	-24
Tracy Pratt[a]	34	0	5	5	90	0	0	0	-18
Gary Smith[a]	211	0	5	5	35	0	0	0	—
Paul Shakes	21	0	4	4	12	0	0	0	-13
Tom Webster	7	2	1	3	6	0	0	0	+3
Ron Boehm[a]	16	2	1	3	10	1	0	0	-5
Angelo Moretto	5	1	2	3	2	0	0	0	+1

Barry Cummins	36	1	2	3	39	0	0	0	-34
Dennis O'Brien	23	0	3	3	31	0	0	0	-13
Del Hall	9	2	0	2	2	0	0	0	-1
Bjorn Johansson[b]	15	1	1	2	10	0	0	0	-13
Tom Thurlby	21	1	1	2	4	0	0	0	-8
Reg Kerr	7	0	2	2	7	0	0	0	0
Ken Baird	10	0	2	2	15	0	0	0	-10
Marv Edwards	35	0	2	2	10	—	—	—	—
Gary Edwards	47	0	1	1	4	—	—	—	—
Lyle Bradley	6	1	0	1	2	1	0	0	-2
Paul Andrea	9	1	0	1	2	1	0	0	-6
Bruce Greig	9	0	1	1	46	0	0	0	-3
Darcy Regier	15	0	1	1	28	0	0	0	-5
Bob Lemieux[a]	19	0	1	1	12	0	0	0	-9
Gary Simmons	89	0	1	1	44	—	—	—	—
Terry Clancy[a]	7	0	0	0	2	0	0	0	-4
Tom Price	10	0	0	0	4	0	0	0	-14
Lyle Carter	15	0	0	0	2	—	—	—	—
Bob Champoux	17	0	0	0	0	—	—	—	—
Barry Boughner	20	0	0	0	11	0	0	0	-3
Chris Worthy	26	0	0	0	6	—	—	—	—
Charlie Hodge[a]	86	0	0	0	4	—	—	—	—
Bob Sneddon	7	0	0	0	0	—	—	—	—
Daniel Chicoine	6	0	0	0	0	0	0	0	-2
Frank Hughes	5	0	0	0	0	0	0	0	-2
Len Ronson	5	0	0	0	0	0	0	0	-3
Ted Tucker	5	0	0	0	0	—	—	—	—
Jeff Allan	4	0	0	0	2	0	0	0	0
Vern Stenlund	4	0	0	0	0	0	0	0	-3
Gary Coalter	4	0	0	0	0	0	0	0	-4
Peter Vipond	3	0	0	0	0	0	0	0	0

Jim Jones	2	0	0	0	0	0	0	0	0
Larry Wright	2	0	0	0	0	0	0	0	-2
Ron Serafini	2	0	0	0	0	0	0	0	-2
Jean Cusson	2	0	0	0	0	0	0	0	-1
Al Simmons	1	0	0	0	0	0	0	0	-1
Hartland Monahan	1	0	0	0	0	0	0	0	0
Neil Nicholson	—	—	—	—	—	—	—	—	—
Bench	—	—	—	—	110	—	—	—	—
All-Time Totals	858	2,296	3,718	6,014	10,052	509	50	229	n.a.

[a]Original Seals draft pick from 1967 expansion draft
[b]Seals / Barons first-round amateur draft pick

Seals / Barons all-time NHL playoff scoring

PLAYER	GP	G	A	PTS	PIM	PPG	SHG	GWG
Al MacAdam	—	—	—	—	—	—	—	—
Dennis Maruk	—	—	—	—	—	—	—	—
Joey Johnston	—	—	—	—	—	—	—	—
Ted Hampson	11	4	5	9	2	2	0	0
Bill Hicke[a]	11	0	4	4	6	0	0	0
Walt McKechnie	—	—	—	—	—	—	—	—
Dave Gardner	—	—	—	—	—	—	—	—
Gerry Ehman	11	3	3	6	0	1	0	0
Rick Hampton[b]	—	—	—	—	—	—	—	—
Carol Vadnais	11	3	5	8	25	3	0	0
Norm Ferguson	10	1	4	5	7	0	0	0
Bob Murdoch	—	—	—	—	—	—	—	—
Ivan Boldirev	—	—	—	—	—	—	—	—
Gary Jarrett	11	3	1	4	10	1	0	1
Gary Croteau	—	—	—	—	—	—	—	—
Wayne Merrick	—	—	—	—	—	—	—	—
Stan Weir	—	—	—	—	—	—	—	—
Bobby Stewart	—	—	—	—	—	—	—	—

Reggie Leach	—	—	—	—	—	—	—	—
Stan Gilbertson	—	—	—	—	—	—	—	—
Mike Laughton[a]	11	3	3	6	0	1	0	0
Craig Patrick	—	—	—	—	—	—	—	—
Mike Fidler	—	—	—	—	—	—	—	—
Hilliard Graves	—	—	—	—	—	—	—	—
Earl Ingarfield	11	5	6	11	6	0	2	1
Mike Christie	—	—	—	—	—	—	—	—
Ernie Hicke	—	—	—	—	—	—	—	—
Jim Neilson	—	—	—	—	—	—	—	—
Doug Roberts	11	0	3	3	40	0	0	0
Bert Marshall	11	0	8	8	32	0	0	0
Gary Sabourin	—	—	—	—	—	—	—	—
Bob Girard	—	—	—	—	—	—	—	—
Dick Redmond	—	—	—	—	—	—	—	—
Greg Smith	—	—	—	—	—	—	—	—
Marshall Johnston	—	—	—	—	—	—	—	—
Dave Hrechkosy	—	—	—	—	—	—	—	—
Ralph Klassen[b]	—	—	—	—	—	—	—	—
Pete Laframboise	—	—	—	—	—	—	—	—
Gerry Pinder	—	—	—	—	—	—	—	—
Larry Patey	—	—	—	—	—	—	—	—
Dennis Hextall	—	—	—	—	—	—	—	—
Morris Mott	—	—	—	—	—	—	—	—
Kris Manery	—	—	—	—	—	—	—	—
Jim Moxey	—	—	—	—	—	—	—	—
Bobby Sheehan	—	—	—	—	—	—	—	—
Ron Huston	—	—	—	—	—	—	—	—
Brian Perry	8	1	1	2	4	0	0	0
Len Frig	—	—	—	—	—	—	—	—
Fred Ahern	—	—	—	—	—	—	—	—

Ted McAneeley	—	—	—	—	—	—	—	—
John Stewart	—	—	—	—	—	—	—	—
Rick Smith	—	—	—	—	—	—	—	—
Warren Williams	—	—	—	—	—	—	—	—
Ron Stackhouse	—	—	—	—	—	—	—	—
Don O'Donoghue	3	0	0	0	0	0	0	0
Charlie Burns	—	—	—	—	—	—	—	—
Dick Mattiussi	8	0	1	1	6	0	0	0
Chuck Arnason	—	—	—	—	—	—	—	—
George Swarbrick	—	—	—	—	—	—	—	—
Frank Spring	—	—	—	—	—	—	—	—
Wally Boyer[a]	—	—	—	—	—	—	—	—
Billy Harris[a]	—	—	—	—	—	—	—	—
Wayne Carleton	—	—	—	—	—	—	—	—
Brent Meeke	—	—	—	—	—	—	—	—
Bob Dillabough	11	3	0	3	0	0	0	1
Tommy Williams	—	—	—	—	—	—	—	—
Jim Pappin	—	—	—	—	—	—	—	—
Harry Howell	4	0	1	1	2	0	0	0
Paul Shmyr	—	—	—	—	—	—	—	—
Charlie Simmer	—	—	—	—	—	—	—	—
Joe Szura[a]	7	2	3	5	2	1	0	0
George Pesut	—	—	—	—	—	—	—	—
Larry Cahan[a]	—	—	—	—	—	—	—	—
Joe Hardy	4	0	0	0	0	0	0	0
Wayne King	—	—	—	—	—	—	—	—
Johnny Muloin	4	0	0	0	0	0	0	0
J. P. Parise[a]	—	—	—	—	—	—	—	—
Alain Caron[a]	—	—	—	—	—	—	—	—
Darryl Maggs	—	—	—	—	—	—	—	—
John Brenneman	—	—	—	—	—	—	—	—

Larry Popein	—	—	—	—	—	—	—	—
François Lacombe	3	1	0	1	0	0	0	0
Tony Featherstone[b]	2	0	0	0	0	0	0	0
Rick Shinske	—	—	—	—	—	—	—	—
Jean Potvin	—	—	—	—	—	—	—	—
Terry Murray	—	—	—	—	—	—	—	—
Gerry Odrowski	7	0	1	1	2	0	0	0
Autry Erickson[a]	—	—	—	—	—	—	—	—
Kent Douglas[a]	—	—	—	—	—	—	—	—
Gilles Meloche	—	—	—	—	—	—	—	—
Juha Widing	—	—	—	—	—	—	—	—
Ken Kuzyk	—	—	—	—	—	—	—	—
Ray McKay	—	—	—	—	—	—	—	—
Gary Holt	—	—	—	—	—	—	—	—
Gene Ubriaco	7	2	0	2	2	0	0	0
Bobby Baun[a]	—	—	—	—	—	—	—	—
Ron Harris[a]	—	—	—	—	—	—	—	—
Brian Lavender	—	—	—	—	—	—	—	—
Tim Jacobs	—	—	—	—	—	—	—	—
John Baby	—	—	—	—	—	—	—	—
Howie Menard	1	0	0	0	0	0	0	0
Rick Kessell	—	—	—	—	—	—	—	—
Phil Roberto	—	—	—	—	—	—	—	—
Mike Crombeen[b]	—	—	—	—	—	—	—	—
Glenn Patrick	—	—	—	—	—	—	—	—
Rick Jodzio	—	—	—	—	—	—	—	—
Bryan Watson	—	—	—	—	—	—	—	—
Randy Holt	—	—	—	—	—	—	—	—
Tracy Pratt[a]	—	—	—	—	—	—	—	—
Gary Smith[a]	11	0	0	0	4	0	0	0
Paul Shakes	—	—	—	—	—	—	—	—
Tom Webster	—	—	—	—	—	—	—	—

Ron Boehm[a]	—	—	—	—	—	—	—	—
Angelo Moretto	—	—	—	—	—	—	—	—
Barry Cummins	—	—	—	—	—	—	—	—
Dennis O'Brien	—	—	—	—	—	—	—	—
Del Hall	—	—	—	—	—	—	—	—
Bjorn Johansson[b]	—	—	—	—	—	—	—	—
Tom Thurlby	—	—	—	—	—	—	—	—
Reg Kerr	—	—	—	—	—	—	—	—
Ken Baird	—	—	—	—	—	—	—	—
Marv Edwards	—	—	—	—	—	—	—	—
Gary Edwards	—	—	—	—	—	—	—	—
Lyle Bradley	—	—	—	—	—	—	—	—
Paul Andrea	—	—	—	—	—	—	—	—
Bruce Greig	—	—	—	—	—	—	—	—
Darcy Regier	—	—	—	—	—	—	—	—
Bob Lemieux[a]	—	—	—	—	—	—	—	—
Gary Simmons	—	—	—	—	—	—	—	—
Terry Clancy[a]	—	—	—	—	—	—	—	—
Tom Price	—	—	—	—	—	—	—	—
Lyle Carter	—	—	—	—	—	—	—	—
Bob Champoux	—	—	—	—	—	—	—	—
Barry Boughner	—	—	—	—	—	—	—	—
Chris Worthy	—	—	—	—	—	—	—	—
Charlie Hodge[a]	—	—	—	—	—	—	—	—
Bob Sneddon	—	—	—	—	—	—	—	—
Daniel Chicoine	—	—	—	—	—	—	—	—
Frank Hughes	—	—	—	—	—	—	—	—
Len Ronson	—	—	—	—	—	—	—	—
Ted Tucker	—	—	—	—	—	—	—	—
Jeff Allan	—	—	—	—	—	—	—	—
Vern Stenlund	—	—	—	—	—	—	—	—
Gary Coalter	—	—	—	—	—	—	—	—

Peter Vipond	—	—	—	—	—	—	—	—
Jim Jones	—	—	—	—	—	—	—	—
Larry Wright	—	—	—	—	—	—	—	—
Ron Serafini	—	—	—	—	—	—	—	—
Jean Cusson	—	—	—	—	—	—	—	—
Al Simmons	—	—	—	—	—	—	—	—
Hartland Monahan	—	—	—	—	—	—	—	—
Neil Nicholson	2	0	0	0	0	0	0	0
Bench	—	—	—	—	2	—	—	—
All-Time Totals	11	31	49	80	152	9	2	3

[a]Original Seals draft pick from 1967 expansion draft
[b]Seals / Barons first-round amateur draft pick

Seals / Barons all-time NHL regular-season goaltending

PLAYER	GP	MIN	W	L	T	SA	SVS.	GA	SV. %	SO	GAA
Charlie Hodge[a]	86	4823	19	44	17	2467	2218	249	.899	3	3.10
Gary Smith[a]	211	11861	62	114	27	6657	5998	659	.901	9	3.33
Ted Tucker	5	177	1	1	1	93	83	10	.892	0	3.39
Gary Simmons	89	5219	27	48	12	2809	2503	306	.891	5	3.52
Gilles Meloche	355	20632	93	191	62	11322	10025	1297	.885	11	3.77
Marv Edwards	35	1983	5	24	3	1149	1011	138	.880	1	4.18
Lyle Carter	15	721	4	7	0	361	311	50	.861	0	4.16
Gary Kurt	16	837	1	7	5	417	357	60	.856	0	4.30
Gary Edwards	47	2696	10	28	8	1444	1248	196	.864	2	4.36
Chris Worthy	26	1309	5	11	3	761	663	98	.871	0	4.49
Bob Champoux	17	922	2	11	3	527	447	80	.848	0	5.21
Bob Sneddon	7	224	0	2	0	127	106	21	.835	0	5.63
All-Time Totals	858	51480	229	488	141	28134[b]	24970	3197[b]	.888[c]	32[d]	3.73

[a]Original Seals draft pick from 1967 expansion draft
[b]Shots against and goals against totals include 33 empty net goals
[c]Save percentage includes empty-net goals
[d]Hodge and Smith shared one shutout (1967–68)

Seals / Barons all-time NHL playoff goaltending

PLAYER	GP	MIN	W	L	T	SA	SVS.	GA	SV.%	SO	GAA
Gary Smith[a]	11	667	3	8	0	361	325	36	.900	0	3.24

[a]Original Seals draft pick from 1967 expansion draft

For a complete list of franchise records, complete game-by-game results, as well as season-by-season scoring and goaltending statistics, please visit www.goldensealshockey.com.

NOTES

1. San Francisco Treat, 1917–1967

1. "New Ice Palace to Open Its Doors," *Oakland (CA) Tribune*, October 1, 1916.
2. "Ice Skating Palace to Be Opened in S.F.," *Oakland Tribune*, October 10, 1916.
3. "Ice Skating Palace."
4. "New Ice Palace to Open."
5. "Seattle Again Trim Canadiens," *Manitoba Free Press* (Winnipeg), March 29, 1917.
6. Quotes taken from an ad in the March 28, 1917, *Oakland Tribune*.
7. "Montreal Hockeyists Win," *Oakland Tribune*, March 31, 1917.
8. "California Dreamin'," *Hockey News*, September 10, 2012, 43.
9. "Hockey Title of World at Stake," *Oakland Tribune*, April 4, 1917.
10. "California Dreamin'."
11. "Golden Gate Fans Fall for Hockey," *Lethbridge (AB) Daily Herald*, April 13, 1917.
12. "LA, San Francisco Get Hockey Teams," *Bakersfield Californian*, April 24, 1961.
13. Kurtzberg, *Shorthanded*, 5.
14. Art Rosenbaum, "The Icemen Cometh to Two Anthems," *San Francisco Chronicle*, November 18, 1961.
15. Stott, *Ice Warriors*, 238–42.
16. Hugh McDonald, "Home Rink Is No Advantage in First Tilt," *San Mateo (CA) Times*, April 27, 1963.
17. "Seattle Pucksters Wallop Seals, 9–1," *Pasadena (CA) Star-News*, May 1, 1963.
18. Merl Moore, "Seals in Last Gasp Tonight," *Oakland Tribune*, May 2, 1963.
19. Moore, "Seals in Last Gasp."
20. Merl Moore, "Near-Riot As Seals Win," *Oakland Tribune*, May 3, 1963.
21. Moore, "Near-Riot."
22. Hugh McDonald, "Seals Go for Title Tonight," *San Mateo Times*, May 6, 1963.
23. KFRC Radio broadcast, May 6, 1963, Bay Area Radio Museum, http://bayarearadio.org/site/sports/.

24. Hugh McDonald, "Record Crowd Sees Seals Do It," *San Mateo Times*, May 7, 1963.

25. KFRC Radio broadcast, May 6, 1963.

26. McDonald, "Record Crowd."

27. Spence Conley, "Mickoski Seals' Savior," *Oakland Tribune*, April 5, 1964.

28. Conley, "Mickoski Seals' Savior."

29. "L.A. Lucky, Says Poile," *San Mateo Times*, April 9, 1964.

30. Hugh McDonald, "Panagabko Playoff Spark," *San Mateo Times*, April 13, 1964.

31. Spence Conley, "Seals Win Patrick Cup Again," *Oakland Tribune*, April 18, 1964.

32. Conley, "Seals Win Patrick Cup."

33. "Seal Loss in Playoffs Protested," *Oakland Tribune*, April 14, 1966.

34. "Seals Are Confident for Opener," *San Mateo Times*, April 13, 1966.

35. "Goalie Request by Seals," *Hayward (CA) Daily Review*, April 15, 1966.

36. Spence Conley, "Seals Seek Clincher over Leafs," *Oakland Tribune*, April 23, 1966.

37. "S.F. Seals Buried by Sad Windup," *Hayward Daily Review*, April 27, 1966.

38. Stott, *Ice Warriors*, 131.

39. Bass, *Great Expansion*, 21.

40. Beddoes, Fischler, and Gitler, *Hockey!*, 91.

41. Beddoes, Fischler, and Gitler, *Hockey!*, 90.

42. Kurtzberg, *Shorthanded*, 5.

43. Bass, *Great Expansion*, 75.

44. Kurtzberg, *Shorthanded*, 4.

45. Bass, *Great Expansion*, 75.

46. Bass, *Great Expansion*, 75.

47. Spence Conley, "Van Gerbig Takes Control of Seals," *Oakland Tribune*, April 21, 1967.

48. Sid Hoos, "3-Year Pattern to Seal Plans," *Hayward Daily Review*, April 21, 1967.

49. Hoos, "3-Year Pattern."

50. Kurtzberg, *Shorthanded*, 5.

51. Ed Schoenfeld, "Oakland Arena Opens Tonight," *Oakland Tribune*, November 9, 1966.

52. Ed Levitt, "A Carpet of Class," *Oakland Tribune*, November 9, 1966.

53. Schoenfeld, "Oakland Arena Opens Tonight."

54. Ed Schoenfeld, "Everyone Agrees: Arena Magnificent," *Oakland Tribune*, November 10, 1966.

55. Spence Conley, "Seals Win Thrilling Debut, 6–5," *Oakland Tribune*, November 10, 1966.
56. Conley, "Seals Win Thrilling Debut."
57. "Gulls Plain Rude to Seals, 11–2," *Oakland Tribune*, April 3, 1967.
58. "Gulls Plain Rude."

2. The Oakland Error, 1967–1968

1. Rick Anderson, "Flowery Harbinger (?) for New Seals Prexy," *Hayward Daily Review*, May 13, 1967.
2. Ed Levitt, "Frozen Optimism," *Oakland Tribune*, February 1, 1967.
3. Kurtzberg, *Shorthanded*, 6.
4. Kurtzberg, *Shorthanded*, 6.
5. Hugh McDonald, "Bert Olmstead of the Seals," *San Mateo Times*, October 7, 1967.
6. McDonald, "Bert Olmstead."
7. Beddoes, Fischler, and Gitler, *Hockey!*, 112.
8. Eskenazi, *Hockey*, 94.
9. "Seal Brass Culls Draft Prospects," *Oakland Tribune*, May 22, 1967.
10. Spence Conley, "Canadien Goalie Picked 1st by Seals," *Oakland Tribune*, June 6, 1967.
11. "Pilous Sues Oakland Seals," *Winnipeg (MB) Free Press*, November 21, 1967.
12. Beddoes, Fischler, and Gitler, *Hockey!*, 112.
13. Proudfoot, *Pro Hockey '69–'70*, 87.
14. Irvin, *In the Crease*, 113–14.
15. *Professional Hockey Handbook*, 102.
16. Willes, *Rebel League*, 241.
17. Baun and Logan, *Lowering the Boom*, 184.
18. Baun and Logan, *Lowering the Boom*, 188.
19. Baun and Logan, *Lowering the Boom*, 189.
20. The cover of the October 14, 1967, issue is mentioned in "Seals Second? Ha!" *Hockey News*, January 24, 1997, 10.
21. "Seal Boss Calls Draft 'Fantastic,'" *Oakland Tribune*, June 6, 1967.
22. McDonald, "Bert Olmstead."
23. Jenish, *NHL*, 193.
24. Spence Conley, "North Stars Beat Seals, 3–1, in First Exhibition Match," *Oakland Tribune*, September 18, 1967.
25. Kurtzberg, *Shorthanded*, 51.
26. "Seals Seek Plante," *Oakland Tribune*, January 13, 1967.

27. Spence Conley, "Plante Hangs Up Skates for Good," *Oakland Tribune*, October 8, 1967.

28. Conley, "Plante Hangs Up Skates."

29. Bruce Levitt, "Olmstead Not Happy," *Cornwall (ON) Standard-Freeholder*, October 11, 1967.

30. Pete Axthelm, "Hockey 1967–68: Crashing into a New Age," *Sports Illustrated*, November 6, 1967.

31. Baun and Logan, *Lowering the Boom*, 194.

32. Axthelm, "Hockey 1967–68."

33. Kurtzberg, *Shorthanded*, 9.

34. Baun and Logan, *Lowering the Boom*, 80.

35. Cory Suppes, "NHL California Seals First Training Camp," Oakland Seals Page, http://www.eskimo.com/~pem/oakseal.htm (defunct link).

36. Baun and Logan, *Lowering the Boom*, 190.

37. Beddoes, Fischler, and Gitler, *Hockey!*, 115.

38. "Big Fines for Seals, Bruins," *San Mateo Times*, December 26, 1967.

39. Beddoes, Fischler, and Gitler, *Hockey!*, 114.

40. Beddoes, Fischler, and Gitler, *Hockey!*, 113.

41. Baun and Logan, *Lowering the Boom*, 190.

42. Laroche, *Changing the Game*, 74.

43. Proudfoot, *Pro Hockey '69–'70*, 87.

44. Podnieks, *Shooting Stars*, 90.

45. "Ice Mishap Claims Life of Player," *Winnipeg Free Press*, January 15, 1968.

46. Kurtzberg, *Shorthanded*, 54.

47. Kurtzberg, *Shorthanded*, 54.

48. "Ice Mishap Claims Life."

49. Rich Roberts, "Harris Walkout to Stir Revolt?" *Long Beach (CA) Press-Telegram*, January 23, 1968.

50. Roberts, "Harris Walkout to Stir Revolt?"

51. Roberts, "Harris Walkout to Stir Revolt?"

52. Baun and Logan, *Lowering the Boom*, 190.

53. "Hawk on the Wing," *Time*, March 1, 1968.

54. McFarlane, *One Hundred Years*, 97.

55. Laroche, *Changing the Game*, 77.

56. "Oakland Owner Says NHL Team Will Stay," *Cornwall Standard-Freeholder*, December 22, 1967.

57. Canadian Press, "B.C. NL Hockey Hopes Soar," *Winnipeg Free Press*, March 13, 1968.

58. Canadian Press, "B.C. NL Hockey Hopes Soar."

59. Kurtzberg, *Shorthanded*, 12.

60. Jenish, *NHL*, 199.

61. Kurtzberg, *Shorthanded*, 12.

62. Scott Graves, "Reorganized Seals to Stay in Area," *Fremont (CA) Argus*, May 25, 1968.

63. Spence Conley, "Seals Lose to Rangers," *Oakland Tribune*, November 2, 1967.

64. Beddoes, Fischler, and Gitler, *Hockey!*, 93.

65. Kurtzberg, *Shorthanded*, 5.

66. Kurtzberg, *Shorthanded*, 7.

67. Rich Roberts, "Kings' Title Hopes Killed," *Long Beach Independent Press-Telegram*, March 31, 1968.

68. Michael Watson, "No Place Like Home . . . But Where Is It?" *Hayward Daily Review*, April 8, 1968.

3. *The Three Musketeers, 1968–1969*

1. Graves, "Reorganized Seals to Stay."

2. Rich Gohlke, "Difficult Task Ahead for Seals," *Fremont Argus*, May 25, 1968.

3. "New Seal Coach Impresses Scribes," *Oakland Tribune*, May 24, 1968.

4. Beddoes, Fischler, and Gitler, *Hockey!*, 116.

5. "New Seal Coach Impresses Scribes."

6. Ed Schoenfeld, "Seals Name Business Manager," *Oakland Tribune*, September 5, 1968.

7. Spence Conley, "Vadnais Is Mod—and Mad," *Oakland Tribune*, September 23, 1969.

8. Ed Levitt, "Carol—Top Puncher," *Oakland Tribune*, December 16, 1969.

9. Baun and Logan, *Lowering the Boom*, 198.

10. Spence Conley, "Seal Boss Applies Some Glue," *Oakland Tribune*, June 8, 1968.

11. Spence Conley, "Seals Open NHL Friday," *Oakland Tribune*, October 6, 1968.

12. Michael Watson, "Great Skating Gives Seals Win," *Hayward Daily Review*, November 2, 1968.

13. Spence Conley, "New Faces, Same Results for Seals," *Oakland Tribune*, November 13, 1968.

14. Spence Conley, "Seals Edge Detroit," *Oakland Tribune*, November 14, 1968.

15. Spence Conley, "Seals Win, in 2nd," *Oakland Tribune*, December 7, 1968.

16. Spence Conley, "Seals Lose Again to Blues, 1–0," *Oakland Tribune*, December 21, 1968.

17. Kurtzberg, *Shorthanded*, 13.
18. Canadian Press, "Latest Seal Move, to Buffalo, Denied," *Winnipeg Free Press*, December 24, 1968.
19. "Buffalo Group Buys Seals," *Winnipeg Free Press*, January 10, 1969.
20. Kurtzberg, *Shorthanded*, 13.
21. Spence Conley, "Seals Future Looking Up," *Oakland Tribune*, March 2, 1969.
22. Kurtzberg, *Shorthanded*, 15.
23. Kurtzberg, *Shorthanded*, 14.
24. "Windup to Seals Sale," *Oakland Tribune*, May 20, 1969.
25. Ronberg, "Freddie's In, Gloom's Out," *Sports Illustrated*, March 10, 1969.
26. Ronberg, "Freddie's In, Gloom's Out."
27. Conley, "Seals Future Looking Up."
28. Kurtzberg, *Shorthanded*, 14.
29. Spence Conley. "Kings Trounce Seals, 8–5," *Oakland Tribune*, February 2, 1969.
30. Rich Roberts, "Kings Live Up to 'Guarantee,' Top Seals in Wild Forum Game," *Long Beach Independent Press-Telegram*, February 2, 1969.
31. "Stick Fight Sets Off Kings-Seals' Feelings," *Hockey News*, February 15, 1969, 7.
32. Kurtzberg, *Shorthanded*, 61.
33. Spence Conley, "Seals Rally; Face Bruins," *Oakland Tribune*, February 27, 1969.
34. Conley, "Seals Rally; Face Bruins."
35. Ed Levitt, "Glover's the Name," *Oakland Tribune*, February 27, 1969.
36. Michael Watson, "Seal 'Bad One' Expected," *Hayward Daily Review*, February 28, 1969.
37. Michael Watson, "'No Duel'-Seal Whiz," *Hayward Daily Review*, March 17, 1969.
38. Thomas LaRocca, "The First All-California Series," April 15, 2009, We Are All Kings, http://kings.nhl.com/club/news.htm?id=456812#&navid =lak-search.
39. Michael Watson, "Seals Gun for Equalizer," *Hayward Daily Review*, April 3, 1969.
40. Michael Watson, "Abscessed Tooth May Be Seal Key," *Hayward Daily Review*, April 4, 1969.
41. Michael Watson, "Next Game Key One for Seals," *Hayward Daily Review*, April 7, 1969.
42. "Seals, Kings, Tied in Playoffs, Meet on Oakland Ice Tonight," *Oxnard (CA) Press-Courier*, April 9, 1969.

43. Hugh McDonald, "Finale Tonight Say Seals," *San Mateo Times*, April 10, 1969.
44. Hugh McDonald, "Finale Tonight Say Seals," *San Mateo Times*, April 10, 1969.
45. Hugh McDonald, "Finale Tonight Say Seals," *San Mateo Times*, April 10, 1969.
46. Michael Watson, "Seals Now Wait for 'Next Year,'" *Hayward Daily Review*, April 14, 1969.
47. Watson, "Seals Now Wait."
48. Watson, "Seals Now Wait."
49. Proudfoot, *Pro Hockey '69–'70*, 27.
50. Proudfoot, *Pro Hockey '69–'70*, 26.
51. Levitt, "Glover's the Name."
52. Levitt, "Glover's the Name."
53. Spence Conley, "Selke, Seal Success Key," *Oakland Tribune*, March 29, 1969.

4. Hung Over, 1969–1970

1. George Ross, "Seals Set Their Course to Lick a Curse," *Oakland Tribune*, October 3, 1969.
2. Levitt, "Carol—Top Puncher."
3. Levitt, "Carol—Top Puncher."
4. Levitt, "Carol—Top Puncher."
5. Ross, "Seals Set Their Course."
6. Ed Levitt, "A Cool Romance," *Oakland Tribune*, February 26, 1970.
7. George Ross, "His Pitch Is Catching," *Oakland Tribune*, October 10, 1969.
8. "Veterans Are Soft Says Coach of Hockey Team," *Ukiah (CA) Daily Journal*, September 30, 1969.
9. "Coach Bum-Rapping Me: Smith," *San Mateo Times*, October 4, 1969.
10. Spence Conley, "Seals, Hawks Mix in Arena," *Oakland Tribune*, October 29, 1969.
11. Spence Conley, "Hampson Fights a Slump," *Oakland Tribune*, October 28, 1969.
12. Conley, "Hampson Fights a Slump."
13. Spence Conley, "Rangers Ride Herd on Seals, 8-1," *Oakland Tribune*, November 8, 1969.
14. Spence Conley, "Bruins Skin Seals," *Oakland Tribune*, November 11, 1969.
15. Graham Cox, "Seals up against Brick Wall," *Cornwall Standard-Freeholder*, January 3, 1970.

16. Hugh McDonald, "Seals' Problem? They Don't Think," *San Mateo Times*, January 8, 1970.
17. McDonald, "Seals' Problem?"
18. Rich Gohlke, "Seals Goalie Keeps Smiling," *Fremont Argus*, January 17, 1970.
19. Michael Watson, "Seals End NY Hex," *Hayward Daily Review*, February 14, 1970.
20. Proudfoot, *Pro Hockey '70-'71*, 102.
21. Michael Watson, "Seal Horses Must Develop More Power," *Hayward Daily Review*, January 8, 1970.
22. Kurtzberg, *Shorthanded*, 114.
23. Spence Conley, "Freak Goal Beats Seals," *Oakland Tribune*, April 9, 1970.
24. Ed Levitt, "A Loser Wins One," *Oakland Tribune*, April 9, 1970.
25. Conley, "Freak Goal Beats Seals."
26. Ed Levitt, "Blame It on Fred," *Oakland Tribune*, April 10, 1970.
27. Levitt, "Blame It on Fred."
28. Levitt, "Blame It on Fred."
29. Hugh McDonald, "Seals Need More Brawn," *San Mateo Times*, April 13, 1970.
30. Kurtzberg, *Shorthanded*, 70.
31. Spence Conley, "New Tune for Old Seals," *Oakland Tribune*, April 16, 1970.
32. Conley, "New Tune for Old Seals."
33. Conley, "New Tune for Old Seals."
34. Proudfoot, *Pro Hockey '69-'70*, 24.
35. Conley, "New Tune for Old Seals."
36. Hugh McDonald, "McDonald's Ice Chips," *San Mateo Times*, April 13, 1970.
37. Conley, "New Tune for Old Seals."

5. Fools' Gold, 1970–1971

1. Levitt, "Blame It on Fred."
2. Kurtzberg, *Shorthanded*, 15.
3. McDonald, "McDonald's Ice Chips," April 13, 1970.
4. Kurtzberg, *Shorthanded*, 15.
5. Proudfoot, *Pro Hockey '70-'71*, 100.
6. Kurtzberg, *Shorthanded*, 15–16.
7. Spence Conley, "Bitter Seal Trial Opening," *Oakland Tribune*, May 24, 1970.
8. Spence Conley, "Ranger-Seal Squabble," *Oakland Tribune*, May 22, 1970.

9. Spence Conley, "Court Finds Seals in Default," *Oakland Tribune*, June 1, 1970.
10. Green and Launius, *Charlie Finley*, 90.
11. "Seltzer Faces Final Hurdle," *Fremont Argus*, June 17, 1970.
12. "Should Seals Wear Spats?" *Newsweek*, June 29, 1970.
13. Jenish, NHL, 202.
14. Kurtzberg, *Shorthanded*, 19–20.
15. Green and Launius, *Charlie Finley*, 22.
16. Green and Launius, *Charlie Finley*, 26–27.
17. Green and Launius, *Charlie Finley*, 56–57.
18. Green and Launius, *Charlie Finley*, 58.
19. Green and Launius, *Charlie Finley*, 114.
20. "Mickey Mantle Quotes," *Baseball Almanac*, http://www.baseball-almanac.com/quotes/quomant.shtml.
21. Green and Launius, *Charlie Finley*, 46.
22. Kurtzberg, *Shorthanded*, 21.
23. Glen Goodhand, "Believe It or Not," *Society for International Hockey Research Newsletter*, March 2013, 9.
24. Kurtzberg, *Shorthanded*, 139.
25. "Should Seals Wear Spats?"
26. "COF: I Know Nothing about Hockey," *Fremont Argus*, July 7, 1970.
27. "California Golden Seals," *Fremont Argus*, October 15, 1970.
28. Steve Tadevich, "Finley Adds More Color to Golden Seals," *Fremont Argus*, October 16, 1970.
29. Tadevich, "Finley Adds More Color."
30. Rich Chere, "Before Lou Lamoriello, Devils Made Waves in NHL, There Was Charlie Finley and His Golden Seals," *NJ.com*, August 15, 2010, http://www.nj.com/devils/index.ssf/2010/08/before_lou_lamoriello_devils_m.html.
31. Chere, "Before Lou Lamoriello."
32. Chere, "Before Lou Lamoriello."
33. John Porter, "Finley Snips at Seals' Red Ink," *Oakland Tribune*, October 2, 1970.
34. Glen Goodhand, "Believe It or Not," *Society for International Hockey Research Newsletter*, November 2011.
35. Greig, *Big Bucks*, 107–8.
36. McDonald, "Seals Need More Brawn."
37. John Porter, "Elusive Lady and the Seal," *Oakland Tribune*, January 26, 1971.
38. Kurtzberg, *Shorthanded*, 122.

39. Adam Proteau, "Hextall's Passion Ran in the Family," *Hockey News*, February 24, 2004.

40. Spence Conley, "Hextall Impresses in Seal Workouts," *Oakland Tribune*, September 17, 1970.

41. John Porter, "Detroit Giggles at Seal Uniforms," *Oakland Tribune*, October 11, 1970.

42. John Porter, "Seals Burn Toronto, 8–4," *Oakland Tribune*, November 7, 1970.

43. John Porter, "Seals Blank Canadiens," *Oakland Tribune*, November 12, 1970.

44. Porter, "Seals Blank Canadiens."

45. Kurtzberg, *Shorthanded*, 23.

46. Kurtzberg, *Shorthanded*, 23.

47. Kurtzberg, *Shorthanded*, 23.

48. John Porter, "Seal Front Office Feud," *Oakland Tribune*, November 13, 1970.

49. Porter, "Seal Front Office Feud."

50. Ross Brewitt, "Frank Selke Jr. Was 1-of-a-Kind," *Thunder Bay (ON) Chronicle-Journal*, March 22, 2013, http://www.chroniclejournal.com /sports/frank-selke-jr-was--of-a-kind/article_e7a7a0ca-dd29-5c77-85bb -5d0977dfd04c.html.

51. Kurtzberg, *Shorthanded*, 23.

52. John Porter, "A Third Hat for Glover," *Oakland Tribune*, November 26, 1970.

53. Porter, "Third Hat for Glover."

54. Chere, "Before Lou Lamoriello."

55. Steve Tadevich, "Finley Adds More Color to Golden Seals," *Fremont Argus*, October 16, 1970.

56. John Porter, "Seals Totter Past Wings," *Oakland Tribune*, December 17, 1970.

57. Hugh McDonald, "Seals Play Aceless Foe," *San Mateo Times*, January 16, 1971.

58. Michael Watson, "Finley Pays for Hat-Trick," *Hayward Daily Review*, January 28, 1971.

59. John Porter, "Seals Trade Hampson to Stars," *Oakland Tribune*, February 24, 1971.

60. Ed Levitt, "Blood on the Ice," *Oakland Tribune*, February 4, 1971.

61. "No Trade in Sight for Sinking Seals," *Oakland Tribune*, February 4, 1971.

62. Milt Richman, "Losing Nightmarish Habit Now for Seals' Glover," *Fremont Argus*, March 24, 1971.

63. Ed Levitt, "A Cold Season," *Oakland Tribune*, March 16, 1971.

64. Proudfoot, *Pro Hockey '71-'72*, 145.

65. Levitt, "Cold Season," *Oakland Tribune*, March 16, 1971.

66. Kurtzberg, *Shorthanded*, 122.

67. Ian MacLaine, "'It Could Be Worse,'" *Cornwall Standard-Freeholder*, April 3, 1971.

68. Levitt, "Cold Season," *Oakland Tribune*, March 16, 1971.

6. Young Blood, 1971–1972

1. John Porter, "Sheehan Excites 'em on Left Side," *Oakland Tribune*, December 17, 1971.

2. Kurtzberg, *Shorthanded*, 145.

3. Kurtzberg, *Shorthanded*, 144.

4. Proudfoot, *Pro Hockey '71-'72*, 144.

5. Kurtzberg, *Shorthanded*, 172.

6. Greig, *Big Bucks*, 70.

7. Kurtzberg, *Shorthanded*, 171.

8. Kurtzberg, *Shorthanded*, 93.

9. Bill Libby, "Hockey Ad Lib," *Hockey News*, November 12, 1971, 8.

10. Proudfoot, *Pro Hockey '71-'72*, 144.

11. Bill Libby, "Hockey Ad Lib," *Hockey News*, March 31, 1972, 8.

12. John Porter, "Seals Blast a Bad Deal," *Oakland Tribune*, September 29, 1971.

13. Porter, "Seals Blast a Bad Deal."

14. "Carleton Proves He's Seals 'Big Man' in Tie with Leafs," *Hayward Daily Review*, October 11, 1971.

15. Hugh McDonald, "'Mystery to Glover,'" *San Mateo Times*, October 16, 1971.

16. McDonald, "'Mystery to Glover.'"

17. Hugh McDonald, "Seals' New Leader Sounds Like Glover," *San Mateo Times*, October 16, 1971.

18. Greig, *Big Bucks*, 95–96.

19. Kurtzberg, *Shorthanded*, 137.

20. Kurtzberg, *Shorthanded*, 111–12.

21. Irvin, *In the Crease*, 133.

22. McDonald, "Seals' New Leader."

23. John Porter, "Seals' Rookie Goaler Meloche Shocks Bruins with Net Play," *Hockey News*, November 19, 1971.

24. John Porter, "Even Novice Beats Seals," *Oakland Tribune*, March 20, 1971.

25. Kurtzberg, *Shorthanded*, 174.

26. John Porter, "Reinstated Pinder Puts Life in Seals with 'Hat,'" *Hockey News*, November 12, 1971, 14.
27. Kurtzberg, *Shorthanded*, 133.
28. Porter, "Reinstated Pinder."
29. Dave Stubbs, "Spotlight: Golden Seals Were Big Deal for Goalie Meloche," *Montreal (QC) Gazette*, January 7, 2011, http://www .montrealgazette.com (defunct link).
30. Geoffrey Fisher, "Meloche Became Goaltender by Volunteering," *Hockey News*, February 8, 1974, 22.
31. Frank Barrett Jr., "Goalie Frustrates B's," *Lowell (MA) Sun*, October 29, 1971.
32. Kurtzberg, *Shorthanded*, 137.
33. John Hickey, "Leafs Look Like Old Seals—New Seals Romp," *Hayward Daily Review*, November 8, 1971.
34. John Porter, "Shaggy Hair and All Redmond Considered Future Seals' Star," *Hockey News*, November 26, 1971, 36.
35. Proudfoot, *Pro Hockey '72-'73*, 120.
36. John Porter, "Unhappy in Oakland, Seals Trade Vadnais," *Hockey News*, March 10, 1972, 2.
37. Kurtzberg, *Shorthanded*, 223.
38. Kurtzberg, *Shorthanded*, 211.
39. Libby, "Hockey Ad Lib," *Hockey News*, November 12, 1971.
40. John Porter, "Rejuvenated Seals Rate as Comeback Team of Year," *Hockey News*, January 7, 1972, 14.
41. "No White Shoes for Seals—Yet," *Hayward Daily Review*, June 30, 1970.
42. Kurtzberg, *Shorthanded*, 143.
43. John Porter, "Seals Face Vancouver," *Oakland Tribune*, January 14, 1972.
44. Tony Cooper, "Seals Were a Bad Team but Good for Laughs," *San Francisco Chronicle*, October 1, 1991.
45. McDonald, "'Mystery to Glover.'"
46. Jenish, *NHL*, 223.
47. Chere, "Before Lou Lamoriello."
48. John Porter, "Now Seals Are Loving It," *Oakland Tribune*, January 31, 1972.
49. Porter, "Now Seals Are Loving It."
50. John Porter, "Young Figures Trade Will Assure Seals of Spot in Playoffs," *Hockey News*, March 17, 1972, 40.
51. Porter, "Young Figures Trade."
52. Libby, "Hockey Ad Lib," March 31, 1972.
53. Michael Watson, "Slumping Seals Stunned," *Hayward Daily Review*, February 24, 1972.

54. Watson, "Slumping Seals Stunned."
55. Watson, "Slumping Seals Stunned."
56. John Porter, "Seals Executive Quits," *Oakland Tribune*, February 27, 1972.
57. Hugh McDonald, "Seals Will Be Up Tomorrow," *San Mateo Times*, March 18, 1972.
58. McDonald, "Seals Will Be Up Tomorrow."
59. Timothy Gassen, "The WHA Invades NYC: Bill Verigan and the Raiders," *World Hockey Association Hall of Fame*, March 17, 2011, http://www.whahof.com/Raiders-feature.html.
60. Proudfoot, *Pro Hockey '72-'73*, 116–17.
61. Proudfoot, *Pro Hockey '72-'73*, 118.
62. John Porter, "Baseball Delays Seals," *Oakland Tribune*, April 12, 1972.

7. Goodbye, Oakland, 1972–1973

1. Milt Dunnell, "NHL Set to Battle New WHA in Court," *Hockey News*, March 10, 1972, 19.
2. Joyce, *Devil and Bobby Hull*, 113.
3. Greig, *Big Bucks*, 13.
4. John Porter, "Baseball Delays Seals," *Oakland Tribune*, April 12, 1972.
5. Cruise and Griffiths, *Net Worth*, 268.
6. Greig, *Big Bucks*, 124–25.
7. Greig, *Big Bucks*, 124.
8. Greig, *Big Bucks*, 124.
9. Greig, *Big Bucks*, 132.
10. Kurtzberg, *Shorthanded*, 173.
11. Greig, *Big Bucks*, 70.
12. Kurtzberg, *Shorthanded*, 126.
13. Eric Prewitt, "Finley Skates on Thin Ice," *Oakland Tribune*, December 1, 1972.
14. John Porter, "Seals Missed Chance to Sign Shmyr Early," *Oakland Tribune*, July 28, 1972.
15. "Finley's Seals Get Glover Back," *Hayward Daily Review*, August 2, 1972.
16. Bill Libby, "Hockey Ad Lib," *Hockey News*, February 22, 1974, 8.
17. "Fickle Finley Plays Managerial Yo-Yo," *San Mateo Times*, August 4, 1972.
18. Kurtzberg, *Shorthanded*, 140.
19. Kurtzberg, *Shorthanded*, 27.
20. "It's Official—Will Serve Dual Post," *San Mateo Times*, August 19, 1972.
21. "Quick on the Draw: Morris Mott," *Brandon (MB) Westman Journal*, February 10, 2010, http://www.westmanjournal.com/article/20100210/brandon0802/302109780/-1/brandon/quick-on-the-draw-151-morris-mott.

22. Mark Mulvoy, "Hockey 72/73: Money Makes the Puck Go," *Sports Illustrated*, October 9, 1972.
23. John Porter, "Losing Seal Happy for A's," *Oakland Tribune*, October 23, 1972.
24. Kurtzberg, *Shorthanded*, 206.
25. Kurtzberg, *Shorthanded*, 201–3.
26. John Porter, "A Hat Trick Ignites the Seals," *Oakland Tribune*, November 4, 1972.
27. Ken McKenzie, "Passing the Puck," *Hockey News*, October 26, 1973, 4.
28. "VP & GM Glover Seeks a Coach," *Oakland Tribune*, November 10, 1972.
29. Kurtzberg, *Shorthanded*, 132
30. Green and Launius, *Charlie Finley*, 178–79.
31. Kurtzberg, *Shorthanded*, 27.
32. "Finley Halves Seals Ticket Prices," *Oakland Tribune*, January 5, 1973.
33. Kurtzberg, *Shorthanded*, 131.
34. Kurtzberg, *Shorthanded*, 132.
35. "Trade Reason 'Simple,'" *San Mateo Times*, December 7, 1972.
36. Hugh McDonald, "Play Time, Pay Time," *San Mateo Times*, December 7, 1972.
37. "Trade Reason 'Simple.'"
38. John Porter, "Charlie O's Angry Blast," *Oakland Tribune*, January 4, 1973.
39. "Finley Halves Seals Ticket Prices."
40. Porter, "Charlie O's Angry Blast."
41. Geoffrey Fisher, "Finley Raps Young for Player Handling," *Hockey News*, January 26, 1973.
42. Porter, "Charlie O's Angry Blast."
43. Geoffrey Fisher, "Young Looking for More Muscle," *Hockey News*, March 22, 1974, 22.
44. Stan Fischler, "Charlie O's Golden Seals Turning to Rust," *Winnipeg Free Press*, December 12, 1972.
45. Porter, "Charlie O's Angry Blast," *Oakland Tribune*, January 4, 1973.
46. "Young Admits His Errors, But . . . ," *Winnipeg Free Press*, January 13, 1973.
47. "Young Admits His Errors."
48. "Young Admits His Errors."
49. "Young Admits His Errors."
50. "Young Admits His Errors."
51. Geoffrey Fisher, "Report NHL Ready to Take Over Seals," *Hockey News*, March 30, 1973, 20.
52. Geoffrey Fisher, "Disillusioned Finley Ready to Unload Seals for Price," *Hockey News*, March 2, 1973, 14.

53. "Mikita Again Terrorizing Goalies after Two Bad Seasons," *Cornwall Standard-Freeholder*, January 8, 1973.

54. "Ex-Seals Place Blame on Finley," *Hayward Daily Review*, January 9, 1973.

55. "Seals' Blanda Gets Tie," *Oakland Tribune*, November 10, 1972.

56. John Porter, "Seal Goalie Blunts Sabres in 5–1 Win," *Oakland Tribune*, November 18, 1972.

57. Kurtzberg, *Shorthanded*, 140.

58. Geoffrey Fisher, "Seals Facing Pathetic but Promising Future in NHL," *Hockey News*, January 12, 1973, 10.

59. John Porter, "Get Seals to Rink on Time," *Oakland Tribune*, January 3, 1973.

60. Lloyd Johnston, "Flames Take Over Second Shutout Maple Leafs," *Cornwall Standard-Freeholder*, January 13, 1973.

61. Ken McKenzie, "Passing the Puck," *Hockey News*, January 19, 1973, 4.

62. Brewitt, *Into the Empty Net*, 115.

63. John Porter, "Seals Shake Hex," *Oakland Tribune*, February 24, 1973.

64. Hugh McDonald, "McDonald's Ice Chips," *San Mateo Times*, March 15, 1973, 21.

65. Hugh McDonald, "McDonald's Ice Chips," *San Mateo Times*, March 17, 1973, 6.

66. Ed Levitt, "Seals Vow Mass Defection to World Hockey," *Oakland Tribune*, March 14, 1973.

67. Levitt, "Seals Vow Mass Defection."

68. Levitt, "Seals Vow Mass Defection."

69. Levitt, "Seals Vow Mass Defection."

70. John Porter, "NHL Would Like Finley to 'Bow Out,'" *Oakland Tribune*, March 15, 1973.

71. Porter, "NHL Would Like Finley."

72. Proudfoot, *Pro Hockey '73–'74*, 168.

73. Proudfoot, *Pro Hockey '73–'74*, 165.

74. Proudfoot, *Pro Hockey '73–'74*, 165.

75. Eric Prewitt, "Finley Skates on Thin Ice," *Oakland Tribune*, December 1, 1972.

8. Big Hats, No Cattle, 1973–1974

1. Geoffrey Fisher, "Team Has Potential, Attitude Must Change," *Hockey News*, April 13, 1973, 17.

2. John Porter, "Off the Ice, Seals Battle Coach," *Oakland Tribune*, January 18, 1974.

3. Kurtzberg, *Shorthanded*, 206.

4. Porter, "Off the Ice."
5. Libby, "Hockey Ad Lib," *Hockey News*, February 22, 1974.
6. Fisher, "Team Has Potential."
7. Bill Libby, "Hockey Ad Lib," *Hockey News*, June 1973, 8.
8. Kurtzberg, *Shorthanded*, 184.
9. Kurtzberg, *Shorthanded*, 198–99.
10. Proudfoot, *Pro Hockey '73–'74*, 165.
11. Geoffrey Fisher, "McKechnie Shaping Up as Seals' New Ice Leader," *Hockey News*, October 19, 1973, 17.
12. Geoffrey Fisher, "'We're Going to Surprise a Lot of People,'" *Hockey News*, October 5, 1973, 8.
13. Proudfoot, *Pro Hockey '73–'74*, 163, 83.
14. "Glover Claims Seals' New Attitude Will Overcome Persistent Sale Talk," *Hockey News*, June, 1973, 18.
15. Ken McKenzie, "Passing the Puck," *Hockey News*, October 19, 1973, 4.
16. "Seals Surprise: Finley's Other Team Is Unbeaten," *Hayward Daily Review*, October 11, 1973.
17. "Seals Surprise."
18. "Seals' Attitude Is Determination," *Hayward Daily Review*, October 13, 1973.
19. Geoffrey Fisher, "It's All in the Mind with the Golden Seals," *Hockey News*, January 11, 1974.
20. Joe DeLoach, "Boldirev Decides It Was Worth It," *Hayward Daily Review*, January 11, 1974.
21. John Porter, "Detroit Lesson Pays for Seals," *Oakland Tribune*, October 25, 1973.
22. Porter, "Detroit Lesson."
23. John Porter, "Meloche Out 2 Months," *Oakland Tribune*, November 29, 1973.
24. Porter, "Meloche Out 2 Months."
25. Porter, "Meloche Out 2 Months."
26. Kurtzberg, *Shorthanded*, 190.
27. John Porter, "Seals Square Off against Broad Street Bullies," *Oakland Tribune*, January 25, 1974.
28. Brewitt, *Into the Empty Net*, 115.
29. Bill Fleischman, "Cummins Regrets Near Tragic High-Sticking of Flyers' Clarke," *Hockey News*, December 21, 1973, 2.
30. Schultz and Fischler, *Hammer*, 99.
31. Fleischman, "Cummins Regrets."
32. Canadian Press, "6 Players Ejected during Brawling Game in Philly," *Cornwall Standard-Freeholder*, December 3, 1973.

33. Canadian Press, "Glover Looking for the Answer," *Cornwall Standard-Freeholder*, December 15, 1973.
34. Hugh McDonald, "McDonald's Ice Chips," *San Mateo Times*, January 10, 1974.
35. Kurtzberg, *Shorthanded*, 227.
36. Hugh McDonald, "McDonald's Ice Chips," *San Mateo Times*, February 7, 1974.
37. John Porter, "Seal Who'd Like to Say So Long," *Oakland Tribune*, February 5, 1974.
38. Hugh McDonald, "Seals' Game Plan: It's Really No Joke," *San Mateo Times*, January 12, 1974.
39. McDonald, "McDonald's Ice Chips," February 7, 1974.
40. John Porter, "Glover Fumes over 7–0 Rout," *Oakland Tribune*, February 26, 1973.
41. "Hull Says Hat Trick a Cinch vs. Seals," *Hayward Daily Review*, January 7, 1974.
42. Hugh McDonald, "Seals, Ice Real Slowpokes," *San Mateo Times*, January 14, 1974.
43. John Porter, "Do Seals Need a Psychiatrist on the Road?" *Oakland Tribune*, January 31, 1974.
44. Geoffrey Fisher, "Seals Head towards All-Time Record," *Hockey News*, January 25, 1974, 20.
45. Porter, "Do Seals Need a Psychiatrist?"
46. Fisher, "Seals Head towards All-Time Record."
47. Geoffrey Fisher, "Seals' Players Hail News Club Will Have New Owner," *Hockey News*, February 1, 1974, 22.
48. Fisher, "Seals' Players Hail News."
49. Fisher, "Seals' Players Hail News."
50. Jenish, *NHL*, 222.
51. "Finley Sells Seals, Admits Failure," *Palm Beach (FL) Post*, February 15, 1974.
52. "Glover Quits as Coach of Golden Seals," *Modesto (CA) Bee*, February 17, 1974.
53. Fisher, "Young Looking for More Muscle."
54. Geoffrey Fisher, "Glover Out As NHL Takes Over," *Hockey News*, March 1, 1974, 23.
55. Leach, *Riverton Rifle*, 62.
56. Fisher, "Glover Out."
57. Kurtzberg, *Shorthanded*, 209.
58. *Professional Hockey Handbook*, 95.

59. Pete Manzolillo, email message to author, December 4, 2013.

60. Kurtzberg, *Shorthanded*, 230.

61. "Streaker Shows at Seals' Loss," *San Rafael (CA) Independent-Journal*, April 6, 1974, 13.

62. Hugh McDonald, "McDonald's Ice Chips," *San Mateo Times*, April 6, 1974.

63. Kurtzberg, *Shorthanded*, 317.

64. Fisher, "'We're Going to Surprise.'"

65. Kurtzberg, *Shorthanded*, 213.

66. Rich Gohlke, "Buy the Seals—Why?" *Fremont Argus*, January 15, 1974.

67. Joe DeLoach, "Learning-to-Win-Again Seals Play to a Deadlock," *Hayward Daily Review*, March 28, 1974, 25.

9. Restoring Pride, 1974–1975

1. "Improving Seals Should Stay Put," *Hayward Daily Review*, February 2, 1975.

2. "Improving Seals Should Stay Put."

3. "Improving Seals Should Stay Put."

4. Kurtzberg, *Shorthanded*, 245.

5. Proudfoot, *Pro Hockey '74–'75*, 142.

6. Joe DeLoach, "MacAdam: Seals' Almost Invisible Man," *Hayward Daily Review*, October 28, 1975.

7. Proudfoot, *Pro Hockey '74–'75*, 141.

8. Proudfoot, *Pro Hockey '74–'75*, 141.

9. Lowell Hickey, "Rather Fight Than Retreat," *Hayward Daily Review*, July 7, 1974.

10. Mark Mulvoy, "These Seals Refuse to Play Dead," *Sports Illustrated*, January 1975, 60–61.

11. Hickey, "Rather Fight Than Retreat."

12. Hickey, "Rather Fight Than Retreat."

13. Gordon Sakamoto, "Seals Showing a Brand New Look," *Fremont Argus*, August 25, 1974.

14. Sakamoto, "Seals Showing."

15. Sakamoto, "Seals Showing."

16. Rich Gohlke, "High Command," *Fremont Argus*, December 12, 1974.

17. Mulvoy, "Seals Refuse to Play Dead."

18. Jim Proudfoot, NHL *Pro Hockey '75–'76*, 182.

19. Lyle Richardson, "Interview with Former NHL Goalie Gary 'Cobra' Simmons," *FoxSports.com*, February 2, 2007, http://community.foxsports.com /Spector/blog/2007/02/02/Interview_with_Former_nhl_Goalie_Gary _Cobra_Simmons_Part_One (defunct link).

20. Kurtzberg, *Shorthanded*, 245.

21. Gary Mueller, "Flyers Back in Form . . . Alley-Fighting Experts," *Sporting News*, November 16, 1974, now available at http://goldensealshockey.com/wp-content/uploads/2016/06/Flyers-Back-in-Form-Brawl-with-Seals-Nov-16-1974.pdf.

22. "Seals, Flyers Battle in 40-Minute Brawl," *Altoona (PA) Mirror*, October 26, 1974.

23. Mueller, "Flyers Back in Form."

24. Schultz and Fischler, *Hammer*, 100.

25. John Porter, "Traded Seals Are Very Happy to Go," *Oakland Tribune*, November 12, 1974.

26. Jack Bluth, "Speaking of Sports: Statistics Not Always Deceiving," *San Mateo Times*, October 17, 1975.

27. Hugh McDonald, "Seals Show Grit . . . Humble Boston," *San Mateo Times*, December 28, 1974.

28. Canadian Press, "Flyers on Top but Good Now," *Lethbridge Herald*, January 2, 1975.

29. John Porter, "Rambunctious Seals Spank the Champs," *Oakland Tribune*, January 6, 1975.

30. Porter, "Rambunctious Seals."

31. Kurtzberg, *Shorthanded*, 260.

32. Joe DeLoach, "Johnston: 'I Stood Up for What I Believed In,'" *Hayward Daily Review*, January 23, 1975.

33. Canadian Press, "Penguins Down Hapless Seals," *Cornwall Standard-Freeholder*, January 23, 1975.

34. DeLoach, "Johnston."

35. Joe DeLoach, "New Coach Says Same Old Things," *Fremont Argus*, January 26, 1975, 14.

36. DeLoach, "Johnston."

37. "Seals Start Grumbling," *Hayward Daily Review*, February 19, 1975.

38. "Seals Host Toronto, Deny Montreal Rumors," *Hayward Daily Review*, January 24, 1975.

39. Ed Schoenfeld, "Seals' Fate by June," *Oakland Tribune*, February 4, 1975.

40. Schoenfeld, "Seals' Fate by June."

41. "NHL Aids Pittsburgh, Eyes Two New Teams," *Elyria (OH) Chronicle-Telegram*, February 2, 1975.

42. Garry Niver, "Coliseum's Iron-Clad Pacts," *San Mateo Times*, February 20, 1975.

43. "Seals Jeopardizing NHL," *Hayward Daily Review*, December 5, 1974.

44. Kenneth Lehn and Michael Sykuta, "Antitrust and Franchise Relocation in Professional Sports: An Economic Analysis of the Raiders Case,"

Antitrust Bulletin, September 22, 1997, *Business Highbeam*, http://Business
.highbeam.com/420683/article-1g1-20374310/antitrust-and-franchise
-relocation-professional-sports (defunct link).

45. "NHL Aids Pittsburgh."
46. Proudfoot, *NHL Pro Hockey '75–'76*, 184.
47. Hugh McDonald, "NHL's Worst Team?" *San Mateo Times*, March 29, 1975.
48. Kurtzberg, *Shorthanded*, 256.
49. Jack Lynch, email message to author, September 7, 2014.
50. Proudfoot, *NHL Pro Hockey '75–'76*, 184.
51. Joe DeLoach, "Seals Wind Down, Survey the Long, Long Season," *Hayward Daily Review*, April 8, 1975.
52. Tony Cooper, "Seals Were a Bad Team but Good for Laughs," *San Francisco Chronicle*, October 1, 1991.
53. "Swig Completes NHL Deal," *Hayward Daily Review*, July 29, 1975.
54. Hugh McDonald, "Swig Submits Offer for Seals," *San Mateo Times*, May 23, 1975.
55. McDonald, "Swig Submits Offer."
56. John Porter, "Seals Fans Hope Swig Is a Modern Moses," *Oakland Tribune*, May 2, 1975.
57. Porter, "Seals Fans Hope."
58. Joe DeLoach, "Seals Must Find Winning Attitude," *Hayward Daily Review*, September 15, 1975.
59. DeLoach, "Seals Wind Down."
60. "Swig Completes NHL Deal."

10. Swig vs. Moscone, 1975–1976

1. Kurtzberg, *Shorthanded*, 213.
2. John Porter, "Seals in Turmoil: Joey Wants Out," *Oakland Tribune*, November 21, 1974.
3. Proudfoot, *NHL Pro Hockey '75–'76*, 183.
4. Kurtzberg, *Shorthanded*, 303–4.
5. "Seals Train sans Pappin," *Oakland Tribune*, September 16, 1975.
6. Proudfoot, *NHL Pro Hockey '76–'77*, 87.
7. Kurtzberg, *Shorthanded*, 312.
8. Joe DeLoach, "Seals Conclude Season on Uncertain Note," *Hayward Daily Review*, April 7, 1975.
9. DeLoach, "Seals Conclude Season."
10. Kurtzberg, *Shorthanded*, 244.
11. Kurtzberg, *Shorthanded*, 186.

12. Eric Prewitt, "Seals Talk Playoffs," *San Mateo Times*, January 28, 1976.

13. John Porter, "Blues Fans Glum after Seal 'Steal,'" *Oakland Tribune*, December 12, 1975.

14. Kurtzberg, *Shorthanded*, 261.

15. Geoffrey Fisher, "Reformed Hitter Stewart Controls Seals' Tempers," *Hockey News*, May 14, 1976, 11.

16. Prewitt, "Seals Talk Playoffs."

17. "Merrick Predicts Cup Berth," *San Mateo Times*, February 3, 1976.

18. "Merrick Predicts Cup Berth."

19. Dick Draper, "Seals Shed Patsy Image," *San Mateo Times*, December 11, 1975.

20. John Hickey, "Wolfe Derails Seals," *Hayward Daily Review*, January 29, 1976.

21. John Hickey, "Montreal Holds Off Late Seal Rally," *Hayward Daily Review*, January 31, 1976.

22. Dick Draper, "Seals Still in Playoffs–Stewart," *San Mateo Times*, February 21, 1976.

23. Draper, "Seals Still in Playoffs."

24. "Seals Flatten Black Hawks," *Hayward Daily Review*, February 23, 1976.

25. John Porter, "Exhausting Standoff for the Seals," *Oakland Tribune*, March 8, 1976, 29–31.

26. Jeff Chapman, "Seals Play Like Team Headed for Playoffs," *Hayward Daily Review*, March 23, 1976.

27. Geoffrey Fisher, "Seals Assault on Records Gives Fans Reason to Cheer," *Hockey News*, April 30 1976, 15.

28. John Porter, "Anatomy of the Improved Seals," *Oakland Tribune*, April 6, 1976.

29. Jeff Chapman, "Seals' Maruk Polishes Off Kings," *Hayward Daily Review*, April 5, 1976.

30. Geoffrey Fisher, "Seals' Girard's Future Bright," *Hockey News*, April 23, 1976.

31. Proudfoot, NHL *Pro Hockey '76-77*, 86.

32. Ken McKenzie, "Passing the Puck," *Hockey News*, April 23, 1976, 4.

33. Geoffrey Fisher, "Moxey Lauds Coach Evans for California Improvement," *Hockey News*, May 7, 1976, 12.

34. Kurtzberg, *Shorthanded*, 32.

35. Kurtzberg, *Shorthanded*, 32.

36. "'Major Cities' After Seals," *San Mateo Times*, May 15, 1976.

37. John Porter, "NHL President: I Won't Lie for Seals," *Oakland Tribune*, May 16, 1976.

38. "'Major Cities' After Seals."
39. Ed Schoenfeld, "Seals Still Owe Rental for Nine Games," *Oakland Tribune*, May 22, 1976.
40. "Seals Deny Talk They're Moving," *Hayward Daily Review*, May 15, 1976.
41. Seth Lerman, "Nine Years with the California Seals," San Jose Sharks website, http://207.222.254.114/sharks/thegame/ca_seals.html (defunct link).
42. Fisher, "Seals Assault on Records."
43. Schoenfeld, "Seals Still Owe Rental."
44. Schoenfeld, "Seals Still Owe Rental."
45. "Seals' Gund Likes Idea of NHL Club's Move Here," *Elyria Chronicle-Telegram*, June 8, 1976.
46. "Seals' Move to Denver Off for Now," *Colorado Springs Gazette-Telegraph*, June 5, 1976.
47. "NHL Franchise in Cleveland's Future?" *Winnipeg Free Press*, June 3, 1976.
48. "Seals Say Good-bye to Oakland," *Hayward Daily Review*, July 15, 1976.
49. John Porter, "The Seals Expire," *Oakland Tribune*, July 15, 1976.

11. Mistake on the Lake, 1976–1977

1. Ross McKeon, "It Was a Short but Colorful History for Golden Seals," *San Francisco Examiner*, January 16, 1997.
2. McKeon, "Short but Colorful History."
3. Beddoes, Fischler, and Gitler, *Hockey!*, 82–83.
4. Beddoes, Fischler, and Gitler, *Hockey!*, 89.
5. "Barons Late for Own Lunch," *Lethbridge Herald*, October 5, 1977.
6. "How the New Barons Logo Was Designed," Cleveland Barons Retrospective website, http://members.dencity.com/clevelandbarons/ (defunct link).
7. Kiczek, *High Sticks*, 181.
8. "The Rebirth of Hockey in Cleveland," Cleveland Barons Retrospective website.
9. Tredree and Bontje, "NHL Entry Draft," 301.
10. Rob Durkee, "A Night of 'Firsts' at Coliseum," *Elyria Chronicle-Telegram*, October 7, 1976.
11. Jerry Rombach, "Big League Hockey Here as Barons Tie in Opener," *Elyria Chronicle-Telegram*, October 7, 1976.
12. "Cleveland Stays Close to Habs," *Cornwall Standard-Freeholder*, December 7, 1976.
13. Terry Goodman, "Barons Get the Bad End … at Home, No Less," *Elyria Chronicle-Telegram*, December 9, 1976.

14. Goodman, "Barons Get the Bad End."
15. "Barons Look for More Scoring from 3M Line," *Elyria Chronicle-Telegram*, January 3, 1977.
16. "Barons Fire Bill McCreary," *Mansfield (OH) News Journal*, January 14, 1977.
17. "Bruins Blitz Barons in Third Period," *Elyria Chronicle-Telegram*, January 22, 1977.
18. Kiczek, *High Sticks*, 198.
19. "Barons Fire Bill McCreary."
20. Kiczek, *High Sticks*, 186–89.
21. "Barons Mull Aid Plan," *Pacific Stars and Stripes*, January 28, 1977.
22. "Barons Mull Aid Plan."
23. "The Socializing of Slap Shots," *Time*, March 21, 1977.
24. "Sobering Side of Pro Sports Now Evident," *Mansfield News Journal*, February 15, 1977.
25. "Pro Hockey Fortunes Slowly Sinking into Oblivion," *Mansfield News Journal*, April 30, 1977.
26. "Players Unpaid; Cleveland Team May Pack It In," *Winnipeg Free Press*, February 2, 1977.
27. "Players Unpaid."
28. "Sobering Side of Pro Sports."
29. "Players Unpaid."
30. "Deal to Save Barons Falls Through," *Elyria Chronicle-Telegram*, February 16, 1977.
31. "Deal to Save Barons."
32. Dick Rosetta, "'New Look' Eagles to Test Barons," *Salt Lake (UT) Tribune*, October 8, 1977.
33. Rosetta, "'New Look' Eagles."
34. "Will the Barons Play Tonight?" *Elyria Chronicle-Telegram*, February 18, 1977.
35. "Barons May Have Played Their Last Game," *Marysville (OH) Journal-Tribune*, February 21, 1977.
36. "Barons' Future Looks Bleak," *Winnipeg Free Press*, February 19, 1977.
37. "Barons Give Swig Ultimatum," *Lethbridge Herald*, February 19, 1977.
38. "Cleveland Barons Franchise Could Fold Today," *Lima (OH) News*, February 23, 1977.
39. United Press International, "'There's Only So Much a Person Can Take,'" *Elyria Chronicle-Telegram*, February 23, 1977.
40. "Barons Stay Alive for Season," *Mansfield News Journal*, February 24, 1977.
41. Robert Dolgan and Rich Passan, "Rescued Again!"

42. "Barons Stay Alive for Season," *Mansfield News Journal*, February 24, 1977.

43. Dolgan and Passan, "Rescued Again!"

44. Rich Passan, "How the Club Was 'Saved,'" *Cleveland (OH) Plain Dealer*, February 24, 1977.

45. Conway, *Game Misconduct*, 192.

46. Conway, *Game Misconduct*, 193–94.

47. Conway, *Game Misconduct*, 193.

48. Conway, *Game Misconduct*, 194.

49. Hollander, *Complete Handbook of Pro Hockey*, 125.

12. One Last Gasp, 1977–1978

1. "Gund Buys Barons for Coliseum Play," *Coshocton (OH) Tribune*, June 26, 1977.

2. Sean Fitz-Gerald, "Cleveland's Rich NHL History Often Forgotten," *Toronto (ON) National Post*, October 13, 2012, http://sports.nationalpost .com/2012/10/13/clevelands-rich-history-in-ahl-nhl-often-forgotten.

3. Ben Olan and the editors of *Hockey Illustrated*, "Previewing the Topsy-Turvy World of the 1977–78 National Hockey League," *Hockey Illustrated*, January 1978.

4. "Gund Buys Barons."

5. "Barons Crown Kings, 3–1," *Mansfield News Journal*, October 20, 1977.

6. "Meloche Is Super as Barons Roll On," *Elyria Chronicle-Telegram*, October 21, 1977.

7. Glenn Cole, "Red Wings, Cleveland Split Weekend Series," *Cornwall Standard-Freeholder*, November 7, 1977.

8. Doug Clarke, "Barons Top Montreal," *Cleveland Press*, November 24, 1977.

9. "Barons Stung by Philadelphia," *Coshocton Tribune*, November 26, 1977.

10. Canadian Press, "Leach Starts Flyers on Road to Victory," *Lethbridge Herald*, November 26, 1977.

11. "Barons Suffer 11–1 humiliation," *Elyria Chronicle-Telegram*, December 12, 1977.

12. Robin Innes, "Barons First to Beat Czechs," *Elyria Chronicle-Telegram*, January 5, 1978.

13. "Barons Rough Up Canucks, 6–1," *Elyria Chronicle-Telegram*, January 7, 1978.

14. Olan and the editors of *Hockey Illustrated*, "Previewing the Topsy-Turvy World."

15. "Barons 'New Look' Paying Dividends," *Elyria Chronicle-Telegram*, January 12, 1978.

16. Robin Innes, "Barons Stun Buffalo," *Elyria Chronicle-Telegram*, January 13, 1978.

17. Mike Harris, "The 'New Look' Barons Roll On," *Elyria Chronicle-Telegram*, January 14, 1978.
18. "Barons End Jinx at Boston," *Elyria Chronicle-Telegram*, January 23, 1978.
19. Mike Harris, "Barons Win Thriller in Final 50 Seconds," *Elyria Chronicle-Telegram*, February 18, 1978.
20. Harris, "'New Look' Barons Roll On."
21. "Barons Win Second in a Row (Honest)," *Elyria Chronicle Telegram*, March 31, 1978.
22. "Barons Win Second."
23. "Barons Win Second."
24. Kiczek, *High Sticks*, 200.
25. Kurtzberg, *Shorthanded*, 300.
26. Kiczek, *High Sticks*, 200.
27. Bob Schlesinger, "Barons Likely to Leave Soon," *Cleveland Press*, June 9, 1978.
28. Kiczek, *High Sticks*, 201.
29. Jenish, NHL, 256–57.
30. Jenish, NHL, 257.
31. Kiczek, *High Sticks*, 201.
32. Kiczek, *High Sticks*, 202.
33. Bass, *Great Expansion*, 84.
34. Jenish, NHL, 257.
35. "Struggle Ends: Barons, Stars Merge," *Winnipeg Free Press*, June 15, 1978.
36. Jenish, NHL, 257.
37. "Struggle Ends."
38. Jenish, NHL, 257–58.
39. "Struggle Ends."
40. Bob Schlesinger, "Some Win, Some Lose as Barons 'Die,'" *Cleveland Press*, June 15, 1978.
41. Bob August, "Barons' Owners Must Provide Stable Direction," *Cleveland Press*, April 3, 1978.

13. The Road Home

1. "Hockey for the Ages," 50th Anniversary Issue, *Hockey News*, September 1997, 64–70.
2. Raider, *Frozen in Time*, 62.
3. Jason Brough, "Bettman: 'We've Gone from the Golden Seals to a Golden Era' in California," May 29, 2013, *Pro Hockey Talk*, http://prohockeytalk.nbcsports.com/2013/05/29/bettman-weve-gone-from-the-golden-seals-to-a-golden-era-in-california/.

4. Kurtzberg, *Shorthanded*, 316.
5. Kurtzberg, *Shorthanded*, 316.
6. Pete Manzolillo, email message to author, September 20, 2015.
7. Kurtzberg, *Shorthanded*, 21.
8. "Midgets Honored," *San Mateo Times*, April 9, 1973.
9. Podnieks, *Shooting Stars*, 90.

BIBLIOGRAPHY

Bass, Alan. *The Great Expansion: The Ultimate Risk That Changed the NHL For-ever.* Bloomington IN: iUniverse, 2011.

Baun, Bobby, and Anne Logan. *Lowering the Boom: The Bobby Baun Story.* Toronto: Stoddart, 2000.

Beddoes, Richard, Stan Fischler, and Ira Gitler. *Hockey! The Story of the World's Fastest Sport.* New York: Macmillan, 1971.

Brewitt, Ross. *Into the Empty Net: Tales of Big League Hockey.* Toronto: Stoddart, 1994.

The California Golden Seals 1975-76 Official Guide and Record Book. Edited by Ron McGrath and Len Shapiro, 1975.

Cleveland Barons 1977-78 Media Guide. Compiled and edited by Edward J. Coen, 1977.

Conway, Russ. *Game Misconduct: Alan Eagleson and the Corruption of Hockey.* Toronto: Macfarlane, Walter & Ross, 1995.

Cruise, David, and Alison Griffiths. *Net Worth: Exploding the Myths of Pro Hockey.* Toronto: Penguin Books, 1992.

Duplacey, James, and Dan Diamond, eds. *Total Hockey.* New York: Total Sports, 1998.

Eskenazi, Gerald. *Hockey.* New York: Grosset & Dunlap, 1973.

Green, G. Michael, and Roger D. Launius. *Charlie Finley: The Outrageous Story of Baseball's Super Showman.* New York: Walker, 2010.

Greig, Murray. *Big Bucks and Blue Pucks: From Hull to Gretzky, an Anecdotal History of the Late, Great World Hockey Association.* Toronto: Macmillan Canada, 1997.

Hollander, Zander, ed. *The Complete Handbook of Pro Hockey, 1978 Edition.* New York: New American Library, 1977.

Irvin, Dick. *In the Crease: Goaltenders Look at Life in the NHL.* Toronto: McClelland & Stewart, 1995.

Jenish, D'Arcy. *The NHL: 100 Years of On-Ice Action and Boardroom Battles.* Toronto: Doubleday, 2013.

Joyce, Gare. *The Devil and Bobby Hull: How Hockey's Original Million-Dollar Man Became the Game's Lost Legend.* Mississauga ON: John Wiley & Sons Canada, 2011.

Kiczek, Gene. *High Sticks and Hat-Tricks: A History of Hockey in Cleveland.* Euclid OH: Blue Line, 1996.

Kurtzberg, Brad. *Shorthanded: The Untold Story of the Seals.* Bloomington IN: Authorhouse, 2006.

Laroche, Stephen. *Changing the Game: A History of NHL Expansion.* Toronto: ECW Press, 2014.

Leach, Reggie. *The Riverton Rifle: My Story—Straight Shooting on Hockey and on Life.* Vancouver: Greystone Books, 2015.

McFarlane, Brian. *One Hundred Years of Hockey.* Toronto: Deneau, 1989.

Podnieks, Andrew. *Players: The Ultimate A-Z Guide to Everyone Who Has Ever Played in the NHL.* Toronto: Doubleday, 2003.

———. *Shooting Stars: Photographs from the Portnoy Collection at the Hockey Hall of Fame.* Toronto: Doubleday, 1998.

The Professional Hockey Handbook. Winnipeg: Greywood, 1973.

Proudfoot, Jim. *Hockey L.N.H. 77-78.* Traduction de *Pro Hockey '77-'78.* Montreal: Quinze, 1977.

———. *NHL Pro Hockey '75-'76.* Markham ON: Simon & Schuster, 1975.

———. *NHL Pro Hockey '76-'77.* Markham ON: Simon & Schuster, 1976.

———. *Pro Hockey '68-'69.* Richmond Hill ON: Simon & Schuster, 1968.

———. *Pro Hockey '69-'70.* Richmond Hill ON: Simon & Schuster, 1969.

———. *Pro Hockey '70-'71.* Richmond Hill ON: Simon & Schuster, 1970.

———. *Pro Hockey '71-'72.* Richmond Hill ON: Simon & Schuster, 1971.

———. *Pro Hockey '72-'73.* Richmond Hill ON: Simon & Schuster, 1972.

———. *Pro Hockey '73-'74.* Richmond Hill ON: Simon & Schuster, 1973.

———. *Pro Hockey '74-'75.* Markham ON: Simon & Schuster, 1974.

Raider, Adam. *Frozen in Time: A Minnesota North Stars History.* Lincoln: University of Nebraska Press, 2014.

Schultz, Dave, and Stan Fischler. *The Hammer: Confessions of a Hockey Enforcer.* Toronto: Collins, 1981.

Stott, Jon C. *Ice Warriors: The Pacific Coast / Western Hockey League.* Surrey BC: Heritage House, 2008.

Tredree, Chris, and Paul Bontje. "The NHL Entry Draft." In *Total Hockey*, edited by James Duplacey and Dan Diamond, 285–348. New York: Total Sports, 1998.

Tremblay, Sebastien. *Goaltenders: The Expansion Years.* Edmonton: Tremblay Sports, 2009.

Willes, Ed. *The Rebel League: The Short and Unruly Life of the World Hockey Association.* Toronto: McClelland & Stewart, 2004.

INDEX

CPSIA information can be obtained
at www.ICGtesting.com
Printed in the USA
LVHW051256020623
748525LV00006B/23